Contemporary Australian Literature

A World Not Yet Dead

Nicholas Birns

SYDNEY UNIVERSITY PRESS

First published by Sydney University Press
© Nicholas Birns 2015
© Sydney University Press 2015

Sydney University Press
Fisher Library F03
University of Sydney NSW 2006
AUSTRALIA
sup.info@sydney.edu.au
sydney.edu.au/sup

National Library of Australia Cataloguing-in-Publication Data

Creator:	Birns, Nicholas.
Title:	Contemporary Australian literature : a world not yet dead / Nicholas Birns.
ISBN:	9781743324363 (paperback)
	9781743324370 (ebook: epub)
	9781743324387 (ebook: mobipocket)
Notes:	Includes bibliographical references and index
Subjects:	Australian fiction--21st century--History and criticism.
	Australian fiction--20th century--History and criticism.
Dewey Number:	820.8092

Cover image: *Thou Majestic : A* (2009) by Imants Tillers. Reproduced with permission from the artist. Image courtesy of Bett Gallery, Hobart.

Cover design by Miguel Yamin

Contemporary Australian Literature

SYDNEY STUDIES IN AUSTRALIAN LITERATURE

Robert Dixon, Series Editor

Contents

Contents

Acknowledgements

Much of this book was conceived while I was a rector-funded visiting fellow at the School of Humanities and Social Sciences (HASS), UNSW Canberra. My thanks to Nicole Moore for inviting me and for her friendship and hospitality; to the HASS Head of School, David Lovell, for his support; and to Marilyn Anderson-Smith, Beibei Chen, Heather Nielsen, Shirley Ramsay, Stefan Solomon and Christina Spittel for their collegiality. "Locals" in Canberra who provided a supportive atmosphere for this project included Belle Alderman, Michael Austin, Sean Burges, Tim Bonyhady, Andrew Clarke and Lee Wallace. Other Australian scholars who have helped with this project are Lachlan Brown, David Carter, Louise D'Arcens, Toby Davidson, Robert Dixon, Delia Falconer, Michael Griffiths, Melissa Hardie, Ivor Indyk, Antoni Jach, Brian Kiernan, Vrasidas Karalis, Lyn McCredden, Fiona Morrison, Brigitta Olubas, Brigid Rooney, Vanessa Smith and Michael Wilding. Non-Australians who provided help are Andrew Arato, Juan E. De Castro, Catherine Gale, Mark Larrimore, Cecile Rossant, Sarah Shieff, Nick Smart, Henry Shapiro, and my parents and other friends and family. I am grateful to Peter Carey and John Kinsella for their kind and understanding advice and to Australian writers in general for being patient with critical scrutiny. I hope this is the book Vivian Smith envisioned when he and I discussed the outlines of this project at Circular Quay in January 2010.

Essays of mine adjacent to this book though not part of it shed light on some figures undertreated here. David Malouf is given a full overview in my essay for the 2014 special issue of the *Journal of the Association for the Study of Australian Literature (JASAL)* on his work, while there is more on Tim Winton in my essay in *Tim Winton: Critical Essays*, edited by Lyn McCredden and Nathanael O'Reilly (University of Western Australia Press, 2014). Christos Tsiolkas' *The Slap* and Elliot Perlman's *Three Dollars*, as well as their precedents in D. H. Lawrence's *Kangaroo*, are examined in my 2009 *JASAL* article "Something to Keep You Steady". Patrick White's relationship to late modernity is examined in "*The Solid Mandala* and Patrick White's Late Modernity" in *Transnational Literature*, November 2011. Other work of mine on Gerald Murnane's recent fiction is to be found in my reviews of *A History of Books* in *Antipodes* and *Southerly*, both published in 2013. More on Stead's *For Love Alone* is to be found in my article in the first issue of the *Chinese Journal of Australian Cultural Studies*, edited by Wang Guanglin of Songjiang University in Shanghai. Shirley Hazzard's United Nations short stories, mentioned with respect to Frank Moorhouse in Chapter 7, are examined in my essay in *Shirley Hazzard: New Critical Essays*, edited by Brigitta Olubas and published by Sydney University Press in 2014. The prehistory of Alexis Wright's representation of Indigeneity in *The Swan Book*, as discussed in Chapter 6, is sounded in two essays in *Telling Stories: Australian Life and Literature 1935–2012*, edited by Tanya Dalziell and Paul Genoni (Monash University Press, 2013), which give background on Aboriginal themes in white writing before the specific onset of "concern" in the post-*Mabo* era. Further treatment of Wright on my part appears in Lynda Ng's casebook on *Carpentaria*, forthcoming in 2016 from Giramondo Publishing, as well as my piece on Australian colonial governmentality, forthcoming in 2016 in *Biopolitics and Memory in Postcolonial Literature*, edited by Michael Griffiths (Ashgate Publishing Group). I am grateful to Philip Mead and Ian Henderson for originally soliciting some of these ideas.

Robert Dixon, as editor of this series, provided detailed and much-needed assistance, drawing on his vast knowledge of Australian literary studies. Robert is not only one of the great contemporary scholar–teachers of Australian literature; he also has a deep concern for the field worldwide. Despite the internet, to work in Australian literary studies outside Australia is still to be at a decided logistical and informational disadvantage, and Robert's diligent and attentive assistance to me helped to remedy this gap. I really appreciate the dedication and professionalism of Sydney University Press, including Susan Murray's expert direction of the project, Agata Mrva-Montoya's timely and enthusiastic interventions, and Denise O'Dea's thorough and percipient copy-editing.

My larger debts to the community of Australian literary scholarship and its pioneering American exponents are recorded in the first chapter. The death of Herbert C. Jaffa, news of which I received while beginning work on Chapter 1, marked the loss of an American who faithfully and selflessly loved Australia and its literature.

In Canberra, I lived near Anzac Parade, and thought continually of the Australian veterans of both world wars, who helped to ensure that we face no more dire problems than those of late modernity and neoliberalism.

This book was partly written on territory historically associated with the Ngunnawal people. I acknowledge them and their custodianship and unceded sovereignty of the land.

Preface

The authors analysed in this book are of different generations, regions, heritages and philosophies. Yet they share a willingness to name the issues of the contemporary, to confront them, but to do so with nuance and poise, to be indirectly and sinuously passionate.

The authors who appear in this book, in both brief and extended roles, were chosen out of a mixture of timeliness, convenience, and my personal familiarity with and affinity for them. I am not proposing them as a set canon of contemporary Australian literature or as a unity for anything but the provisional purposes of this book. But I do believe that these writers, in their different ways, all testify to the persistence of imaginative hope in the aftermath of a free-market ideology that seeks to degrade humanity into automatons of profit and loss, success and failure.

Both poets and novelists have been included because I wish to demolish the old canard that, whereas fiction pertains to society and can be a reading of the culture, poetry speaks to inward states of experience. Both genres can do this, but they can also assume other roles, and the novelists presented in this book – above all the nonpareil Gerald Murnane – speak to private experience, while the poets – above all Ouyang Yu and John Kinsella – are as publicly engaged as any contemporary writer. In the twenty-first century, the aesthetic and the public have to mix; they cannot be cordoned off from each other.

This book is largely concerned with the economic philosophy of neoliberalism. Neoliberalism proposes a utopian confidence in the free market and a valuation of human life only as it is or is not successful in market terms. I do not wish to make the argument that literature, as such, can or should be a privileged mode of resistance to neoliberalism and the inequality that comes in its wake. The novel is, nevertheless, a form that contributes to a reading of the culture, and as such uses its particular modes of empathic identification to register with great sensitivity the really existing contemporary situation of its characters. In this book, we will see the persistence of Christos Tsiolkas' Danny Kelly through castigation as a loser; the loutish valour of Tim Winton's Tom Keely in belatedly refurbishing his family's role of social honour; the way Alexis Wright's Oblivia cares for others while being vulnerable herself; the healing after complex trauma that Gail Jones permits her troubled characters. All these writers testify to how we can conceive life differently than merely valuing one another by our financial conditions.

This is not to say neoliberalism does not have some positive aspects: cultural diversity, a greater variety of lifestyle, entertainment and aesthetic choice, and wider networks of communication are among them, as well as, necessarily, the greater viability of democratic institutions in the post–Cold War world. Stephen Greenblatt wisely urges us to avoid a "sentimental pessimism" that "collapses everything into a global vision of domination and subjection".[1] But, like all periods of history, the current one involves forms of injustice and dogma that writers must defy, evade or circumvent. The assumption behind this book is that writers always have to struggle against their cultural context, or, in Greenblatt's words, to "make imaginative adaptations" in their work, no matter their manifest cultural position or the apparent benignity of the ruling forces.[2] This era's writers have a unique challenge, and this book tells the story of how, in Australia, they have responded to this challenge.

I am not saying that these are the only contemporary Australian writers who can provide this testimony, nor that those Australian writers who cannot be read in this way are either not worth reading or not of aesthetic value. This book offers one map of what is going on today; other critics would draw other maps. Furthermore, Australian literature is different from that of the UK and USA in that it has never had a set canon. As important as figures such as Henry Lawson, Judith Wright, Patrick White and Peter Carey have been, the reader who does not wish to engage with these writers has always been able to navigate around them. In turn, no one person can read all of Australian literature or be conversant with its full range: it is too large and too diverse for that. Australian poetry has had more of a set canon than Australian fiction – certainly in the mid-twentieth century no anthology of Australian poetry could exclude Kenneth Slessor, David Campbell or R. D. Fitzgerald – but today of those three only Slessor still plays a central role in the national literary conversation. The fortunes of Adam Lindsay Gordon – *the* Australian poet in the nineteenth century, but ranked below his contemporaries Charles Harpur and Henry Kendall by the late twentieth century – testify to the openness of the Australian canon, an openness that has only increased as Indigenous, migrant and expatriate writers, as well as those working in languages other than English, have more recently stretched the very definition of what it is to be Australian. Meanwhile, the contemporary availability of digital and print-on-demand technologies has expanded the mathematical possibility of what can be canonical and, along with a more tolerant cultural agenda, has meant we have more books to choose from than ever before.

Australian literature, because of its traditional pluralisms, is well equipped to handle this new contingency. I attribute part of this to the fact that Australia has had no single dominant metropolitan area. Whereas London and New York have defined British and American literature far more than any other city in those countries, Sydney and Melbourne have kept up with each other, while Perth and Brisbane have held their own in a smaller compass. Canberra plays a key role in this book, not just as site of much of its composition (while I was a visiting fellow at the Canberra campus of the University of New South Wales), but as a potential ground of re-emergent Australian idealism – reflecting the fact that there is no single metropolitan space for the artificially built national capital to rival. The plurality of Australian literature is its great joy, and one of the qualities that enable it to be resilient against the threats to the imagination with which this book is so concerned.

---

1   Stephen Greenblatt, *Marvelous Possessions* (Chicago: University of Chicago Press, 1991), 152.
2   Greenblatt, *Marvelous Possessions*, 152.

Australian Literature: From Modern to Contemporary

1
Australian Literature in a Time of Winners and Losers

Immortal Democratic Moment

In 1985, at age twenty, I turned to the study of Australian literature, seeking a world that was not yet dead. I sought a horizon of hope, a milieu of greater generosity and charity, tolerance and flexibility. Three years later, in 1988, in the consummate gesture of the New Historicist school of criticism, Stephen Greenblatt said, "I began with a desire to speak with the dead".[1] Greenblatt sought to understand the past, to study how people of previous generations might have thought in their own terms. My interest in Australia was motivated by a similar freewheeling curiosity about a locale from which I was separated not by time but by space. I had no organic ties to Australia, had never been there and knew next to nothing about it. I knew where it was and that was about all. Yet Australia seemed an alluring alternative for a young American in despair over the corrosive and cruel effects that the policies of the Ronald Reagan administration were having on my country, turning it into a place where a sharp divide between economic winners and losers categorised everybody.

The same year, the Australian historian Stuart Macintyre published a book entitled *Winners and Losers*. It explored the theme of social justice in Australian history in an optimistic manner, as if, despite challenges and a history marred by hierarchy, there were more social justice to come.[2] One hundred years earlier, in *On the Genealogy of Morals*, Friedrich Nietzsche had discussed the displacement, at some point in the ancient world, of the dichotomy of "good" and "bad" (a distinction based on opinion or taste) by "good and evil" (a dichotomy seen as metaphysical and unalterable). Malcolm Bull and Corey Robin have linked the rise of social inequality from the 1980s to a new Nietzscheanism.[3] Nietzsche as a thinker is hard to pin down, but his sense of the good as "the noble, the superior, the powerful and the high-minded", possessed by "the ones who felt themselves to be good",

---

1 Stephen Greenblatt, *Shakespearean Negotiations: The Circulations of Social Energy in Renaissance England* (Berkeley: University of California Press, 1988), 1.
2 Stuart Macintyre, *Winners and Losers: The Pursuit of Social Justice in Australian History* (Sydney: Angus & Robertson, 1986).
3 Malcolm Bull, *Anti-Nietzsche* (London: Verso Books, 2011); Corey Robin, "Nietzsche's Marginal Children: On Friedrich Hayek", *Nation*, 27 May 2013, 27–36.

implies the division of humanity into an elite overclass and an underclass.[4] It might be argued that the 1980s saw a revision to Nietzsche, with a shift from good versus evil to winners versus losers. After about 1980, what one stood for mattered less than whether or not one was winning. The "ones who felt themselves to be good", in Nietzsche's words, felt so not because they believed their values were superior, but simply as a consequence of brute success.

At a time when, in America, there was a sharp and growing divide between economic winners and losers, Australia seemed an alluring alternative. The Australian difference I perceived was not so much the fact that a Labor government, led by Prime Minister Bob Hawke, was in power as that Australia seemed to have a more humane society and even literary culture. It seemed a place where living, not dead, values predominated.

My turn to Australian literature was not inspired by illusions of mateship or working-class solidarity. My impressions of Australia were gleaned not from any understanding of Australian society, either real or fanciful, but from my immersion in two of Australia's most important writers. Patrick White was still living and was still a force. No one could see White as an optimistic writer in a naive sense, certainly not in political terms. As Peter Wolfe, the American author of one of the first books on White, put it, "No social historian he."[5] White's books were either about visionary failures (Voss stranded in the desert, Waldo and Arthur Brown locked in mutually destructive kinship, the valorous madness of Theodora Goodman, the mock crucifixion of Himmelfarb) or qualified successes (Stan and Amy Parker with their Job-like endurance, Hurtle Duffield's achievement of artistic clarity through, and despite, his tortuous pain, Ellen Roxburgh's discovery of a deeper self amid catastrophic displacement and Elizabeth Hunter's adamance even in the face of death). All these characters were quintessentially modernist losers who nonetheless won.

Yet by the 1980s, when (to use Lauren Berlant's phrase) the "cruel optimism" that for most of the twentieth century had been a hallmark of the totalitarian left shifted over to the right, White's complex sense of the moral integrity of failure (or qualified success) seemed reassuringly human.[6] When White chose not to publish any work in 1988, in protest against the inaptness of Australia's bicentennial celebrations while Indigenous Australians were still mistreated and marginalised, he seemed not the Jungian or Nietzschean that some critics argued, but someone in whose creative soul art and conscience could coexist, even if they did not exactly coincide.

White had won the Nobel Prize in 1973 and by the 1980s was as much a household name as any Australian writer. Yet he never wished to be a straightforward hero. In 2010, the poet Vivian Smith, who knew White, told me over lunch at Circular Quay that White had always been gracious and kind to him. The public orneriness White displayed in later years – his dropping of former friends and his prickliness about the reception of his work – was, said Smith, a perhaps necessary, if unpleasant, consequence of his late political and postmodern turn. To some 1980s tastes, White's novels might have seemed like superannuated blockbusters, tethered to an immobile conception of "the mythic". But the half-lifting of White's authorial mask during his last decade, as well as his openness about his sexuality

---

4   Friedrich Nietzsche, *On the Genealogy of Morals: A Polemic*, trans. Douglas Smith (New York: Oxford University Press, 1996), 12.

5   Peter Wolfe, *Laden Choirs: The Fiction of Patrick White* (Lexington: University Press of Kentucky, 1983), 11.

6   Lauren Berlant, *Cruel Optimism* (Durham: Duke University Press, 2011).

in *The Twyborn Affair* (1979) and *Flaws in the Glass* (1981), made the sage of Centennial Park, in all his ornery idiosyncrasy, someone not just honourable but exemplary.

The other major writer who introduced me to Australia was just beginning to make a worldwide impression. Les Murray – who, at that point, signed himself "Les A. Murray" – astonishes with his braiding of linguistic complexity and personal feeling; his sense of the world and of the word transcends naive lyricism, preening formalism, or avant-garde posturing. This very much set him apart from the zeitgeist of the time.

In the spring of 1986, *American Poetry Review* published a portfolio of poems by Murray, including "Physiognomy on the Savage Manning River", Murray's portrait of Isabella Mary Kelly, a sadistic landowner who "rode beside / her walking convicts three days through the wilderness / to have them flogged half-insane in proper form / at Port Macquarie and Raymond Terrace". Kelly, in Murray's portrayal, is cruel and haughty, telling the convict who "dragged her from swift floodwater / 'You waste your gallantry / You are still due a lashing / Walk on, croppy'".[7] Writing from his home territory of Bunyah, on the mid-north coast of New South Wales, after spending his young adulthood in Sydney, Murray is unyielding in portraying the struggle of convicts and Highland immigrants as they try to make their way in a post-settlement Australia still willing itself into existence. But his Isabella Kelly is no stock villain. Murray is more interested in how Kelly, scarred either by being jilted back in Dublin or by some innate evil in her soul, is turned into a "useful legend", a substratum of history, destined to be confused with Kate Kelly, sister of the outlaw Ned. It would have been easy for Murray to see the convicts as victims and Isabella Kelly as a mere symbol of what David Scott later called "colonial governmentality".[8] Murray avoids a dichotomy of winners and losers, preferring the drama of a shared, toughening history. He also avoids a metaphysic of good and evil, despite being a convinced Christian. Indeed, in two poems published shortly after "Physiognomy on the Savage Manning River", "Easter 1984" and "Religion and Poetry", Murray gave us a Christ who does not impose upon us, but whom we cannot resist, one whose divinity "would not stop being human". Murray offers a vision of religion and of poetry as both "given and intermittent", both present and absent, an oscillation vital for Murray, but which he understands not everyone invests with the same credence. Murray is a populist, opposed not only to the residual colonial establishment but also to the entitled, leftist "Ascendancy". He asks his reader not only to think and to contemplate but also to know. If we have not read widely in history, anthropology and religion, we lose much of Murray's implication. Yet Murray is not elitist. He believes that the vast majority of us can know. This makes him unusual in a time of widening inequality when, as the French economist Thomas Piketty observes:

> The most striking fact is that the United States has become noticeably more inegalitarian than France (and Europe as a whole) from the turn of the twentieth century until now, even though the United States was more egalitarian at the beginning of this period.[9]

---

7   Les Murray, *The Daylight Moon* (Sydney: Angus & Robertson, 1987). All of the Murray poems quoted in this chapter were accessed via the e-text of *The Daylight Moon*. www.poetrylibrary.edu.au/poems-book/the-daylight-moon-0572000.

8   David Scott, "Colonial Governmentality", *Social Text* 43 (1995): 191–220.

9   Thomas Piketty, *Capital in the Twenty-First Century*, trans. Arthur Goldhammer (Cambridge: Harvard University Press, 2014), 292.

Murray, whatever his politics, is egalitarian in spirit. He demonstrates a faith not just in the compassion of what he calls the "vernacular republic", but also in its intellectual resourcefulness. He insists that knowledge and imagination can abide in what he terms, in his poem "1980 in a Street of Federation Houses", an "immortal democratic moment".

Murray insists that those who fail are not losers, that even those who treat others cruelly also suffer – his Isabella Kelly brings to mind the repressed spinster Miss Hare in *Riders in the Chariot* – and that a strictly economic measurement of humanity, which partitions us into those who succeed and those who do not, is truly, on a moral level, impoverishing.

From these two icons, White and Murray, I rapidly branched out. For whatever reason, Columbia University's Butler Library had a strong collection of Australian material. This was not to support a teaching interest: Columbia offered no courses in Australian literature. In this respect it was very different from its downtown competitor, New York University, which boasted the senior American Australianist Herbert C. Jaffa, humanities library bibliographer George Thompson and guest faculty including Thomas Keneally and Peter Carey. Nonetheless, the Columbia library housed an impressive Australian collection, not only of books but also of serials. Journals I read regularly included *Poetry Australia*, under the editorship of Grace Perry, and *Scripsi*, the all-too-short-lived journal under the rambunctious editorship of Peter Craven and Michael Heyward that had a vision of Australia as at once distinct and cosmopolitan.

A Time of Indigo-Maroon

But the books were the heart of it. I read widely and ravenously and somewhat unsystematically. The library had many of the University of Queensland Press editions of the collected works of prominent Australian poets, so in the dark of the stacks I readDavid Rowbotham (whom I would later meet at his Brisbane home) and Thomas Shapcott (whom I would later meet and edit). Thomas Keneally was widely known and respected in the USA and on a drizzly Saturday in March 1986 I was reading his *Confederates*, fascinated, as I still am, by his uncanny ability to capture the American Civil War from "outside" and by his talent for depicting warfare with both drama and integrity. Little did I know that, on the same campus, a group of Australianists and one actual Australian – Brian Kiernan of the University of Sydney – was meeting with the intent of founding an American association of Australian studies. This was yet another example of the "missed appointments" that have plagued the American rendezvous with Australia. A couple of years later, however, I joined the organisation.[10]

The genesis of the American Association of Australasian Literary Studies (AAALS) occurred when Kiernan gave a paper on Patrick White at a Modern Language Association convention in the early 1980s. In the audience was Robert L. Ross, a Texas-based academic and founding editor of *Antipodes*. Ross suggested that he and Kiernan collaborate to form an organisation devoted to Australian literary study. Although a curiosity about the land and people of Australia was a major motivation, Ross was also interested in South Asian

---

10 Nicholas Birns, "Missed Appointments: Convergences and Disjunctures in Reading Australia Across the Pacific", in *Reading Across the Pacific: Australia–United States Intellectual Histories*, eds. Nicholas Birns and Robert Dixon (Sydney: Sydney University Press, 2010), 91–103.

writing and more broadly in what was then termed "Commonwealth literature". Although he was not theoretically inclined and his work did not have the same conceptual breadth attained by the work of John Thieme, Gayatri Chakravorty Spivak and Homi K. Bhabha, Ross' instincts, like those of comparable Australian figures such as Ken Stewart and Julian Croft, were more or less in line with what would later receive academic codification as "postcolonial" criticism.

I was also pleased to meet the visiting Australian scholars at those first few conferences. They included Bull Ashcroft, Livio Dobrez, Margaret Harris, Susan Lever and John McLaren. Ashcroft's presence was especially notable as *The Empire Writes Back* (1989), which he co-authored with Gareth Griffiths and Helen Tiffin, was a leading text in postcolonial theory. Australians performed much of the theorising of the postcolonial in the Anglophone academy, even if Australia took a back seat to regions such as the Caribbean and South Asia, whose postcolonial struggles were more urgent and more recent. There was a marked contrast between these scholars' work and the position of academics such as Stewart and Croft, who were associated with the more nationalist tendencies of the Association for the Study of Australian Literature (ASAL), which had been founded in 1977. To me at the time, both those perspectives were breaths of fresh air.

Significantly, even while these scholars sought to promote and further to understand Australian classics, they were also open to more recent writing, especially by women. If there was one writer aside from White who united AAALS in its earliest days, it was Thea Astley, with Elizabeth Jolley not far behind. The women writers of the day were often "late bloomers" who entered the field of serious fiction writing in their forties or fifties (much like the first novelists of the eighteenth century, Defoe and Richardson). Writers such as Astley, Jolley, Jessica Anderson, Barbara Hanrahan, Olga Masters and Amy Witting were not the bright young things the culture industry favours. Much in the spirit of the Patrick White Award, which White endowed specifically to support under-recognised older artists, they contravened the market's preference for youth and trendiness. Although feminism's place in mainstream Australian literature was hardly uncontested – the 1980s saw many gender-based battles for voice and position – by the time I arrived on the scene a feminist perspective was manifest. Then there was the superb Aboriginal poet Colin Johnson (who also wrote under the name Mudrooroo), whom poetry editor Paul Kane included in the spring 1988 *Antipodes*, the first issue of the journal I read. In his lyric "Dalwurra" Johnson asks, hearkening back to an archetypal Dreaming, "Was there ever a time of indigo-maroon?", and then answers his own question, speaking of Indigenous people "surviving, surviving in the time of indigo-maroon".[11] The Dreaming is there, not in the remote past; it is now, however compromised that "now" may be.

Australian literature seemed to constitute an ideal world, especially in contrast to the USA, which in the 1980s was already becoming what Thomas Piketty would later call a "hypermeritocratic society". In this society, a few "winners" would dominate and even, in Piketty's words, "succeed in convincing some of the losers" that this was justified.[12] In contrast, Australia seemed more a land of possibility, of a latter-day "time of indigo-maroon" where people of all backgrounds could affirm a sense of belonging in the world.

This was, of course, an illusion, one of many illusions brought to the Australian continent from people outside of it, starting perhaps from settlement. Gerald Murnane was

---

11   Colin Johnson, "Dalwurra", *Antipodes* 2, no. 1 (1988): 3.
12   Piketty, *Capital*, 265.

another writer I read in these early years. In his 1983 short story "Land Deal", Murnane speaks, from an imagined Aboriginal perspective, of European settlement as "a dream, which must now end".[13] Although this dream hardly ended after the *Mabo* decision of 1992, that verdict's epochal affirmation of Indigenous land rights, its jettisoning of the principle of *terra nullius* through which white occupation of the land had been justified, meant that justice for Indigenous Australians could no longer be ignored. When, in 1997, it was revealed that Colin Johnson had misunderstood his own ancestry and was not, in fact, of Aboriginal descent, this disclosure seemed but an element in the unravelling of a "pre-*Mabo*" moment that, however promising and honourable, was in the end a false synthesis because it did not fully foreground the Indigenous issue.[14]

My view of Australia was not as romantic as that propagated by the popular Anglo-Australian novelist Nevil Shute, whose *On the Beach* (1957) imagined Australia as the last place to avoid nuclear devastation, or his lesser-known and weirder *In the Wet* (1953), which envisioned Australia embracing the royal family after Britain had turned republican. But I was still, like Shute, hoping that Australia would resist a trend that was advancing, in the end inexorably, worldwide.

The Global Comes to Australia

This fallacious hope may even be seen as a structural principle, embedded in capitalism. In the USA and the UK, the monetarist economic policies of the ruling parties in the 1980s had pushed inflation very low, leaving American investors used to high bond yields to look elsewhere. In 1985, the First Australia Prime Income Fund was founded, with former prime minister Malcolm Fraser and a former governor of New South Wales, Sir Roden Cutler, among the directors. The fund promised international investors higher yields than were available in the USA, but was never in fact a financial success, as under the policies of Labor treasurer Paul Keating inflation was controlled in Australia too. Australia turned out not to be nearly so far removed from global trends as many thought.

In the late 1980s and the 1990s, Australian publishing houses such as McPhee Gribble and Angus & Robertson, and Australian branches of world houses that had maintained a resolute Australian presence, such as Penguin, were taken over or amalgamated with global conglomerates and were as a result no longer as interested in promoting a distinctive Australian voice. In the 1980s, the Australia Council had sponsored "familiarisation tours" to Australia for American academics and had supported New York publicists such as Selma Shapiro and Pearl Bowman, whose function was to promote not specific Australian writers but Australian writing generally. These initiatives were all gone from the scene by 2000, reflecting what many saw as a more general waning of a distinctively Australian publishing space. Mark Davis speaks of the "decline of the literary paradigm" in this period, a yielding to neoliberal logic. A few literary books might still be unexpected hits, but the publishing industry's commitment to publishing serious literature had, in Davis' view, attenuated.[15] When I began as reviews editor of *Antipodes* in the mid-1990s, I worked with a num-

---

13 Gerald Murnane, "Land Deal", in *Velvet Waters* (Ringwood: McPhee Gribble, 1990), 55–60.
14 See Nicholas Birns, "Pre-*Mabo* Popular Song: Icehouse Releases 'Great Southern Land'", in *Telling Stories: Australian Life and Literature 1935–2012*, ed. Tanya Dalziell and Paul Genoni (Melbourne: Monash University Press, 2013), 392–97.

ber of Australian publishing houses that were responsive – Penguin, Angus & Robertson, University of Queensland Press, Magabala, Spinifex – and understood the purpose of a small, USA-based academic journal. By 2000, only University of Queensland Press, under the editorship of Rosie Fitzgibbon, remained as a reliable partner willing to send books to a small scholarly journal that often took over a year to get books reviewed. By 2000, Michael Wilding was warning of the impending disappearance of Australian publishing culture.[16]

Larger political and cultural developments were also operative. The election of the conservative Coalition government under Prime Minister John Howard in 1996 coincided with a series of scandals that seemed to delegitimise multiculturalism and social critique. Among these was the furore over the prize-winning novel *The Hand That Signed the Paper*, purportedly by a young Ukrainian-Australian woman named Helen Demidenko, who was revealed to be, in fact, of English descent and named Helen Darville, and the allegation that the leftist Australian historian Manning Clark had accepted the Order of Lenin from the Soviet Union. These scandals were symptomatic of a turn in the cultural conversation away from the subversive. During the 1980s, cultural and critical theory had had a growing impact in Australian academia, as seen in the work of Graeme Turner, John Frow and Kay Schaffer. In the early 1990s, there had been a series of theoretically inclined books: Bob Hodge and Vijay Mishra's *Dark Side of the Dream* (1992), Ross Gibson's *South of the West* (1992) and the cultural anthropology of Stephen Muecke and Eric Michaels. These books were the culmination of an Australian interest in Continental critical theory and its potential Australian application that had been evident since the early 1980s.[17] They augured a more philosophical turn for Australian literary studies, which, as Leigh Dale argued in *The English Men*, had been shaped by generations of British and Anglophile professors with an empirical, canonical outlook.[18] This theoretical phase, however, was eclipsed by the conservative turn in Australian culture and by the backlash against theory worldwide. By the late 1990s the academic study of Australian literature was overshadowed by commentary by critics such as Peter Craven and Andrew Riemer, who wrote for newspaper literary supplements and presumed a belletristic, if stylish and accomplished, view of literature. Theirs was the approach to Australian literature that now reached the world via the internet.

The internet did wonderful things for Australia, connecting it to the rest of the world and finally making possible an intellectual union of the English-speaking peoples. What James Bennett called "the Anglosphere" reached its full potential in the 1990s and 2000s.[19] In earlier eras, major writers and movements had erupted in Australia without even registering in the USA and literary contact between the two countries had depended on rogue

15   Mark Davis, "The Decline of the Literary Paradigm in Australian Publishing", in *Making Books: Contemporary Australian Publishing*, ed. David Carter and Anne Galligan (St Lucia: University of Queensland Press, 2007), 116–31.

16   Michael Wilding, "On Australian Publishing in a Global Environment", *Antipodes* 14, no. 2 (2000): 152–54.

17   Delys Bird, Robert Dixon and Christopher Lee date the emergence of theory to 1986 and the publication of Graeme Turner's *National Fictions*; see Bird, Dixon and Lee, *Authority and Influence: Australian Literary Criticism 1950–2000* (St Lucia: University of Queensland Press, 2001), xxiii.

18   Leigh Dale, *The English Men: Professing Literature in Australian Universities* (Toowoomba: Association for the Study of Australian Literature, 1997). A revised edition was published as *The Enchantment of English: Professing English Literatures in Australian Universities* (Sydney: Sydney University Press, 2012).

19   James C. Bennett, *The Anglosphere Challenge: Why the English-Speaking Nations Will Lead the Way in the Twenty-First Century* (Lexington: Rowman and Littlefield, 2007).

alliances and chance affinities: Miles Franklin, Christina Stead and Shirley Hazzard made connections while living in the USA; Ben Huebsch at Viking in New York developed an enthusiasm for Patrick White; John Ashbery took an ironic delight in the poems of "Ern Malley". With the advent of the internet, however, there could be a much more efficient exchange of literary culture. A book successful in Australia could now reasonably hope for publication, if not necessarily commercial success, not only in the USA and the UK but also worldwide in translation.

The fall of Soviet communism had much to do with this, dispelling as it did the last vestiges of that curiously Australian naive confidence in Soviet benignity. This confidence was very different from that of American fellow-traveller and proletarian writers, who were geographically much closer to the Soviet Union. Although Nevil Shute's vision of an Australia isolated, if only temporarily, from a worldwide nuclear conflagration was a conceit, for Australian writers of the left in the mid-twentieth century the Soviet Union was so distant that it could be imagined as a fantasy land. This was true of writers such as Judah Waten, Jean Devanny, Katharine Susannah Prichard, Mary Gilmore and Manning Clark. As the recent work of Nicole Moore and Christina Spittel has demonstrated, Australian writing received enough of a reception in communist-ruled East Germany to buoy the hope of certain leftist writers of garnering public acclaim there.[20] The fall of the Berlin Wall was the final blow to this long-atrophied dream. Henceforth, if Australian writers were to find an international readership, they would need to look to the West. Furthermore, the biggest obstacle for Australian literature on the world scene had been irrelevance: the fact that Australia seemed protected behind the curtain of global conflict. Although clearly in the American camp politically, Australia seemed too minor to be important in a Cold War divide between good and evil. But if the polarity was reframed as winners vs losers, gifted individual Australians might stand a chance. Their Australian identity need no longer define or hold back at least selected individual Australians who sought to bestride the world stage.

The 1990s saw the lapse of much of the postcolonial rhetoric of the 1980s, when Australian literature had frequently and fruitfully been compared with the literatures of other former British colonies in South Asia, Africa and the Caribbean. Journals such as *New Literatures Review* (originally *New Literature Review*) and Anna Rutherford's *Kunapipi* had made these links explicitly. Far from the robust assertions of Australian autonomy made in the 1980s, the pertinence of the former coloniser re-emerged. Juan De Castro has argued that the late twentieth century saw a resurgence of Spain as the centre of the Spanish-speaking world, as a newly democratic and culturally revitalised Iberian Peninsula became the hub of all the former colonies.[21] The internet aided this; the more information became dispersed and instantaneous, the more cultural capital accreted to the former coloniser.

The same was true with respect to Australia and Britain. Although by the late 1990s Australia had a conservative government, in Britain the ascendancy of Tony Blair's "Cool Britannia" gave a tremendous boost to the prestige of Australia. The Western Australian poet and gadfly Hal Colebatch could write *Blair's Britain* (1999) and not once reveal that he was Australian. Similarly, a British novelist, Louis de Bernières, could write *Red Dog* (2001), set in Western Australia, without seeming particularly appropriative. Frieda

---

20 Nicole Moore and Christina Spittel, eds., *South by East: Australian Literature in the German Democratic Republic* (London: Anthem Press, 2015).
21 Juan E. De Castro, *The Spaces of Latin American Literature* (New York: Palgrave Macmillan, 2008).

Hughes, in *Wooroloo* (1998), and Matthew Kneale, in *English Passengers* (2000), contributed to this new canon of British literature written about Australia (and were sometimes even assumed to be Australian by a world readership uninterested in fine distinctions).

In the 1990s and 2000s, Australian literature tended to reach international readers via Britain. American and other readers discovered Australian writing through prizes such as the Booker and through publications such as the *Times Literary Supplement* and *Granta* (which published a special Australian issue in 2000). Murray Bail's *Eucalyptus* (1998) gave a sense of the Australian landscape, making the proliferation of different eucalyptus species a central plot device. Bail's book, which combined a deep sense of Australia with a sense of fictive sophistication, was taken up with enthusiasm in the USA. But its most prominent American review, in the *New York Times*, was written by the noted British critic John Sutherland.[22]

Similarly, Les Murray attained his greatest fame in the USA after building a much bigger fan base in the UK. Murray's verse epic *Fredy Neptune* appealed to late 1990s sensibilities; the travails of its eponymous hero accorded with the idea that the twentieth century had strayed onto the wrong path through the mid-century decades of war, totalitarianism and trauma, but now, in an age of restored capitalist prosperity, was being providentially healed.[23] Similarly, Bail's *Eucalyptus* could be seen as a riposte to the apocalyptic rhetoric that had reigned for most of the twentieth century: a "eucalypse" in which history ends with regeneration rather than catastrophe; an unexpectedly happy ending. (This sense that the twentieth century had been a cauldron of calamity and that the millennium could provide a healing respite was also evident in British works such as Ian McEwan's 2002 novel *Atonement*.) *Fredy Neptune*, like Bail's book, was reviewed for the *New York Times* by a British critic, the poet Ruth Padel. Every Australian text that reached the world seemed, metaphorically if not literally, to have to transfer through Heathrow Airport in order to arrive there.

Millennium and Crisis

In 2000, I took over the editorship of *Antipodes* from Robert Ross. At the time, Herbert Jaffa, by then long retired from New York University and a great source of counsel for so many younger scholars, telephoned me and said that his contacts in Australia had told him Australian writers no longer felt the need for a specialised magazine of Australian literature. Now that Australians felt that the broadest reaches of world exposure – *Granta*, the *New Yorker*, the *Times Literary Supplement* – were open to them, Jaffa explained, *Antipodes* seemed small-fry and parochial. Jaffa had served in World War II in Australia and New Guinea, and his Australian contacts were his contemporaries – they were not the sort of voices that a conformist media might privilege, swaggering young upstarts hoping to make it big on the world scene. These were sober and weathered veterans, including many senior

---

22 Fifteen years later, the *New York Times* turned to Sutherland to review Patrick White's *The Hanging Garden*. In 2014, the *New York Review of Books* asked the British critic James Walton to review Eleanor Catton's *The Luminaries*, with a side comment on Richard Flanagan's *The Narrow Road to The Deep North*. Although both Australians and Americans were available to review these books, the mainstream US organs kept turning to British critics, in a gesture of either sage transnationalism or residual colonial submission.

23 Piketty, *Capital*, 98.

or retired academics, not likely to be lured by the latest fad. If they said Australia was going global, you could be confident that it was.

This "global" turn, of course, largely involved Australian writers embracing the West and affirming Australia's place within it. While the work of writers such as Alex Miller, Nicholas Jose and John Mateer approached Asia, most Australian writers were still writing within European traditions. The era of Australian isolation was definitely over. Yet there was a danger that, as Antigone Kefala put it, the "inflated presentation" of these years, characterised by the hegemony of an "infinitely seductive" English, would lead to a "closed in" system that would not allow for "wider cultural truths".[24]

This raised the question: just what was the value of *Antipodes*? In 2001, having taken over the editorship, I visited Australia for the first time. I was reassured by academics I respected that the journal was still relevant, which it hopefully continues to be. As of 2015, I have made six extended trips to Australia, visiting every capital city except Adelaide and Hobart and seeing a good deal of regional New South Wales, Queensland and Western Australia. Visiting Australia did not in itself significantly change my thinking about Australian literature. But it did, necessarily and immeasurably, deepen my experience of reading Australian writing. Moreover, the *Tampa* crisis of August 2001 made me acutely aware of the refugee issues that were to dominate Australia's sense of itself for the next generation.

In that same year, 9/11 shattered the global consensus that had emerged during the 1990s. At first, the common experience of terrorism and its convulsive aftermath seemed to unite Australia and the USA. Novels such as Andrew McGahan's *Underground* (2006) and Richard Flanagan's *The Unknown Terrorist* (2006) registered an Australian response to 9/11. But 9/11 and the war in Iraq ended up diminishing the sense of an Anglophone utopia that had been a feature of the previous decade. The political right brandished the idea of an Anglophone coalition for militaristic purposes, but Emily Apter has argued that the American literary world became more interested in translation during this period, in an attempt to understand a world that suddenly seemed catastrophic.[25]

Nonetheless, Australia now had a definite place in world literature. This was witnessed in transnational novels by Australian writers, such as Kirsten Tranter's *The Legacy* (2010), which takes place in both Sydney and New York leading up to and just after 9/11. It was also evident in books by non-Australians featuring Australian characters and themes. The American novelist Claire Messud's *The Emperor's Children* (2006) included an Australian character, Ludovic Seeley, a pilgrim to New York in a postmodern utopia, a latter-day version of Christina Stead's picaresque travellers. Both books captured a sense that Australia was at the outer edge of the world and yet very much a part of it.

In a society based on what Piketty calls "the hierarchy of labor and human capital", cultural products and their reception often seem to offer "a hymn to a just inequality".[26] The reception of Australian literature in the Anglophone North in the 1990s and 2000s mirrored this: it was all about picking winners and scorning or ignoring losers. Although both Les Murray and Murray Bail eminently deserved their fame, other writers of equivalent stature, such as Gerald Murnane, Helen Garner, Robert Adamson and Jennifer Maiden,

24 Antigone Kefala, *Sydney Journals* (Atarmon: Giramondo Publishing, 2008), 51.
25 Emily Apter, *The Translation Zone: Towards a New Comparative Literature* (Princeton: Princeton University Press, 2005).
26 Piketty, *Capital*, 419–22.

were published internationally only by small presses or not at all. This fixation on picking winners was an example of what Piketty calls a "meritocratic hope", which masks the reality of inequality. Andrew Leigh, writing on Piketty in the June 2014 issue of the *Monthly*, observed, "When I speak with audiences about inequality, I sense that Australian values like egalitarianism, mateship and the fair go are still strongly held."[27] If Australia continues to become more unequal – as Piketty's capital theory suggests it might – then it will become increasingly difficult to hang on to these values.

This crisis in Australian values was paralleled by a crisis in the public image of Australian literary studies. If academic literary study always has an asymmetrical relation to literature actually being produced, a crisis in one usually betokens at least an unease in the other. In December 2006, Rosemary Neill, writing for the *Australian*, dramatically announced that Australian literary studies in the academy were dead or at least in extreme peril.[28] Neill did not necessarily blame academics, but other media did. Generally, the right seemed to blame the left, accusing it of diverting literary study into identity politics. Anthony Hassall blamed the rise of cultural studies: "As cultural studies increased its parasitic stranglehold on the host discipline of literature, departments of English disappeared into schools of English and cultural studies and then into larger, more diverse and even less meaningful conglomerates".[29] Andrew Bolt, a conservative commentator, went further and blamed certain authors for the state of "Australian literature" as a whole, writing, "When our top literature prize can these days be won by works such as Shirley Hazzard's *The Great Fire* and Andrew McGahan's *The White Earth*, it's clear the books just are not good enough."[30] Bolt's odd pairing of examples – a transnational book by a seventy-five-year-old expatriate and a novel deeply concerned with Indigenous land rights by a forty-year-old author – proved that opprobrium could be flung far and wide. A more dispassionate observer, however, might conclude that the apparent death of Australian literary study in the early 2000s was a result of global economic forces and their magnetic draw of cultural energies towards the world's financial centres. By 2015, both the Australian literary scene and Australian publishing seemed livelier, but they still had to contend for visibility in a global arena that privileged those who already had fame, power and status.

Today's Australia

Yet one might argue that Australia had changed for the better between 1985 and 2015 and all because of greater international connections: dining, wine, clothing, shopping are all improved, as is the general cultural vitality and intellectual climate. Furthermore, Australian culture is more visible globally than ever before. It would seem churlish to whinge about apparently minor asymmetries in this generally beneficial situation. Australians often reproach themselves for "tall poppy syndrome", and the related problem of what A.

---

27   Andrew Leigh, "An Australian Take on Thomas Piketty's *Capital in the Twenty-First Century*", *Monthly*, June 2014.
28   Rosemary Neill, "Lost for Words", *Weekend Australian*, 2–3 December 2006, 4–6.
29   Anthony Hassall, "Whatever Happened to Australian Literature in the Universities?", *Quadrant* 55, no. 10 (2011): 30–34.
30   Andrew Bolt, "The Great Unread Australian Novel", *Andrew Bolt Blog*, 2 December 2006. http://blogs.news.com.au/couriermail/andrewbolt/index.php/couriermail/comments/ the_great_unread_australian_novel/.

A. Phillips diagnosed as the "cultural cringe": the national habit of assuming that culture produced "overseas" must be better than that coming out of Australia.[31] The global success of certain Australian writers might seem to offer an opportunity to redirect Australian self-scrutiny in the direction of *amour-propre*.

What this vindication of Australian *amour-propre* misses is that Australia has changed for the better but the world has changed, too. If these Australian cultural exports had arrived in America in the period before 1980, during the era of what Lane Kenworthy has termed "American social democracy",[32] so far to the good. But they did not; instead, the tall poppy syndrome was weakened at a time when "winning" no longer entailed mere recognition and acceptance, but had become a corollary of what Piketty calls "the indefinite increase of the inequality of wealth".[33]

How *Mabo* Changed Australian Literature

During the same period, Australia has paradoxically seen the most consequential changes in the political consciousness of Indigenous peoples. After the *Mabo* decision and the revelation of the Stolen Generations – the Aboriginal children taken away from their families in the mid-twentieth century in order to assimilate them into white society – Indigenous issues had surged to the forefront in an unprecedented way.[34] As John Frow puts it, *Mabo* and its aftermath drew attention to "quite incommensurate structures of value and historicity", ones which engaged both modernisation and counter-modernisation and thus did not direct or predicate time in only one way.[35] After *Mabo*, scholars were even freer to explore multiple European temporalities in Australia, as was seen in Louise D'Arcens and Stephanie Trigg's work on Australian discourses of the European Middle Ages as at once a temporal alternative to progressive optimism and a potential displacement of Indigenous deep time.[36]

Before *Mabo*, the prevailing left-of-centre mentality thought that Aboriginality could be seamlessly attached to a more open, humane Australia and in this its hopes were too shallow. As Ian MacLean has argued, a laudable tendency for white artists to identify with the Australian land also led to less benign appropriative impulses towards Aboriginal culture. This impulse could be seen in the Jindyworobak movement, in the poetry of Judith Wright, and in Les Murray's *The Buladelah-Taree Holiday Song Cycle*.[37] After *Mabo*, it was clear that Aboriginal identity was not there for whites to appropriate. In addition, the dismantling of the White Australia Policy in the 1960s and 1970s, and the subsequent

---

31 A. A. Phillips, "The Cultural Cringe", *Meanjin* 9, no. 4 (1950): 299–302.

32 Lane Kenworthy, *Social Democratic America* (New York: Oxford University Press, 2014).

33 Piketty, *Capital*, 518.

34 For background on the history wars, see Stuart Macintyre and Anna Clark, *The History Wars* (Melbourne: Melbourne University Press, 2004).

35 John Frow, *The Practice of Value: Essays on Literature in Cultural Studies* (Nedlands: University of Western Australia Press, 2013), 258.

36 Louise D'Arcens, *Old Songs in a Timeless Land: Medievalism in Australia* (Nedlands: University of Western Australia Press, 2013); Stephanie Trigg, ed., *Medievalism and the Gothic in Australian Culture* (Melbourne: Melbourne University Press, 2005).

37 Ian McLean, *White Aborigines: Identity Politics in Australian Art* (Cambridge: Cambridge University Press, 1998).

development of a polity that was multilingual, egalitarian and pluralistic (although still predominantly European) had made Australia more diverse.[38]

Today's Australia is a crossroads for people from all over the world. Moreover, Australia today is approaching the racial diversity of countries that lifted immigration restrictions earlier, such as Canada and the USA.[39] Was hyper-capitalism the price required in order to achieve racial justice? If so, was it one we should be prepared to pay? Here, I would differ from Walter Benn Michaels' analysis of recent American literature in *The Shape of the Signifier*, in that from my perspective cultural diversity is not, as Michaels argues, simply an illusion proffered by a protean and transmogrifying capitalism, but an ideal genuinely to be honoured.[40] Racial justice, if it had occurred, would justify any extreme of capitalism or inequality. But is there racial justice in Australia today, in the aftermath of the 2007 Northern Territory intervention and the prevalence of anti-Aboriginal rhetoric in political campaigning, popular journalism and talkback radio? And what is the likelihood of racial justice in a world where only money and social status are valued? In Alexis Wright's *Carpentaria* (2006), the glaring rapacity of a mining company pushes the crisis in the Indigenous community to the surface, where it is visible; the mining company's greed both precipitates the crisis and offers a possible redemption from it. Neoliberalism may pay lip-service to diversity, but it often deepens the social inequality that is racism's legacy.

Nonetheless, and despite the push and pull of party politics, on racial issues Australia has generally presented an increasingly inclusive face to the world. But the broader world is not an unchanging monolith, and it has its own dynamics. The most sophisticated portrayals of contemporary Australia register these complexities. Gail Jones' *Five Bells* (2011) depicts reparation and provisional healing for victims of trauma from Ireland and China. Jones wrote about the Aboriginal Stolen Generations in *Sorry* (2007) and alludes to them in *Five Bells* by the presence of the Indigenous didgeridoo player in Circular Quay. Present-day Australia becomes a refuge from the tumult in the larger world, a place for what Patrick Morgan called "getting away from it all".[41] The Irish Troubles, the Chinese Cultural Revolution and the other religious and cultural backgrounds of Jones' various itinerants are understood both as coherent cultural legacies and as contingencies inflected by specific political events.[42] Jones acknowledges both the luminosity of individual consciousness and the inescapability of political events.

Contemporary Australian Literature: A World Not Yet Dead does not mean to urge an elegiac perspective on contemporary Australia. One can believe that the changes in recent decades have all been to the good and still arguably find something rewarding in this book. But a prerequisite for this reward requires understanding that the world *has* changed in the past forty years: that the contemporary is different from the past. Periodisation is of course problematic. As David Scott's work on colonial governmentality indicates, Australia may not yet be postcolonial, notwithstanding its glib classification as such by English

---

38   On the decline of the White Australia policy and its residual influence, see Laksiri Jayasuriya, David Walker and Jan Gothard, eds., *Legacies of White Australia* (Crawley: University of Western Australia Press, 2003).

39   On the anti-Islamic and asylum-seeker issues, see Suvendrini Perera, *Australia and the Insular Imagination: Beaches, Borders, Boats and Bodies* (New York: Palgrave Macmillan, 2009).

40   Walter Benn Michaels, *The Shape of the Signifier: 1967 to the End of History* (Princeton: Princeton University Press, 2006).

41   Patrick Morgan, "Getting Away from It All", *Kunapipi* 5, no. 1 (1983): 73–87.

42   Gail Jones, *Five Bells* (New York: Picador, 2012), 113.

departments since the early 1990s. Frow addresses this revaluation of reductive historicism when he says that the "historicity of texts is not a matter of the *singular* moment of their relation to a history that precedes them, because that moment is in turn endowed with meaning in a succession of later moments, as well as in the lateral movement of texts across cultural boundaries".[43] Moreover, periodisation in literature is only important as far as the field of writers, texts and readers constitutes it and/or reacts against it. Periods have no particular ontological reality; they are discursive constructs. Furthermore, one cannot neatly pin down the present; any attempt to do so risks what Les Murray, in "Four Gaelic Poems", called the "connoisseurship of outsets" – trying to know what today's Australia is before it has finished happening.[44] Nevertheless, this book will address Australian literature at a certain time, and is addressed to as general an audience as possible given the inevitably specialised nature of the subject. Three terms that will be used in the argument require definition. They are neoliberalism, late modernity and Australian literature.

Neoliberalism

Although "neoliberalism" is increasingly used in the mainstream media – John Lanchester used it in the *New Yorker* in 2014 without feeling he had to define the term, and the magazine's scrupulous editors let him do so – it is still not quite a household word.[45] Part of the issue is that the word "liberal" in the USA, and at times in other countries, means "left-wing", whereas neoliberalism is (to resort to the analogy whose tedium was exposed by Les Murray in "The Vol Sprung from Heraldry"), if anything, right-wing. Even "liberalism" in the nineteenth-century sense, with what Harold Laski described as its "concentration upon the powers and possibilities of the free entrepreneur", has an aura of freedom and progress, of looking forward to liberation.[46] Neoliberalism, by contrast, has tended to emphasise a residual sense of sovereignty, dismissing much of the twentieth century as an unfortunate detour.

Neoliberalism is defined by David Harvey as:

> a theory of political economic practices that proposes that human wellbeing can best be advanced by liberating individual entrepreneurial freedom and skills within an institutional framework characterised by strong private property rights, free markets and free trade.[47]

Harvey sees the beginnings of neoliberalism in the aggressive free-market policies pursued by the illegitimate and authoritarian Pinochet regime in Chile after the 1973 coup that brought it to power. But Harvey defines the years 1978–80 as a "revolutionary turning point" in the advance of this doctrine, with the all-important turning of China towards economic liberalisation under the leadership of Deng Xiaoping and the rise of pro-free-market politicians such as Ronald Reagan and Margaret Thatcher in the USA and the

---

43 Frow, *The Practice of Value*, 221.
44 Les Murray, *Collected Poems* (Melbourne: Black Inc, 2006), 148.
45 John Lanchester, "Money Talks: Learning the Language of Finance", *New Yorker*, 4 August 2014, 31.
46 Harold Laski, *The Rise of European Liberalism* (London: Allen & Unwin, 1936), 168.
47 David Harvey, *A Brief History of Neoliberalism* (New York: Oxford University Press, 2005), 18.

UK.[48] There is a general recognition that these years marked a turning point; Christian Caryl, in 2013, saw the year 1979 as "the birth of the 21st Century", while George Packer's *The Unwinding: An Inner History of the New America* saw this unwinding as stemming from the election of Ronald Reagan in 1980.[49]

Neoliberalism is often associated with transparency and democracy, as opposed to the authoritarian regimes of the right or left that it replaced in Latin America and Eastern Europe. Yet neoliberalism has also taken root in countries such as Singapore and Dubai, polities that have been reluctant to implement full democracy in the Western sense. The USA, with its traditional inclination towards deregulation and low taxation, may well be the *fons et origo* of neoliberalism. But, as Peter Josef Mühlbauer points out, the term is not widely used in the USA, where the word "libertarianism", which is associated with far less governmental authority than neoliberalism, is more often used.[50]

Notably, Piketty himself never uses "neoliberalism", although he speaks at times of "liberalisation". What Piketty does offer, however, is a vision of this liberalisation that is not intellectually descended from Marxism, as Harvey's is. Furthermore, although Piketty, a rigorous, quantitative economist, supplies statistical proof that Harvey does not, he understands that the impact of recent changes has not been only economic but also moral, redefining what humanity seeks and how we see ourselves.[51] Like Piketty, I am interested in questions of ethics and agency as well as economics.

Rob Nixon describes "neoliberal ideology" as one that "erodes national sovereignty, and turns answerability into a bewildering transnational maze". In such a maze, it becomes impossible to look to a single nation for sanctuary, as I did to Australia in the 1980s.[52] Neoliberalism for Nixon leads to "occluded relationships" and to a "slow violence", which operates indirectly and often unobservably (as in the case of environmental degradation, or the diminution of middle-class wages).[53] It is through "slow violence" that neoliberalism – ostensibly emphasising merit, transparency and technology – evokes what Jacques Derrida called the "occulto-mystic" idea of authority that operates alongside a "maximum intensification of a transformation in progress".[54] Neoliberalism, in promising us freedom from the rigid constraints of statist late modernity, ends up reducing humanity to an object of incalculable force.

Key to this paradox is how neoliberalism sees itself as liberating and populist, benefitting everyone by unleashing the dynamic power of capital. In the early 1990s, the American academic Jerome C. Christensen spoke of a "corporate populism" in neoliberal culture, which has only accelerated since.[55] Behind much denunciation of neoliberalism is

---

48   Harvey, *Neoliberalism*, 1.

49   Christian Caryl, *Strange Rebels: 1979 and the Birth of the 21st Century* (New York: Basic Books, 2013); George Packer, *The Unwinding: An Inner History of the New America* (New York: Farrar, Straus, & Giroux, 2013).

50   Peter Josef Mühlbauer, "Frontiers and Dystopias: Libertarianism and Ideology in Science Fiction", in *Neoliberal Hegemony: A Global Critique*, ed. Dieter Plehwe et al. (London: Routledge, 2009), 155.

51   Neil Brenner, "Berlin's Transformations: Postmodern, Postfordist ... or Neoliberal?", *International Journal of Urban and Regional Research* 26, no. 3 (2002): 635–42.

52   Rob Nixon, "Neoliberalism, Slow Violence, and the Environmental Picaresque", *Modern Fiction Studies* 55, no. 3 (2009): 444.

53   Nixon, "Neoliberalism, Slow Violence, and the Environmental Picaresque", 445.

54   Jacques Derrida, "Force of Law", *Cardozo Law Review* 11, nos. 5–6 (1990): 929, 933.

55   Jerome Christensen, "From Rhetoric to Corporate Populism: A Romantic Critique of the Academy in an Age of High Gossip", *Critical Inquiry* 16, no. 2 (1990): 438.

a Marxist animus against capitalism as such; as a result, the term neoliberalism is sometimes applied to what is in fact liberalism more generally. In this book I do not equate neoliberalism with more inclusive forms of capitalism; what is needed is a more targeted critique of neoliberalism, focusing on the way its financialisation of reality has led to a reduction of subjectivity and a desiccation of interior life.

In Australia, the term "economic rationalism" is often used to describe what elsewhere is called "neoliberalism". This phrase was associated most strongly with the Howard government, although it had been used even in the Hawke–Keating era; in 1991, Michael Pusey published *Economic Rationalism in Canberra: A Nation Building State Changes Its Mind*.[56] By the mid-1990s, the phrase "economic rationalism" was common parlance in Australia. Although the University of Queensland economist John Quiggin used the term "neoliberalism" as early as 1999, it did not catch on in Australia the way "economic rationalism" did.[57] Although some might suppose "neoliberalism" is simply the American or international equivalent of "economic rationalism", "economic rationalism" operates strictly in the realm of public policy whereas neoliberalism, as Harvey suggests, offers a more broad-reaching worldview. Neoliberalism is the "pure reason" to the "practical reason" of economic rationalism, more theoretical and fundamental. Neoliberalism thus has a greater presence than economic rationalism in the sphere of culture and imagination to which this book is dedicated. It seeks to define humanity in a new way.

The poet Fiona Hile grasps this when she asks:

> But what if love unfolds with the synchronous
> Cruelty of your lips, the parameters of unlikely
> Incision gelded to private property and the right
> to that property?[58]

The novels of Elliot Perlman also evoke the new neoliberal mankind, a humanity drained of any motive but profit-seeking. In *Three Dollars* (1998), *Seven Types of Ambiguity* (2003) and *The Street Sweeper* (2011), Perlman is not interested in economic rationalism merely as an influence on policy and party politics; he is concerned with how humanity is now defined. Other Australian writers to depict neoliberalism are David Malouf, in his short-story collection *Every Move You Make* (2007) and his nonfiction treatise *The Happy Life* (2011), and Malcolm Knox, in his novels since *Summerland* (2000). J. M. Coetzee – once South African, now Australian – fiercely denounces neoliberalism by name, or at least his close-to-autobiographical persona does, in *Diary of a Bad Year* (2007), as I will discuss in Chapter 5. But my argument goes beyond such explicit depictions of neoliberal economics to talk about how the mentality of the age has inflected the Australian novelistic imagination.

Neoliberalism is also a term of temporality, what Mikhail Bakhtin called a chronotope, as much as it is a term of political economy. Neoliberalism asserts that a) there was once

56 Michael Pusey, *Economic Rationalism in Canberra: A Nation-Building State Changes Its Mind* (Cambridge: Cambridge University Press, 1991).

57 John Quiggin, "Globalisation, Neoliberalism, and Inequality", *Economic and Labour Relations Review* 10, no. 2 (1999): 240–59.

58 Fiona Hile, "A Portable Crush", *Overland* 216 (2014): 100.

a time when a more collective view of society predominated; and b) a more pro-market view has now superseded it. Although Harvey focuses more on the state apparatuses that support neoliberalism than on those who have been directly or indirectly victimised by it, my focus goes beyond this. Both internationally and in Australia, writers such as Martha C. Nussbaum, Raimond Gaita and Robert Manne have argued that literature must necessarily speak of the bypassed and the overlooked, the scorned and the dismissed. Literary criticism, despite being bound at times to its intellectual high horse, must as well.

Another term often used alongside "neoliberalism" is "globalisation". The phrase is problematic for a few reasons. First, "the global" existed long before 1980: people before 1980 were not parochial homebodies. Neoliberalism did not usher in the global: there was a modernist globalism, a romantic globalism, certainly an Enlightenment globalism. Even Stalinism, as the Australian-born Slavic scholar Katerina Clark has pointed out, had cosmopolitan aspirations.[59] The very idea of the various Socialist Internationals (the social-democratic Second, the Stalinist Third and the Trotskyite Fourth) made clear the global dimensions of Marxism as an ideology, which twenty-first-century free-market capitalism mimics.

Globalisation in the twenty-first-century sense has elicited a range of responses. Arjun Appadurai takes an optimistic view: while he admits the potential of globalisation to elevate those who are already privileged, he argues that it can also lead to "knowledge transfer and social mobilisation".[60] Giovanni Arrighi, meanwhile, offers a lacerating critique: he sees globalisation as basically another word for imperialism and notes the convergence of the idea of there being "one indivisible, global economy" with "the revival of neoutilitarian doctrines of the minimalist state".[61] Lisa Rofel, though not endorsing neoliberalism, sees it as "an on-going experimental project that began in the global south", but nonetheless defines neoliberalism as a uniform plan to "produce a new human nature".[62]

"A new human nature": neoliberalism's definition of success is also temporal. A success under neoliberalism is not someone who simply makes a lot of money, but someone who is in touch with the times. A loser – as seen in the novels of Christos Tsiolkas – may or may not be poor, but he will almost always, like Don Quixote in early modernity, be out of touch with the times.

There are those who view neoliberalism in positive terms, who value, as Aihwa Ong puts it, neoliberalism's propensity to "induce self-animation and self-government so that citizens can optimise choices, efficiency and competitiveness".[63] Others, however, believe neoliberalism mandates a crass materialism, "making the market a model for all modern freedoms", as Pauline Johnson writes.[64] Some critics argue that this threatens, in the words

59   Katerina Clark, *Stalinism, Cosmopolitanism, and the Evolution of Soviet Culture, 1931–1941* (Cambridge: Harvard University Press, 2011).

60   Arjun Appadurai, ed., *Globalization* (Durham: Duke University Press, 2002), 3.

61   Giovanni Arrighi, "Globalisation and Historical Macrosociology", in *Sociology for the Twenty-First Century: Continuities and Cutting Edges*, ed. Janet M. Abu-Lughod (Chicago: University of Chicago Press, 1999), 118.

62   Lisa Rofel, *Desiring China: Experiments in Neoliberalism, Sexuality, and Public Culture* (Durham: Duke University Press, 2007), 2.

63   Aihwa Ong, *Neoliberalism as Exception: Mutations in Citizenship and Sovereignty* (Durham: Duke University Press, 2006), 7.

64   Pauline Johnson, "Sociology and the Critique of Neoliberalism: Reflections on Peter Wagner and Axel Honneth", *European Journal of Social Theory* 17, no. 4 (2014): 517.

of Hans Christoph Schmitt am Busch, "the material and moral wellbeing of a large number of citizens".[65] The most menacing of these threats is a reductive division of the world into winners and losers that crushes any idea of what the phenomenologist Edmund Husserl called the *Lebenswelt*, the life-world, as relentlessly as did earlier materialisms such as Stalinism.

Geordie Williamson links the erosion of Australian literature as a category to the "individual competition" and "atomisation of traditional groupings" of neoliberalism, a word Williamson, unlike Piketty, uses.[66] Williamson is one of the few commentators to juxtapose neoliberalism with Australian literature. His frequent use of the term as a characterisation of the current climate shows how concentrating on neoliberalism is more radical and useful than emphasising the end of postcolonialism, which has become too preoccupied by the arrival of Australian literature on the world scene. As David Scott has noted, "a teleological historicity of transition from the evils of colonialism to the promised virtue of the sovereign nation" is now "exhausted" and "played out" and needs to be "suspended" in favour of recognition of more tragic conditions. Until this tragic awareness occurs, the teleological optimism of postcolonialism cannot admit the turbulence of the inequality that neoliberalism has caused.[67]

For the French critic and polemicist Viviane Forrester, inattention to the consequences of neoliberalism is, notably, part of the neoliberal ideology: "achieving general indifference is more a victory for the system than gaining partial support".[68] Tom Whyman has spoken of a "cupcake fascism": the contemporary popularity of cupcakes for adults, he argues, represents an "infantilisation" that forestalls a "critical and thus transformative stance towards one's environment" and so keeps one from being a "fully cognitive adult".[69] In this atmosphere, the workings of neoliberalism pass beneath the notice of the distracted consumer. In the same subterranean way, the institutions in which writers and intellectuals typically dwell have been almost invisibly infiltrated by neoliberal assumptions. As was noted by Simon Marginson and Mark Considine in *The Enterprise University* (2000), the contemporary university has been susceptible to these rationalising pressures.[70] But academia has always been the last best hope of any opposition to neoliberalism, more so than the futile activism of demonstrations. As Les Murray puts it, "Nothing a mob does is clean". Demonstrations are rarely as effective as academic critiques such as Harvey's or Piketty's.[71] The academic enterprise of "Australian literature", by having its own logic within the matrix of universities, refereed journals and grants proposals, can counter market pressures.

---

65 Hans-Christoph Schmitt am Busch, "Can the Goals of the Frankfurt School be Achieved by a Theory of Recognition?", in Busch and Christopher F. Zum, eds., *The Philosophy of Recognition: Historical and Contemporary Perspectives* (Lanham: Lexington Books, 2010), 280.

66 Geordie Williamson, *The Burning Library: Our Great Novelists Lost and Found* (Melbourne: Text Publishing, 2012), 5.

67 David Scott, "The Tragic Vision in Postcolonial Time", *PMLA* 129, no. 4 (2014): 806.

68 Viviane Forrester, *The Economic Horror* (London: Polity Press, 1999).

69 Tom Whyman, "Beware of Cupcake Fascism", *Guardian* online, 8 April 2014, http://www.theguardian.com/commentisfree/2014/apr/08/beware-of-cupcake-fascism.

70 Simon Marginson and Mark Clonidine, *The Enterprise University: Power, Governance and Reinvention in Australia* (Cambridge: Cambridge University Press, 2001).

71 Les Murray, "Demo", *Selected Poems* (New York: Farrar, Straus, & Giroux, 2007), 187.

Late Modernity

This book uses the term "late modernity" to denote that which came before neoliberalism. Eras are not sealed tight, and some major figures in Australian literature – for instance the poets Bruce Dawe and Barry Hill – continued to manifest a serene vision that was more or less late-modern even while the world as a whole careered helter-skelter towards neoliberalism.

"Late modernity" can be used in a different sense: to denote a late form either of modernism as an artistic mode – as in Tyrus Miller's book on the subject – or of the modern in an industrial sense.[72] But here I use it above all to mean what came before neoliberalism in society. The settings of Elizabeth Harrower's fiction, for example, are late-modern because they take place (in the 1950s and 1960s) just before neoliberalism and are distinct from it. There is of course no decisive temporal boundary. The late-modern did not suddenly stop in 1980 and the shift from late-modern to neoliberalism did not take place at the same time, or in the same way, in every country. Much like the psychiatrist Jean Piaget's four stages of child development, in which the various stages do not necessarily occur at the exact same age in every child, but always occur in sequence, late modernity came before neoliberalism and was replaced by it.[73] In this book I describe Christina Stead's fiction as modern and Harrower's and White's as late-modern, not simply because they wrote in the years between 1930 and 1980 – the period generally identified with high and late modernity – but because they afforded a definition of humankind that neoliberalism has altered. I will say more about this, and about late modernity more generally, in Chapters 2 and 3.

Australian Literature

Many presume that, today, great Australian writers do not need to be distinctly or vocally Australian; in some quarters, a collective Australian identity has become an embarrassment. As Herbert Jaffa noted to me circa 2000, the notion of "Australian literature" as a category has been destabilised under neoliberalism because individual Australian writers are now expected to be successful under their own steam. Williamson connects the vogue for transnationalism in Australian literary study with the perceived crisis of Australian literature that was often lamented in journalistic circles in the early 2000s. Classic Australian texts were out of print, there were few academic chairs in Australian literature within Australia, and "the transnational researches increasingly undertaken in the academy" arguably squeezed out Australian writing.[74]

Transnationalism, however, might no longer see Sydney as the periphery and New York or London as the metropolis; it would recognise Sydney as a significant metropolis alongside New York and London, and alongside Mumbai and Singapore for that matter. One is reminded of this knowing passage from Ada Cambridge's memoir of a century ago, *Thirty Years in Australia* (1903), in which she describes her experience as the wife of an English clergyman who embarks for Australia:

---

72 Tyrus Miller, *Late Modernism: Politics, Fiction, and the Arts between the World Wars* (Berkeley: University of California Press, 1999).

73 Jean Piaget, *The Theory of Stages in Cognitive Development* (New York: McGraw Hill, 1969).

74 Williamson, *The Burning Library*, 5.

G. was an English curate for a few weeks, and an English rector for a few more. It was just enough to give us an everlasting regret that the conditions could not have remained permanent. Doubtless, if we had settled in an English parish, we should have bewailed our narrow lot, should have had everlasting regrets for missing the chance of breaking away into the wide world; but since we did exile ourselves, and could not help it, we have been homesick practically all the time – good as Australia has been to us. At any moment of these thirty odd years we would have made for our native land like homing pigeons, could we have found the means; it was only the lack of the necessary "sinews" that prevented us.[75]

What would have seemed parochial had Cambridge stayed in England became an object of nostalgia once she was in Australia, as though she felt she was missing out on something at "home". Transnationalism does not just mean having a passport tattered from frequent use; it also entails, as Vilashini Cooppan argues in *Worlds Within*, an emotional sensibility.[76] It can prompt a feeling of melancholy as well as of victory, and, as the passage from Cambridge shows, conjure a longing for roads not taken.

To define "Australian literature" requires reading Australian books and then deciding either what is best or what is most interesting. Neoliberalism, however, demands a different type of sorting: it wants winners, not in the old canonical sense of "Great Books" (as championed by Harold Bloom), but in the sense of "successful" books, as measured in cultural capital. If, as Piketty puts it, "wealth and merit" can be "totally unrelated", and if, as Colleen Lye, Kent Puckett and C. D. Blanton have argued, cultural capital has undergone "financialisation" in the neoliberal era, so that critical acclaim can be leveraged in ways that at once monetise and inflate it, success in the twenty-first century is neither transparent nor innocent.[77] Allegedly "meritorious" individual works rise to the top, but questions about the arbitrariness of this process inevitably recur, while the idea of a national literature is left behind.

Understanding a national literature requires reading not only what Williamson calls "writers … whose works still glow brightly today" but also those "gone in the grate".[78] Indeed, I would argue there is a third category crucial to the constitution of a national literature: writers who are worthy, if not world class. When, in 1986, I began to read the University of Queensland Press editions of Shapcott and Rowbotham, I was conscious that, although their work was good, they were probably not important to world literature in the way Les Murray and Patrick White were. As Harold Bloom puts it, "There is never enough time for reading", and in reading these authors I was giving up the chance to read others and to deepen my knowledge in important areas.[79] But I was also aware that Rowbotham and Shapcott were accomplished, insightful poets with technical command and moral integrity, and that if I read them, even at the cost of not reading some world classics,

75 Ada Cambridge, *Thirty Years in Australia* (1903; Sydney: Sydney University Press, 2006), 6.
76 Vilashini Cooppan, *Worlds Within: National Narratives and Global Connections in Postcolonial Writing* (Redwood City: Stanford University Press, 2009).
77 Piketty, *Capital*, 447; C. D. Blanton, Colleen Lye and Kent Puckett, eds., *Representations – Special Issue: Financialisation and the Culture Industry* 126 (2014): 1–8.
78 Williamson, *The Burning Library*, 14; A. D. Hope, "Standards in Australian Literature", *Current Affairs Bulletin* (Nov. 1956).
79 Harold Bloom, *How to Read and Why* (New York: Scribner, 2000), 24.

I would not be making a wasteful choice. One of the advantages of the plurality of Australian literature is that one gets to proclaim one's idiosyncracies of taste, and to affirm the importance of that literature which is more significant than what Sianne Ngai called "the merely interesting", even if it is not necessarily "world class" in Williamson's sense.[80]

That Australian literature is not just one thing but many also makes tracking its progress much harder, but there is one certainty: Australian literature cannot offer a sanctuary from the questions of the era. This book will consider whether Australian writers whose work made some sort of world news between 2010 and 2015 can offer a new sense of life, one that defies deadening attempts to divide people into winners and losers. Although I am an American who is among other things a scholar of Australian literature, and although much of my sense of the global reverberation of Australian literature is anchored in an American context, I do not see this project as "an American take on Australian literature". One can be an Australianist literary scholar from anywhere in the world. The national adjective applies to the body of literature or to a national horizon of reading, not necessarily to the critical apparatus used to study it. This book is definitely from a *non-Australian* perspective, but only incidentally from a specifically American one.

Although many comparisons will be made with American authors, British, Latin American and French comparisons will also frequently be drawn. Any idiosyncrasies in this account likely pertain less to my nationality than to my own interests as a critic. Australian literature as a category will also be stretched to include one New Zealand writer, Eleanor Catton, whose work and world reception raise many of the same questions with respect to form, genre and the world market as that of her Australian contemporaries. Catton made news worldwide by winning the 2013 Man Booker Prize and by explicitly critiquing neoliberalism and its ravages in the antipodes. At times, there will be digressions on writers from other places and times, intended to place today's Australian writers in the widest possible literary context – as the quality of their work demands.

Exploring the Contemporary

This book will consider recent Australian fiction and poetry, but also go one or two generations back, to the midpoint of the twentieth century. As the Australian-born art theorist Terry Smith has suggested, the "superficial contemporariness" often favoured by the contemporary art world is far less rewarding than what he calls "a more measured layered take on our contemporaneity".[81] Previously Smith has spoken about the Fordist paradigm in twentieth-century economics, stating that the assembly-line mass production in Henry Ford's automobile factories had only a "short life" in its pure form, but persisted through the balance of the century as a "symbolic paradigm".[82] The period I am calling late modernity has much in common with what Smith (inspired, of course, by Antonio Gramsci) terms Fordism, and neoliberalism shares features with what is sometimes called post-Fordism or post-Keynesian, when the socioeconomic framework of late modernity began to crack, to be replaced by a rhetoric of individual initiative, innovation and freedom – all

---

80 Sianne Ngai, "Merely Interesting", *Critical Inquiry* 34, no. 44 (2008): 777–817.
81 Terry Smith, *Thinking Contemporary Curating* (New York: Independent Curators, 2012), 219.
82 Terry Smith, *Making the Modern: Industry, Art, and Design in America* (Chicago: University of Chicago Press, 1994), 3.

of which, in their own way, end up being at least as restrictive as the Fordist paradigm. Although neoliberalism arrived after late modernity, there is no clear chronological break, and the two modes can exist side-by-side, just as, in fourteenth-century Italy, a resident of Florence might be at once medieval and renaissance; as revealed in the stories of Boccaccio, she might travel to the countryside and see jousts, or roam the city and witness the mercantile and artistic activity of an urban commune.[83] Philip Jones speaks indeed of a "medieval renascence" that circumambulated the conventionally defined Italian renaissance. One could similarly speak of a "late-modern neoliberalism", as the two modes sometimes appear at the same time.[84] This book goes as far back as the 1940s and 1950s in its purview because this era comprises the necessary antecedents of our own, and because critiques of the dominant paradigms of those decades by writers such as Stead and Harrower foreshadow many of our current aspirations. Moreover, even very recently composed Australian novels, such as Alex Miller's *Coal Creek* (2013) and Steven Carroll's Glenroy novels, explore this era in ways that are not simply "historical".

This book is an excursion into various aspects of this layered contemporaneity. It is not an attempt at a broad literary-historical overview of the period, unlike Ken Gelder and Paul Salzman's trenchant *After the Celebration*, nor does it seek to rescue Australian literature as an aesthetic category, as Williamson's coruscating *The Burning Library* does.[85] I make no attempt to proclaim a fixed canon of Australian literature, and many excellent writers will be mentioned only in passing. My focus is on the extent to which Australian literature might be able to make the world after neoliberalism one that is not yet dead: a world in which people can matter on their own terms and care for others, where they are not relentlessly subjugated to dehumanising market forces, and where commodification is not the only route to significance. In such a world, nature itself would not be undermined and exhausted, and boundaries of class, gender and race would be more fluid. This book, however, is chiefly concerned with the division between social winners and losers in contemporary Australian fiction and the question of who wins and loses by this division.

---

83   Daniel Philip Waley, *The Italian City-Republics* (New York: McGraw-Hill, 1969), 52.

84   Philip Jones, *The Italian City State: From Commune to Signoria* (New York: Oxford University Press, 1997), 3.

85   Ken Gelder and Paul Salzman, *After the Celebration: Australian Fiction 1989–2007* (Melbourne: Melbourne University Press, 2009); Williamson, *The Burning Library*, 19.

2
Christina Stead: Australian in Modernity

In the early 1970s, when Les Murray wrote *Poems Against Economics*, it was axiomatic that he was writing them against leftist economics.[1] To be economic then was to speak of the left. The right was irrelevant, so much so that in *The Liberal Imagination*, Lionel Trilling could write that the "sole intellectual tradition" of the United States was of the left.[2] A generation later, any Australian poet writing *Poems Against Economics* would have been assumed to be opposing neoliberalism and by extension the right. Murray's positioning of poetry against economics was part of his early aesthetics, which privileged literary language, but in a way that left room for other forms. Murray's willingness to accept "poemes" (by which he means "fusions of thought and dream" that may find expression in poetry but also through analogous forms, including in politics and religion) and his idea of imaginative "interest" not entirely divorced from the economic meaning of the term, implied a juxtaposition of art and economics, even if, in the case of art, an unremunerated one lacking ulterior motives.[3] Despite his identification with the political right (he has served as poetry editor of *Quadrant*), Murray's aesthetic does not isolate art from economics. It posits that the differences that exist between art and economics reveal the important links between the two.

Occupying a very different part of the political spectrum and a generation older than Murray, Christina Stead (1902–1983) had a keen sense of both art and economics at a time when the left reigned among intellectuals. Unlike more impressionistic twentieth-century Marxists, she had, through her own work and that of her husband, the economist and radical thinker William Blake, a real knowledge of how modern economies worked. As opposed to other twentieth-century writers who worked in or had some affiliation with business – such as Wallace Stevens or T. S. Eliot – she was committed to an ideology that could not see art and economics as two separate spheres. The ambition of Stead's novels is so massive and her achievement so nearly matches her ambition, that her Australian origins have seemed to some critics quaint or embarrassing.

---

1 Les Murray, *Poems Against Economics* (Sydney: Angus & Robertson, 1974).
2 Lionel Trilling, *The Liberal Imagination* (New York: New York Review Books, 2008), xv.
3 Les Murray, "Poemes and the Mystery of Embodiment", *Meanjin* 47, no. 3 (1988): 519–33; and "First Essay on Interest", *Collected Poems* (Melbourne: Black Inc., 2006), 166.

In this chapter I will argue that Stead's perception of the world she encountered was more astute because she was an Australian. She was at once an insider and an outsider on the American and British literary scenes, and her political affiliation brought together, in Simon During's phrase, "Stalinism, world literature and the nation".[4] Rebecca Walkowitz has argued that modernism incarnated a "cosmopolitan style" that was suspicious of "epistemological privilege".[5] Stead's work embodies this cosmopolitanism: it was equally at home in Australia, the USA and the UK and even in Germany and France; stylistically, it was influenced by the Russian novel as much as by anything else; and it was attuned to the transnational rhythms of financial and intellectual capital. But its critical reception necessarily followed more parochial channels, namely those of the London and New York press. Susan Stanford Friedman has argued that for many years, Western cultural chauvinism prevented recognition of "Muslim modernities".[6] A more minor and less premeditated prejudice prevented the recognition of an Australian modernity by the world. The success of Eleanor Dark's *Timeless Land* (1941) in America, and the concomitant American neglect of her more modernist novels such as *Prelude to Christopher* (1934) and *Return to Coolami* (1936), suggest that the gatekeepers of modernity – particularly the book critics and academics of New York – were not able to recognise Australia as modern.

This book locates modernity in the early to mid-twentieth century, bounded more or less by the two world wars. In the UK, the modern period was preceded by the Victorian and romantic periods; in Australia by the colonial and federation periods. In a larger sense, however, as Greenblatt and other scholars have argued, modernity stretches back to the renaissance, to the era of Gutenberg, Columbus and Shakespeare. There is an important distinction to be drawn between modernity – a state of being in the modern world, which any person or text in the twentieth century exemplifies – and modernism, an aesthetic, avant-garde mode that was often critical of the technological and political priorities of modernity even as it rebelled against the modern representational preference for what Ian Watt termed "formal realism".[7] Esther Gabara speaks of "peripheral modernisms", which are often seen as "rejecting modernity". Yet, as Gabara notes, the reality is more complicated.[8] Stead takes the modern world as her subject but offers a lacerating critique of it. Her settings are modern and, despite her realistic frames, she has often been accepted by critics as being in some way modernist.

Stead is often described as an expatriate writer. This is so, in that the prime of her life was spent in Europe, the USA and the UK. Critical discussions of Stead's relationship with Australia, however, are unusual when compared with the treatment of other expatriate or displaced writers. Willa Cather, for example, is seen as a quintessentially Nebraskan writer, although not more than half of her fiction is set there and she lived there for a relatively small portion of her life. She arrived in Nebraska at age eight and left permanently after age

---

4   Simon During, *Exit Capitalism: Literary Culture, Theory, and Post-Secular Modernity* (London: Routledge, 2009), 57.

5   Rebecca Walkowitz, *Cosmopolitan Style: Writing Beyond the Nation* (New York: Columbia University Press, 2007), 2.

6   Susan Stanford Friedman, "Unthinking Manifest Destiny: Muslim Modernities on Three Continents", in *Shades of the Planet*, eds. Wai Chee Dimock and Lawrence Buell (Princeton: Princeton University Press, 2005), 62.

7   Ian Watt, *The Rise of the Novel* (Stanford: Stanford University Press, 1957), 117.

8   Esther Gabara, *Errant Modernism: The Ethos of Photography in Mexico and Brazil* (Durham: Duke University Press, 2008), 17.

twenty-three; although she returned for extended visits, she never again lived there in the sense in which the word is usually used. Yet Cather's admirers do not shrink from identifying her with Nebraska, even though she moved permanently away. In the second major attempt to revive Christina Stead's reputation in the United States, by contrast, Jonathan Franzen said that Stead "fled the country decisively" at age twenty-five.[9] Cather is never said to have "fled" Nebraska, and the contrast is striking, especially in light of the fact that Stead returned to Australia in 1968 and lived there for the last fifteen years of her life, while Cather died in New York City. Or one could compare Stead to James Joyce, certainly an expatriate but one enthusiastically claimed by Ireland and the Irish tourist industry. Joyce left Ireland at twenty-three and returned only for occasional visits, eventually dying in Zurich, but is he ever said to have "fled" Ireland "decisively"? Hazel Rowley makes the parallel with Joyce in her 2007 article on Stead.[10] But she blames Australians' indifference towards Australian authors more than the world's. Franzen's comment suggests that the latter might also have something to do with it. The implication in Franzen's remark is that Australia is parochial and that staying there or being interested in it is only for parochial people. If this were Franzen's informed opinion – if he had made an extensive study of the Australia of the 1920s and decided that it were so – no one could object. The problem is, he clearly did not.

This is not Franzen's fault. To be an adept of Australian literature you must learn a whole literary history, including catchphrases such as "cultural cringe", "pretentious and illiterate verbal sludge", "dun-coloured journalistic realism", "Jindyworobak" and "Ern Malley". To understand Australian literature one has to learn a new geography, metaphorically but also literally. One has to, in a general sort of way, know how far Sydney is from Melbourne, just as one has to know how far Moscow is from St Petersburg to understand Russian fiction. One must know the Northern Territory to read Xavier Herbert's *Capricornia* much as one must know the Caucasus to read Lermontov's *A Hero of Our Time*. In both cases, what Murray might call the "poemes" of the novels' material origins are important backgrounds to understanding the novels artistically. Of course, a reader can enjoy *Vanity Fair* without understanding the precise cultural topography of early nineteenth-century London. But paying attention to this topography does not provincialise the book; it does not make one's perspective hopelessly Londonish, or stop one from seeing the book on a universal scale. Stead's Australian origins, by contrast, are not seen as important. This is not because there was anything unique about Stead's relationship to Australia. She left her home country, as did Ernest Hemingway and Gertrude Stein, D. H. Lawrence and Robert Graves, in an age when literature was often associated with expatriation, exile and internationalism.

As an individual, Franzen may well be willing and able to consider the cultural context of Stead's novels. Franzen's oeuvre as a novelist, after all, shows a consummate craft and an ability to work up large subjects. In writing about Stead for the general American public, however, he does not expect his readers to do so. In this, Franzen follows Randall Jarrell, whose 1965 preface to the Holt, Rinehart & Winston reissue of *The Man Who Loved Children* declared it a canonical world novel. In explaining Stead's novel, Jarrell was more

---

9 Jonathan Franzen, "Rereading *The Man Who Loved Children*", *New York Times Book Review*, 6 June 2010. In fact, according to Stead's biographer, Hazel Rowley, Stead left Australia at twenty-six. Hazel Rowley, interview with Leonard Lopate, WNYC radio, 22 August 2005.
10 Hazel Rowley, "The Mocking Country", *Weekend Australian*, 25–26 August 2007, 8–9.

comfortable using Russian references than Australian ones. This reflected the fact that Russian fiction was familiar to American readers, whereas Australian fiction was not – but it was also, for all Jarrell's downplaying of the political aspects of Stead's work, a Cold War gesture: Russia, unlike Australia, was in 1965 important in world affairs.[11] So, although the Australia Stead left had produced John Shaw Neilson, Miles Franklin, Christopher Brennan, Henry Handel Richardson, Katharine Susannah Prichard, Mary Gilmore, Vance and Nettie Palmer and, in the rising generation, Kenneth Slessor, Eleanor Dark and Xavier Herbert – among them symbolists, modernists, feminists and socialists – it is dismissed as parochial, and the international reader is presumed to be so incurious as to accept that proposition.

Stead herself, as Robert Dixon demonstrates, distanced herself from Australian nationalist critics, even accomplished ones such as Nettie Palmer, whose physical appearance and intellectual perspicuity Stead mocked.[12] Stead did not wish to be bound by Australia. But she is Australian, and knowing something about Australia helps us to read her. Stead's first novel, *Seven Poor Men of Sydney* (1935), was a great work of Australian social realism, written in Paris and influenced by *Ulysses* (as any portrait of a modern city written after Joyce was likely to be). The fact that it was social-realist did not mean that it was not also modernist. As Hazel Rowley pointed out in a 2005 radio interview with Leonard Lopate, *Seven Poor Men of Sydney*, the only book of Stead's set totally in Australia, was, along with *The Salzburg Tales*, her best received book internationally, more than *The Man Who Loved Children*.[13] Dixon notes that these books were published internationally in the USA and UK in the 1930s, but not in Australia until the mid-1960s, after Australian academics had begun to notice Stead.[14]

Franzen also downplays the importance of Stead's gender and the pertinence of feminist criticism to her work. Franzen calls Stead's allegiance to feminism "dubious" and quotes her as saying that she wished to "write 'like a man'", although he then says that she was not enough of a "man" to do so successfully. Yet being a woman was Christina Stead's "other country", even if she did not see herself as a feminist or as an advocate for the collective experience of women: it is an aspect of what Hannah Arendt called "natality", "the most general condition" of her existence.[15] Rowley notes that Stead "wrote beautifully" about "being a woman".[16] Franzen has expressed surprise that *The Man Who Loved Children* is not a "core text" in "women's studies courses". If its feminist interpretability is repeatedly played down, however, such will be the case.[17]

Probably too much has been made of Stead's anti-feminism – which was notably evident in interviews she gave in the early 1970s – just as too much has been made of her expatriation. She was an Australian woman writer, and even when she did not write

---

11   Like Jarrell, Franzen was also writing an introduction to a reissue of the book, but, given its shorter length and Franzen's greater fame, it unsurprisingly found publication in the *New York Times Book Review* as well.

12   Robert Dixon, "Australian Fiction and the World Republic of Letters, 1890–1950", in *The Cambridge History of Australian Literature*, ed. Peter Pierce (Melbourne: Cambridge University Press, 2009), 223.

13   Hazel Rowley, interview with Leonard Lopate, WNYC radio, 22 August 2005.

14   Dixon, "Australian Fiction", 248.

15   Hannah Arendt, *The Human Condition* (Chicago: University of Chicago Press, 1958), 9.

16   Hazel Rowley, interview with Leonard Lopate, WNYC radio, 22 August 2005.

17   In the weeks after Franzen's article appeared, several feminist academics wrote responses pointing out that they did teach the book in their courses.

explicitly about those identities, her take on global twentieth-century history derived from them. But Stead wrote in an era when – unlike both the late twentieth century and the late nineteenth century – female voices and feminist perspectives were not in favour. War and economic catastrophe had foregrounded more "masculine" concerns and the literary mainstream was often misogynistic.[18] In addition, Stead happened to have a satisfying marriage to a man she loved and respected. In this she was like other Australian women writers of the era, including Eleanor Dark (called by During "the best stay-at-home comparison with Stead"), Judith Wright and Gwen Harwood.[19] As Simon During points out, for Stead "romantic heterosexuality was a source of empowerment and pleasure for women as well as exploitation".[20] Like Wright, Stead tended to see feminism as anti-male, a stance neither woman wished to endorse in part because of the roles their husbands played in their lives.

Interpreting Stead's work in light of her life experiences is not to contort her words, but to recognise the wider horizon that acknowledging her gender and her Australian origins can afford. But the tradition in which Franzen writes is as uninterested in gender as it is in nation; it registers no impact from the critical work of feminist academics, whether Australian or North American, such as Diana Brydon, Judith Kegan Gardiner, Margaret Harris, Joan Lidoff, Susan Sheridan and Louise Yelin. The Jarrell-led revival, in contrast, had been inflected and given a more political slant by critics such as Michael Ackland, Jonathan Arac, Ann Blake, Simon During and Anne Pender.[21] Indeed, the Australian academic revival of Stead began before Jarrell's 1965 preface was published, as instanced in R. G. Geering's 1962 *Southerly* article, "The Achievement of Christina Stead", although Jarrell's piece registered no awareness of this.[22]

The tendency, fostered by Jarrell, to see Stead as a neglected modernist, has led critics to downplay other aspects of her identity, suggesting a cosmopolitanism far more untethered than she actually practised. By not rushing to distance Stead from her natal contexts, I will instead locate her in a modernity whose failures help to explain the rise of neoliberalism. This entails a revaluation of Stead as a writer.

The Limits of Revival

The Man Who Loved Children has always been subject to a debate about whether the transposition of its setting from Sydney Harbour to the Chesapeake denudes it of its local pertinence, or makes it meaningful to the lives of millions by giving it a transnational

---

18   Sandra M. Gilbert and Susan Gubar, *No Man's Land: The War of the Words* (New Haven: Yale University Press, 1989).
19   During, *Exit Capitalism*, 79.
20   During, *Exit Capitalism*, 73.
21   Margaret Harris, ed., *The Magic Phrase: Critical Essays on Christina Stead* (St Lucia: University of Queensland Press, 2000); Susan Sheridan, *Christina Stead* (London: Harvester Wheatsheaf, 1988); Judith Kegan Gardiner, *Rhys, Stead, Lessing, and the Politics of Empathy* (Bloomington: Indiana University Press, 1989); Louise Yelin, *From the Margins of Empire: Christina Stead, Doris Lessing, Nadine Gordimer* (Ithaca: Cornell University Press, 1988); Michael Ackland, "Hedging on Destiny: History and Its Marxist Dimension in the Early Fiction of Christina Stead", *Ariel: A Review of International English Literature* 41, no. 1 (2010): 91–109; Anne Pender, *Christina Stead, Satirist* (Altona: Common Ground Publishing, 2002); During, *Exit Capitalism*.
22   R. G. Geering, "The Achievement of Christina Stead", *Southerly* 22, no. 4 (1962): 193–212.

scope. Louise Yelin asserts that *The Man Who Loved Children* "bears the marks of its origins".[23] Although Stead may have tried to jettison any Australian trappings at the behest of her publisher (as Hazel Rowley puts it, Simon & Schuster insisted Stead do it for "marketing reasons")[24], the novel's first reviewers registered its background nonetheless. Charles Poore, in the *New York Times*, captured two aspects of the book that Franzen and Jarrell both miss: its Australian qualities and its severe critique of traditional family power structures. Poore wrote in his review of "overtones of other places" and "undivulged roots"; he knew, biographically, that Stead was from Australia, but he was also observing that the book itself feels spliced and splayed, and that Australia is its absent centre, its displaced subconscious.[25] This is a richer reading than either lamenting the book's displacement from Australia or hailing its transnationalism; Poore understands that the displacement, the half-exposed roots, are part of the book's complex literary value. Necessarily, all of Stead's possible settings are transnational. Had she been allowed by her publishers to set the book in Sydney, she would inevitably have been influenced by fictional portrayals of European cities; even a novel by a lifelong Sydneysider would thus contain transnational elements.

The headline of Poore's review, "A Bureaucrat at the Breakfast Table", brilliantly plays on the title of Oliver Wendell Holmes' 1858 essay collection, *Autocrat at the Breakfast Table*, to insinuate how Sam Pollit's domestic tyranny is also inflected by the bureaucratic practices of twentieth-century totalitarianism, later to be anatomised by Arendt. Poore, a workmanlike daily journalist, writing in the darkest days of World War II, saw Stead's deep, disturbing critique of traditional institutions, amid the pessimism of a world that seemed to have lost its moorings, something later critics, writing in more sedate times, have missed.

Fiona Morrison, in much more detail, follows up Franzen's important point that Jarrell's revival of Stead failed. Stead, argues Morrison, has not been successfully revived in that people with literary tastes generally do not read Stead; she is not widely taught in university English classes; she is not an author firmly ensconced in the global literary tradition.[26] The more recent Stead revival, in focusing so squarely on *The Man Who Loved Children*, and in insisting that this book must be seen first as a novel about the vagaries of family life, rather than about social and political injustice, suggests a wish to revive Stead in a manner that has already failed. The very fact that she still needs reviving is proof of the failure of this approach. When in 2005 Hazel Rowley discussed Stead on New York Public Radio, for example, she failed to cause a sensation, although she spoke intelligently (and with more acknowledgement of Stead's Australian aspects than either Jarrell or Franzen).[27] This does not mean that *The Man Who Loved Children* has not reached many individual scholars and readers. But as Morrison states, the book is still not in the canon and During forecasts that the most the novel will attain is a "quasi-canonical" status.[28] Perhaps the enthusiasm for *The Man Who Loved Children* is simply overdone. It may be a fine, original

---

23 Hazel Rowley, interview with Leonard Lopate, WNYC radio, 22 August 2005.
24 Yelin, *From the Margins*, 31.
25 Charles Poore, "Books of the Times: The Critic on the Hearth", *New York Times*, 18 October 1940, 19.
26 Fiona Morrison, "Unread Books and Christina Stead's *The Man Who Loved Children*", in *Republics of Letters: Literary Communities in Australia*, eds. Peter Kirkpatrick and Robert Dixon (Sydney: Sydney University Press, 2013), 127–36.
27 Hazel Rowley, interview with Leonard Lopate, WNYC radio, 22 August 2005.
28 During, *Exit Capitalism*, 93.

book, but one whose advocates have overstated their case. Alternatively, perhaps they have gone about making their case the wrong way.

Psychic Bloodlands

Both Jarrell and Franzen see Stead's main subject as the family and applaud her for, in a Tolstoyan way, writing about this fertile ground for character, motive and emotion. (Not withstanding that *Anna Karenina* is not so much about family as it is about marriage; it is not a book about "parenting" the way *The Man Who Loves Children* is.) Yet the behaviour of Sam Pollit in the novel leads to the question: can and should the family continue as an institution? Can the family survive after we have seen it enabling such sadism and narcissism? Is the story of the Pollit family a harrowing exposé, or simply a comic mock-epic about a quirky family and a gruff, eccentric father who is at once impossible and endearing? The latter is hardly how Sam Pollit is portrayed by the book or perceived by most critics. Louise Yelin has spoken helpfully of Stead's novel as a "national family romance" that emphasises the affinity between family and nation, and thus by implication – although Yelin does not stress this – the homology between Sam as patriarch of the family and the modern idea of the national, ideological autocrat.[29] Paul Giles describes Sam as "quite literally, the voice of the nation" as he contemplates a career in radio.[30] But this is not how Franzen and Jarrell describe the book. Although Franzen aptly identifies the novel's "private language" and "psychological violence", in his reading the book is mainly about a "patriarch" who is a "crackpot". *The Man Who Loved Children*, however, goes much further, questioning the viability of one of the central institutions of human society in a way no other novel has done. In this sense *The Man Who Loved Children* could be, to the modern family, what Orwell's *Nineteen Eighty-Four* was to the modern state, representing the height of the minatory aspects of modernity.

Terry Eagleton has argued that praising psychological depth assumes that well-drawn characters are essentially more good than bad.[31] This assumption can act as a straitjacket, favouring as it does multi-dimensional, quirky characters in whom the good ultimately balances or outweighs the bad. To interpret Sam Pollit this way would be to misread him. Stead endows him with an aspect of the buffoon, which makes his aspirations for dominance seem ludicrous. But comic touches have often been used in portrayals of Hitler, from Charlie Chaplin onward; the susceptibility to comic portrayal does not make the underlying subject any less menacing.

Stead was a political writer.[32] Michael Wilding has, as Margaret Harris puts it, "argued for the coherence of Stead's leftist vision" and has criticised what he termed the "depoliticisation" of Stead's vision in Hazel Rowley's biography. Brigid Rooney has linked Stead's early novels to the Popular Front atmosphere of 1930s Paris.[33] Giles says aptly that Franzen did Stead a "profound disservice" by his determination to "privatise ... the novel's sphere

---

29 Yelin, *Margins of Empire*, 35.
30 Paul Giles, *Antipodean America: Australasia and the Constitution of US Literature* (New York: Oxford University Press, 2013), 353.
31 Terry Eagleton, *How to Read Literature* (New Haven: Yale University Press, 2013), 55–61, 171–73.
32 Brigid Rooney, "Christina Stead", in *A Companion to Australian Literature Since 1900*, eds. Nicholas Birns and Rebecca McNeer (Rochester: Camden House, 2007), 235. Rooney describes Stead as a member of "the left intelligentsia".

of activity"[34] Indeed, Stead's leftist politics may be said to be her third country, after Australia and her gender.[35] Jarrell could revive her no earlier than 1965 because previously, McCarthyism had stanched the reputation of writers known to be on the left; Jarrell's focus, in his introduction to *The Man Who Loved Children*, on its treatment of the intimate and domestic might reflect not only his own well-known preoccupations, but also the need to dampen Stead's politics in order to rescue her for an aesthetic, rather than social, agenda. Indeed, Jarrell was needed to lead Stead's revival because Stead's long-time advocate, Stanley Burnshaw, a man perfectly well equipped in critical terms to do the job himself, was known for being on the left (he had been a political antagonist of Wallace Stevens in the 1930s). Jarrell, in During's phrase, was "the mainstream charismatic ex-leftist", widely seen as a middle-of-the-road aesthete, whose endorsement might recover Stead's reputation.[36]

As During points out, Stead was on the far left, a weird kind of "committed, if heretical, Stalinist".[37] If her portrait of Sam is meant to be a send-up of New Deal liberalism or of the Australian Labor enthusiasm of her father, it takes aim at its targets, at least nominally, from the left. Yet, although Stead persistently displayed what Michael Ackland calls "a lifelong interest in the socialist movement", she remains politically difficult to define.[38] Stead was politically aware, and displayed a concrete engagement with Northern Hemisphere geostrategic stakes that writers who set their novels in Australia, such as Dark and Prichard, did not possess, although their political views were similar to Stead's. As Rowley notes, *The Man Who Loved Children* was not only transposed geographically, but also temporally: it was originally set during the Edwardian years before World War I.[39] Had it kept this setting, Sam Pollit might have seemed a wayward Victorian paterfamilias, a variation on Edmund Gosse's description of his father in *Father and Son* (a portrait Peter Carey would later draw on in *Oscar and Lucinda*). Instead, because Sam is thrust forward into the mid-twentieth century, we read his attitudes in the light of twentieth-century dictatorships and mass social control. Stead's Marxism assisted her understanding of the family as not a natural but a contingent unit. In Stead's sense of it, the family is a society in which power, if exploited by the wrong people, is arbitrary, unmotivated by any sense of the plural good. This has been concealed by Jarrell's and Franzen's readings, which, as Ackland puts it, concentrate on the novel only as "an unforgettable, rarely equalled portrayal of family life" but miss the political dimensions of her work.[40]

The historian Timothy Snyder has eloquently spoken of the "bloodlands" of Central Europe during World War II and the Cold War, the interstitial plains where the contest between the two great totalitarian European powers played out.[41] *The Man Who Loved Children* may be said to depict the psychic bloodlands of the twentieth century, the places

---

33   Margaret Harris, ed., *The Magic Phrase: Critical Essays on Christina Stead* (St Lucia: University of Queensland Press, 2000), 19; Brigid Rooney, "Loving the Revolutionary: Re-reading Christina Stead's Encounter with Men, Marxism and the Popular Front in 1930s Paris", *Southerly* 58, no. 4 (1998): 24–102.
34   Giles, *Antipodean America*, 353.
35   There is a pun here involving "left" in the sense of leaving her country and "left" in political terms. Stead did not leave Australia for the USA, for Europe, for the UK; she left it for the left.
36   During, *Exit Capitalism*, 75.
37   During, *Exit Capitalism*, 57.
38   Michael Ackland, "Realigning Christina Stead: A 'Red Stead'", *Overland* 192 (2008): 49.
39   Hazel Rowley, interview with Leonard Lopate, WNYC radio, 22 August 2005.
40   Ackland, "Realigning Christina Stead", 49.
41   Timothy Snyder, *Bloodlands: Europe between Hitler and Stalin* (New York: Basic Books, 2010).

where a person like Sam, with a modern sense of autonomy unaccompanied by a modern sense of democracy, could put out the autonomous aspirations of those near and allegedly dear to him. The feeling that orthodox family structures are a trap is seen in many twentieth-century Australian novels: David Malouf's *Remembering Babylon*, Kate Grenville's *Lilian's Story*, much of Patrick White's work. There must be more here than an allegorical rejection of Mother (or Father) England. Stead wrote about marriage, relationships and family in ways that appear to be more literal than they are, yet are not purely allegorical, either.

Stead wrote in a modern global context, in which Australia was beginning to have diplomatic, economic and cultural relationships with countries other than Britain, but before the hegemony of the United States and its representational practices (as anatomised by Michael Hardt and Antonio Negri in *Empire*). Her greatest novels were written before the Cold War bipolar consensus had hardened, when it appeared, at various junctures, that Germany, Japan, the United States and the Soviet Union would all be major world powers. Stead's books of the 1940s were written in a post-imperial yet unstable and multipolar world. In the world in the background of Stead's fiction, the minor regime can speak to the major; the domestic martinet can exemplify the national or transnational hegemon. It is significant that Sam is at once Australian – a scientist like Stead's own Australian father – and American, both in his name, which evokes Uncle Sam and Samuel Langhorne Clemens, aka Mark Twain (Sam was also the name of Stead's own grandfather) and in his aggressive, colloquial vulgarity, suffused with an American sense that authority need not be dressed up in a polite accent.

Stead refuses to "other" totalitarianism entirely, or to pretend that it cannot exist in the English-speaking world. Indeed, an alternative title for the book could be, to borrow the title of Sinclair Lewis' 1935 alternative history, *It Can't Happen Here*. Stead shows us that, within the Pollit family, it can, whether the "here" is on Sydney Harbour or Chesapeake Bay. Graham Huggan has suggested that Stead's novel is more about "the brutal logic of eugenics" than about patriarchy.[42] This is concomitant with the possibility, far more evident in the twenty-first century than in Stead's day, of seeing Australian and American practices of "colonial governmentality" as differing more in degree than in kind from those of totalitarianism.[43] This is a point made by Doris Pilkington Garimara in *Follow the Rabbit-Proof Fence* (1996), with its clear analogy between the eugenic and assimilationist practices of A. O. Neville, Chief Protector of Aborigines in Western Australia, and the way similar bureaucracies operated in Europe and Asia to assist authoritarian governance.[44] The Australian government policy of severing Aboriginal parents from their children is emblematic of this. Another instance is seen in certain novels of Carmel Bird, particularly *The White Garden* (1995), in which religious and moral institutions betray the trust of those they are supposed to ward, much as occurred in Europe. In these examples, as in Stead's novel, the protection of children's welfare becomes an excuse for the wielding of fearsome and unwelcome force. In the world of *The Man Who Loved Children*, democratic

---

42 Graham Huggan, *Australian Literature: Postcolonialism, Racism, Transnationalism* (Oxford: Oxford University Press, 2007), 87.

43 David Scott, "Colonial Governmentality", *Social Text* 43 (1995): 195.

44 Doris Pilkington Garimara, *Follow the Rabbit-Proof Fence* (St Lucia: University of Queensland Press, 2013); see also Tony Barta, "Discourses of Genocide in Germany and Australia: A Linked History", *Aboriginal History* 25 (2001): 37–56.

polities do not represent the antithesis of totalitarianism but a palliated version of it; this totalitarianism may be confined to the family, but it is nonetheless latent in society.

As Louise Yelin points out, even Sam Pollit's Labor-supporting "public spiritedness" has an "Australian provenance in the values of the new middle-class".[45] In mid-century modernity, all ideologies, even reformist liberalism, are contaminated by the presence of totalitarian regimes. This is not to say that Stead was being relativistic, but to say that even the most benign society at the time was inflected by the dangers of authoritarianism, even if these dangers became acute only in certain contexts. Stead might possibly have admired social-democratic Sweden as much as she would any democratic polity, yet, as Alberto Spektorowski and Elisabet Mizrachi have argued, the Swedish welfare state practised eugenics as part of its efforts to mould a just society, and saw no contradiction in this.[46] Roberto Bolaño playfully speculated about fictional American fascist writers in *Nazi Literature in the Americas* (1996), and the Pollits could well be included in a dictionary of *Nazi Families of the Americas* (or *of the Antipodes*). The Australian latencies in Stead's fiction have as much to do with totalitarianism as they do with colonialism.

Little-Womey

Most critics of *The Man Who Loved Children* have concentrated on Sam's relationship with his wife, Henny, whom he dominates until she unexpectedly gets her own back, or with Louie, the bright, proactive daughter who brilliantly withstands her father's denigration and bullying, a figure modelled on Stead herself. Louie leaves the family home – or family prison – and, despite her ungainliness and low self-esteem, confidently enters the world. Meanwhile Ernie, the eldest son, finds his precious moneybox has been stolen by his mother, desperate for funds, and realises that the self-proclaimed omnipotent Sam is in fact incompetent and impecunious. Ernie hangs himself in effigy as a mode of protest, a gesture that puts him well on the way to self-determination. A younger son, "Little Sam", along with Saul, one of the twins, surprises his father by refusing to clean up a mess, thus protesting in a larger sense against the mess his father has made of all of their lives.

I wish, however, to consider Sam's relationship with his second daughter, Evie, whom he nicknames "Little-Womey", or little woman, in an act of gender derogation and infantilisation. Little-Womey might seem pathetic, or just unlucky, like the victims of totalitarian regimes who simply did not get out in time. What the novel shows, however, is Evie's resistance. When Louie stands up to Sam by denying his claim that he makes it rain, Evie is "puzzled". Prompted by Sam to back him up, she says uncertainly, "I dunno."[47] This may mark her as a compliant guinea-pig for Sam's preposterous claim that, in effect, he is God. Sam sees himself not just as a *paterfamilias* but also as a deity, a creator of meaning and sustenance. This is far more than the overweening behaviour of a bossy or paternalistic father; it is psychosis and augurs, on the personal level, the claims that totalitarian states

45   Yelin, *From the Margins*, 34.
46   Alberto Spektorowski and Elisabet Mizrachi, "Eugenics and the Welfare State in Sweden: The Politics of Social Margins and the Idea of a Productive Society", *Journal of Contemporary History* 39, no. 3 (2004): 333–52.
47   Christina Stead, *The Man Who Loved Children* (Melbourne: Melbourne University Press, 2010), 293. All subsequent references are to this edition and appear in parentheses in the text.

made in the twentieth century: that their ideological leaders were in effect God-kings. Sam is effectively founding a "political religion" (as the historian Michael Burleigh has used the term) with himself as a godhead, using the family as a cult.[48]

But even if she lacks her older sister's gumption and intelligence, Little-Womey is not as compliant as she appears. As her father continues robustly to press his grandiose claim, she looks scared, "thinking about her own incredulity" (294). She is potentially taken in, but she is aware of her potential to be taken in – and to be conscious of one's own incredulity is the first step from gullibility to scepticism. If Louie is the dissident who leaves the totalitarian society early, Little-Womey is the beguiled dupe in the deluded crowd, as portrayed in Thomas Mann's *Mario and the Magician*, Elias Canetti's *Auto-da-Fé* and Czeslaw Milosz's *The Captive Mind*. The beguiled dupe may be manipulated or gratified or subjugated at first. But her eventual disaffection is undeniable proof of the failure of the system.

Jarrell and Franzen miss this about Evie's slow but palpable disaffection because they see Sam's extreme behaviour as just a piquant example of how quirky and captivating family life can be. Yet Sam's behaviour is so outlandish, so extreme, it is hard to think of the family as an institution surviving it, much as a previously stable mode of rule often cannot survive a particularly brutal despot. To measure the full impact of Sam's behaviour, it is deleterious to focus exclusively on Louie, whose individual aptitude will get her, as it might a Dickens hero, out of the prison cell and towards outward progress or self-fulfilment. A reading that focuses solely on Louie might conclude that exceptional ability is the only brake on systemic brutality, or the only mode of escape from it. But it is Little-Womey (who, unlike Louie, has an archetypally feminine name in Evie), whose resistance, when it slowly comes, will break all the malevolent hopes of perpetual domination for which Sam stands. In a way later to be made familiar by Michel Foucault, her resistance stands within the system that it challenges. Note this exchange from the book, as quoted and critiqued by Franzen:

> More and more clearly, though, Louie emerges as Sam's true nemesis. She begins by challenging him on the field of spoken language, as in the scene in which he's expatiating on the harmonious oneness of future mankind:
>
> "'My system,' Sam continued, 'which I invented myself, might be called Monoman or Manunity!'
>
> "Evie [Sam's younger, favored daughter] laughed timidly, not knowing whether it was right or not. Louisa said, 'You mean Monomania.'
>
> "Evie giggled and then lost all her color, became a stainless olive, appalled at her mistake.
>
> "Sam said coolly, 'You look like a gutter rat, Looloo, with that expression. Monoman would only be the condition of the world after we had weeded out the misfits and degenerates.' There was a threat in the way he said it."[49]

---

48 Roger Griffin, ed., *Fascism, Totalitarianism and Political Religion* (London: Routledge, 2013). Griffin is sceptical about some of the excesses of the theories of Burleigh and, before him, Elie Kedourie. Such religious-based theories will inevitably be more popular on the right than on the left, but the basics of them are difficult to deny.

49 Jonathan Franzen, introduction to *The Man Who Loved Children* (Melbourne: Melbourne University Press, 2010), xii.

What Franzen misses is that while Louie may be the one who challenges Sam, it is Evie who at first joins in her elder sister's derision of their father, then retreats once she realises that the centre of authority does not think it funny. When the favoured part of a subject people begins to dissent, the regime knows its goose is cooked. Here Evie resembles the awakening populace of an authoritarian regime: she may be cowed, but she is not quelled or stilled.

Franzen makes the debatable contention that "abuse" is a "natural" or "potentially comic" feature of the family landscape. This is to read the book as the product of a less politically correct time when people were more relaxed about parental prerogative – less concerned, as the young Hillary Rodham Clinton put it in her pioneering work on children's rights, that "children should have the right to be permitted to decide their own future if they are competent".[50] But the language of "incredulity" that Stead uses in Little-Womey's slow, hesitant but nonetheless steady resistance to her father shows that she was writing a parable of unwarranted authority within the family, or, more aptly, saying that unwarranted authority had become so widespread in the 1940s as to infect even the allegedly private reserve of the family.

Louie is the leader of the resistance in her family, but she does not have to do it alone; she is not the only person who can envision a world not yet dead under Sam's hegemonic sway. Stead's portrayal of Little-Womey reveals both the breadth of Sam's ambition and the hidden reserves of obdurate yet insensate resistance, a resistance that makes possible Sam's undoing, even if Louie and Henny are the most visible agents of that undoing. If Evie did not resist, the book would celebrate only the exceptional resisters, not the ordinary ones: it would introduce a dichotomy of winners and losers even in the depths of the totalitarian cauldron.

Weird Public-Mindedness: *For Love Alone*

There is a danger, for the critic, of inadvertently dividing Stead's canon into winners and losers: of giving so much attention to *The Man Who Loved Children* that the other novels suffer from neglect. Rowley and another American novelist who has championed Stead, Jonathan Lethem, have however extolled Stead's entire oeuvre. Lethem has said that Stead's *I'm Dying Laughing* (published posthumously in 1986) influenced his own portrayal of the fraught emotional lives of communists in *Dissident Gardens* (2013).[51] In this spirit, I will briefly discuss Stead's two other mid-career novels, *For Love Alone* (1944) and *Letty Fox: Her Luck* (1946).

For Love Alone is a female *Bildungsroman* that charts the progress of its heroine, Teresa Hawkins, from a stunningly evoked Sydney Harbour to London, where she follows her former teacher, Jonathan Crow, a man with "modern" intellectual aspirations whom Teresa eventually sees through. In his combination of insecurity and arrogance, Crow could be a younger version of Sam Pollit. Instead, Teresa turns to an American businessman, James Quick – a clear analogue to Stead's husband, Blake – but not before a fleeting "jump to

50   Hillary Rodham, "Children's Rights: A Legal Perspective", in *Children's Rights: Contemporary Perspectives*, eds. Patricia A. Vardin and Ilene N. Brody (New York: Teachers College Press, 1979), 21.
51   "Which Writers Influenced Jonathan Lethem? 'You've Got to Be Into Old, Weird Books'", *The Globe and Mail*, 8 November 2013. (No author given.)

the third" with a man named Harry Girton (which unsettles any complacency the reader might feel about drawing parallels with Stead's own life). Crow's addled utopian-reformism gives way to Quick's more savvy critique of the market from within.

Throughout the book – and here the title of Les Murray's *Poems Against Economics* is once again pertinent – modernity is defined in terms of socialist economics, not symbolist aesthetics or stream-of-consciousness narration. The London depicted in the book's second half is the Bloomsbury of John Maynard Keynes, not that of Virginia Woolf. It is very different from our era of what Yann Moulier Boutang has called "cognitive capitalism", a renascent, contemporary capitalism based on the harvesting of mobile and digitally manifested knowledge.[52]

Simon During has said that Stead was so far left that she was off the map politically in a way that liberated her, and that her literary power was indeed occasioned by a hatred of capitalism. Free from a "soft-progressivist" New Deal desire to humanise capitalism or to make it more equitable, she could rove outside the capitalist paradigm entirely.[53] This raises the question of Stead's attitude to the social-welfare state. With its avoidance of dogmatic socialist realism on the one hand – despite Stead having praised just that in her essays – and its flagrant experimentation on the other, Stead's distinctive style could be said to fit into Michael Szalay's category of New Deal modernism, which in the work of James Agee, for example, harnessed literary craft with social concern.[54] But not only did Stead apparently not pay close attention to the Roosevelt administration in any respect other than its posture towards the Soviet Union, but her villains, including Sam Pollit and Jonathan Crow, could well (as Arac has pointed out) be seen as representatives of the New Deal: technocrats, improvers, modernising engineers.[55]

In turn, Stead's most famous American admirers, Jarrell and Franzen, seem to be drawn to her work partially by its criticism of twentieth-century statism. The Jarrell who wrote, "From my mother's sleep I fell into the State, / And I hunched in its belly till my wet fur froze", and the Franzen whose engaging first novel, *The Twenty-Seventh City* (1988), can be read as an allegory of excessive governmental power, may have found succour in Stead's guying of people who, in their private lives, want to maintain regimes that put weaker people in a state of dependence, often via the rhetoric of solidarity and democracy.[56] In the early twenty-first century, the only people with any voice in the public sphere who were critiquing moderate-left statism were from the right. With her critique of Sam Pollit, Stead offered a critique of statism from the radical left.

Susan Sheridan speaks of a sense of "material or spiritual impoverishment" in Stead's fiction.[57] Sheridan further asserts that most of Stead's characters are petit bourgeois: they may be getting by economically, but they are hardly in a position to influence society. The pretensions of Sam Pollit and Jonathan Crow reveal their powerlessness. Jonathan travels to London, where his ideology is exposed as not up to the rigour of the modern world.

---

52 Yann Moulier Boutang, *Cognitive Capitalism* (Cambridge: Polity Press, 2012).

53 During, *Exit Capitalism*, 69.

54 Michael Szalay, *New Deal Modernism: American Literature and the Invention of the Welfare State* (Durham: Duke University Press, 2000).

55 Jonathan Arac, *Impure Worlds: The Institution of Literature in the Age of the Novel* (New York: Fordham University Press, 2010), 53.

56 Randall Jarrell, "The Death of the Ball Turret Gunner" (1945), quoted in Diana Fuss, *Dying Modern* (Durham: Duke University Press, 2013), 62.

57 Sheridan, *Christina Stead*, 61.

Sam, for all his egoism, is a worker for the government, a cog in the system. Even as he tries to mime governmental authority within the family, he knows that, career-wise, he is but a mid-level civil servant.

Yet for all her mockery of Sam Pollit's enthusiasm for Roosevelt's New Deal and its petty-bureaucratic reform, Stead had her own New Deal moments. In 1942 she proposed a project for a Guggenheim Fellowship, a book described by Rowley as an anthology of "legends and contemporary lore from diverse regions in the United States".[58] The proposal could not have been more New Deal: it closely resembled the Workers' Progress Administration guides to individual states that proliferated in the 1930s, overseen by the government's Federal Writers' Project. Stead's Guggenheim project does indicate a certain mid-centuriness, not, incidentally, just in the populist interest in folklore but in the idea of the anthology itself, with its incorporation of multiple modes, seen again in the picaresque frame with which Stead so often surrounds her accounts of modern experience. If, as Claire Seiler argues, a predominant trope of the mid-century was "suspension", a sense of equipoise, deadlock and stilled transition, the picaresque can be seen as the form of extended narrative that can most readily accommodate suspension, in a way that brings the representational novel as a form into the twentieth century.[59] This perhaps is what leads During, after stressing Stead's uncompromising hatred of capitalism, to call her nonetheless a "soft progressivist".[60]

Within this soft-progressivist suspension, we may see that Teresa's love for Crow, as disconnected from reality as it might be, has positive consequences. It enables her to find a community of shared interests and concerns, not just of geographical proximity. Knowledge does not so much pierce the naivete of love as allow love to flow outward, ramified and reticulated. Jarrell said in his introduction to *The Man Who Loved Children* that a novel is a prose fiction of some length with something wrong with it: it lacks the perfection, and the desire for perfection, that is found in the lyric poem or the short story. The asymmetrical and uneasy imbalance of love and knowledge is the aspect of Stead's novel that feels "wrong" – awkward, unbalanced, distracting – and that therefore makes the novel as a whole a success.

The melange of passion and worldliness of *For Love Alone* creates an alternative public space. This is something Stuart Sayers discerned when reviewing *For Love Alone* for the *Age* on its Australian reissue in 1969. Sayers wrote that "an entire universe coalesces about the chief character".[61] Teresa never rejects a vision of a modern community, even after she realises Crow's vision is fatuous. Like Stead herself, Teresa arrives at her public-mindedness by a weird route (Crow's faux-progressivism, Blake's outlandish Stalinism), but her trajectory is applicable to many other people of her time. In her sense of social panorama and of complex interpersonal relationships, Stead proposes a public-mindedness different from one premeditated by a conscious progressive ideology.

In her one sustained piece of literary theory, Stead spoke of herself as writing the "many-charactered novel" and also the "novel of strife".[62] The greatest strength of the

---

58   Rowley, *Christina Stead*, 282–83.
59   Claire Seiler, "The Mid-Century Method of *The Great Fire*", in *Shirley Hazzard: New Critical Essays*, ed. Brigitta Olubas (Sydney: Sydney University Press, 2014), 103.
60   During, *Exit Capitalism*, 59.
61   Stuart Sayers, "Books You Just Listen To", *Age*, 23 August 1969, 10.
62   Christina Stead, "Uses of the Many-Charactered Novel", in *Selected Fiction and Nonfiction*, edited by R. G. Geering and A. Segerberg (St Lucia: University of Queensland Press, 1994), 196-99.

community of *For Love Alone* is, paradoxically, that it is so adversarial. The failed relationship of Teresa and Crow limns an antipathy that yet implies a world of dependency, vulnerability and mutual caring. Teresa's acceptance of a complex world, a world she once thought was animated by love alone, is informed by her romantic disillusionment, but this does not represent an utter disappointment. The modernity described by the novel is multi-layered and multipolar, and although its heroine struggles with gender hierarchies and ideologies, she still manages to navigate forward within its systems. The sense of individual agency brings us forward from modernity to late modernity, and heralds Stead's next heroine, who finds herself even less comfortable amid modern systems than does Teresa.

Letty Fox : Australian Unconscious in Late Modernity

Letty Fox, like its two predecessors, is a long novel composed in the United States featuring a young female protagonist who grows out into the world during the novel's course. Letty, however, is the most adult and self-assured of the three protagonists, and she is most symptomatic of trends that would continue later in the twentieth century. Stead's first novel was composed after the end of World War II, and its action extends into 1946. It synthesises the pre-modern picaresque with the nineteenth-century *Bildungsroman*, adding a modern sexuality so shocking that, as Nicole Moore has discussed, it was censored in Australia.[63]

In *Letty Fox*, Stead employs what seems like an amalgam of prose styles, an askance and frenetic version of T. S. Eliot's "ideal order", André Malraux's *musée imaginaire* or Joseph Frank's "spatial form", all the while rendering a split portrait of a New York whose sophistication is admired – particularly when it is coupled with anti-establishment politics – yet is built on misogyny.[64] Robert Genter has spoken of late modernity as featuring elaborate symbolic systems, confident in their self-constitution and thus not needing to admit history.[65] Letty is embedded in these forms but she is not at home in them; she yearns for a more direct historical causation, and this both makes her relationship to her milieu less viable than Teresa's and positions her as a forerunner of a future mentality.

It is with *Letty Fox* that Stead enters what this book terms late modernity. This late modernity was premised – to riff on Eliot's *cri de coeur* that he was Anglo-Catholic in religion, classicist in literature and royalist in politics – on being socialist in economics, static in temporality and still patriarchal in gender politics. Late modernity is here juxtaposed against a neoliberalism that is libertarian in economics, dynamic in temporality and – it must be said in the current era's favour – allows for a wider range of gender roles and expressions. Late modernity was recently described by Nick Pearce in the *New Statesman* as a time when "The huge inequalities of the *belle époque* gave way to a more egalitarian distribution as capital was destroyed, taxed or nationalised to pay for the war effort and

---

63 Nicole Moore, *The Censor's Library: Uncovering the Lost History of Australia's Banned Books* (St Lucia: University of Queensland Press, 2012).
64 Joseph Frank, "Spatial Form in Modern Literature: An Essay in Two Parts", *The Sewanee Review* 53, no. 2 (1945): 221–40; André Malraux, *Le musée imaginaire* (Paris: Albert Skira, 1947).
65 Robert Genter, *Late Modernism: Art, Culture, and Politics in Cold War America* (Philadelphia: University of Pennsylvania Press, 2011).

the building of public services and social security".[66] Gender equity, however, was not yet a priority.

The young New York socialite Letty Fox, as Stead presents her, would be a happier character in the neoliberal era, with its frank exaltation of selfishness and personal fulfilment as defined by material gain. But she is a more interesting character when her buccaneering self-realisation faces the constraints of late modernity, and the genius of Stead is to recognise the fascination of this character within these conditions. Jill Lepore has dissected the contemporary rhetoric of disruptive innovation, the way any novelty is deemed by neoliberalism to be progress and therefore desirable for its own sake.[67] It is no accident that Joseph Frank's essay on "spatial form" was so influential on the late-modern era's idea of what constituted literary innovation; far from the neoliberal dynamism excavated by Lepore, what was new in modernist poetics was, after its initial innovations of modernism, stasis.

Stead's prose in *Letty Fox* epitomises this late-modern stasis. Yet *Letty Fox* is a picaresque novel, in which its title character makes a rogue's progress through a jaded and cosmopolitan New York society. The picaresque seems inherently progressive, or at least serial, as one incident must succeed another and the hero is always trying to get somewhere, even if he or she usually fails. But on a deeper level, the picaresque is static because the landscape of the picaresque is never historically inflected. If the tableau of the picaresque were historically variable, the picaresque hero would not be able to make any sort of progress. Roguish or not, he or she would be bewildered and at a loss.

I wish to connect this to Fiona Morison's argument that luck is a crucial structural principle in the novel. Luck, for Morrison, fills the otherwise potentially paralytic gap between individual agency and systemic coherence.[68] The randomness connoted by this theme of luck, however, might lessen any sense of political pertinence. Anne Duchene's 1978 review in the *Times Literary Supplement* – in an instance of Stead's own authorial luck, the novel's first review in that august journal – cites the references to fascism and communism as "peripheral anachronisms".[69] Although this is too harsh, their overt mention is far less tacitly integrated into the novel than is the tacit presence of totalitarianism in *For Love Alone* and *The Man Who Loved Children*. Furthermore, Letty's fate depends on the amorality of, as the subtitle denotes, luck, and she does not even make the presumption that Bernard Williams called "moral luck"[70] – that is, the belief that you are good because you are fortunate.

If Letty's inability to change a static world is emblematic of late modernity, her habit of invoking "luck" while privately crediting her progress to her own merits is consummately neoliberal. Letty would thrive in a world where, to use Piketty's phrase, "meritocratic extremism" means that those who strive the most are lauded because they are the only ones who seem to represent positive energy in an atmosphere dominated by the accumulated privilege of inherited wealth. Or she might have thrived in the nineteenth century, when,

---

66   Nick Pearce, "Thomas Piketty: A Modern French Revolutionary", *New Statesman*, "Cultural Capital" blog, 3 April 2014. http://www.newstatesman.com/2014/03/french-revolutionary.

67   Jill Lepore, "The Disruption Machine: What the Gospel of Innovation Gets Wrong", *New Yorker*, 23 June 2014. http://newyorker.com/magazine/2014/06/23/the-disruption-machine.

68   Fiona Morrison, "The Rhetoric of Luck in Christina Stead's *Letty Fox: Her Luck*", *Antipodes* 28, no. 1 (2014): 111–22.

69   Anne Duchene, "Victors of Love", *Times Literary Supplement*, 8 September 1978, 985.

70   Bernard Williams, *Moral Luck* (Cambridge: Cambridge University Press, 1982).

as Piketty remarks, novelists such as Balzac described a world in which "inequality was to a certain extent necessary: if there had not been a sufficiently wealthy minority, no one would have been able to worry about anything but survival".[71]

In Balzac's world, wealth and privilege allowed for choice and aspiration, as opposed to merely getting by. In Letty's era, with a large aspirational bourgeoisie, the circle of choice was widened. Privilege does not make her extraordinary or give her more agency than others. The notion of luck allows Letty to exploit others without assuming a malicious intent. In the egalitarian Fordism of late modernity, when even Ford's automobile workers could and did see themselves as middle class and even well off, Letty is a fish out of water, so much so that she has to go back to a tradition even older than the bourgeois novel – the picaresque – in order to find a mode in which her adventures can at once stand out from those of others and not truly harm anyone.

Letty was born too soon for neoliberalism. She must make do with the givens of a world whose main ideological pillar, Freudianism, she finds deeply disillusioning, because it seems to dim her individual agency. She scoffs at the psychiatrist who says her problem is a fixation on her father; Letty accuses vulgar Freudianism of invoking parent-fixations as the source of every problem, even though, given Letty's propensity for significantly older men, the psychiatrist might have a point, even if only in the same way as a stopped clock is right twice a day. The relationship between Letty's sister Jacky with the scientist Gondych, whom at one point Letty nicknames "Father Gondych", cries out for Freudian explication, as does Letty's amoral and will o' the wisp desire to steal Gondych from Jacky, who actually cares about the pathetic old man. If people live vulgar-Freudian lives, they will invite vulgar-Freudian analyses. Stead is not out simply to gore Freudian clichés but also to pinion the empty urbanity that gives rise to them.

The book might reject Freudianism, but it arguably has an Australian unconscious. Brigid Rooney, discussing Shirley Hazzard's depiction of Naples in *The Bay of Noon*, writes of "the trace of the antipodean province", a trace that is also present in Stead's rendition of New York.[72] The nation-state unexpectedly haunts this transnational book. Paris is a city, in Stead's eyes, as much beyond the vulgarity of nationhood as is New York. But neither of the book's two cities, nor the nations in which they are embedded, represents an ideal of nationhood in *Letty Fox*. This role is assumed, bizarrely, by Liberia, by the territory which is to become Israel, and by what will later become Indonesia. Letty speaks of herself as "taking up the question of Zion and Liberia", likening the idea of resettling Jews in Palestine and that of the nineteenth-century resettlement of Americans in Africa as visionary movements that looked to the past for inspiration for a national future. Letty dates a young African American man, Jeff Mossop, and seems interested in Africa not as a land of racial uplift as envisioned by the Jamaican political leader Marcus Garvey, but as a new arena for industrialisation (a premonition of how, later, India and China would be seen by the West).

Zion and Liberia both turn out to be illusions for Letty, but they are more tempting sirens than either Marx or Freud, because they inspire, in her view, real passion in their adherents, unlike the affectations of Susannah Ford, the pseudo-liberated mother who in-

---

71   Piketty, *Capital*, 416.
72   Brigid Rooney, "'No One Had Thought of Looking Close to Home': Reading the Province in *The Bay of Noon*", in *Shirley Hazzard: New Critical Essays*, ed. Brigitta Olubas (Sydney: Sydney University Press, 2014), 41.

sists that her son enter analysis in order to be free of all hang-ups. The national temptation is renewed when Letty meets her last serious boyfriend before her marriage, Cornelis De Groot, a middle-aged Dutchman who is in line to be the next governor of Curacao and, he hopes, "Surinam, Celebes. And, later, much later ... Java".[73] The spectre of colonial governance in South-East Asia inevitably brings to mind Australia. In *Letty Fox*, however, Stead alludes more overtly to the colonial world of *Max Havelaar* than to that of *For the Term of His Natural Life*.

Among Letty's boyfriends, Cornelis is especially significant. She is with him at the beginning of the narrative, which then lopes back before skipping forward; she ultimately leaves him for Bill van Week (another Dutch name). The name "De Groot" itself has an Australian valence: Francis de Groot, an Australian right-wing paramilitary leader who could have stepped from the pages of D. H. Lawrence's *Kangaroo*, famously disrupted the opening of the Sydney Harbour Bridge in 1932. The irony is further compounded by the fact that New York itself is a former Dutch colony.[74] It is with Cornelis De Groot that the novel comes closest to naming Australia, and the Dutch connection reminds us that Stead became more of a "New York" writer than an American, Australian or transnational one. As During points out, the patronage of Stead by middlebrow American intellectuals such as Clifton Fadiman diverted her from the cosmopolitan social realism of the 1930s and led her to write books that were more parochially anchored in a New York familiar to her intended reader. In the 1940s, Stead was displaced but also secondarily localised, and at times her novels pointed back indirectly to her first locality: Australia.

Both Liberia and Zion are outward projections from the imaginations of people living elsewhere – African Americans and Jews respectively – and these are the places, rather than Paris or New York, that most tug at Letty's heart and most tempt her to arrest her picaresque progress. Zion and Liberia are both anti-diasporic. They represent a temptation considerably deeper than Marx or Freud, as they are intimately bound up with the men Letty tries to love. And here is where Australia comes in, not just in its proximity to Celebes and Java, but in the way the Dutch colonies, along with Israel, Liberia and Australia, are all still settler colonies, at various stages of securing independence. In 1946, Liberia was an always tottering experiment that the USA worried would be annexed by Britain or France; Palestine was still under the British mandate; Indonesia was struggling to free itself from Dutch control. Israel is an especially interesting example. Paul Keating described Australia as "a multicultural nation in Asia" and Israel similarly is a multicultural yet predominantly European country in Asia. In evoking these other colonial societies, Stead gestured to an Australia to which she felt a deep, almost libidinal attachment but which, for her, was not yet manifest in history. It ironically constitutes the absent centre of *Letty Fox*'s surprisingly circular conception.

Australia is evoked throughout the novel by indirect references. The most compelling is the name of Letty's father (a man long divorced from her mother), who in Letty's mind is completely exempt from Oedipal fixation: Solander Fox. Daniel Solander was the botanist aboard Captain Cook's first *Endeavour* voyage, which, in European terms, discov-

---

73   Christina Stead, *Letty Fox: Her Luck* (Melbourne: Melbourne University Press, 2012), 472. All subsequent references are to this edition and appear in parentheses in the text. One also thinks of the Cornelius involved in the wreck of the *Batavia* during the seventeenth-century proto-exploration of Australia by the Dutch.

74   Morrison, *Antipodes*, points out the Dutch etymology of the word "luck" itself.

ered Australia. Cape Solander at Botany Bay, an important place of arrival and departure, is named after him and is visible from Stead's childhood home, Lydham Hall. (Stead's own father, as mentioned earlier, was a biologist.) Hazel describes Solander's lover, Persia, as "Stead's idealised fictional self", and this name gestures towards a country then in the thick of geopolitical competition among world powers. Interestingly, Persia was also the name of the nineteenth-century Australian poet Henry Kendall's daughter, to whom he dedicated a poem:

> I have given my darling the name
> Of a land at the gates of the day,
> Where morning is always the same,
> And spring never passes away.
> With a prayer for a lifetime of light,
> I christened her Persia, you see ...[75]

Kendall's poem "Bell-Birds" was a pedagogical staple in Australian girls' schools in the early twentieth century, and Stead may well have encountered "Persia", with its sense that Persia somehow mysteriously gestured to Australian landscapes.

In *Letty Fox*, a subterranean Australia emerges, glimpsed in the references to Solander, to other colonial settlements, and even in the expression "Such is life!" At the book's end, Uncle Percival Hogg (another botanist, and a misogynist) charters a ship, the USS *Sons of Liberty*, to take men bound by alimony payments from the USA to Paraguay, "to set up his colony, Parity, Paraguay". Uncle Perce explains, "They have the smallest ratio of women to men in the world due to Lopez, who almost extinguished their manhood in his wars; it's impossible for women to tyrannise over men" (506). In a still-patriarchal late modernity, Perce senses an incipient decolonisation in gender terms threatening, analogous to the impending independence of Israel and Indonesia. So he runs off to Paraguay, an independent but deeply wounded nation. In the nineteenth century, Paraguay had suffered the authoritarianism of the dictator Francia (as vividly chronicled by the novelist Augusto Roa Bastos), followed by Solano Lopez's pitiable aggression and then, in the 1930s, the Chaco War. Paraguay's large indigenous Guarani population took it further out of the European orbit than Australia.

In Australian terms, however, Paraguay represents something more. In the 1890s it was the site of William Lane's expedition to found a utopian "New Australia",[76] a quest that has parallels with Stead's sense that she had to travel outside Australia in order to be Australian. Paraguayan society also contains elements – white supremacism, socialism, patriarchy – that crop up in *Letty Fox*, in its evocation of what is, to later eras, an odd amalgam of left and not-so-left. By mentioning a country bound up with Australian history, Stead let clued-in readers – at that point, almost exclusively Australian readers – know that, imaginatively speaking, she still in some ways called Australia home. If *For Love Alone* explicitly announces its Australian basis and then gravitates to the transnational centre of

---

75   *The Poems of Henry Clarence Kendall* (Melbourne: Robertson, 1903), 177.
76   Anne Whitehead, *Paradise Mislaid: In Search of the Australian Tribe of Paraguay* (St Lucia: University of Queensland Press, 1998).

London, *Letty Fox* evokes a hidden Australian identity from within the transnational maw of New York, a city W. H. Auden called "the great Rome / to all those who lost or hated home".[77]

It is a tribute to Christina Stead's consummate ingenuity as a writer that she finds, in the synchronic vault of late-modern prose, a new Australia. Stead's importance as a writer lies in the way she approached the challenges and calamities of the twentieth century from an acutely Australian angle. By the time she died in 1983, late modernity had run its course and society was about to turn the corner into neoliberalism. The endemic frustrations of late modernity will be the subject of the next chapter.

---

77   W. H. Auden, *Collected Poems*, ed. Edward Mendelson (New York: Random House, 2007), 235.

3

"Medium-sized Mortals": Elizabeth Harrower and the Crisis of Late Modernity

Revivals: From Heroic to Systemic

In *The Field of Cultural Production*, Pierre Bourdieu argued that, in the symbolic network of modernity, "losers win".[1] A novelist like Flaubert, who did not enjoy much commercial success, is far more esteemed than a more commercially successful writer, not just in spite of Flaubert making less money but *because* he made less money. The ratio between financial and imaginative success was inverse. One can see this in the counterculture as late as the 1960s, when the American bohemian writer Seymour Krim could say, "if you are a proud, searching 'failure' in this society, and we can take ironic comfort in the fact that there are hundreds and thousands of us, then it is smart and honourable to know what you attempted …".[2] Honourable failure – conceived as smart, proud, searching – was seen as superior to success in bourgeois terms, which focused on money, status and power. There was an asymmetry: those who were losers in the real world were winners in the symbolic world Krim sketches.

In neoliberalism, the asymmetry between the winners in the real world and the winners in the symbolic world is eliminated. There is no gap: the relationship between the real and symbolic worlds is one of reproduction, mimesis or miniaturisation, not inversion. Neoliberalism claims that the old obstacles to success have been removed, and that people are now assessed, as Thomas Piketty observes, on "the basis of their intrinsic merits" – not on inherited wealth, class, gender or race.[3] If there is nothing to stop anyone succeeding, those who do not must be failures – not losers who win, but losers who merely lose. If symbolic capital swirls the other way from real capital in a kind of uncertainty principle, art thus might be able to resist the pressures of capitalism. In any event this is what

---

1   Pierre Bourdieu, *The Field of Cultural Production*, ed. Randal Johnson (New York: Columbia University Press, 1994), 154.
2   M. G. Stephens, "The Dogs of Literature – Seymour Krim: Bottom Dog Part I", *The Hollins Critic* 51, no. 5 (2014): 8.
3   Thomas Piketty, *Capital in the Twenty-First Century*, trans. Arthur Goldhammer (Cambridge: Harvard University Press, 2014), 334.

the late-modern mentality hoped and assumed. Here I discuss the works of Elizabeth Harrower and, at the conclusion of the chapter, Patrick White as emblematic of the last stage of modernity before neoliberalism arrived to replace it.

In the novels of Elizabeth Harrower (born in 1928), for the most part the protagonists lose; they are victimised or constrained by society. But they also in some way win, even if only by increasing our estimation of them. The reader looks down on those who oppress or limit these characters. In most cases gender is involved: female characters are brutalised or led astray by men in whom they have trusted and invested too much. Despite the welfare state and a seeming general tendency towards social equality, the patriarchal forces so evident in Stead still persist.

Harrower may continue the dynamics at play in Stead's work, but her route back to canonicity has been very different. The revival of Christina Stead has been heroic, closely associated with specific individuals who, through the force of their personal reputations, have pulled her work onto the international stage. This was in the tradition of earlier revivals, particularly T. S. Eliot's engagement with the seventeenth-century metaphysical poets. Although the twentieth-century interest in the baroque was Europe-wide, the revival of these poets largely depended on Eliot's personal taste and discernment. The revival of Elizabeth Harrower, however, followed a different pattern.

Beginning in the late 1970s, there had been a series of revivals of previously neglected female writers. Although the writers concerned were women, their revival was not an explicitly feminist one. It can be differentiated from the republication of neglected twentieth-century female writers such as Antonia White and Rosamond Lehmann by Britain's Virago Press (led by the Australian Carmen Callil) in the 1980s, which garnered notice in academic and activist circles but not among general readers.

Unlike the concurrent revival of female writers for explicitly feminist reasons, these women writers were associated more with arch moral sagacity than with feminist activism, and were revived by publishers and belletrist critics. Some were still living, though elderly, when their works were revived: Barbara Pym in the UK, Paula Fox in the USA.[4] Some had been dead for many years, such as Dawn Powell, the American comic novelist whose publication by Steerforth Press was paradigmatic of the revival process: a writer known in her own day but only perceived as a secondary talent, revived a generation after her death as a major American writer. Powell had died recently enough (1965) for her works still to be in copyright. In the USA, copyright lasted fifty years after the death of the author (in 1998, thanks to pressure from the Walt Disney Company for the protection of Mickey Mouse, new legislation extended this to seventy years). If a book had gone out of print, the rights might have reverted to the author or to her estate, but the work would still be under copyright. If the original publisher reasserted its rights, or if some other publisher acquired them, no other house could publish the book without permission. Steerforth agreed to have Dawn Powell be published by the Library of America, a clear win–win proposition for both publishers as they served such different markets.

---

4   Tim Parks, *Translating Style: The English Modernists and Their Italian Translators* (London: Cassell & Co., 1997), 172. Parks speaks of "the revival of her fortunes" in 1977. Enough time has passed since then for Laura Miller, writing in a March 2013 *Slate*, to call for a revival of Pym's revival. Jonathan Lethem, *The Ecstasy of Influence* (New York: Vintage Books, 2012), 389, speaks of the revival of Paula Fox as being "the most encouraging revival since Dawn Powell".

This was the general pattern for the revived novelist, and Harrower's revival largely followed it. Before 2012 or so, Harrower was remembered only in Australia, but her ensuing Australian and international rediscovery, led by her Melbourne-based publisher, Text, followed the paradigms already established by the cases of Powell and Fox. Moreover, Harrower was revived in an international way, not along the lines of the nationally defined feminism adumbrated in, for example, Susan Sheridan's *Nine Lives*, which focused on postwar Australian women writers.[5]

There was also an invisible distinction between writers from the more distant past, who tended to be championed by critics with cutting-edge theoretical agendas, and those from the near past, whose revival was associated more with general readers and their literary pleasure. Text forthrightly says on its webpage that it believes "that reading should be a marvellous experience, that every book you read should somehow change your life if only by a fraction".[6] This wording serves to distance Text's books from how-to manuals or trashy potboilers, but also and more pertinently from books seen as ideologically didactic. It also suggests that books exist above the market, even though the phrase is itself in part – if not solely – a marketing device. This commercial imperative distinguishes the revival of authors such as Powell, Fox and Pym from writers from the more distant past, whose work was out of copyright and could be taken up by multiple publishers. When eighteenth-century writers such as Frances Burney or Charlotte Lennox came back into academic vogue as a result of feminist and new historicist criticism, multiple publishers could and did publish their works. With Powell and Harrower, however, specific publishers held the rights and led their revival. Steerforth and Text adopted Powell and Harrower respectively as their signature authors; in doing so, the publishers sought to promote not only the author's work but also the company's own profile. Furthermore, although these revivals were not as closely associated with single champions as those led by Eliot and Jarrell had been, there were still individuals involved: Gore Vidal and the literary and music critic Tim Page in the case of Powell; Jonathan Franzen and David Foster Wallace in the case of Fox; Philip Larkin in the case of Pym. The academic revivals had tended to be more collective. (The case of the African American writer Zora Neale Hurston, revived on an individual basis by Alice Walker but then widely taken up within academia, may be said to split the difference here.)

Text Publishing's revival of a series of Australian books, which as of 2015 numbered well over 100, could also be said to diverge from the usual pattern.[7] Text's emergence was part of a revival of independent Australian publishing that included Black Inc., Scribe, Giramondo, Puncher & Wattmann and Sleepers, and helped to counter the conglomerate-heavy scene of the early 2000s described in Chapter 1. Text in particular, led by publisher Michael Heyward, has ramified the current literary market by acquiring books no longer in circulation and energetically promoting them, both at home and internationally. Text also published Geordie Williamson's *The Burning Library: Our Great Novelists Lost and Found* (2012), a survey of Australian fiction that features, although not exclusively, many writers who have been revived by Text. Text, however, has not focused solely on writers still in copyright: the Text Classics series includes late eighteenth-century accounts of the earli-

5   Susan Sheridan, *Nine Lives: Postwar Women Writers Making Their Mark* (St Lucia: University of Queensland Press, 2011).

6   https://www.textpublishing.com.au/about.

7   https://www.textpublishing.com.au/text-classics.

est white Australian settlement by Watkin Tench and Matthew Flinders, as well as works by Miles Franklin, Henry Handel Richardson and Joseph Furphy, all long out of copyright and available in editions by other publishers. The series also features books first published in the past few decades, such as Kate Grenville's *The Idea of Perfection* (first published in 1999) and J. M. Coetzee's *Diary of a Bad Year* (2007). The inclusion of these recent books, written by currently active and internationally celebrated authors (Grenville won the Orange Prize; Coetzee the Nobel) has made the Text Classics series both more prestigious and more newsworthy than the smaller set of Australian classics published by Angus & Robertson, now a subsidiary of HarperCollins, which concentrates on older, out-of-copyright works, or the Sydney University Press print-on-demand Australian Classics series, which features new editions of Australian classics with scholarly introductions intended largely for an academic audience.[8] As the star of the Text series, Harrower, in contrast, is very much in the tradition of Fox and Pym: a writer still alive when revived, who is seen to belong to the recent rather than distant past and to offer something different from what is currently being produced and reviewed.

Losers Who Win

Stead and Harrower may both have been revived for the twenty-first century, but they are two very different writers. Harrower's novels are short to medium in length, largely domestic in setting and concerned chiefly with relationships. Although they are full of philosophical and social resonance, they lack the realistic heft of much of Stead's work. And whereas Stead had been revived once before, Harrower's revival in the 2010s was the first time her work had been considered since its initial publication in the 1960s. Like Stead at the time of her first revival in 1965, Harrower was alive (although no longer writing fiction) at the time of her rediscovery. But whereas Stead's first revival in the mid-twentieth century was meant to redress the perceived defects of that era, Harrower's revival in the 2010s reflected a new nostalgia for the 1960s and 1970s. Against the backdrop of neoliberalism, the era in which Harrower wrote her fiction was suddenly seen fondly as a bygone period of postwar reconstruction and of moves towards equality and social improvement.

Harrower's view of late modernity is as dystopian as it is utopian. But her work very obviously pertained to a decisively different era, one that by the 2010s was no longer the near past (which is always likely to be disparaged by those who historicise) and had moved into the middle distance. Paradoxically, the fact that she seemed far removed from the market-dominated energies of the twenty-first century made Harrower marketable. This new late-modern chic was not confined to literature. The positive reaction to a 2014 exhibition of Australia's quintessential modernist architect, Harry Seidler, at the Museum of Sydney emblematised it.[9] Part of this is cyclical and inevitable, more mathematical than hermeneutic, propelled by a constant demand for novelty: eventually, every era gets its

---

8   More recently, HarperCollins has expanded its A&R Classics series to include contemporary writers such as Steven Carroll, Geraldine Brooks and Janette Turner Hospital.
9   Lenny Ann Low, "Harry Seidler's Life and Legacy Explored in New Exhibition at the Museum of Sydney", *Sydney Morning Herald*, 28 October 2014. http://www.smh.com.au/entertainment/art-and-design/
harry-seidlers-life-and-legacy-explored-in-new-exhibition-at-the-museum-of-sydney-20141030-11d19d.html.

turn, much as, in Pascale Casanova's *World Republic of Letters*, each nation is bound to have its vogue as long as it bides its time. Casanova says, "Every work from a dispossessed national space that aspires to the status of literature exists solely in relation to the conse-crating authority of the most autonomous places."[10] Harrower's reputation was dependent on international acclaim as much as Australian, and her revival was also dependent on the mood of the current time and whether it would condescend to take an interest in the era in which she wrote. The reassessment of late modernity is akin to the reassessment of indi-vidual nations or regions by the literary academy, as when it was decided in the 1980s that the literature of Poland had been underrated and deserved more acclaim. The renewed interest in the late-modern period, however, was not random. It was symptomatic of a growing scepticism, in the wake of the 2007–08 Global Financial Crisis, about capitalist economic policies.

In 2012, Text brought out paperback editions of Harrower's *The Watch Tower* (1966) and *The Long Prospect* (1958). *Southerly* published a special issue on mid-century women writers with an article on male hysteria in *The Watch Tower* by Naomi Riddle.[11] In the *Australian*, Stephen Romei commented:

> in our article last week, the most mentioned "book of 2012" was Elizabeth Harrower's 1966 novel *The Watch Tower*, republished forty-six years later as part of the Text Classics initiative. With the likes of Helen Garner and Delia Falconer naming it the best book they read in 2012, *The Watch Tower* has rocketed up my holiday reading list.[12]

Williamson devotes an illuminating chapter to Harrower in *The Burning Library*. Seem-ingly hopelessly irrelevant at the turn of the millennium, Harrower had surged back to prominence.

Text also made Harrower's titles available as ebooks that could be purchased by readers in the USA and UK, not just Australia. Text sent the first instalments of the Australian Classics series for review to a number of North American newspapers. In June 2013, Michael Dirda, the book critic for the *Washington Post*, wrote a long and appreciative consideration of Harrower, singling her work out among the series of books sent to him and concentrating on *The Watch Tower*.[13] By August 2013 the first two Harrower novels were in major independent bookstores in New York, receiving as much exposure as Stead, who had been heralded by Franzen three years before, and as much even as Peter Carey, who has lived in New York since 1989. In 2013, Harrower's *Down in the City* (1957) was re-released, followed in 2014 by *The Catherine Wheel* (1960) and *In Certain Circles*. The latter was written in the late 1960s but had not previously been published. In November 2015, Text published a collection of Harrower's short stories, *A Few Days in the Country*.

The Harrower phenomenon was a victory for genuine transnationalism. Text, based in Melbourne, reached readers in the USA without going through an American corporate intermediary. Now, it must be admitted that Harrower had had an international presence

---

10 Pascale Casanova, *The World Republic of Letters*, trans. M. B. Debevoise (Cambridge: Harvard University Press, 2007), 109.
11 Naomi Riddle, "Turning Inward on Himself: Male Hysteria in Elizabeth Harrower's *The Watch Tower*", *Southerly* 72, no. 1 (2012): 204–13.
12 Stephen Romei, "Books of the Year", *Weekend Australian*, 21–22 December 2012, 14.
13 Michael Dirda, "Book World: Elizabeth Harrower's *The Watch Tower*", *Washington Post*, 19 June 2013. http://tiny.cc/dirda_2013.

since the beginning of her career: she lived and wrote in London in the late 1950s and early 1960s, and *The Watch Tower* was published in 1966 by Macmillan in London and St Martin's Press in New York (only in 1977 was it published "locally" in Australia, by Angus & Robertson). The Angus & Robertson editions, in particular, did have a modest international circulation. But this small-scale transnational success had long been eclipsed and what little attention Harrower received in the 1980s and 1990s was by academics working within Australia. The transnational Harrower of the 2010s was a new phenomenon.

The Harrower wave peaked in October 2014 when James Wood, the renowned chief book critic of the *New Yorker*, published a lengthy, discerning and appreciative essay on Harrower in that magazine. Wood describes Harrower's writing as "witty, desolate, truth-seeking and complexly polished". The title of his essay, "No Time for Lies: Rediscovering Elizabeth Harrower", embodies all the factors discussed above: the sense of revival and rediscovery and of the active role of publishers and critics in implementing the rediscovery; the perceived moral honesty Harrower shares with Powell, Fox and Pym; and, playing on the other meaning of time, as temporality, that the time of Harrower's novels, now so conspicuously different from the contemporary, is coming back into view.[14]

In January 2015, the *New Yorker* published a short story of Harrower's, "Alice". (Harrower told the magazine that she couldn't remember when she had written the story, but that she had stopped writing fiction in "1971 or 1972".) Furthermore, Harrower's work is influencing contemporary writers in a felt, idiomatic way, as seen in Fiona McFarlane's story "Art Appreciation", published in the *New Yorker* in 2013.[15] Written by an Australian and first published in America, the story captured a sense of frustration with love and life in 1960s Sydney that was recognisably influenced by Harrower in tone and setting. Harrower is now a world writer. This is a far cry from even 2009, when a responsible survey such as Ken Gelder and Paul Salzman's *After the Celebration* called Harrower a middlebrow, socially committed novelist.[16] Harrower is more than that. Through a scrupulous focus on prismatic localities of experience, which has a far wider tacit scope than it would first appear, Harrower's narratives hew to a taut twentieth-century stylistic lyricism. In this mode, she pinpoints the tragic situations of the "medium-sized mortals" she depicts.[17]

If one had to choose a governing scheme for Harrower's fiction, it would be constriction. Letty Fox was able to burst out of her confines through sheer force of will. Harrower's more wan and easily discouraged characters feel more compelled to yield. "The 1950s were the time for the growth of systems", says the Norwegian writer Karl Ove Knausgaard in Book Three of *My Struggle*.[18] Harrower's importance is, in the largest sense, political, not necessarily in a partisan or electoral way (in Australia, the 1950s and 1960s saw the electoral lockhold of the conservative Robert Menzies and his like-minded successors), but in portraying the collective possibilities available to people at a given time.

---

14   James Wood, "No Time for Lies: Rediscovering Elizabeth Harrower", *New Yorker*, 20 October 2014, 66–70.

15   Fiona McFarlane, "Art Appreciation", *New Yorker*, 13 May 2013. http://wwww.newyorker.com/magazine/2013/05/13/art-appreciation.

16   Ken Gelder and Paul Salzman, *After the Celebration: Australian Fiction 1989–2007* (Melbourne: Melbourne University Press, 2009), 201.

17   Elizabeth Harrower, *The Watch Tower* (1966; Melbourne: Text Publishing, 2012), 17. All subsequent references are to this edition and appear in parentheses in the text.

18   Karl Ove Knausgaard, *My Struggle: Book 3*, trans. Don Bartlett (New York: Macmillan, 2014), 3.

We often find the deep past more accessible than the near past. It is easier to desire to speak with the long dead than to reach out to those, like Harrower, who are still living or those like Patrick White, who died only within the last few decades. The hybrid nature of the near past, caught between past and present, is vexing. As suggested by Johannes Fabian in his discussion of the denial of coevalness, another problem is the way people use temporality as a mode of dismissal.[19] Saying someone is outdated is a more acceptable way of saying you dislike them. This became a particular issue in the early 2000s, when some castigated what they called "seventies feminism", as if to tag feminism as outdated was the first step in further delegitimising it (in the process hiding sexism behind a form of ageism).[20] Because the present has seen itself as neoliberal, or involved in the questioning of what were previously established left-wing or welfare-state assumptions, the dismissal of the near past has been associated with a rejection of the left. The near past has been seen, in Francis Fukuyama's phrase, as a modern or late-modern "great disruption", a statist aberration that has been cured by a neoliberal "reconstitution".[21]

The issue becomes complicated with respect to Australian literature. Through the course of various paradigms – nationalist, postcolonial, internationalist – there has been tremendous pressure to validate the Australian literary project, to see it as emerging from British precedent. Though one understands that this sort of hortatory rhetoric is needed in order to secure arts funding and to galvanise peak bodies, it has led us to emphasise a view that new always means better. This was true as far back as Miles Franklin's rejection of modernism at a time of cultural nationalism; it is evident in her disappointment in Stead (after *Seven Poor Men of Sydney* and Stead's expatriation) and in Henry Handel Richardson, who was an internationalist despite staying closer to home and with whom Franklin was "not temperamentally attuned".[22]

This had the baleful consequence of bringing Franklin perilously close to the pro-Nazi Australia First movement, although, as Jill Roe relates, she rejected this movement; Franklin adhered to an "old-fashioned evolutionary nationalism", while Australia First, in Roe's account, was "modernistic, antidemocratic, and looking for the main chance".[23] Although the malevolent male narcissists of Harrower's fiction do not share the rightist politics of Australia First, those adjectives could well apply to them, showing the conjunction of late modernity with power-hungry, ideological narrowness. This linkage between vulgar nationalism and swaggering masculinity played into certain media and pop-cultural stereotypes. The 1994 film *Sirens* portrays a visit by a British Anglican clergyman to the rural retreat of the artist Norman Lindsay as an allegory of Pommie uptightness versus Australian vitality. Lindsay is ribbed and lampooned. He is subject to prudish censorship. But on his own property he is king. Australia is on its own, and happy about that.

---

19 Johannes Fabian, *Time and the Other: How Anthropology Makes Its Object* (New York: Columbia University Press, 2002), 33.
20 See Kellie Bean, *Post-Backlash Feminism: Women and the Media Since Reagan–Bush* (Jefferson: McFarland & Company Inc., 2007).
21 Francis Fukuyama, *The Great Disruption: Human Nature and the Reconstitution of Social Order* (New York: The Free Press, 1999).
22 Jill Roe, *Her Brilliant Career: The Life of Miles Franklin* (Cambridge: Harvard University Press, 2009), 315.
23 Roe, *Her Brilliant Career*, 410. See also David Bird, *Nazi Dreamtime: Australian Enthusiasts for Hitler's Germany* (London: Anthem Press, 2014), 372, for more discussion on the convergence between Australian nationalism and fascism.

Today, transnationalism is often proposed as a solution that will bring happiness where nationalism failed.[24] In Harrower's work, although the national is no longer the solution, the transnational cannot yet be that. In *The Watch Tower*, a male officemate of the young Clare Vaizey tells her she is not reading the "real" news when she reads Australian newspapers and offers to lend her his papers from England. When he leaves Sydney to return to Britain, he promises to "send you some of ours when I get back". Clare, jaded and unexcitable, responds, "Thank you. But don't bother. It doesn't matter. It makes no difference." When the man remarks of Australians, "You get a bad press in London", Clare ripostes, "Do we? Never mind." This is not about Australia not needing Britain any more, or standing on its own feet, but about the malaise Clare sensed as too endemic to be solved by a change of venue or a breath of fresh air from the metropolis.

Although Harrower's novels (except for *The Catherine Wheel*, which is set in London) are precisely and observantly set in specific Australian locales (Sydney in *Down in the City*, *In Certain Circles* and *The Watch Tower*; Newcastle, where Harrower lived for the first eleven years of her life, in *The Long Prospect*), her characters are past the point where landscape or national identity can matter. They were born too late to be euphoric about nationalism and either too early or too prescient to be euphoric about globalisation. Harrower's books give a sense of a society that confines without satisfying. Her world offers no categorical liberation from mid-century industrialism, suburbia or domesticity. This is a world where people will allow themselves to fester in a stasis if it helps them to control others. Harrower's texts have both the virtues and the liabilities of being in the middle. They are middle-class (although her books range from the shabby industrial boarding houses of *The Long Prospect* to the cultivated radical-chic of *In Certain Circles*), and they are in the middle in the sense of being hemmed-in.

There is no neoliberal bimodality between winners and losers here. Even the winners are losers, and the losers are winners if they just endure with some cognition of the horror of their circumstances. This dovetails with the books' generally suburban settings, and a sense that suburbia provides an index of the shift from modernity to late modernity, as seen in the difference between Stead's largely urban settings and Harrower's suburban ones. As Nathanael O'Reilly argues, suburbia was at once a characteristic setting for mid-century Australian fiction but also a target of its sometimes splenetic critique.[25] Harrower's fiction has to be seen as a kind of extension of Patrick White's Sarsaparilla novels. White was a supporter of her work, and the sense of stasis and paralysis seen in *The Solid Mandala* resembles that of Harrower's characters, although no one in her books is as cruel as Waldo Brown or as innocent as his brother, Arthur. Harrower avoids polarities. But her characters have so few options that the reader almost wishes for the emergence of such extremes.

---

24   Michael Jacklin points out that, in the first decade of the twenty-first century, "transnationalism" largely replaced "multiculturalism". See Jacklin, "The Transnational Turn in Australian Literary Studies", *Journal of the Association for the Study of Australian Literature*, Special Issue 2009. http://openjournals.library.usyd.edu.au/index.php/JASAL/article/view/10040.
25   Nathanael O'Reilly, *Exploring Suburbia: The Suburbs in the Contemporary Australian Novel* (Amherst: Teneo, 2012).

Chocolate Factories and Grandmothers: *The Watch Tower* and *The Long Prospect*

In *The Watch Tower* Laura Vaizey feels fixed, confined, in a Manly so parochial it refers to itself as "the village" (31), although it is just across the harbour from Sydney, a major world metropolis. The very title *The Watch Tower* evokes a mixture of T. S. Eliot's line, cribbed from Gérard de Nerval, "*La prince d'Aquitaine dans le tour abolie*" and Foucault's iteration of Bentham's Panopticon, a juxtaposition memorably captured in the title of Philip K. Dick's alternative history novel *The Man in the High Castle*. All these images combine privilege with stasis. This is the Australian condition in Harrower's works, and the white house in which Laura comes to live yokes privilege and paralysis. Harrower's Australia is one where the future is "a boundary" rather than an opportunity, and in which the future of women who lack a man in their lives is absorption into "strange institutions" (12). In Laura's case this is the chocolate factory in which she works (a realistic antipodal obverse of Willy Wonka's in Roald Dahl's 1964 *Charlie and the Chocolate Factory*), where, more through inertia than anything else, she becomes engaged and then married to its proprietor, Felix Shaw.

Felix turns out to be an opportunistic self-promoter. In Williamson's phrase, he is a "perfect beast" who, despite not being really well off or successful, concocts an enabling myth of himself as a self-confident, secular, modern man, a myth that proves disabling for his new and swiftly disillusioned wife.[26] Far from being a stable man of affairs, Felix is a self-pitying, impecunious madman, whose greatest delusion is that he is not mad. Stella, Laura's mother, is lost in dreams of being rescued from her Australian mediocrity by a return to wealth, England, or both; Clare, "remorselessly expectant" (93), is the one who is not totally controlled by the social determinism to which her mother and sister too readily succumb and which Shaw personifies (108). Against the background of World War II, the dangers Shaw presents might seem parochial, yet Harrower convincingly shows that his delusions are symptomatic of the age. Fiona Capp, in the epigraph to her 2013 novel *Gotland*, quotes the British psychoanalytic thinker Adam Phillips as saying, "Because erotic life rearranges the world it is political."[27] Through Eros, Felix malevolently rearranges the lives of his wife and thereby his sister-in-law and so is malevolently political.

The reader takes a savage delight in how little works out for Felix. We are appalled by his decline into penury, failure and the "male hysteria" diagnosed by the critic Naomi Riddle. But we are also vindictively pleased by his failure, not because we do not feel sorry for Laura or, collaterally, Clare, but because Harrower convincingly reveals how often people get it wrong. The world makes idols of anyone who seems moderately successful, but a few turns of fortune's wheel sees them topple. As Nicholas Mansfield points out, this is a world in which nobody really has any individual power.[28] Harrower and the reader collusively chuckle over the folly of it all even as we gnash our teeth about how much waste results from wrong decisions and misalliances. Clare uses a young Dutchman named Bernard to detach herself from Felix and her emotionally bludgeoned sister, but Bernard has to destabilise Felix's authority first; Felix is still adamant in his self-belief despite his

---

26 Williamson, *Burning Library*, 166.
27 Fiona Capp, *Gotland* (Sydney: Fourth Estate, 2013), 166.
28 Nicholas Mansfield, "The Only Russian in Sydney", *Australian Literary Studies* 15, no. 3 (May 1992): 131.

inexorably diminishing circle of influence. Clare escapes from her oppressors, but the air is one of respite rather than liberation:

> More outer suburbs and more time: hills and valleys of roofs, grey-blue gravelled streets, blue-black tarred roads, square miles of brick, corrugated iron, gravel, concrete, hard dry substances, hard shapes, graveyard architecture and landscape. Still time and suburbs passed.
>
> Abruptly the road by the train lines changed colour and character; it was a bush track – bright clay. And there were trees suddenly, swift-moving past – blossoming eucalyptus, pines. Alone in the compartment, Clare jerked the window up and leaned out into the day. The light was wonderful. Waves of air beat against her face, and it smelled of grass, or clover, or honey. (334)

The journey out of the late-modern suburbs brings healing, but the hardness, the constraint, still looms in the background.

Both Clare and Emily in *The Long Prospect* are heroines who, though very young, have ceased to have definitive or determinate hope for the world. This is both because they have been traumatised and because they have seen what self-delusion – a lack of self-knowledge – has done to the older people who oppress them. Lilian is Emily's grandmother, but Emily never calls her by that name and there is little affection between them. Lilian looks after Emily because Emily's mother, Paula, is unwilling to, but she does so only just enough to ensure that she will not be deprived of the girl, like a bad leader doing just enough administration to avoid being booted out. Lilian's unsavoury liaison with her boarder, Rosen, outrages Emily, who finds an ally in Max, the kindly, introspective quondam lover of Lilian's former best friend Thea. The setting may be conventionally domestic, but the particular congeries of relationships are very unusual. *The Long Prospect* is narrated through the third-person perspective of Emily's consciousness, in a way in tune with the period's formal dogma, influenced by Henry James, of the well-made novel – one sees particularly the influence of Frankie in Carson McCullers' *The Member of the Wedding*.

This is another trait Wood remarks upon: Harrower's emulation of Henry James, particularly in her use of third-person limited point of view. This Jamesian predilection was shared by novelists such as Elizabeth Bowen and Glenway Wescott, who were a generation older, but Harrower's last contemporarily published book, *The Watch Tower*, appeared after Wayne Booth's *The Rhetoric of Fiction* (1961) had exploded this Jamesian paradigm. Yet the wounded lyricism of Harrower's writing combines with its astonishing philosophical depth to ask such insoluble questions as: if people are to be judged by equal standards yet are born with different levels of moral character, how is one to square the circle? This moral horizon goes well beyond the frame of taut, austere, technically accomplished realism. To speak of Harrower as a domestic, politically committed or social-realist writer is to perceive the surface but miss the depths. She is politically committed because the domestic relations she depicts – between husband and wife, between guardian and child – are so oppressive, authoritarian and unjust as to become political. Her social commitment lies in her recognition that the denial of human freedom and potential in these situations is but an instance of how, as Shakespeare put it in *Pericles, Prince of Tyre*, "the earth is thronged by man's oppression". As Geordie Williamson remarks, Harrower's vision contains "intimations of Auschwitz" and of "nuclear annihilation", allusions that only need to be dropped lightly, so close in tenor is the domestic tyranny and abuse depicted here to those external political nightmares.[29]

In *The Long Prospect*, even the minor characters are vividly etched. They include Billie, the middle-aged housewife who appeals to Max to go off with her and, when he rejects her, falsely accuses him of indecent relations with little Emily, setting off the sad chain of events that leads to what can only be called the young girl's emotional incarceration. Emily is in an unorthodox situation for a child of any era. Her precocity, combined with Lilian's belief that she too is still in the game of love, precipitates a rivalry between them more intense than most mother–daughter, let alone grandmother–granddaughter, relationships. In comparison, Emily's relationship with her actual parents seems remote, as though they are only deputies for Lilian, who by book's end has in effect restored their broken marriage solely in order to control Emily. Marriage and worldly authority are shams, as is property. Well-intentioned people like Max go just a bit too far and inspire emotions in Emily that are inappropriate; intellect and books are valued but are far out of reach of most people condemned to a life of drudgery and manipulation. Authority within the family is used to control rather than to nurture. Both Felix Shaw and Lilian are authoritarian personalities who are also strangely weak and dependent; despite their absolute self-assurance they lack resourcefulness, inventiveness and self-confidence. Felix may represent, as Michelle de Kretser puts it, "grab-all materialism", yet he is a risible failure in building, just as his pseudo-machismo covers, as de Kretser asserts, "repressed homoeroticism".[30] They are bad eggs in intrinsic terms, but they are also representative of a way of life that does not foster positive outcomes for most people. The institutions of mid-century life – the industrial factory, the welfare state, the black-and-white television serials evoked *en passant* in *The Long Prospect*, expressions of the lower-middle-class culture that was assumed to be the norm – all stifled creativity but made people understand how difficult it was to disestablish authority.

The neoliberal era has given us the illusion that we can disestablish authority simply by cutting taxes for wealthy people and for business, when all that does is consolidate and intensify authority. Harrower's realistic understanding of the malign tendencies of the welfare state suggests that neoliberalism will not cure them. This does not mean we can look to Harrower's fiction for leftist nostalgia or for simple caricatures. Some characters are better than others, and some outcomes are preferable, but, as Brigid Rooney observes, "in Harrower, every choice is marred".[31] The only political hope in Harrower is to realise there is no way out, at least in the short term. Gelder and Salzman read Harrower as a strictly naturalistic and social novelist, while Williamson is so determined to concentrate on Harrower's aesthetic aspects that he scants the novel's social horizons, although he is aware of them. From whatever perspective, however, Harrower's social thought is one of profound and lacerating pessimism.

The Long Prospect does offer some possibilities for dissent and growth, but it treats them ironically or distances them from the foreseeable canvas. Emily champions the Spartans as losers of history, a stance that is similar to Sylvia/Dora's defence of the Carthaginians in Marcus Clarke's *For the Term of His Natural Life*, and in context it makes us think more darkly of Max's motives as Dawes, an adult, ends up having overtly romantic

---

29   Williamson, *The Burning Library*, 171.
30   Michelle de Kretser, "*The Watch Tower* by Elizabeth Harrower", *Monthly*, June 2012, 63.
31   Brigid Rooney to Nicholas Birns, 16 January 2013.

feelings for the young girl. While Clarke's nineteenth-century story has a tragic but emotionally cathartic ending, Harrower's twentieth-century novel is more equivocal but also more ambiguous. Like any great book, *The Long Prospect* is full of wisdom above and beyond the situations of its characters, such as Max's admonitions on what one can and cannot expect to get from a university education. But Harrower will not allow Max to be an unambiguously good figure, a figure the reader probably yearns for as much as Emily does. Instead, Max is like a hybrid of two Patrick White characters, Himmelfarb in *Riders in the Chariot* – an émigré intellectual factory worker, a man whose wisdom is wasted among the complacent and limited – and Waldo Brown in *The Solid Mandala*, whose artistic pretensions are mingled with a self-destructive perversion.

Harrower's female characters are stymied in their choices, and even their potential saviours are flawed. In the twenty-first century, realistically depicted female characters would have many more choices due to the expansion of women's rights and roles (and because there is simply more choice generally). Like Stead's portraits of Sam Pollit and Jonathan Crow, Harrower's evocation of authoritarian males reminds us that the late twentieth and early twenty-first centuries, with their libertarian emphasis on individual volition, did serve to break down not only the patriarchy but also certain restrictively macho renditions of masculinity. This is not to credit neoliberalism with promulgating feminism or with bringing down the patriarchy. As Nancy Fraser has pointed out, feminism can be co-opted by neoliberalism and turned into something very different from its original collective and altruistic spirit. Fraser, a long-time feminist theorist and activist, has accused feminism of being no less than "capitalism's handmaiden".[32] But if the defect of neoliberalism is an excessive polarisation between winners and losers and the equation of human achievement with worldly success, then late modernity, with its preoccupation with system and circularity, was prone to a wielding of male authority and control. We see this in Felix, although Harrower extends this authoritarian principle to female characters such as Lilian in *The Long Prospect*.

The Victims of Late Modernity: *Down in the City* and *The Catherine Wheel*

Although Harrower's women can be tyrants like Lilian, or insensitive absentees like Stella Vaizey in *The Watch Tower*, most of them are victims. In Harrower's first novel, *Down in the City*, Esther Prescott is a seemingly willing victim: on the shelf at thirty-three, she jumps at the chance to wed Stan Peterson, whose uncouth life-force is inversely appealing. Stan represents two principles characteristic of late modernity. First, he appeals to Esther as a man who "had to make his own chances" without culture or cultivation. This may just be masculine sex appeal, making Stan a mundane version of the early Marlon Brando or James Dean. (Harrower mentions "American crooners", and Stan notably drives an American car.) But Stan is also, in Bourdieu's sense, a loser who wins. He is socially disadvantaged but, in an era anxious to smooth things out socially, this disadvantage becomes an advantage: his roughness is valued as virile, energetic, charismatic and subversive. Stan is totally unlike the modernist aesthetes who conventionally benefit from Bourdieu's in-

---

32 Nancy Fraser, "How Feminism Became Capitalism's Handmaiden – and How to Reclaim It", *Guardian*, 14 October 2013. http://www.theguardian.com/commentisfree/2013/oct/14/feminism-capitalist-handmaiden-neoliberal.

verted economy, but he partakes in the modernist reversal of accustomed winners and losers. He participates in the air of "fostered disreputability" that Harrower sees in the neighbourhood of Kings Cross, and his appeal is the product of an analogous sort of inverse valuation. In an era so concerned with, in Max Weber's phrase, "the routinisation of charisma" – a tendency Edward Mendelson sees as a concern in the early works of Thomas Pynchon – the charisma of men like Stan, and like Christian in *The Catherine Wheel*, is a rare commodity.[33] These men's charisma manifests itself so repugnantly because their society, seeking to inhibit all extremes and originalities in the interest of systemic egalitarianism, represses it so much.

Stan is unimaginative, authoritarian in his view not only of himself but of the world (not unlike his namesake, Stanley Kowalski, in Tennessee Williams' *A Streetcar Named Desire*): "How came man on earth? Stan neither knew nor wondered. If he had been asked, he might have said that things were as they had always been."[34] This sense of stasis, of circularity, is heightened by Stan's belief that "politicians born of other politicians – a great racket but a closed one" (77), govern the world. For all the potential dynamism of what Delia Falconer calls his "aggression",[35] Stan is not a threat to the system, nor does he wish to be. His aggression is narrowly channelled against his wife, Esther, so that it becomes a form of control. For all his energy, Stan is just as governmental a figure as a welfare-state bureaucrat, although in Stan's eyes such a person would be laughably effete. Stan, insofar as he has any politics at all, is hardly on the left. But he channels any potential disruptive energy – energy that is indeed felt by Esther during their two-week courtship as disruptive in a sexual way – into governance. This makes his way of life amenable to a socialist or social-democratic mentality. In late modernity, this mentality was predominant, whichever party happened to rule in whichever country.

Another element that might elsewhere be liberating – the city itself – is confining in Harrower's novel. Wood remarks that Harrower's titles have a slightly ironic feeling, as "parodic fabrications" in the manner of Nabokov or Anthony Powell, novelists famous for inventing titles of fictional books within their oeuvres that are more or less meant as satiric indications of second-rate works.[36] While I agree with Wood as to the constricted and possibly self-parodic aura emanating from the titles, I do not attribute this to Harrower's talent not extending from the representative into the titular; rather, her books evoke a deliberate constriction, one that is both enabling and limiting, laden with a felt inadequacy but drawing its touch, its palpability, from that felt inadequacy. If, as John Welchman has argued, titles of paintings are "invisible colours", so might titles of books be invisible characters, exemplifying a deliberate sense of constraint just as Felix and Laura, and Lilian and Max, do.[37] The very title of *Down in the City* suggests that being in the city is not a liberation, but

33 Edward Mendelson, "The Sacred, the Profane, and *The Crying of Lot 49*", in *Individual and Community: Variations on a Theme in American Fiction*, ed. Kenneth Baldwin and David Kirby (Durham: Duke University Press, 1975), 186.

34 Elizabeth Harrower, *Down in the City* (1957; Melbourne: Text Publishing, 2013), 77. All subsequent references are to this edition and appear in parentheses in the text. One also thinks here of course of Satan's "We know no time when we were not as now", from *Paradise Lost*, Book V, line 859.

35 Delia Falconer, "Elizabeth Harrower's *In Certain Circles* Is a Triumphant Final Fugue", *Weekend Australian*, 26–27 April 2014, 20.

36 Wood, "Rediscovering", 92.

37 John Welchman, *Invisible Colors: A Visual History of Titles* (New Haven: Yale University Press, 1997).

an act of abasement or subordination. The titles *Down in the City* and *The Watch Tower* are neatly paired: a watch tower is precisely the vantage point from which one can see people being "down in the city" and potentially keep watch over them. Appropriately, Felix in his chocolate factory is a more articulate version of Stan in the earlier novel. The city does not represent possibility in this book, but boundedness:

> The city, to her, meant a few particular blocks – the best blocks – lying together in a neat rectangle, linked by arcades and department stores, three streets one way, cut by four at right angles, bounded at the top by gardens, self-enclosed at the bottom and either end. (15)

Elsewhere, several male characters are described as working in "cool, straight buildings" (131). The city is rectilinear, spatial; it does not yield any sort of growth or progress. It is enclave as much as metropolis, representing immurement as much as potential. It is more a Borgesian labyrinth than the sort of postmodern conduit of possibility – realisable either as dark anarchy or dynamic plurality – described by Suketu Mehta in his book on twenty-first-century Mumbai, *Maximum City*.[38] Esther marries Stan in an effort to escape this. But although she sees their union as "dangerous and dark", Stan is no Prometheus, able to rend the bounds of urban limitation, but merely "a distorted giant". He is to some degree parasitic on constraint. Accusing Stan of dishonesty in business, Esther's brother, a prominent lawyer, says, "new regulations of all kinds appear to inspire your ingenuity, so that you are at the same time able to overcome them, and increase profit" (177). Stan illegally evades government regulations, but he could not do so if they did not exist; even while he is violating them, he is in another way being governed by them. He is hardly a pure entrepreneur who operates outside government control or who would benefit from deregulation. He is the sort of businessman who complements the welfare state and even depends on it, even if his business is not strictly legal. As such, even while he cheats others, Stan is also ensnared, and, much as Esther dreams of escape from his abusiveness, so does Stan wish for a different situation, at one point yearning for the unbound, if frigid, spaces of the South Pole. Although Stan is "proud of his ability to make money", he is also "not self-sufficient". He is not who he wants to be. He punishes Esther for this, grinding her down until her autonomy and integrity are imperilled. In marrying an outsider, Esther was seeking to be special, but Stan only hems her in even more.

The conformism of the late-modern welfare state is one of the reasons neoliberalism, with its rhetoric of choice, was able to make such inroads. It is best to see this above the fray of party-political affiliations, elections and ideology. This catchall quality of neoliberalism can be seen in the case of the British novelist Zadie Smith. With the publication of *White Teeth* in 2000, Smith emerged as a novelist who represented a hip, multicultural Britain. Set, in an ambitious and rambunctious way, among lower-middle-class migrant communities, Smith's novel was presented as the obverse of the traditional British novel. Multicultural, anti-racist, but also postmodern, Smith's was a radical voice, a voice at once imaginative and from the cultural left. In a commencement address to the New School in New York in May 2014, however, Smith offered a different analysis of her own generation. In its rejection of the collective and its privileging of individuality, she said, her generation had participated in the free-market rhetoric of neoliberalism even if, in overt political

---

38   Suketu Mehta, *Maximum City: Bombay Lost and Found* (New York: Vintage Books, 2005).

terms, it opposed it: "For the most part we were uninterested in what we considered to be unglamorous pursuits. We valued individuality above all things." Smith spoke of initially spurning ancestors and relatives who worked with their hands, only to end up valuing, in chastened midlife, their expression and continuance of time-honoured tradition: "It feels good to give your unique and prestigious selves a slip every now and then and confess your membership in this unwieldy collective called the human race."[39]

But Smith's earlier avowal of a libertarian self declaratively reveals that neoliberalism can include even the hip, the radically diverse and the superficially left wing. It was not just about white men in suits. It was an entire mentality that, like the characters in Elizabeth Harrower's novels, feared the constraining, cyclical mesh of late modernity. The difference is that Harrower sees relief from these conditions as possible only on an individual basis, as depicted in the trajectory of Clare Vaizey in *The Watch Tower*. Smith's generation hoped, paradoxically, for a collective overthrow of late modernity that would unleash individualism. It is this collective overthrow of the collective that I am calling neoliberalism, although it can be called other things – Zygmunt Bauman's "liquid modernity", for instance, or Ulrich Beck's "risk society".[40] To highlight Zadie Smith's partial co-option by neoliberalism is not to castigate multiculturalism for complicity with late capitalism, as Walter Benn Michaels does, or to hanker for the return of an all-pervasive working-class solidarity. The paradigm of late modernity, which as Harrower's work reveals had many problems, is burst, and we cannot go back to the way things were fifty years ago. But Smith does cogently offer proof that what I am calling neoliberalism was all-pervasive and was not just a function of a particular party platform or administrative practice.

As Smith described it, neoliberalism, in shattering the constraining systemic structures of late modernity, created a situation in which to be valued you had to be special, to be special you had to be a winner, and to be a winner you needed other people to lose. There was none of the late-modern sense of "losers who win". In 1957, when Harrower published *Down in the City*, the type embodied by James Dean, Marlon Brando or even Stanley Kowalski may not have had money or social respectability. But he had cultural capital. He was cool. Under neoliberalism, you could be a writer or a businessman, a musician or an entrepreneur. You could be whatever you chose. But you had to be better at it than other people, and the only way to be the best was, as Smith observed, to "value individuality above all things".

It is appropriate that England comes into the picture here, as Harrower devotes one of her books, *The Catherine Wheel*, to a depiction of London society in the generation before Zadie Smith's. The late 1950s was a time of systematic Australian migration to Earls Court, as depicted in novels such as Barbara Hanrahan's *The Albatross Muff* (1977). Harrower's novel, however, is set in the slightly more posh London district of Bayswater. Here, young Clemency James looks to London as "the centre of the universe" and celebrates "the brilliance of the winter season".[41] But Clemency has very low self-worth, as shown by her externalisation of value into London in a sort of non-metropolitan self-abasement. This

---

39 Zadie Smith, commencement speech to the New School, 23 May 2014. https://youtu.be/pjdmo6EKn8I.

40 Zygmunt Bauman, *Liquid Modernity* (London: Polity Press, 2000); Ulrich Beck, *World at Risk* (Cambridge: Polity Press, 2009).

41 Elizabeth Harrower, *The Catherine Wheel* (1957; Melbourne: Text Publishing, 2014), 3. All subsequent references are to this edition and appear in parentheses in the text.

leads her to fall into the trap set by the contumacious Christian. Christian is young, married and, relative to Clemency, lower-class: a handyman, an "employee", whereas she is a "tenant" (19). Although Clemency discerns that Christian's "premeditation" and "boldness" are bogus (20), she eventually succumbs to his charisma and begins an affair with him, even though she knows it will be destructive.

A superficial reader of Harrower might ask, with Robert Graves, "Why have such scores of lovely, gifted girls" taken up with "impossible men"?[42] The answer has to do with the allure of any charisma in a paralysed late-modern age: in a society that has tried to bind everything into system and mediocrity, a charismatic figure can more easily gull a certain number of people. Setting aside the issue of sex – which, although it is undoubtedly the vehicle of Harrower's moral concern, is not necessarily its subject – the more apt question becomes, "Why do self-aware, democratically inclined liberal individuals take up with people who are authoritarian, controlling and malign?" Again the answer comes back to Clemency's own sense of inadequacy. The dynamic recalls Yeats' "The Second Coming": "The best lack all conviction, while / the worst are full of passionate intensity". Clemency has the moral capacity of the liberal individual – she is after all a law student – but not the self-belief. Christian has the self-belief, but his charisma is easily punctured. The illusion of his charisma is produced by the contradictions of late modernity, which empower people to believe they are important, but then drop the floor out from under them at the first hint of stress or pressure.

Clemency fears the malice of people who exist "several feet off the ground" (184). Perhaps, however, she is so firmly on the ground as to be too humble, humble to the point of humiliation. In this state, she must contend not only with Christian but also with a group of self-elevating people, people who make her wish for a "normal intelligent neurotic with whom it was possible to speak a common language" (185). The phrase "normal intelligent neurotic" exhibits a late-modern presumption not of universal happiness but of a society composed of individuals who maturely admit their flaws and live constructively in spite of them. The word "neurosis", used five times in the novel, signifies a flaw serious enough to be disabling individually, but not socially catastrophic. Some people may even turn their neuroses in a positive direction. But Christian, and others such as his friend Rollo, are unable to give up their illusions of self-superiority. They embody the charismatic energy that the systems of late modernity have tried to suppress. The difference between Christina Stead's modernity and Elizabeth Harrower's late modernity may lie in the way Sam Pollit, to beguile and suppress Henny, has to be at once autocrat and clown. In Harrower's fiction, amoral but charismatic people merely have to seem to blend in for the moment; it is people who, like Clemency, sincerely try to be normal (in the terms of the time) who are most vulnerable to their menace. Clemency settles too much for mediocrity. She then feels her own mediocrity attacked by the appeal of those she had hoped would cure it, but who in fact exacerbate it.

---

42   Robert Graves, "A Slice of Wedding Cake", *Selected Poems*, ed. Paul O'Prey (New York: Penguin, 1986).

Beyond Late Modernity? *In Certain Circles* and *The Hanging Garden*

The title of *In Certain Circles* would seem to indicate the late-modern stasis that is Harrower's hallmark, and indeed the last lines of the novel – Zoe Howard Quayle's affirmation that she can move on, "having pierced that stasis" as Claire Vaizey did in *The Watch Tower* – confirm late-modern stasis as the default mood of the book. Yet the phrase "in certain circles" also relates to cultural capital, to reputation, gossip, connections, all things that are redolent of neoliberalism and its preoccupation with mobility. Neoliberalism offers a solution to the problems in Harrower's fiction: males are no longer charismatic under-achievers, but super-proficient nerds; women can achieve on their own and need not find their identity through men. But neoliberalism also brings with it perdition and obloquy for those who cannot win on these terms. Harrower's characters – holding on to a perilous middle – would, in a neoliberal world, fall by the wayside. Where late modernity manifests a critique of existing constraints, neoliberalism is more prone to celebrate its sense of un-trammelled freedom; it glorifies those who are what Wood calls, with reference to Zoe and Anna of *In Certain Circles*, "free agents" who go out to "meet the oncoming present" of the era succeeding their own.[43] One era, the era of the setting of Harrower's fiction, fosters critique through stasis. The other, the era of Harrower's rediscovery, employs dynamism only to forestall radical critique. There is a possible parallel here with climate change: the 1950s was often seen as an era of global cooling, while in succeeding decades temperatures began to rise again.[44] Similarly, Harrower's caesura of standstill and stasis was pierced by an age of unleashed free agency.

Harrower's characters are necessarily driven by factors in their own present, not a future that their choices may anticipate. Wood notes that Harrower's books are partially driven by "anti-bourgeois animus".[45] This seems particularly true of the heroines, with their willingness to put themselves into the clutches of unsuitable, dishonourable men. The men they take up with are not just the objective correlative for these women's masochism. They are desirable because they are brutal and because they are anti-bourgeois. In the three paradigmatic Harrower works with male antagonists – *The Watch Tower*, *Down in the City* and *The Catherine Wheel* – the tyrannical men are at once abusive and insurgent. This becomes subtler in *The Long Prospect* and *In Certain Circles*.

In *The Long Prospect*, the antagonist is the grandmother Lilian, and Max expresses this anti-bourgeois masculinity in a more sensitive and vulnerable way, albeit in the form of a younger and more sensitive Humbert Humbert. Stephen Quayle of *In Certain Circles* is similarly a more sympathetic male outsider than Felix of *The Watch Tower*, although both are anti-bourgeois. Wood's remarks on "anti-bourgeois animus" place Harrower with such writers as Richard Yates, whose anti-suburban excavations Wood mentions, and with more radical contemporaries such as Sylvia Plath and Jack Kerouac. In a different way these anti-bourgeois qualities also participate in a long Australian tradition of anti-puritanical bohemianism, as seen particularly in the work of M. Barnard Eldershaw, the public profile of cultural figures like Dulcie Deamer and the Andersonian tradition of the Sydney Push.[46]

---

43 Wood, "Rediscovering", 94.
44 Mark Maslin, *Global Warming: A Very Short Introduction* (Oxford: Oxford University Press, 2008), 27.
45 Wood, "Rediscovering Elizabeth Harrower", 94.

This anti-bourgeois attitude is also reminiscent of Patrick White's Sarsaparilla novels, with their sense of spiritual aspiration amid ruinous deadlock and paralysis.

Whereas Stead can benefit by a strategic Australian reading, Harrower sets her books in Australia but is more interested in the quandaries of late modernity than in Australia in particular. The world of Harrower's fiction is not only in the Menzies era, before the generation of '68 and Gough Whitlam, but in an age before neoliberalism; in this longer view, it was not rock and roll but leveraged buyouts that were the true successors and antithesis of Harrower's world of late-modern authoritarianism. What Wood calls the "anti-bourgeois animus" shared by Harrower's victims and victimisers would yield to bourgeois bohemians.

If, in the neoliberal era, women are liberated by being free to show leadership and initiative, men are also liberated by being free to be less brutal and more articulate, free to work with their minds, not just their bodies. But the price of this freedom, as Nancy Fraser asserted, is an all-pervasive economism and the disappearance of the zone where working-class and middle-class milieus once came into contact, a zone depicted in Harrower's fiction, albeit uneasily and unheroically. Wood and Williamson both register the social aspects of Harrower's work, while seeing her in broader moral and aesthetic terms than Gelder and Salzman, who tend to pigeonhole her as merely naturalistic. *In Certain Circles*, to which Wood devotes the most space, is not Harrower's best book, but it is the best-suited to this mode of analysis, as it finds itself poised between stasis and dynamism, paralysis and nobility.

More than any other of Harrower's books, *In Certain Circles* is preoccupied with class. The two pairs of siblings, Russell and Zoe Howard, and Stephen and Anna Quayle, are contrasted by class. The Howards are established, wealthy, of a sophisticated and cosmopolitan mien, whereas the Quayles are misfits from the lesser suburbs who are the objects of the Howards' patronage and compassion. Russell Howard is known for his altruism, a quality that is half genuine concern for other people, half moral vanity. This reflects the ambiguities of the welfare state itself, the combination of succour and authority that is the collective version of the more individualised phenomena Foucault labelled "pastorship".[47] Russell invests in a printing factory in order to issue the broadsides and pamphlets that further his social causes. For Stephen Quayle, his business partner and brother-in-law, however, the printing business is just a business – but one that, like Felix's chocolate factory in *The Watch Tower*, he will use in order to conceal his personal flaws. The factory itself – half in the industrial era, half in the information age – is itself indicative of how *In Certain Circles* anticipates the neoliberal era. Zoe's "sheltered life" is reminiscent of the Bentwoods in Paula Fox's *Desperate Characters*, the epitome of a revived book by a living writer and of the paradigm that Text's success with Harrower has emulated.

---

46   For the latter, see Jill Dimond and Peter Kirkpatrick, *Literary Sydney: A Walking Guide* (St Lucia: University of Queensland Press, 2000), 155–56. The authors say that the Push put the libertarian philosopher John Anderson's ideas into practice "through a bohemian lifestyle which disregarded middle-class careerism in favour of pub symposia and sexual freedom". It might be said that Harrower's heroines, when they take up with the unsuitable Stan, Felix and Christian, are disregarding middle-class careerism without even the compensatory virtue of sexual freedom, as ephemeral and ultimately disappointing as that freedom may have been for those able to procure it.

47   See Theresa Man Ming Lee, *Politics and Truth: Political Theory and the Postmodernist Challenge* (Albany: State University of New York Press, 1997), 102.

Zoe, as a daughter of a purportedly liberal man of science, resembles Louie in *The Man Who Loved Children*, although Charles Howard is the real deal as far as science is concerned and his wife Nicole, unlike Henny Pollit, is his peer and collaborator. Throughout the book, biology and medicine are representative of careers that allow women to evade the confinements of marriage. When Russell and Lily's daughters decide to go to England and be ballet dancers rather than doctors, Lily experiences it as an almost Lear-like betrayal; she feels that all the sacrifices she has made for them were not worth it. Lily should have listened to her mother-in-law, Russell and Zoe's mother, Nicole, who warns Zoe against investing her life in individuals, invoking her own work as a biologist as an example of a greater systemic preoccupation.

But as the paradigm shifts from the systemic to the individual, from late modernity to neoliberalism, perhaps the granddaughters, like Stead's Letty Fox, are simply doing what they can to flourish in the emergent order. Both Zoe and Anna undertake artistic careers; Anna's photography, strengthened by her experience of loss and an invigorating trip to the Canadian Rockies, becomes particularly important. *In Certain Circles*, of all of Harrower's novels, values art and the artistic process the most highly.

Although *In Certain Circles* shares major themes with Harrower's previously published works, it also differs from them in ways that might explain why Harrower chose not to publish it sooner, and that suggest a shift away from the givens of late modernity. Anna may not be able to attain happiness in marriage, but she takes herself seriously as an artist. Charles and Nicole Howard may be mocked as *bien-pensant* leftists, somewhat like the Folliots in Stead's *Seven Poor Men of Sydney*, but Harrower – who has made clear that her political sympathies are on the left – also admires their genuine desire to make the world better. Their social activism, although laced with hypocrisy and self-congratulation, is not sourly castigated. Russell, their son, is genuinely compassionate, as is shown when he walks away from a science project because a young woman involved has been bullied into suicide by her team members.

The presence of suicide in the novel, both this young woman's and the apparent suicide of Anna towards the end of the book, portends a far more urgent sense of crisis than the qualified escape or dour stasis with which Harrower's previous novels concluded. Harrower was so dissatisfied with *In Certain Circles* that she refused to publish it at the time of its completion circa 1970 and gave up writing fiction for many years. Although she has not given a reason for this, one might speculate that she felt that the suicide scare was an excessively melodramatic gesture, one that violated the taut, humdrum precision of her earlier fictions. Anna's putative suicide, although it turns out not actually to have happened, is disturbing and gives the book an unsettling tone.

The title *In Certain Circles* might connote constrained circularity. But to move "in certain circles" is not to be confined, but to be known, to have a reputation among certain groups, groups that are in one or another way selective. The novel's circles centre upon the bonds between the siblings Anna and Stephen and Zoe and Russell. Stephen retains his sense of being an outsider despite marrying the more upper-class Zoe; being known in certain circles does not allow him to transcend class differences entirely. But the barrier between his world and Zoe's is more permeable than that between Stanley and the Prescott family in *Down in the City*, and looks forward to Zadie Smith's era, when artistic prestige can provide as much social mobility as financial success. *In Certain Circles* explores a terrain different enough from Harrower's previous novels to constitute a semi-crisis in her mode of fictional representation, a sense that the paradigm whose contradictions she had so mordantly rendered was changing.

In late modernity, bourgeois and anti-bourgeois – in broad terms, corporate drudge and hippie rebel – cancelled each other out, or held each other in a standstill. In every instance in Harrower's work of a bourgeois woman marrying a subaltern, striving man, the woman expects to be liberated by the marriage but is not. The men, and the masculinity of the era, are to blame. Within a deadlocked system, anti-systemic forces can neither rupture the system nor be squelched by it. Adam Davidson has said that late modernity offered "moderate rewards and limited risks".[48] Under neoliberalism, the "bourgeois bohemian", to use David Brooks' phrase, emerged and sought to break the deadlock.[49] Bohemians and rebels are no longer losers who win, but winners in slightly different clothing. The success of a corporate executive such as Bill Gates and of a writer such as Zadie Smith are different only in degree. Yet there was a quantum difference between the success of a Samuel Beckett, a Jorge Luis Borges or an Allen Ginsberg and the success of a mid-twentieth-century corporate executive such as Charles Wilson, who famously said in the 1950s that what was good for General Motors was good for America. In late modernity, the only way a writer might be seen to rival a corporate magnate in importance was as a loser who won. In neoliberalism, losers who win are non-starters. There are only outright winners and losers, although the scale of the winners' success may vary drastically.

Patrick White and the Waning of Late Modernity

In *In Certain Circles*, Harrower anatomised one era with unmatched precision while sensing the onset of its successor. Patrick White's posthumously published *The Hanging Garden* (2012) presents the even more tantalising spectre of an unfinished novel of the then-present by a late-modern master who sensed the coming of a new age. *The Hanging Garden* describes the childhood meeting in Sydney of Gilbert Horsfall, a boy fleeing from the Blitz in Britain, and Eirene Sklavos, a cultivated Greek-Australian expatriate who has been displaced from her home in Greece by the German invasion. It was to have been White's next novel after *The Twyborn Affair* (1979). *The Twyborn Affair* was White's belated coming-out, as it were, as gay and postmodernist, and there is a clear relationship between the two novels. In *The Hanging Garden*, the sibling-like relationship of Eirene and Gilbert recalls the mingling of genders depicted in Eddie/Eudoxia/Eadith Twyborn. Eirene's Greek name, meaning "peace", echoes the Shakespearean synthesis of conflicting energies that occurs at the end of *The Twyborn Affair*.

The Hanging Garden also takes up the migrant theme seen in *The Twyborn Affair* and in many of the short stories in *The Burnt Ones* (1964), White's first collection of short fiction. In stories such as "The Evening at Sissy Kamara's" and "Being Kind to Titina", White sets narratives entirely within milieus of Greeks and Greco-Australian migrants, a world to which he had access through his relationship with Manoly Lascaris. In "Miss Slattery and her Demon Lover", White's demi-villain is a refugee from the Soviet suppression of

48   Adam Davidson, "Welcome to the Failure Age!", *New York Times* magazine, 21 November 2014, MM40.
49   David Brooks, *Bobos in Paradise: The New Upper Class and How They Got There* (New York: Simon and Schuster, 2000).

the Hungarian Revolution.[50] In these stories, White represented experiences that writers of actual migrant background were later to explore more organically. *The Hanging Garden* continues White's exploration of these themes, and one cannot but appreciate how central it could potentially be to White's ouevre, even in the incomplete form we now have.

In comparison to these stories and to *The Twyborn Affair*, *The Hanging Garden* is more traditional and even sentimental in tone. If one were to venture why White never published the book in his lifetime, one might speculate that it was not just that he thought the book was not good enough, nor that, as David Marr's afterword indicates, he preferred in his last decade to focus on politics and theatre. Perhaps White realised that he was writing at a cusp of cultural change, and that the time was no longer ripe for his novelistic vision. Or, perhaps he sensed that *The Hanging Garden* would have provided his oeuvre with a lyrical late synthesis that might have been too pat for his liking. With its juvenile protagonists and its sense of psychological ease (in comparison to White's earlier, more stormy works), *The Hanging Garden* resembles Ingmar Bergman's final feature film as director, *Fanny and Alexander* (1983) (given the composition dates, the similarities must represent a coincidence rather than an influence). In both cases, authors known for pessimistic and introspective works produced a final, far more optimistic narrative of childhood.

Eirene, the young Greek-Australian protagonist, discovers that back in Australia, she is not seen as an educated aristocrat but as a refugee. The question of who is Australian and who is not is scrambled in a manner that alludes to White's relationship with Lascaris, perhaps reflecting a desire to splice and suture the differences between the two partners. Furthermore, *The Hanging Garden* is set during a period (the 1940s) when White was not in Australia, and during which he first met Lascaris. In his blissful portrayal of a prepubescent heterosexual relationship in pastoral Australia, White transplants his relationship with Lascaris from its actual genesis in wartime Egypt. *The Hanging Garden* is the first of White's novels after *The Tree of Man* to be dominated by a heterosexual couple (no, neither Voss and Laura in *Voss* nor Waldo and Dulcie in *The Solid Mandala* counts). After the coming-out of *The Twyborn Affair* and its confirmation in his memoir *Flaws in the Glass* (1981), White returned to a luxuriant if poised modernist-realist style to portray a heterosexuality uninhibited by compulsoriness. Indeed, had *The Hanging Garden* been published when it was written – that is, after *The Twyborn Affair* and *Flaws in the Glass*, and before *Memoirs of Many in One* (1986) – its lyricism would have anchored those other books, providing a steady counterpoint to their experimentation.

Why then did White not publish? The answer is perhaps to be found in a note he jotted down on the manuscript, to the effect that Gilbert would be "14 in 1945, 50 in 1981".[51] *The Hanging Garden* was to have been the first part of a triptych. Portending that the next section would focus on Gilbert and Eirene meeting again in adulthood, White's codicil committed him to writing a realistic fiction set in the 1980s. Now, White himself was sixty-nine in 1981. For him, the 1980s would be an autumnal period, preoccupied with memoirs, theatre and political activism. Gilbert and Eirene, however, would be in their fifties in the 1980s, still at the peak of their lives; they would likely be intimately engaged with the decade's culture and politics. The projected time-frame would demand a realistic rendition of the 1980s, something White might have felt unable to attempt.[52] The children's landlady and custodian, Mrs Bulpit, is a classic late-modern figure, reminiscent of Mrs Reardon in

---

50 Patrick White, *The Burnt Ones* (London: Eyre & Spottiswoode, 1964, republished by Penguin, 1974).
51 Patrick White, *The Hanging Garden* (New York: Picador, 2013), 224.

David Rowbotham's poem "Australian Scene 1938": bumptious, unlikeable but basically decent and reliable, an embodiment of the late-modern welfare state. If White had taken the novel into his present, he would have had to create characters evocable in a similar comic-realist vein, and it is likely that he shrank from this long prospect, not for lack of artistic potency but for totally comprehensible reasons of aesthetic measure.

In addition, by 1981, a new political paradigm was emerging. White may have been focused on what he saw as the perfidy of Malcolm Fraser, but he could not help but have noticed the rise of Reagan and Thatcher, or the more subtle shift from late modernity to neoliberalism. Gough Whitlam's dismissal in 1975, the successive re-elections of the Fraser government, and the beginning of the Hawke era in 1983 created a rapid sense of political change that may have made White feel he could no longer act as an up-to-date chronicler of contemporary Australia. As with Harrower's *In Certain Circles*, perhaps the non-publication of *The Hanging Garden* reflected an awareness that society was on the verge of a paradigm shift, and an unwillingness to take the artistic risk of representing a time beyond the author's own.

Why was *The Hanging Garden* finally published in 2012? It was the centenary of White's birth, but it was more than that: as signalled by the revival of Harrower, there was a renewed interest in late modernity (especially in the wake of the Global Financial Crisis) that gave White more currency. *The Hanging Garden* did not receive universal acclaim. Geordie Williamson, whose treatment of the book in *The Burning Library* was one of the first full-length responses to it, and David Marr, who wrote the afterword to the published edition, seemed to have their doubts. Andrew Riemer found the book inconsistent and suggested that White's reputation might have been better off had it not been published.[53] But the general international reaction was enthusiastic enough to show that a writer once thought out-of-date was now back in style.[54]

For all the loyalty and security Gilbert Horsfall and Eirene Sklavos discover in the book, however, late modernity was too enmeshed in ideologies of control for its resurrection to be desirable. The revivals of White and Harrower were a symptom of neoliberalism. But they were not a signal that late modernity could be recouped. There was no road home.

---

52   This is different from Andrew Riemer's supposition that White "probably felt too ill and infirm to tackle a large-scale novel" ("The Last Word", *Sydney Morning Herald*, 24 March 2012). The fact that White published three plays and the story collection *Three Uneasy Pieces*, worked with David Marr on Marr's biography and participated in political activism shows that even eight years before his death he was hardly exhausted.

53   Riemer, "The Last Word".

54   See, for example, Brigitta Olubas and Elizabeth McMahon, eds, *Remembering Patrick White* (Amsterdam: Rodopi, 2010), and Ian Henderson and Anouk Lang, eds, *Patrick White Beyond the Grave* (London: Anthem, 2015).

4
The Long and the Short of It: The Shape of Contemporary Australian Literature

Big and Australian

Mega biblion, mega kakon, pronounced the Alexandrian sage Callimachus in the early third century BC: "Big book, big problem." Callimachus was not speaking metaphorically. It was a literal complaint about the lengthy efforts of his contemporary and rival, Apollonius of Rhodes, whose epic on Jason and the Argonauts, written in deliberate imitation of Homer, was all the rage in the court of the early Ptolemies. Since Apollonius' book has never quite made its way into the central literary nexus (Harold Bloom, for instance, did not include it in his list of masterworks in *The Western Canon*), Callimachus' quip might be said to have won the day. Yet various versions of Apollonius' work have, as of 2015, more than twenty reviews on Amazon.com; various translations of Callimachus, only five. Callimachus' epigram may have prevailed. But Apollonius is still, as it were, laughing all the way to the bank.

In this chapter I will discuss the relationship between the length of Australian books of the past generation and their reception. Is a big book necessarily a great book? When Australian novelists announce themselves to the international market, do lengthy books fare better than concise ones? For the purposes of this chapter, a short novel is shorter than 250 pages, a medium-length novel 250 to 450 pages, and a long novel anything more than 450.[1] These divisions are not categorical. Ideally, word count rather than page count would be the surest metric, but word count is still not always easy to determine without counting words manually. As digitisation becomes more widespread, word count should replace page count as the indicator of a book's length. Indeed, page count is notoriously misleading, as leading and type size can be manipulated to make books appear longer or shorter than their word count might suggest. Anyone comparing the published versions of Richard Flanagan's and Peter Carey's novels can see that the typeface is larger in Flanagan's books, meaning fewer words per page. Page count is nonetheless significant because, even if it does not correlate to the actual number of words in a book, it gives the reader an impression of how long the book is and therefore what its potential cultural heft might be.

---

1 The page extents cited in this chapter are those listed by the publisher and used in reviews of the first edition.

This question of size is especially relevant in the marketing of Australian literature. Australian literature has always felt the pressure to speak for an entire continent. The size of the *Macquarie PEN Anthology of Australian Literature*, edited by Nicholas Jose (2009), and its wide representation of authors, speak to this (the book is nearly 1500 pages long; although, interestingly, the equivalent New Zealand anthology is nearly the same length).[2]

Richard Eder, in his review of David Malouf's short-story collection *Dream Stuff* (2000), noted that "no contemporary literature is more permeated by the spirit of the land than Australia's".[3] Other books published around that time, such as those by Luke Davies, Christos Tsiolkas, Justine Ettler and Shane Maloney, might have countered this observation, but the statement still represents an intelligent American critic's view at the turn of the century. And literature about the land was expected to be as massive and awe-inspiring as the land itself. The title of Baz Luhrmann's 2008 film *Australia* speaks for itself, and captures the aura of what in Latin America has been called the "total novel", a work of fiction expected to sum up a country's entire history, society, culture and imagination. A big book from Australia promises the international reader "all of Australia". Describing the mainstream reception of world fiction, Pascale Casanova has identified what she terms "The World Republic of Letters", a global field of literary circulation.[4] But this republic can become what Vilashini Cooppan calls "the geopolitical sense of an institution that makes maps yet misses places, encloses the world yet loses the political, either by occluding the nation or miming it".[5] Thus books about Australia must be big because the continent is big, or because people know so little about Australia that they want to take it all in in one gulp. This goes back at least to the 1930s and 1940s, when Eleanor Dark and Xavier Herbert attempted to sum up the Australian settler experience in books that were well received in the larger Anglophone countries. As Patrick Buckridge argues, however, both Dark in *Sun Across the Sky* and M. Barnard Eldershaw in *Plaque with Laurel* wrote books about "great authors" (necessarily, great male authors), both manifesting and to some extent satirising what Buckridge calls the "canonical anxiety" of Australian literature.[6] Novels that ostentatiously aspired to greatness, such as Dark's *The Timeless Land* (1941) and Herbert's *Capricornia* (1938), inevitably had a middlebrow quality, which the aesthetic stringency of late modernity – as seen in Harrower's taut, Jamesian novels – discouraged. In the 1980s, however, postmodernism, the allure of receptive world markets and magic realism changed matters, and the search for, in Buckridge's terms, "the Great Australian Novel" resumed.

This expectation that Australian literature should be lengthy was reinforced in the era of postmodernism, when Australian literature was more exposed to the world, and when long books – by members of the "Latin American Boom", as well as by writers such

---

2   Nicholas Jose, ed., *Macquarie PEN Anthology of Australian Literature* (Crows Nest: Allen & Unwin, 2009); Jane Stafford and Mark Williams, eds., *The Auckland University Press Anthology of New Zealand Literature* (Auckland: Auckland University Press, 2012).

3   Richard Eder, "Wary and Unsettled in Their Ghost-ridden Land", *New York Times*, 5 July 2000. http://tiny.cc/eder_2000.

4   Pascale Casanova, *The World Republic of Letters*, trans. M. B. DeBevoise (Cambridge: Harvard University Press, 2007).

5   Vilashini Cooppan, *Worlds Within: National Narratives and Global Connections* (Stanford: Stanford University Press, 2007), 30–31.

6   Patrick Buckridge, "Greatness in Australian Literature in the 1930s and 1940s: Novels by Dark and Barnard Eldershaw", *Australian Literary Studies* 17, no. 1 (1995): 29–37.

as Salman Rushdie, Thomas Pynchon, John Barth, Joyce Carol Oates and Toni Morrison – received widespread acclaim. In previous decades, the short, finely wrought novella (Conrad's *Heart of Darkness*, Glenway Wescott's *The Pilgrim Hawk*) had often been held up as the ideal. Although *Ulysses* is the most famous modernist book, it is Joyce's shorter *A Portrait of the Artist as a Young Man* that was celebrated as the paragon of modernist form. But in the mid-twentieth century, ingenious, experimental work was prized – Borges, Nabokov, Robbe-Grillet and Beckett. With rare exceptions, such as Nabokov's *Ada*, these writers wrote at short to medium length. This was a reaction against the length of the eighteenth- and nineteenth-century novel – a length encouraged by market forces such as serialisation and the three-decker format favoured by the circulating libraries. The reaction had arguably begun in the late 1840s, when Edgar Allan Poe argued for the superiority of the short story to the novel due to its concentrative effect. By the twentieth century, the novella had come into favour, particularly as perfected by such French writers as Gustave Flaubert and, later, André Gide, with whose name the genre of the *récit* – the short novel that is deceptively simple but which raises fundamental interpretive questions – is associated. Generally, the Australian novelists who have written short to medium works yet succeeded on the international stage, such as David Malouf, have written *récits*. (The special cases of the later work of Tim Winton and Richard Flanagan will be discussed at the end of this chapter.)

It was only when this consensus was dissolved that it became possible for Australian writers to offer big synecdoches of all of Australia to the world. Previous attempts to do so, such as Rex Ingamells' 1951 epic poem *The Great South Land*, had foundered on a sense of aesthetic inappropriateness. They were too sprawling, too centred around data, for modernist taste. Had Ingamells written his book in 1991 rather than 1951, he might have garnered international respect for his ambition. Long novels became associated with Australia in the post-1980 Anglophone marketplace in part because Australian fiction became more popular abroad at a time when long novels were seen as "highbrow".[7] After the postmodernism of Pynchon, Rushdie, Morrison and the Latin American novelists, it was widely accepted that, as Chris Andrews puts it, "A 'great book' is often a big book, one whose text is long, whose story is extensive in space and time, and that gives an impression of exhaustiveness."[8]

In the late-modern period, when the finely crafted, limited third-person viewpoint, often said to be in the tradition of Henry James, was in vogue, Australian fiction, with the singular exception of Patrick White, was hardly visible on the world stage. It was not that Australian novelists were not writing late-modern novels, and writing them well – Harrower's work appeared in the late stages of this vogue. But extending the imaginative franchise to Australia would have meant being daring and imaginative. And an exacting, finely honed caution – even, as seen in our discussion of Harrower, a constraint – was at the heart of the elevation of the "Jamesian" mode.

That White was the one exception to the general neglect of Australian fiction during this period may appear surprising, as his major novels are inarguably on the long side. *Voss* (1957) clocks in at 448 pages in the Penguin paperback edition, *Riders in the Chariot*

---

7 In earlier eras, Clarke's *His Natural Life*, Henry Handel Richardson's *The Fortunes of Richard Mahony* and Dark's *The Timeless Land* had been popular abroad, but by the 1980s they had been largely forgotten.
8 Chris Andrews, *Roberto Bolaño's Fiction: An Expanding Universe* (New York: Columbia University Press, 2014), 24.

(1961) at 643 pages, *The Vivisector* (1970) 640, *The Eye of the Storm* (1973) 608, *A Fringe of Leaves* (1975) a comparatively brief 405 and *The Twyborn Affair* (1979) at 432. White's work became shorter as he became more postmodern in mode, most obviously in the last three books published in his lifetime, with their overtly queer subjects and their dissolution of the line between life and art. He wrote his longest books at a time when readerly taste (as exemplified by books like Percy Lubbock's *The Craft of Fiction*) still insisted on brevity and restraint. This may be one of the reasons why White, despite his worldwide acclaim, sat uneasily with many international readers' understanding of what Australian writing should look like in a way that, later, Peter Carey did not. Carey's novels are about as long as White's: *Illywhacker* is 600 pages, *Oscar and Lucinda* 538, *The Unusual Life of Tristan Smith* 432. But Carey was writing at a time when long, highly literary novels were also bestsellers, and when the difference between the literary and the popular, which had been maintained so adamantly in the high-modernist era, was beginning to erode.

The *New York Times* and the Booker Prize

I will now survey the role that length played in the reception of Australian fiction in the USA and the UK from 1980 to 2014. For the USA, my main source of evidence will be, from 1980 to 1989, the *New York Times Book Review*, supplemented thereafter by the annual bibliography of Australian books published in North America, compiled by H. Faye Christenberry and annually published in *Antipodes*. In the UK, the data pool is a looser one. The Booker Prize, long seen as the principal mediator of Australian fiction to the broader Anglophone world, has accumulated in its shortlists and, from 2001, its longlists, a convenient archive of Australian fiction that has been deemed canonical.[9] Both the *New York Times Book Review* and the Booker Prize may be seen as self-reinforcing, as the consumerist idea that one should get one's money's worth from a book may prevail in these institutions that mix commercial and aesthetic appeal. They have a vested interest in seeing literature as flourishing, and longer books might seem to portend a healthier literary culture. On the other hand, really long books may be seen as too daunting for the average reader. When Eleanor Catton's *The Luminaries* won the Man Booker Prize in 2013, its length – 864 pages – was much discussed.

As opposed to the American women, such as Joyce Carol Oates and Toni Morrison, who published long books in the 1970s and 1980s, the Australian women writers reviewed in the *New York Times* during the 1980s nearly all published short books, and their brevity was at times noted as a virtue. Elizabeth Jolley, especially, was extensively reviewed in the *New York Times* during this period. Reviewing the 224-page *The Sugar Mother* in 1988, Stephen McCauley noted that the book demands "to be taken on its own terms", and compared Jolley to Evelyn Waugh and Barbara Pym.[10] Reviewing Jolley's *Palomino* (260 pages) in 1987, Josephine Hendin praised the novel's "gift for wryness" and its "lyricism and bitterness", again characterisations that can be code words for brevity and control; the words "ambitious" or "prolific" are not used of Jolley, although Jolley was as prolific as Hall.[11] In

---

9   Established in 1968, the Booker-McConnell Prize was commonly known as the Booker Prize. From 2002 it became the Man Booker Prize for Fiction.
10   Stephen McCauley, "Pedant in Love", *New York Times*, 10 July 1988. http://www.nytimes.com/1988/07/10/books/pedant-in-love.html.

reviewing Thea Astley's 208-page *It's Raining in Mango* in 1987, Rosellen Brown found the novel "compressed" and "frustratingly elliptical". There is a distinct connotation that more sprawl (as Les Murray might put it), more largesse, would have aired the canvas out a bit and extended the novel's "quick external summary".[12]

This complaint may also have had to do with Astley's inclusion of Aboriginal themes, which were so foreign to American reviewers that they seemed to require more exposition. A short book may assume more background cultural knowledge on the reader's part. Astley's *Reaching Tin River* (1990), with its evocation of a librarian's obsession with a long-dead politician, Gaden Lockyer, might have excited more attention if Lockyer had been depicted in a three-dimensional and historical way, as Cass Mastern was in a model for Astley's book, *All The King's Men* by the American writer Robert Penn Warren. This would have made Astley's book much longer than its lean 224 pages; in such a short book, any historical evocation was probably bound to seem, to use Brown's phrase, quick and external. Helen Garner is another female Australian writer whose work has been neglected in America. The brevity of books such as *Monkey Grip* (1977, 245 pages) and *The Children's Bach* (1984, 96 pages) may have been a factor; in 1986, Gina Mercer vigorously argued that Garner's fiction had been discounted in Australia because of its length.[13] In the USA, Garner's work was not just discounted; unlike Astley's and Jolley's work, it was not even published, until her 1995 nonfiction book *The First Stone*.[14]

In between, in terms of length, there is Thomas Keneally, whose early books reviewed in the *Times* varied in length from the relatively short *The Chant of Jimmie Blacksmith* (1972, 178 pages), to *Gossip from the Forest* (1975, 222 pages), to *Blood Red, Sister Rose* (1974, 368 pages). Keneally's documentary style and his ability to consider historical issues within a terse and austere frame gave him an appeal that had more to do with subject matter than with style – but he had style enough to shelter his subject matter from self-indulgent sprawl. In the 1980s, however, Keneally's work was consistently longer: *Schindler's Ark* was 400 pages long, *A Family Madness* 353, *The Playmaker* 310 and *To Asmara* 308. It was this "longer" Keneally who was taken seriously as a novelist and as a storyteller, as an artistic and moral force as well as a commercial one. Meanwhile the rambunctious and often farcical historical epics of Rodney Hall were frequently reviewed in American periodicals in the 1980s, where their length was often seen as a correlate of their ambition.

The exception here is David Malouf, second only to Carey in literary and artistic impact in the USA, whose *Harland's Half Acre* (1984) was extravagantly well received in the USA, although it was a mere 214 pages long. Malouf, however, communicated a sense of the national in those 214 pages, as witnessed by Michael Gorra's description in the *New York Times* of the novel's evocation of "a new world, shaped by settlers exiled from the old, by the absence of an inherited culture and the corresponding need to create one to fill it", which Gorra compared to nineteenth-century America. Here we see one source of the tacit demand that Australian fiction be long: an assumption that Australian fiction, as

---

11   Josephine Hendin, "Perfecting Woman", *New York Times*, 19 July 1987. http://www.nytimes.com/1987/07/19/books/perfecting-woman.html.

12   Rosellen Brown, "Travels in the Quirky Latitudes", *New York Times*, 22 November 1987. http://www.nytimes.com/1987/11/22/books/travels-in-the-quirky-latitudes.html.

13   Gina Mercer, "Little Women: Helen Garner Sold by Weight", *Australian Book Review* 81 (June 1986): 26–28.

14   If the 1982 film of *Monkey Grip* had done better abroad, perceptions of the early 1980s Australian film boom would have been very different.

Buckridge has traced, should recapitulate the search for the Great American Novel, whose prerequisite in all but a few cases (such as *The Great Gatsby*) is length. Malouf has enjoyed significant international success – in 1993 he won the inaugural IMPAC Dublin Literary Award for *Remembering Babylon*, a book that was also named *Time* magazine's best book of the year – but perhaps he might have done even better had his books been longer. (When Daniel Mendelsohn reviewed Malouf's *Dream Stuff* for *New York Magazine* in 2000, he remarked that Malouf was "inexplicably underappreciated", and that people of Mendelsohn's acquaintance had even confused Malouf with the Egyptian Nobel Laureate Naguib Mahfouz.)[15]

When one looks to the UK, meanwhile, one sees that although in recent years Australian literature has been closely associated with the Booker – John Miller in 2010 wrote of "Australian authors gaining success in international awards such as the … Booker" – in the 1980s only Carey's *Illywhacker* and *Oscar and Lucinda* and Keneally's *Schindler's Ark* (published in the USA as *Schindler's List*) were shortlisted (*Oscar and Lucinda* and *Schindler's Ark* both won).[16] In the 1970s, Keneally had been shortlisted three times, but no other Australian was mentioned. The "lost" Booker shortlist for books published in 1970, which was not awarded until 2010, did feature two Australians, Patrick White and Shirley Hazzard. But in reality there was nothing to prevent either of these books from being considered for the prize in 1971; their inclusion in the 2010 shortlist should not be taken as evidence that Australian writers were strong contenders for the prize in its early years.

In the 1990s, there was a stronger Australian presence on the shortlists: Malouf (for *Remembering Babylon* in 1993), Winton (*The Riders*, 1995), Madeleine St John (*The Essence of the Thing*, 1997) were all nominated, but none of them won (fifteen years later, after her premature death and critical neglect, St John would be included in the Text Classics series). In the 2000s, Carey won again (for *True History of the Kelly Gang* in 2001), as did D. B. C. Pierre, a writer who was born in Australia but had not lived in the country since early childhood, and whose prize-winning book, *Vernon God Little*, was not set in Australia. Other shortlistees that decade were Kate Grenville (*The Secret River*, 2006), Tim Winton (*Dirt Music*, 2002), Steve Toltz (*A Fraction of the Whole*, 2008), M. J. Hyland (*Carry Me Down*, 2006) and J. M. Coetzee (*Summertime*, 2009; Coetzee had become an Australian citizen in 2006). The 2000s longlists include a few more Australians: Shirley Hazzard for *The Great Fire*, Carey for *Theft: A Love Story* and Michelle de Kretser for *The Lost Dog*. (One is tempted to count Claire Messud's *The Emperor's Children* for its one millennially portentous Australian character; Messud is an American of Canadian extraction.) In 2010, Peter Carey was shortlisted for *Parrot and Olivier in America*, and Christos Tsiolkas was longlisted for *The Slap*. In 2014, the first year in which novels from the USA were formally eligible for the prize, Richard Flanagan won for *The Narrow Road to the Deep North*. Flanagan's victory seemed to answer fears that the new rules would crowd out books from the Commonwealth.

The Booker has unquestionably created possibilities for Australian fiction that would not have existed without it. James English has contended that in the English-speaking world, the Booker is now more newsworthy than the Nobel – and the Booker's success,

---

15   Daniel Mendelsohn, "Uneasy Pieces", *New York Magazine*, 7 August 2000. http://nymag.com/nymetro/arts/books/reviews/3594/.
16   John Miller, *Australia's Great Writers and Poets: The Story of Our Rich Literary Heritage* (Wollombi: Exisle Publishing, 2007), 87.

English argues, has been associated with scandal.[17] Even if the scandals have not involved Australian books, they have made the prize newsworthy and therefore noteworthy. What is striking about the list above, aside from the revelation that the Booker, although it has unquestionably made Australian fiction more visible internationally, has not featured as many Australian authors as many Australians might think, is that the Australian novels longlisted for the prize have generally been short. Hyland's *Carry Me Down* was 192 pages long, St John's *The Essence of the Thing* 234, Gail Jones' *Sixty Lights* 256, and Coetzee's *Summertime* 224. Carey's *Theft*, at 260 pages, was considerably shorter than those books of his that won.

There were exceptions: de Kretser's *The Lost Dog* was 352 pages, Tsiolkas' *The Slap* 496 pages, and Toltz's *Fraction of the Whole* 576 pages. Toltz's book may seem at first glance to have made it onto the shortlist precisely because it was long. It was certainly promoted that way: its British publicity, according to Frank Cottrell Boyce's review in the *Guardian*, heralded it as "rollicking".[18] Yet, as the same review remarked, the book is actually rather intimate, concentrating on the father–son relationship between Jasper and Martin Dean. The novel is not "many-charactered" in the sense that Christina Stead used that term. Furthermore, it seems worried about its own length: in the last paragraph, Jasper says he has "run out of time anyway" and wonders, even on a catastrophically overpopulated earth, who will be there to read it. *Tristram Shandy*-style, Toltz's book refrains from unfolding its own plot. The title itself indicates a renunciation of any attempt to conjure the whole; a part might be able to do this, but hardly a mere fraction.

Luke Strongman, meanwhile, has argued that novels from Australia, New Zealand and Canada that have *won* the prize have generally reflected these countries' struggles to form a national identity.[19] And such books have tended to be lengthy. Perhaps journalistic critics deemed more room necessary to discuss these issues, to provide the scope for what Timothy Brennan called "the national longing for form".[20]

Of course, Booker juries do not speak for the entire world. Lily Brett's huge sales in Germany and her 2014 winning of the Prix Medicis Étranger far outpaced her reputation in her adopted city of New York, where her themes of survival, dislocation and memory among European refugees were not what was expected from Australia. Peter Goldsworthy's *Maestro* (1989), also featuring European subject matter, was translated into German by Susanne Costa in 2007 and did exceedingly well. Mandy Sayer and Robert Drewe garnered more notice in translation in Spain than they did in their own language in North America. In general, European countries were more receptive to migrant writers and to shorter, more psychologically oriented novels than were critics in the USA. In India, more notice was accorded to Australian Indigenous writing (Alexis Wright's participation in the 2008 Jaipur Festival seemed a turning point). Chinese academics, in contrast, seemed still to focus on more mainstream writers, although writing by members of the Chinese diaspora in Australia became more popular, and a growing interest in Australian minority and Indigenous literature abetted curiosity about culturally subordinated elements in Australian life.

---

17   James F. English, *The Economy of Prestige: Prizes, Awards and the Circulating of Cultural Value* (Cambridge: Harvard University Press, 2005), 205.
18   Frank Cottrell Boyce, "*A Fraction of the Whole* by Steve Toltz", *The Guardian*, 21 June 2008.
19   Luke Strongman, *The Booker Prize and the Legacy of Empire* (Amsterdam: Rodopi, 2002), 170.
20   Timothy Brennan, "The National Longing for Form", in *Nation and Narration*, ed. Homi Bhabha (London: Routledge, 1990), 45.

In the USA, dispelling stereotypes of Australian fiction proved more problematic. At 264 pages, Murray Bail's *Eucalyptus* was far leaner than Carey's *Illywhacker* or *Oscar and Lucinda*. While Carey was compared to writers practising magic realism such as García Márquez and Rushdie, for Bail the natural point of comparison was Borges – elliptical, parabolic, fond of telling stories about stories, a master of style, erudition and irony. Bail's tale of a father who forces his daughter's potential suitors to name all the possible varieties of eucalyptus trees, for all its dry elaboration of various species, tells an engrossing story. As Peter Craven argued, readers of *Eucalyptus* could see the story on two levels: as a wry modernist parable or as an exotic tale of Australian nature.[21] Even though *Eucalyptus* is not concerned with the identity of Australia, it does foreground a vivid feature of the Australian landscape: the variety of eucalyptus species and the tree's omnipresence on Australian soil. The nation is deflected into the tree. The long novel can become shorter.

There was a similar sense of synecdoche in the emphasis on Tasmania in the late 1990s, when the early work of Richard Flanagan became widely appreciated in the USA. His works were significantly shorter than Carey's breakthrough books: *Death of a River Guide* was 326 pages long and *The Sound of One Hand Clapping* 425, a difference perhaps attributable to Tasmania being only a part of Australia, occupying, as Hamish Dailey puts it, "a problematic place in the Australian imagination".[22] Flanagan's concentration on a part of the country that is geographically marginal – as Flanagan put it in his 2014 Booker Prize acceptance speech, "an island at the end of the world" – dimmed demands that Australian novels should contain all of Australia.[23] In 1999 Julia Leigh's short, parabolic novel *The Hunter* (170 pages), also set in Tasmania, described a multinational corporation's attempt to corral and clone the last thylacine (Tasmanian tiger); the story operated as a trope not just of ecological catastrophe but of capitalist possession. This further cemented the idea that there was room for brevity in Australian writing, and that one could write not about a massive island-continent, but about a much smaller fraction of the whole. By the turn of the century, the 1980s demand for lengthy Australian books had eased, and international readers had grown more tolerant of shorter Australian works.

The *Récit* and the Total Novel

Some Australian books that might have been expected to do well internationally, based on the experience of the 1980s, did not do so well in the 1990s. Merrill Findlay's *The Republic of Women* (1999) was as philosophical as any Australian novel of that time, and was hailed rapturously by Murray Waldren in the *Australian*.[24] Its social speculations and redeployments of world history are reminiscent of those of Peter Carey and Rodney Hall. Yet Findlay's novel was not picked up internationally, perhaps because its manifest feminism made international publishers shy away. In addition, its portrait of Melbourne bohemian life, like Helen Garner's in *Monkey Grip*, did not fit international preferences for

21 Peter Craven, "Murray Bail: The Homemade Modernist Finds a Heart", *Heat* 9 (1998): 75–91.
22 Hamish Dailey, *The Postcolonial Historical Novel: Realism, Allegory and the Representation of Contested Pasts* (New York: Palgrave Macmillan, 2014), 174.
23 James Walton, "Star Fiction", *The New York Review of Books*, 4 December 2014. http://www.nybooks.com/articles/archives/2014/dec/04/luminaries-star-fiction/.
24 Murray Waldren, "Distaff Side of Plato", *Weekend Australian*, 4–5 September 1999, 14.

rip-roaring yarns set in the bush. At 280 pages, *The Republic of Women* was longer than many of Garner's novels, but it was still a short book. On the other hand, David Ireland's *The Chosen* (520 pages) was, in Buckridge's terms, a Great Australian Novel if ever there were one. It told the story of an entire town in rural Australia in ways that were representative and, as Ron Blaber has argued, even populist.[25] It was the capstone novel by one of Australia's most inventive and original novelists, a writer with both thematic heft and experimental verve. Yet it made no impact internationally. In marketing terms, perhaps Ireland, who was seventy when he published the novel, was simply too old. The publicity generally associated with the hefty novel is largely a young man's affair; youth connotes vigour, promise and abundance. Furthermore, Ireland's novel was far more about explaining Australia to itself than explaining Australia to the world.

Ireland's experience illustrates that length is no guarantee of international success. What is needed is to be long and to be written by a reasonably marketable author, or by an author who is already famous. Mid-list authors who write big books face an uncertain course. John A. Scott is a distinguished Australian novelist and poet whose verse novel *St Clair* (1986) was one of the principal contributors to the flourishing of the verse novel in Australia in the 1980s, along with Alan Wearne's *The Nightmarkets* (1986) (an early response to neoliberalism) and Laurie Duggan's regional montage on the east Victorian region of Gippsland, *The Ash Range* (1987). Transgressive formally and politically, Scott's work has received attention in the USA – *What I Have Written: A Novel of Erotic Obsession* (240 pages) was published in 1994 in New York by Norton – but he is not as well known as he deserves to be. In 2014, the independent Australian publisher Brandl & Schlesinger released Scott's novel *N*, a dystopian alternative history of an Australia that had surrendered to the Japanese in World War II. It is a long (600 pages), ambitious and allusive book. Compared by its blurbers to Pynchon and to Rodney Hall's *Kisses of the Enemy*, it remains to be seen whether it will win Scott the international reputation his work warrants, or whether, as in the case of Ireland, ambition attracts fewer rewards later in a writer's career.

In the twenty-first century, the expectation that literary fiction be long has diminished. Latin American fiction was dominated from the 1960s to the 1980s by the "total novel". The Peruvian novelist Mario Vargas Llosa, who wrote several total novels himself, in 1971 praised García Márquez for writing novels that were "simultaneously, many things believed to be mutually exclusive: traditional and modern, local and universal, fantastic and realistic".[26] By the 1990s in Latin America, however, the "total novel" was being replaced by shorter forms. Although the Chilean-Mexican-Spanish novelist Roberto Bolaño attained his greatest fame for the blockbusters *The Savage Detectives* (1998) and *2666* (2004), his first and in a way most characteristic achievements were the shorter *By Night in Chile* (2000), *Distant Star* (1996) and *Nazi Literature of the Americas* (1996), brief novels characterised by a clipped, disillusioned asperity. Even shorter were the *micronovelas* of the Argentine César Aira and the Chilean Alejandro Zambra, whose narratives were often in the neighbourhood of 100 pages. For these writers, the rejection of the total novel was a rejection of the claims of totality; it represented an ascetic shying-away from aspirations to speak for a whole nation, region or era. Although it was often aesthetically highly wrought,

---

25   Ron Blaber, "The Populist Imaginary in David Ireland's *The Unknown Industrial Prisoner* and *The Chosen*", *Journal of the Association for the Study of English Literature* 5 (2006): 58–71.
http://openjournals.library.usyd.edu.au/index.php/JASAL/article/view/10038.
26   Sabine Köllmann, *A Companion to Mario Vargas Llosa* (London: Tamesis Books, 2014), 30.

Zambra's fiction bore some resemblance to the *testimonio* genre, a mode of nonfiction that involves bearing unembellished witness to the reality of events in their aftermath. Although the most famous writer of *testimonio*, the Quiché Guatemalan writer Rigoberta Menchù, is now somewhat discredited because her stories were not necessarily authentic, and although the testimonial novels of the Mexican writer Elena Poniatowska are no longer *de rigueur*, the *testimonio* form has had a substantial influence on Latin American novelists born in the 1960s and 1970s. *Oblivion* (2006), the acclaimed memoir of the Colombian writer Hectór Abad Faciolince, at 273 pages tells in a comparatively restrained frame the huge story of the political murder of the author's father.

To understand this phenomenon, we need to bring back the category of the *récit* – the short, apparently simple but inherently open-ended novella perfected by Flaubert and Gide. There is a relation between the *récit* and the *testimonio*. This seems incongruous, as the *testimonio* is ostensibly nonfiction, about things that have actually happened, with direct political bearing, while the *récit* is associated with a pure formalism. In both cases, however, not only brevity but also a deceptive clarity pertains. For all its claims to authenticity, the *testimonio* depends so much on the reliability of its recounting voice that the threat of unreliable narration hangs like a dagger above its heart. There is an awareness of the twists and turns of memory, and of the way memory never gets us entirely to the truth. The truth of the *récit*, similarly, is apparent only superficially; it ultimately has to be decided by the reader. That their meaning is not stable is why *récit*-like texts – *The Great Gatsby*, *Heart of Darkness*, *A Portrait of the Artist as a Young Man* – are so teachable. The *récit* has a lyric aspect, evoking the indefinable nuance of song rather than the articulated agenda of epic. The mystery at the heart of the *récit* is something it also has in common with the detective story (Gide himself admired the hardboiled detective novels of Dashiell Hammett), which also depends on brevity – an inheritance from Poe – for its effect.

Conversely, the total novel, as flagrantly inventive as it might be, always refers in some way to the external world. Fuentes, Rushdie and Carey can spin an engrossing tale while registering history in their multifarious narratives. Even Bolaño, the author of short novels such as *By Night in Chile* and *Distant Star*, seems to privilege the longer novel when, in *2666*, he has Guerra, a young pharmacist, express a preference for short fiction: Guerra rates "*Bartleby* over *Moby-Dick* and *A Simple Heart* over *Bouvard et Pecuchet*". Amalfitano, the third-person narrator, disdains Guerra's preference, lamenting that "now even bookish pharmacists are afraid to take on the great, imperfect, torrential works, books that blaze paths into the unknown. They choose the perfect exercises of the great masters".[27] The total novel values imperfection, dovetailing with what Hamish Dailey has described as "the postcolonial historical novel", which went "beyond anti-realism" into a mode that braids history and fiction, reality and representation.[28] Yet – and crucially for our discussion of Australian literature – just as it is only the claim to truth that distinguishes the *testimonio* from the *récit*, so is the claim to be fictional, the overt engagement with meta-textual games and other self-conscious devices, the main distinction between postcolonial historical novels and the ordinary sort. It is its advertisement of its fictiveness that renders the total novel different from the works of Edward Rutherfurd, James A. Michener and Bryce Courtenay, all of whom attempt a similarly large canvas and who also mix historical and invented characters. In Carey's total novel *Illywhacker*, Herbert Badgery's claim that "ly-

---

27 Roberto Bolaño, *2666*, trans. Natasha Wimmer (New York: Farrar, Straus and Giroux, 2008), 27.
28 Dailey, *The Postcolonial Historical Novel*.

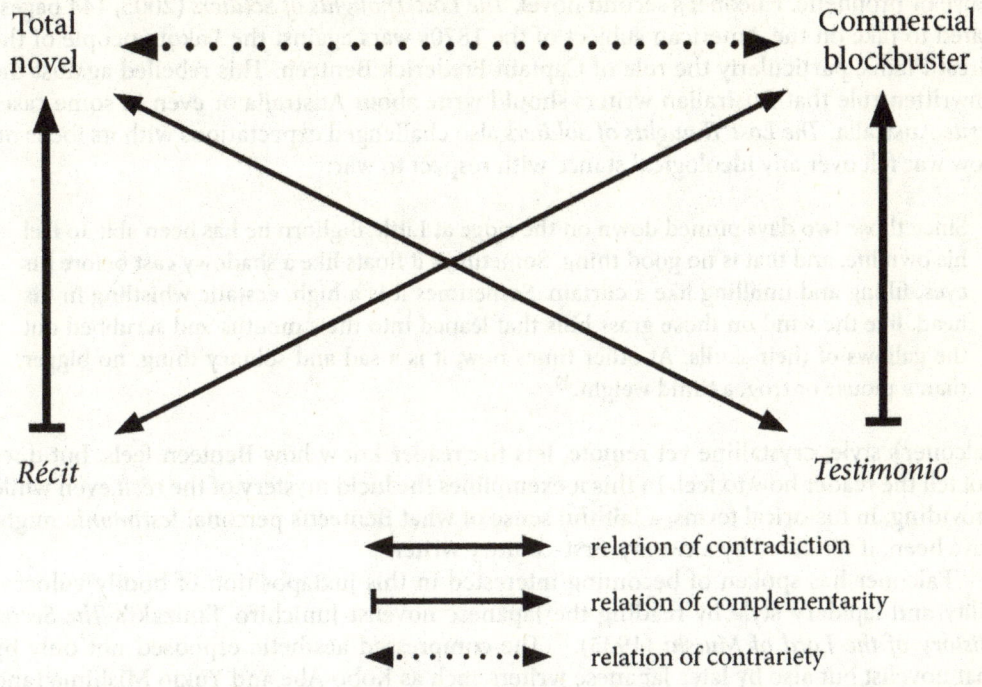

The relationship between four genres, mapped using Algirdas Greimas' "semiotic square".

ing is my main subject, my specialty, my skill" enables the reader to have a sort of double vision, consuming both history and fiction at the same time. The total novel thus relies on referentiality, even if it is the assertion of its fictiveness that distinguishes it from more commercial blockbusters. The total novel is the self-conscious version of the commercial blockbuster – both are long and filled with often-tangential information – just as the *récit* is the self-conscious form of the *testimonio*: both are short and want the reader to puzzle out questions using what information is available on the surface. One can graph the relationship between the four genres in this way using Algirdas Greimas' "semiotic square".

The total novel cannot be hurt by assertions of factual error, narrative ambiguity or flagrant falsehood, because part of its appeal is a freewheeling independence from pedantic notions of accuracy. Briefer novels, in contrast, can be hurt by accusations of inaccuracy or incompleteness. One can see this in the response to novels such as Thea Astley's books, which never claim to be anything but fiction. In finding Astley's work "frustratingly elliptical", the *Times* reviewer felt that the account of historical events in the novel was insufficient. Similarly, the Australian novelist Barbara Hanrahan wrote books that were deeply personal, embodied and subjective. As her journals show, Hanrahan's fiction captured these states in detached ways that were not necessarily straightforward transcriptions of her literal states of mind. The reader had to decide, to work actively, not just to ingest a totality. Similarly, Delia Falconer's *The Service of Clouds* (322 pages), a bestseller in Australia, was published in 1998 by America's leading literary publisher, Farrar, Straus & Giroux, but, despite receiving generally positive reviews, seemed to puzzle readers by leaving them to decide whether the aesthetic vision of the photographs of Harry Kitchings was naive or prophetic. Falconer's second novel, *The Lost Thoughts of Soldiers* (2005, 144 pages) dared to take on the American subject of the 1870s wars against the Lakota people of the Great Plains, particularly the role of Captain Frederick Benteen. This rebelled against the unwritten rule that Australian writers should write about Australia or even in some cases *write* Australia. *The Lost Thoughts of Soldiers* also challenged expectations with its focus on how war felt over any ideological stance with respect to war:

> Since those two days pinned down on the ridge at Little Bighorn he has been able to feel his own life, and that is no good thing. Sometimes it floats like a shadowy cast before his eyes, filling and unfilling like a curtain. Sometimes it is a high, ecstatic whistling in his head, like the wind on those grass hills that leaped into their mouths and scrubbed out the gallows of their skulls. At other times now, it is a sad and solitary thing, no bigger than a mouse or frog, a timid weight.[29]

Falconer's style, crystalline yet remote, lets the reader know how Benteen feels, but does not tell the reader how to feel. In this it exemplifies the lucid mystery of the *récit* even while providing, in historical terms, a faithful sense of what Benteen's personal *testimonio* might have been, if rendered by a twenty-first-century writer.

Falconer has spoken of becoming interested in this juxtaposition of bodily vulnerability and lapidary style by reading the Japanese novelist Junichiro Tanizaki's *The Secret History of the Lord of Musshi* (1935).[30] The compressed aesthetic espoused not only by that novelist but also by later Japanese writers such as Kobo Abe and Yukio Mishima (and conspicuously rebelled against by the "hefty" Haruki Murakami) provides an interesting alternative to the total novel, a mode of *récit*. Elements of the Japanese aesthetic, such as the idea of *mono no aware*, the sense of an indiscernible, bittersweet quality of life and art, lend themselves to pithier, more understated narrative. Some of the best-known Chinese (*The Journey to the West*; *The Dream of the Red Chamber*) and Japanese (*The Tale of Genji*; *Heike monogotari*) literature is lengthy. But many other major works from these countries are not, and it has been argued that the primary place of "the short lyric, with its values of immediacy, brevity, and momentariness", may be crucial to the difference between Western and Chinese aesthetics.[31] If, as heralded by Mabel Lee's translations of the 2000 Nobel Laureate Gao Xingjian, more and more of what the Anglophone world receives as world literature is Asian, the demand for size, heft and national significance may fade, and the work of Falconer, whose art, although it often interacts with social concerns, is rigorously artistic, will rise higher in the canon. Nicholas Jose's *The Red Thread* (2001), a metafictive turn on the middle-Qing Dynasty classic *Six Chapters of a Floating Life*, tells a story of epic dimensions in a modest 324 pages. Even Carey's *Illywhacker* posits the Japanese as the antitype of the boisterously Australian, as Japan takes over the country economically and Herbert Badgery's son is given the Japanese name of Hissao. A book that so ingratiatingly reaches out to an American audience by presenting a rollicking, happy-go-lucky image of Australia ends by warning this audience that its standards are not the only ones.

---

29 Delia Falconer, *The Lost Thoughts of Soldiers* (New York: Soft Skull, 2006), 6.
30 "Open Page with Delia Falconer", *Australian Book Review*, no. 333, July–August 2011. https://www.australianbookreview.com.au/about/56-july-august-2011/445-open-page.
31 Pauline Yu and Theodore Huters, "The Imaginative Universe of Chinese Literature", in *Chinese Aesthetics and Literature*, ed. Corinne H. Dale (Albany: State University of New York Press, 2004), 9.

Other Australian works of note have clearly not appeared on the world radar as visibly as they should have in part because of their length. Like Falconer, David Foster (along with Morris Lurie, one of Australia's great comic novelists) has questioned customary conceptions of masculinity in an offbeat way. That this most "male" of novelists, who consciously writes about men and men's lives, has been persistently championed by the feminist critic Susan Lever says something about his originality, yet Foster's work has largely been neglected by the North American market.[32] His best chance at penetrating this market was probably *Testostero* (1987), published at a time when Carey and Keneally, and to a lesser extent Rodney Hall, were prominent on the American scene. Yet that headstrong and funny book is only 188 pages long. Foster's 1996 novel *The Glade within the Grove*, by contrast, is well over 400 pages long – but by then Foster was fifty-two years old, well over the hill for an established mid-list author at a time when the 33-year-old David Foster Wallace was having massive success with the 1079-page *Infinite Jest*.

Eyrie: *Récit* contra Neoliberalism

Tim Winton (born in 1960) was a younger writer who attracted global attention shortly after Peter Carey but, for all his commercial success in Australia, and his three Miles Franklin wins, has remained in Carey's shadow internationally. Like *Illywhacker*, 1991's *Cloudstreet* (426 pages) spanned several generations of two quirky families and gave a lively sense of, in this case, the Western Australian scene. But, compared to *Illywhacker*, it is far less of a "total novel". It lacks the total novel's self-reference and ironic sense of national destiny, traits with which Carey's novel is laden. Winton's novels sell well and are frequently assigned in high schools, but he is not widely regarded as highbrow. In his review of Winton's *The Riders* in the December 1995 *Antipodes*, Jack Turner said he could not support Winton's literary project because Winton was too "middlebrow".[33]

Winton's early work might be Faulknerian in its quirky regionalism, but it generally reflected a representational, if at times slightly surreal, aesthetic. His work since the 2004 short-story collection *The Turning*, however, has been more opaque and challenging. Before *The Turning*, although Winton's writing shared a sense of the offbeat and the idiosyncratic with Faulkner, it lacked both Faulkner's formal experimentation and its immersion in tragic conflict, particularly as race, although present in *Cloudstreet*, did not play nearly as prominent a role in Winton's work as it does in Faulkner's. From *The Turning* onward, Winton filled every page with nuance and implication; his books are medium-sized but seem longer because of their moral and intellectual complexity. In *Breath* (2008, 215 pages) we see a turning away from the kind of minor total novel Winton attempted with *Cloudstreet*, where any complexity is put before the reader, to a book lingering between *testimonio* and *récit*. As an adult, Bruce Pike tries to make sense of events in his adolescence that have traumatised him. Pike sees risk as something at once sublime and repulsive, to be by turns admired and shunned. There have been several analyses of the novel in light of Ulrich Beck's theories of risk society, a key analytic coefficient of neoliberalism.[34]

---

32   Susan Lever, *David Foster: The Satirist of Australia* (Amherst: Cambria Press, 2008).
33   Jack Turner, "Tim Winton's *Riders* Sends Father on a European Quest", *Antipodes* 9, no. 2 (1995): 148–49.

Winton's next book, *Eyrie* (2013, 432 pages), is long but intimate. It centres on the relationship between Tom Keely, a middle-aged man adrift in a Fremantle highrise, and Gemma Buck, a woman he knew in childhood who moves into the apartment building with her young grandson, Kai. Keely, in Lyn McCredden's words, is a "nauseous, self-pitying, unlovable failure".[35] Many years before, his mother, Doris, protected Gemma's family. Winton's description of Keely's Fremantle apartment building is a miniature ekphrasis of late modernity: "It was a classic shitbox, beige bricks, raw concrete galleries, ironbar railings, doors and windows like prison slots. Hard to credit that fifty years ago some nabob thought it a grand idea, a harbinger of progress".[36] Winton's account of Kelly's building skewers a late-modern vision of progress, once hopeful but now grotesque or absurd (a transformation that recalls Winton's portrait of Perth suburbia in *Cloudstreet*). A few pages earlier, Keely's interior monologue captures how late modernity has been transformed by neoliberalism and the contemporary Australian love of good coffee:

> After all that he'd finally totter onto the little avenue of self-congratulation that everyone called the Cappuccino Strip. Fifty umbrellas around which a certain civic pride once rallied. In the seventies the Strip had been a beacon of homely cosmopolitanism, a refuge from the desolate franchise dispensation stretching from sea to hazy hills. (17)

Much like the misfits in Harrower's novels, the people who once sought out these coffee houses are looking to evade the calcifying corporate and bureaucratic conformity of late-modern stasis. But this search for idiosyncrasy and dissent degenerates into an orgy of elitism:

> But that was before it calcified into smugness. Somewhere along the way the good folks of the port settled in the wisdom that coffee was all the culture and industry a town required. Butcher shops, hardware stores, chandlers and bakeries had steadily been squeezed out and supplanted by yet more cafes, new spaghetti barns. Rents were extortionate, house prices absurd. The city had become a boho theme park. (19)

No writer, Australian or otherwise – even Coetzee in his animadversions on neoliberalism in *Diary of a Bad Year*, to be discussed later – has provided a more powerful thumbnail sketch of how neoliberalism has changed the urban landscape. Even in *Cloudstreet*, Winton chronicled the cultural topography of change from the residually colonial to the modern; in his books of the twenty-first century, he continues this with respect to the change from modernity to neoliberalism.

Winton is often regarded as chronicling the lives and concerns of the typical Australian bloke. This was always an under-reading of him, but it became a farcical one after the achievements of *The Turning* and *Breath*. *Breath*, through its depiction of risk and its

---

34 Nicholas Birns, "A Not Completely Pointless Beauty: *Breath*, Exceptionality and Neoliberalism", in *Tim Winton: Critical Essays*, eds Lyn McCredden and Nathanael O'Reilly (Nedlands: University of Western Australia Press, 2014), 263–83.

35 Lyn McCredden, "The Quality of Mercy", *Sydney Review of Books*, December 2013. http://www.sydneyreviewofbooks.com/the-quality-of-mercy/.

36 Tim Winton, *Eyrie* (New York: Farrar, Straus & Giroux, 2014), 21. All subsequent references are to this edition and appear in parentheses in the text.

false exaltation, as represented by extreme sports and extreme sex, allegorically depicted the depredations of neoliberalism. According to the Australian Treasury, the "Gini co-efficient", an economic metric that measures inequality, increased in Western Australia drastically between 2008 and 2013.[37] *Eyrie* tackles neoliberalism and inequality head on, as they seismically impact Winton's home state. It depicts Australian masculinity as a trope, one compromised and imperilled by neoliberalism and its monotonous smugness.

Keely is portrayed as a failed environmental activist. Timothy Clark has described the Anthropocene as the era during which humanity became a "decisive geological and climatological force".[38] One can, however, read the environmental crisis itself as a symptom of the Anthropocene. Such a reading would see the crisis as the product of the human re-framing of nature in a way that can also include the goal of free-market capitalism as an attempted human remaking of human nature: a universal designation of everyone as either a winner or a loser. The Anthropocene in climactic terms represents a human remaking of the earth. In the same way, neoliberalism represents a remaking of society, by which social solidarity, compassion and caring for others become conceptually impossible. As Dipesh Chakrabarty argues, awareness of the Anthropocene has allowed us to see that humans are "a part of the natural condition", and has thus made problematic traditional accounts of human agency that saw the volition of humanity as counterposed to the inanimate force of nature.[39]

In *Eyrie*, Keely's failure as an ecological activist can be put in the grain of the book's larger mission: to shake us out of any sense of comfort with our times. As a critique of neoliberalism, however, the novel is not straightforward. The villain of the novel, Kai's creepy, drug-addicted father, Stewie, is hardly a smooth corporate operator. He is a hungry lower-middle-class menace who has it in for Kai and Gemma. We should not assume that convincing narratives about neoliberalism must always have as their villain a corporate executive or a stockbroker. Some novels, such as Elliot Perlman's *Three Dollars* (1998) do just that. But this sort of simplistic critique has the potential to reduce the problems of neoliberalism to melodrama, in which an endearing dreamer wins out over the cold forces of corporate capitalism. Such a narrative risks underestimating the diffuse power of neoliberalism.[40]

In *Grub Street Irregulars* (2008), Jeremy Lewis, the British man of letters, notes that at a certain point in the 1980s, one stopped being able to know just who was in control in publishing, or who was making what decisions.[41] The newspaper headlines told of conglomerates, mergers and synergies, but the post-apocalyptic hierarchy was not clear even to an old publishing hand such as Lewis. Neoliberalism is not a conspiracy, not a cartel of

---

37   Michael Fletcher and Ben Guttmann, "Income Inequality in Australia", in *Economic Roundup* 2 (Canberra: Treasury of Australia, 2013). http://www.treasury.gov.au/PublicationsAndMedia/Publications/2013/Economic-Roundup-Issue-2/Economic-Roundup.

38   Timothy Clark, "Nature, Post-Nature", in *The Cambridge Companion to Literature and the Environment*, ed. Louise Westling (New York: Cambridge University Press, 2010), 79.

39   Dipesh Chakrabarty, "The Climate of History: Four Theses", *Critical Inquiry* 35, no. 2 (2009): 214. Chakrabarty's essay is dedicated to the memory of the Australian scholar Greg Dening and Australia is mentioned as one of the ecologically vulnerable areas of the globe in Chakrabarty's article.

40   Perlman's 2005 novel *Seven Types of Ambiguity* was a fierce critique of neoliberalism and one that also saw a way beyond neoliberalism's ideological grasp – but its heft (640 pages) paradoxically played into some of the neoliberal era's marketing prejudices.

41   Jeremy Lewis, *Grub Street Irregular: Scenes from the Literary Life* (London: HarperCollins, 2008), 43–44.

meanies. It is thoroughly systemic even though, paradoxically, it manifests itself unsystematically. Felix, the owner of the chocolate factory in Harrower's *The Watch Tower*, with his top-down mentality, was a model of failed late-modern charismatic authoritarianism. In the late-modern period, this mentality was seen on a larger scale in both corporate boards and Communist Party presidia. In that era, one could point confidently to Felix, or to the system of power in which he was invested, as the problem. Neoliberalism, in contrast, as Mark Bevir notes, makes its centres of power diffuse.[42] Thus casting a corporate lawyer or a stockbroker as *Eyrie*'s villain would have oversimplified the problems it is considering. This does not make the novel's indictment of neoliberal excesses any less savage. Winton makes it clear both that Stewie is a vicious scoundrel, and that he is the by-product of larger, systemic issues. He is what happens when society is drastically and arbitrarily divided into winners and losers. That the villain is a fellow victim of the system underscores the variable and unintended consequences of today's cultural climate.

In Stewie, Keely finds someone more or less on his own scale to oppose. Keely's relationship with Gemma and Kai is not just a romantic reawakening for a man who, adrift in a large, anonymous apartment building, had seemed severed from life and from love. It also allows him to transition from (in the New Zealand writer John Mulgan's famous phrase) "Man Alone" into a person who exhibits concern and care for others. Indeed, Keely does this in a more authentic way than his mother, Doris, a classic welfare-state carer who has always put the needs of others first and who now has nothing to show for it.

Winton's earlier books described an Australian working-class masculinity that in a previous era would have been organised, whether in labour unions or, as Falconer's *Lost Thoughts of Soldiers* reminds us, in war. But these men are now roving free agents, and *Eyrie* unsentimentally captures what happens when one of them learns how to care. That Keely is not inherently or apodictically virtuous adds force to his moral awakening. Winton does not preach.

Although *Eyrie* is as long as the total novel *manqué* that was *Cloudstreet*, it is much more a *récit*. The *récit* is better equipped to address the contradictions of neoliberalism than the total novel. Neoliberalism brings opposing elements so close to each other and makes them so dependent on each other that they are hard to separate, making it not easily susceptible of a coherent opposition. Even the most determined critic of neoliberalism has sipped a first-rate cappuccino. Moreover, as discussed above, neoliberalism does not have agents or executives of the sort found in late modernity and depicted by Harrower. In plumbing this social nexus, the *récit*, with its clarity, its stylistic rigour and its fostering of the reader's independence, takes on the urgency of a *testimonio*.

The image of the eyrie that gives the novel its title refers to the birds that Keely and Kai together care for; as we will see in considering Alexis Wright's *The Swan Book* in Chapter 6, an extension of care to animals seems to be concomitant with a rethinking of altruism in the twenty-first century. But "eyrie" also connotes inhuman sublimity and speaks to the strange liminal state in which Keely is in at the beginning of the novel – ensconced at the hub of a prosperous city, in another sense cast off in a world of desperation and anomie, untethered, unmoored.[43] Birds can be birds of prey as well as songbirds. The eyrie represents aspiration, but also elitism; soaring freedom, but also the danger of independence from concern.

---

42   Mark Bevir, "Governance and Governmentality after Neoliberalism", *Policy and Politics* 39, no. 4 (2011): 457–71.

In his 2013 article on class in the *Monthly*, Winton offers a clear account of the differences between late modernity and neoliberalism in Australia:

> The culture that formed me was poorer, flatter and probably fairer than the one I live in today. Class was more visible, less confusing, more honestly defined and clearly understood. And it was something you could discuss without feeling like a heretic. The decency of our society used to be the measure of its success. Such decency rescued many of us from over-determined lives. It was the moral force that eroded barriers between people, opened up pathways previously unimagined. Not only did it enlarge our personal imaginations but it also enhanced our collective experience.[44]

Indeed, Winton goes on to argue that even Australia's material prosperity is due to this decency, not to neoliberal deregulation. I will leave this to the economists to decide, but it is notable how much Winton resists his own era, even to the point that, as Robert Dixon has noted with respect to *Cloudstreet*, he could be accused of nostalgia.[45] Winton's anti-elitism resembles Les Murray's; he is opposed not just to the hyper-elite but also to the pretentious intellectual class that often emerges as the only vocal opposition to the hyper-elite (this is clear in his portrait of the arrogant and complacent Toby Raven in *Cloudstreet*). Yet *Eyrie* differentiates between late modernity and neoliberalism (which it describes as "the new managerial dispensation"), even though both are characteristically urban, and finds a model of resistance through care. This is another reason why it is important that the villain is the drug-abusing, working-class Stewie, rather than a more mercantile figure. Had Winton set Keely in opposition to a slick, citified elite, the book would suggest nothing more nuanced than a longing for a blokey renaissance. Instead, Keely realises by the end of the book that, in order to carry on his mother's legacy of compassion, he must climb out of the eyrie and live in the contemporary world.

To cement these fine distinctions, Winton repurposes the medium-length novel. Rather than seeking to embrace the whole, his narrative circles in a finite way upon its preoccupations. Nevertheless, most reviewers treated *Eyrie* either as the same old macho, vernacular Winton, seen as routine and unspectacular, or just as a baffling conundrum. *Eyrie* did not receive the Miles Franklin Literary Award, was not shortlisted for the Booker, and did not come close to page one in the *New York Times Book Review*. Catherine Blyth, in the UK *Telegraph*, called *Eyrie* "overextended and underdeveloped".[46] Wendy Smith, writing in the American online magazine *Daily Beast*, called it "brilliantly written but ultimately frustrating".[47] The novel seemed too parabolic, too riddling, to these reviewers; it did not sufficiently parade its evident meaning. This played into a general pattern for the

---

43 For a similar reading of Peter Carey's *The Tax Inspector*, see Robert Dixon, "Closing the Can of Worms: Enactments of Justice in *Bleak House*, *The Mystery of a Hansom Cab* and *The Tax Inspector*", *Westerly* 37, no. 4 (1992): 37–45.

44 Tim Winton, "Some Thoughts about Class in Australia", *Monthly*, December 2013, 24–31.

45 Robert Dixon, "Tim Winton, *Cloudstreet* and the Field of Australian Literature", *Westerly* 50 (2005): 240–60.

46 Catherine Blyth, "A Heartfelt Story of Disillusion and Salvation Fails to Soar", *Telegraph*, 18 June 2014. http://www.telegraph.co.uk/culture/books/bookreviews/10894457/ Eyrie-by-Tim-Winton-review-overextended-and-underdeveloped.html.

47 Wendy Smith, "Tim Winton's Beautiful, Baffling *Eyrie*", *The Daily Beast*, 18 August 2014. http://www.thedailybeast.com/articles/2014/08/18/tim-winton-s-beautiful-baffling-eyrie.html.

reception of Australian literature. As Antigone Kefala once remarked, "the editor found my piece too small. Length, length is what they want".[48]

The Narrow Road to World Reception

In 2014, two events occurred that countered the association of the large with the Australian. One was James Wood's review of Harrower, which drew a writer of taut domestic fiction to the attention of millions of readers. The other was Richard Flanagan's Booker win for *The Narrow Road to the Deep North*. It might seem odd to think of Flanagan as a writer of *récits*, given the epic size of *Gould's Book of Fish* (2001, 480 pages). But Flanagan's 2007 *The Unknown Terrorist* was spare (336 pages), intense and contemporary, violating expectations that Australian novels be large, lush and historical. It also was not a particular success internationally, perhaps because readers found disconcerting Flanagan's portrait of The Doll – a tough, manipulative, no-nonsense exotic dancer who is an embodiment of neoliberal self-interest. De-idealising the present instead of selectively idealising the past is not a recipe for global success. *The Narrow Road to the Deep North*, however, is different. It is historical, but it is concerned with history within living memory, namely Australian prisoners of war forced by the Japanese Army to build a railroad north from Burma. The Australians' Japanese captors know that Japan, "overstretched, under-resourced, is losing" – as, with the benefit of hindsight, does the reader.[49] This subject matter can still be sensitive, as seen in the review of Flanagan's novel in the *Japan Times*, which takes pains to point out moral equivalences to Japanese wartime conduct among other great powers.[50] Flanagan has made clear that his own father, who was a prisoner of war, supplied inspiration for the novel. His relation to the material thus has a personal, lyrical cast.

The novel is more a *récit* than a total novel, not only because it is relatively slim (334 pages) but also because of this fundamental lyricism. Flanagan takes his title from a book of haiku by Basho, the great Japanese poet of the eighteenth century. It is a book that is prized by the sadistic prison-camp commandant, Major Nakamura, and here Flanagan is also musing on how aesthetic and authoritarian impulses can reside within the same heart, something frequently noted with respect to both European and Asian authoritarianism. The title thus alludes not only to an Asian literary work, but to a literary genre invented and overwhelmingly practised by Asian writers. Like Nicholas Jose and Delia Falconer, Flanagan does not just take Asia as his subject matter – as did earlier Australian writers such as Christopher Koch and T. A. G. Hungerford – but is formally influenced by Asian modes, taking the Australian novel away from the boisterous reoccupation of European forms that has long been Australia's assigned role in the world literary sphere. Flanagan has stated that he does not come out of a national literary tradition.[51] Yet his sense of a

48   Antigone Kefala, *Sydney Journals: Reflections 1970–2000* (Artarmon: Giramondo Publishing, 2008), 178.

49   Richard Flanagan, *The Narrow Road to the Deep North* (New York: Knopf, 2014), 21. All subsequent references are to this edition and appear in parentheses in the text.

50   Roger Pulvers, review of *The Narrow Road to the Deep North*, *Japan Times*, 9 November 2013. http://www.japantimes.co.jp/culture/2013/11/09/books/book-reviews/the-narrow-road-to-the-deep-north/#.VkFx178YNqF.

51   Quoted in Walton, "Star Fiction". http://www.nybooks.com/articles/archives/2014/dec/04/luminaries-star-fiction/.

literary tradition in another language provides *The Narrow Road to the Deep North* with moving reverberations. Flanagan contrasts the Japanese and British literary inheritance by strategic quotations from Tennyson's *Ulysses* and Kipling's "Recessional". He saves these quotations from cliché by placing them in felt emotional contexts, yet they also show the English predilection for grandiloquence, in contrast to the Japanese restraint.

The title has other resonances. It describes the railroad the men are building, north towards China, a country Japan is still trying to subdue at the outset of the novel. In the 1990s, there was much talk of Australia seeing Asia not as the "Far East" but as the "Near North" (a term used originally as early as 1948).[52] The "Deep North" of the novel's title evokes a time before economic convergence, when Asia seemed to Australians a closed, ineffable realm. The novel does not treat Asia as a monolith, however. Flanagan understands that there are many Asias. *The Narrow Road to the Deep North* portrays a Korean sergeant, Choi Sang-Min, who despite being the object of Japanese prejudice participates in the sadistic cruelties of the Japanese forces. The novel recognises that a Korean officer might at once feel oppressed by the Japanese and be driven to try to excel in a system stacked against him from the beginning. As a Korean soldier in the Japanese Army, he is a member of the "precariat" (to use Guy Standing's term).[53] Choi must exceed if he hopes to be treated as ordinary, to be seen as anything but despicable and abject by his oppressors.

The novel's chief character, Dorrigo Evans, is a man of paradoxes. As a doctor he tries to care for his fellow prisoners and as an officer he has some authority over the enlisted men. Accepting the Prime Minister's Literary Award in December 2014 (he was joint winner with Steven Carroll, for *A World of Other People*), Flanagan said that the theme of *The Narrow Road to the Deep North* – in defiance of all the hierarchies of neoliberalism – is that the strong should care for the weak. Dorrigo's physiological and psychological solicitude for his patients, his fellow detainees, embodies this.

Dorrigo is a man involved in traumatic public events; his pain has an identifiable source. Yet in his heart his deepest lost is that of his first beloved, Amy, who is married to his uncle Keith Mulvaney (the husband of Dorrigo's deceased aunt on his father's side, although there is nonetheless a soupcon of incest sufficient to make the relationship slightly anomalous). Dorrigo marries the conventional and amiable Ella, but Amy – her very name connoting "love" – remains his principal emotional attachment, inspiring him during his imprisonment, lingering in his heart even after her reported death in an Adelaide pub fire in 1945. "Amy" is an anagram of "may", and there is an element in the Amy plot of possibility and the subjunctive.

Flanagan also uses the love story between Amy and Dorrigo to demonstrate the selfishness of their partners, who are determined to hold Amy and Dorrigo back – the lies they tell to do so are like soul-murders. This conduct is akin to that of Rooster MacNeice in the camps, a proto-neoliberal figure who also puts self-interest first. It involves secrets back in Australia, and losses other than those inflicted by combat. The revelation that one of Dorrigo's fellow prisoners, Darky Gardiner, was in fact Dorrigo's nephew, the child of his brother Tom and a half-Aboriginal woman, Ruth Maguire, demonstrates that cultural encounter and historical trauma occur within Australia as well. Whereas Flanagan's earlier books looked at history moralistically, his later work, like that of Winton, is more nuanced.

---

52 R. J. Gilmore and D. Warner, *Near North: Australia and a Thousand Million Neighbours* (Sydney: Angus & Robertson, 1948).
53 Guy Standing, *The Precariat: The New Dangerous Class* (London: Bloomsbury Academic, 2011).

In *Gould's Book of Fish*, Flanagan came close to seeing the abusive nature of the Australian convict system as tantamount to critical reason itself. In *The Narrow Road to the Deep North*, there is a still a critique of linearity. Dorrigo draws a circle as a gesture of protest against the line in which he is forced to march in, a circle twice visually reproduced in the book. The line is described as "something that proceeded from one point to another – from reality to unreality, from life to hell" (22). But Dorrigo is deeply analytical, and is willing to scrutinise all that challenges him, both in public and in private.

In *Gould's Book of Fish*, Flanagan flailed against the rational and privileged the multitudinous. In *The Narrow Road to the Deep North*, he privileges the private over the public. The novel's private dimension indicates that its depiction of the experience of war does not insist on reality. Flanagan unfolds this in the preposterousness of Imperial Japanese ideology, and in the way Dorrigo is temporarily part of "a slave system that had at its apex a divine sun king led him to understand unreality as the greatest force in life" (288). Recalling his medical schooling in Melbourne, Dorrigo observes that conventional white Australians lived in a condition they thought was reality but in fact was "a fiction greater than anything Trollope had ever attempted" (11). History is not, as in traditional or even magical realism, seen as a bedrock of reality upon which imagination can play; history is composed of unreality. The real does not actually have to happen to be felt as real. The Amy plot suggests that the problem of wartime trauma is impossible to solve definitively. Unlike the romance Dorrigo tries to read at the end of the book, Dorrigo's story cannot "end well, with the hero and heroine finding love, with peace and joy and redemption and understanding" (334). Instead it is a riddle, a puzzle that cannot be (and is not meant to be) solved, but still tantalises the reader with hints of a possible solution.

It is not the international success of Flanagan's novel that is surprising – since the late 1990s he has had a devoted readership in the USA and the UK – but the fact that he successfully challenged the stereotypical formulae of what Australian novels must do if they are to appeal to what Malouf has called "the great world". Flanagan wrote an Australian story that did not presume to be *the* Australian story, proving that Australian fiction does not have to be (to quote from his American publisher's description of *Death of a River Guide*) as sprawling and compelling as the land and people it describes. In doing so, Flanagan took Australian letters a significant step further along the narrow road to world reception.

The Affects of Contemporary Australian Literature

5
The Ludicrous Pageant: Challenging Consensus Through Rancour

If globalisation can lead to hype and inequality in literary reception, as shown in the previous chapter, the two earlier chapters, on Stead and Harrower, have shown that there can be no return to the deadlocked reassurances of late modernity. One cannot, in other words, simply lament the free market and indulge in a nostalgic wish for the era of the welfare state; that era, even if it was better than Stead and Harrower unsparingly show it to be, is gone forever. Instead, I am proposing that, rather than any sort of polemical antidote to neoliberalism, the solution to the problems of the contemporary lie in affect: in conditions of feeling that can fight back, albeit indirectly, against contemporary inequalities. Affect here occupies an anomalous role, as it is not primarily a social or political condition, but finds itself operating in the social and political spheres by virtue of the discursive unavailability of other, more obvious alternatives. With writers unable or unwilling to affirm a more rousing but naive vision, affect assumes an unexpected role: feeling takes up, imperfectly and asymmetrically, the ethical burden previously borne by more direct modes of social comment. The three emotions I examine in this section, rancour, idealism and concern, contradict but also complement one another. They are not the only possible literary emotions, but, I will argue, they are the main ones that Australian literature is using to fight back against the problems of the contemporary.

In the next three chapters, I will explore states of affect in contemporary Australian literature. Sianne Ngai has explored "aesthetic categories" that are unpleasant, ambiguous, recalcitrant or, in Ngai's terms, "minor and generally unprestigious", and usually seen as troubling.[1] The work of Vilashini Cooppan has linked affect to ideologies of globalisation. Cooppan's idea of "worlds within" limns intermediate identities between the personal and the global, "ambivalent forces of desire, identification, memory, and forgetting". Her model defines affect as a border zone between sovereignty and desire, individual will and social force.[2] Such intermediate constellations of identity, between the individual and the social, can have an effect on how literature manifests feeling. In an era when the only opponents of the neoliberal consensus are on the political fringe, modes of affect become the most

---

1   Sianne Ngai, *Our Aesthetic Categories: Zany, Cute, Interesting* (Cambridge: Harvard University Press, 2013); and *Ugly Feelings* (Cambridge: Harvard University Press, 2005), 6.
2   Vilashini Cooppan, *Worlds Within: National Narratives and Global Connections in Postcolonial Writing* (Stanford: Stanford University Press, 2009), xvii.

palpable and constructive imaginative response to the cruelty and inequality promoted by the dominant socioeconomic mode.

Emotions straddling the line between the individual and collective can reveal aspects of literature distinct from those rendered by either traditional close reading or the various practices of distant reading, whether they be in the style of the statistical analyses of Franco Moretti, or older practices of ideological critique, which, in a cruder way, attempted a strategic distance from the weave of the text.[3]

Emotional analysis stands in a sort of middle distance between text and context, lingering in a zone that cannot entirely be evidence-based, as both close-reading and distant-reading practices are. As Kathleen Stewart argues, affects are "the varied, surging capacities to affect and to be affected that give everyday life the quality of a continual motion of relations, scenes, contingencies, and emergences".[4] Affect is a realm between the specific and the general, a realm of the radically experiential that is generalisable into theory, yet not a synthesis or a concrete universal. It is an indefinite realm of emotions where, as Christine Berberich puts it, "the haptic and the critical" can fuse.[5] This is especially true, as both Ngai and Cooppan note, of the current era, in which the hyper-marketisation of value and the destabilisation of accreted identities give middle-distance emotional categories a relevance they lacked in more hierarchical days. The three emotions I will explore, rancour, idealism and concern, are all laden with such ambiguities. They are not easy to see as unambiguously good or bad, and in that way escape the simple market moralism of winners and losers.

Of these three emotions, rancour may seem the least ambiguous. Paradoxically, this is not because it is uniformly negative, but because it seems determinate. To hate someone or something is almost invariably to reduce, to be inflexible, to see something in only one way. It is the argument of this chapter that rancour need not hew to one firm viewpoint; it can be open, creative, and through the very force of its anger and spite spur dialogue. This chapter discusses rancour in Australian fiction, beginning with A. D. Hope, who, though of an earlier period, is crucial in defining the affect of contemporary rancour with which the chapter is concerned, and continuing with writers who in different ways are both major writers in today's Australia yet outsiders in relation to the mainstream Australian literary world: the novelist Christos Tsiolkas, the poet and novelist Ouyang Yu, the poet John Kinsella, the novelist and essayist J. M. Coetzee, and the poets Pam Brown and Jennifer Maiden. These writers are all willing to use anger and contumely to speak truth in the face of contemporary piety. The emphasis here will not be on rancour as a mode of spite or of denunciation so much as rancour as a refusal to be a genial dinner guest at the table of culture. By refusing to be happy with the way things are, rancour can destabilise our sense of winners and losers, of what it means to succeed and to fail in contemporary culture. Andrew McCann exemplified this in his 2004 *Overland* essay, "How to Fuck a Tuscan Garden", a splenetic exception to the inculcated Australian, and Australianist, habit of barracking for any sort of literary success regardless of the implications for literary standards.[6]

---

3 Franco Moretti, *Distant Reading* (London: Verso Books, 2012).

4 Quoted in Christine Berberich, ed., "Introduction", *Place, Memory, Affect* (Lanham: Rowman & Littlefield, 2015), 7.

5 Berberich, *Place, Memory, Affect*, 5.

6 Andrew McCann, "How to Fuck a Tuscan Garden", *Overland* 177 (2004): 22–24.

Rancour interjects discord into literary debate in order to maintain some awareness of those standards.

True Hope Is Swift: Australia's Great Satirist

The work of A. D. Hope embodies this idea of rancour as an emotion that at once puts paid to the idea that Australia has escaped the maladies of the world, and yet sustains, within its spite and contempt, a deep resilience. In the hands of Dryden, Pope, Swift and Johnson, satire became the premier mode of English poetry, as these generally conservative satirists inveighed against the fashionably meretricious thought of the day. In Pope's hands, satire became a form of literary criticism, skewering bad writing. The fiery indignation (*saeva indignatio*, a phrase associated with Swift) of these writers illustrates one of the key paradoxes of satire. Satire irreverently attacks current institutions and modes. Yet, in doing so, it eulogises an old order that these satirists implied was far superior to the current one. As Michael Seidel points out, satire in this era often redeployed ideas of violence from epic, making them seemingly less consequential but keeping their rancour and instability.[7] Furthermore, as Robert Elliott asserted in *The Power of Satire*, the form's potential for critique is so powerful that whatever its overt nostalgic aims, it has the potential to be a catalysing rhetoric.[8]

Hope's work was urbane and neoclassical. But it was also harsh, rancorous and rebarbative. This did not dim its popularity or appeal. Indeed, in an age when little attention was paid in America to Australian poetry, Hope gained some traction in the USA, where poets writing in a similar mode, such as Yvor Winters, wielded influence in the 1950s and 1960s. It is not to downplay Hope's ability or appeal to speculate that his surname may have had something to do with this. The Australian literary scene was often bewilderingly non-navigable for American readers, but the word "hope", with its promise of idealism, had a resonance, whatever the rancour of the actual poetry. Hope was not above playing on his name, as is seen in his appropriation of these lines from Shakespeare in the dedication of *Dunciad Minor*:

> To the Memory of the late Ambrose Philips,
> esquire and the somewhat later Arthur Angell Phillips,
> esquire, the onlie begetters of these ensuing verses
> True Hope is swift, and flies with swallow's wings;
> Kings it makes gods, and meaner creatures Kings![9]

Hope also rhymes with Alexander Pope, the poet Hope most tried to emulate. Yet although classicists valued Hope's work, they were not the only ones. Harold Bloom, who more than any other critic is associated with romantic ideals of creative genius, not only approved of

---

7   Michael Seidel, *Satiric Inheritance: From Rabelais to Sterne* (Princeton: Princeton University Press, 1979).

8   Robert Elliott, *The Power of Satire* (Princeton: Princeton University Press, 1972).

9   A. D. Hope, "An Heroick Poem", *Dunciad Minor* (Melbourne: Melbourne University Press, 1971).

Hope but ascribed to Hope's evocation of Christopher Marlowe's "argument of arms": this was the vital inspiration for Bloom's sense of influence as a battlefield, an epic struggle.[10] In a 1987 interview with Imre Salusinszky, Bloom perhaps surprised some readers by speaking positively of Alexander Pope's poetry, praising the energies in it as romantic by other means.[11] Similarly, Hope's satire is not mechanical: it is full of verve.

This was recognised by Kevin Hart, the contemporary Australian poet most enthusiastically embraced by Bloom. Hart wrote a book about Hope that praised his Orphic drives, something not normally associated with a cerebral classicist.[12] The sense of Hope as a romanticist in classicist garb, or someone who made classicism a mode of emotion as expressive as romanticism, can also be seen as a way to reconcile Bloom's later, more humanistic and generalist work with his earlier, more arcane and antithetical production. That Bloom's later writing, widely seen in the USA as a defence of traditional canons, garnered praise in Australia from Robert Dessaix as "multicultural", shows how in Australia, rancour and idealism, contempt and enthusiasm, are not always easily distinguished.[13]

Ann McCulloch comments that Hope's satire "is made less polemical and more ambiguous by his irony".[14] This is true of *Dunciad Minor*, a work that tries to duplicate Pope's rendering of what Ngai termed "stuplimity" – an amalgam of stupidity and sublimity – on the Australian scene of its day. Robert Darling, Hope's most faithful American exegete, used the word "rancour" to describe *Dunciad Minor*.[15] Darling was an arch-formalist and did not see Hope in the nuanced way that Bloom did. One might expect that *Dunciad Minor*, an Augustan critique of modern follies, would have garnered Darling's approval. But *au contraire*: he saw it as a distinctly minor and unsatisfying work, and barely allotted it two paragraphs in his critical book on Hope.

The key here may be Darling's remark that if the deconstructionists had been around when Hope wrote the poem, Hope would have made mincemeat of them. But the deconstructionists were not around then, or at least were not yet part of the academic canon, although Derrida's early writing was indeed published when Hope was at the height of his acclaim. The people Hope satirises, F. R. Leavis among them, were often invoked as the humanistic precursors – and sane alternative – to the deconstructionists. Rather than letting himself be conscripted into an anti-theory mob, Hope hewed to his own critical line, and in his 1992 memoir *Chance Encounters* again identified Leavis, rather than critical theory in general, as his main opponent.[16] It is interesting that Hope's principal contemporary proponent has been Hart, a confirmed deconstructionist. Hope had an animus against modern innovation. But it may be more useful to see his use of rancour as a refusal to participate complacently in a dutiful celebration of modern innovation. He resisted the mid-century habit of praising Joyce, Woolf and Eliot not out of genuine enthusiasm, but because they were considered current and acceptable.

Graham Huggan compares Hope's "vigorous challenge" to modernism with the "experimental fiction" of Patrick White.[17] This is a notable instance of how time smooths

10   Harold Bloom, ed., *Hart Crane* (New York: Chelsea House, 2009), 10.

11   Imre Salusinzky, "An Interview with Harold Bloom", *Scripsi* 4, no. 1 (1986): 69–88.

12   Kevin Hart, *A. D. Hope* (Melbourne: Oxford University Press, 1993).

13   Robert Dessaix, "An Interview with Harold Bloom", *Australian Book Review* 169 (April 1995): 17–20.

14   Ann McCulloch, *Dance of the Nomad: A Study of the Selected Notebooks of A. D. Hope* (Acton: Australian National University Press, 2010), 26.

15   Robert Darling, *A. D. Hope* (Boston: Twayne Publishers, 1997), 30–31.

16   A. D. Hope, *Chance Encounters* (Melbourne: Melbourne University Press, 1992), 59.

all oppositions, for Hope had memorably excoriated White's fiction as "pretentious and illiterate verbal sludge". In his essay collection *The Cave and the Spring*, Hope deplored "activist" poetry, poetry that "requires the writer to write in such a way that he promotes something".[18] Yet his willingness to associate poetry with argument is strikingly activist. Hope did not remain in a formalist cocoon. He observed that "many of the greatest works of literature have a perfectly deliberate social or religious or artistic purpose". Although in part Hope's essay was an attack on left-wing literary activism – he particularly singled out social realism – he was too broadminded to reduce it to a simple matter of left versus right. Indeed, in many ways the hero of the essay is Shelley, a poet who was a radical political activist, but whose work soared beyond that into "something beyond any possible anticipation". Nor did all of Hope's didactic poetry warn against modish pretension. "The Cetaceans", as Tracy Ryan points out, is an early instance of an ecological poem.[19] Hope's argumentation is plural and polymathic.

In his essay "The Argument of Arms", Hope takes a line from Marlowe's *Tamburlaine* – spoken by the great conqueror himself, when he stabs his once pacifist son Calyphas in order to prove his dedication to a warrior ethos. Tamburlaine is an activist if ever there was one. Hope finds admirable, in Marlowe's language, "a poetry so splendid as to compel understanding", the same opulent relentlessness with which Tamburlaine enunciates his rhetoric of conquest.[20] This points to a self-identification between Hope and Marlowe, as between Marlowe and Tamburlaine, even though Hope's own poetry directs its energy towards tearing things down, not building things up.

Moreover, Hope comes close to naming himself in his own essay. Tamburlaine announces his intention to "cut a channel" to "both the Red Sea and the Terrene" (the Mediterranean),[21] foreshadowing the Suez Canal, whose eventual completion in the nineteenth century connected Australia to the British imperial polity more directly. Moreover, Tamburlaine speaks of "our antipodes" (although here he means South America, not Australia, since he is in Persia rather than England). Tamburlaine presaged the British imperialism that would one day lead to a man named Alec Hope living in the twentieth century in the Great South Land.

Hope himself accentuated this sense of challenge to the consensus. His iconic poem "Australia" vindicates a continent the poem had previously scorned as desiccated and derivative, conjecturing that "still from deserts the prophets come", evoking an almost Byronic tone. *Dunciad Minor* also enacts this sense of being an outsider, although in a secondary and deflective fashion. *Dunciad Minor* is in fact longer than Pope's *Dunciad*, and tries to be more of an epic than a mock epic. It is also dialogic. Hope uses mock footnotes attributed to "A. P." and "A. A. P." – the Augustan Ambrose Phillips and the twentieth-century Australian critic A. A. Phillips, who coined the phrase "cultural cringe" – in which they dispute with the main narrative. In addition, Hope himself, most unlike Pope, cites his own classical and modern sources. The book is as much pedagogical – Hope was a

---

17   Graham Huggan, *Australian Literature: Postcolonialism, Racism, Transnationalism* (Oxford: Oxford University Press, 2007), 85.
18   A. D. Hope, *The Cave and the Spring: Essays on Poetry* (1965; archived online at http://setis.library.usyd.edu.au/ozlit/pdf/sup0002.pdf/), 31.
19   Tracy Ryan, "Cold Greed and Rankling Guilt: A Re-reading of A. D. Hope's 'The Cetaceans'", *Southerly* 69, no. 1 (2009): 146–69.
20   Hope, *The Cave and the Spring*, 99.
21   Christopher Marlowe, *Four Plays* (New York: Bloomsbury, 2014), 142.

famed teacher – as satiric. Mikhail Bakhtin might have described it as "double-voiced". Even today, the open-ended quality of Hope's rancour is notable. He is not attacking a single target, but using rancour to expose the contradictions in his world. Even less than Pope, who as Bloom observed often exhibits a conflict between his ideology and his poetic passion, is Hope a dogmatist.

Hope was modern even as he virulently criticised the modern. He could not conceive of modernity as being vulnerable to annulment or repeal. In "The Argument of Arms" Hope writes, "kings have fallen into such disrepute that to aspire to sovereignty over others has come to be regarded as a disgraceful if not actually a criminal ambition".[22] To us, there seems an innocence in this sentence. Hope was writing from within modernity, from within the welfare state, from within an egalitarian consensus – a consensus he did not necessarily like or accept, but whose existence he perceived no alternative to acknowledging. In his poem "Observation Car", the routine conformity of modern transportation is at once seen as a limit and a condition; train travel, with its lack of charm and loss of individual sovereignty, acts as a classical restraint on the poet's extravagant desires. In the twenty-first century, however, as the work of Giorgio Agamben attests, sovereignty has returned with a vengeance, as a "power which decides not between the licit and the illicit but the originary inclusion of the living in the sphere of law", a force that arbitrarily decides whose humanity will be recognised and whose will not be, who wins and who loses.[23]

Even if this contemporary sovereignty does not literally take the form of a monarchy, the powerful can coerce the powerless through the exercise of status. From refugees in detention centres to the unwaged and minimally waged precariat, what Simon During calls "unstable and diverse conditions of deprivation and insecurity" proliferate in the contemporary era.[24] Hope, on the other hand, perceived his own era as an age of egalitarianism. He may have mocked this egalitarian consensus, but he accepted it as real, and perhaps even fostered it in his role as a caring supervisor of graduate students at the Australian National University, many of whom were first-generation university graduates. Hope may have been a conservative, but he was not a reactionary.

This is seen in Hope's interpretation of Marlowe's protagonists as not dynastic or aristocratic but self-made and meritocratic. Hope's "Argument of Arms" shows that the coercive exercise of power by such self-authored individuals can if anything be even more menacing than that exercised by dynastic hegemons. But Hope did not envision this mentality returning; indeed, it was omening so far in the past that modern people, living in a radically different life-world, inevitably misunderstood Marlowe's poetry.

As theorists of satire like Elliott have noted, rancour must come from a minority perspective to be cogent; otherwise, it is simply the consensus enforcing itself through spleen. In Hope's day, his attitudes were beleaguered by trendy social optimism; in a later era, social optimism was itself beleaguered. Hope's satiric protest was directed against a modern or late-modern world of egalitarianism, formal experimentation, and the welfare state. The next generation of Australian satirists, especially those who used rancour more broadly to protest against social conditions, were reacting against a different world: one of rampant capitalism, bimodally distributed status, and a resurgence of sovereignty, although sover-

---

22 Hope, *The Cave and the Spring*, 99.
23 Giorgio Agamben, *Homo Sacer*, trans. Daniel Heller-Roazen (Stanford: Stanford University Press, 1998), 127.Hope, *The Cave and the Spring*, 99.
24 Simon During, "From the Subaltern to the Precariat", *Boundary 2* 42:2 (2015): 57–84.

eignty exercised only by certain privileged individuals and the state formations that served them. In this milieu, rancour was not an alternative to social activism, but an example of it, and the satiric pressure came, broadly speaking, from the left, as it was the left that was now out of power.

Rancour and Competitiveness: Christos Tsiolkas

If Hope embodied this sort of enabling rancour in his own, late-modern, generation of Australian writers, in subsequent generations the baton was taken up by migrant and ethnic writers. While many rather stereotypical accounts of Australian landscape, such as Nikki Gemmell's *Alice Springs* (1999), were launched on the world market in the 1990s and early 2000s, it was paradoxically the often confrontational work of Christos Tsiolkas that garnered world acclaim. Tsiolkas is the grumbling guest at the party, rancorously reminding us of what is still wrong, making no concessions to genteel taste. Nor does he assume the role of "the submissive foreigner" that Toula Nicolacopoulos and George Vassilacopoulos argue is often expected of Greek-Australians.[25]

Tsiolkas certainly defies this stereotype in his 2013 novel *Barracuda*, in which he takes on the world of privileged achievement in Australia. He does so through Danny Kelly, a half Scottish, half Greek boy who, despite his migrant origins, bears an iconically Australian name, and whose ascribed identity has more to do with class than with ethnicity or sexuality. Danny's homosexuality is not problematised or highlighted, and Australian society is not depicted as particularly homophobic. Danny's straight friends accept his sexuality. Andrew McCann, writing of Tsiolkas's *Dead Europe* (2011), described Tsiolkas' dual themes as "the disintegration of left-wing politics in the face of consumer culture and neoliberalism" and "the confluence of sexuality and power".[26] *Barracuda*, while not forgetting the latter, decidedly emphasises the former.

Danny is hazed and discriminated against because of his ethnic and working-class origins. He tells himself, and is told by others, that if he is an outstanding swimmer this stigma will go away – that extraordinary achievement will dispel the threat of what Rob Nixon calls the "slow violence" of neoliberalism.[27] But if excellence is necessary to avoid discrimination, where does that leave working-class ethnics who do not have an exceptional talent? Even for Danny, all the skill in the world only serves to neutralise society's disdain for where he comes from; he is tolerated but not embraced. To be considered a viable person, an outsider must excel; to qualify as "ordinary", he must be extraordinary. This is what happens when equality of opportunity is considered the only important equality, and when the only social solidarity is one of mutually self-congratulatory winners.

Danny becomes unhinged and commits the assault that will send him to jail when Martin Taylor calls him "a fucking loser."[28] This is the biggest insult, the most stigmatising ignominy. At the peak of his promise, Danny may be a winner, but that status is always

---

25   Toula Nicolacopoulos and George Vassilacopoulos, "The Making of Greek-Australian Citizenship: From Heteronomous to Autonomous Political Communities", *Modern Greek Studies* 11 (2003): 172.

26   Andrew McCann, "Discrepant Cosmopolitanism and the Contemporary Novel: Reading the Inhuman in Christos Tsiolkas' *Dead Europe* and Roberto Bolaño's *2666*", *Antipodes* 24, no. 2 (2010): 135–41.

27   Rob Nixon, "Neoliberalism, Slow Violence, and the Environmental Picaresque", *Modern Fiction Studies* 55, no. 3 (2009): 445.

vulnerable. Like financial investments, social status fluctuates; it can never be presumed to be permanent. Being called a loser hurts Danny so severely because his entire identity is built upon being a winner. He is not a failed meritocrat who pursued achievement because of a conscious choice, or an aristocrat who desired to earn his own spurs. Nor is he a "loser who wins", a beatnik, bohemian or *poète maudit*. Winning is Danny's only way out of a condition of inferiority. The advocates of meritocracy have it right that exceptional achievement is a way out of disadvantage. But it is wrong that it should be the *only* way out.

The only way someone from Danny's world can have even a normal life is if they achieve excellence. For them it is, to use the old Australian saying, "Sydney or the bush": total victory or total loss. Neither patience nor luck offers an alternative route. Unlike in a Dickens novel, where a loser can become a winner through luck and pluck, Martin's comment to Danny renders being a loser an ontological state of being, in the same way that gender, ethnicity and sexuality are often ontologised. Martin says, "You know what we thought? We thought you were a loser. You didn't have the balls then and you don't have the balls now. That's why you're not there tonight, that's why you'll always be a fucking loser" (250). Danny's status as a loser makes other people uncomfortable, especially when they have to see him or speak to him. In the pub, Danny feels that the other people there "wanted to be celebrating, having fun" but cannot because of their sense of embarrassment, their discomfort that a loser such as Danny is in their presence (228).

Danny, for all his athletic potential, does not make it to the 2000 Sydney Olympics, and does not have the drive to follow through on his aspirations as a swimmer. But in calling him a loser, Martin is not criticising a wrong decision or an opportunity missed. He is implying that Danny is a loser innately. This is strangely antithetical to the doctrine of the free market, which lauds mobility and justifies inequality with the promise that those less well off can hope to move up. It is also antithetical to the very idea of sport, which recognises that even talented athletes often lose; mathematically, for every winner there must be at least one loser, and merit alone does not guarantee winning. But, in Martin's judgement, nothing can ever clear Danny of being a loser: he *is* a loser in the same way that one *is* a woman or an ethnic minority or a homosexual. He is inextricably bound to a subordinate identity. Martin's calling Danny a loser is in one way a socially acceptable substitute for such offensive terms as a "wog" or a "reffo"; in another way it represents the displacement of all anterior ethnic, racial or gender differences by the one universal binary of winners and losers.

Martin calling Danny a loser might be said to be the epicentre of critiques of neoliberalism in contemporary Australian literature. In past eras, Danny would have been denigrated for reasons of class or ethnic origin, for his sexuality or, like a Patrick White character, for simply not fitting in. In respect to Nietzsche's dichotomies examined in Chapter 1, if one is "bad" or "evil" one is always that. But if one is a loser presumably there is a hope of one day being a winner. In the world of *Barracuda*, however, being a winner or a loser is predestined, like Calvinistic grace. It is because Danny is condemned to this eternal category that he snaps and pummels Martin with rage, responding to Martin's "slow violence" with a more traditional fast violence.

Tsiolkas, as Andrew McCann has pointed out, is a consummate excavator of the "fissures and inequities underpinning notions of cosmopolitan freedom".[29] It is a major fissure,

---

28 Christos Tsiolkas, *Barracuda* (Crows Nest: Allen & Unwin, 2013), 302. All subsequent references are to this edition and appear in parentheses in the text.

if not a gulf, that even as the identities – gender, ethnicity, sexuality – that traditionally kept people back have been eliminated or stripped of their old significance, a new, equally oppressive category has emerged. There is no affirmative action for losers. But, as with those other categories, being labelled a loser can enrage those who stake their identities on being the opposite. For Martin and the other young men in the pub, the physical presence of a "loser" injects rancour into their celebration. It is an impingement on those who suppose themselves winners. Just as attacks on gay men are sometimes committed by macho assailants who panic that they, too, might be homosexual, the very presence of a loser makes winners worry that they might, in fact, be losers as well.

As Liliana Olmos, Rich Van Heertum and Carlos Torres have argued, the United States has seen "education as a panacea for its social ills for most of its history".[30] In Danny Kelly's Australia, the situation is becoming much the same. The welfare state has lost credibility, and government-led solutions to inequality are no longer *de rigeure*; in 2012 Joe Hockey, then shadow treasurer, declared "the end of the age of entitlement".[31] Hockey, born in 1965, is an exact contemporary of Tsiolkas, and their generation did not grow up with an expectation of universal social welfare as the generation before them did. As early as the late 1940s, when the transition from modernity to what we are calling late modernity began, education became the preferred way to ameliorate inequality. In Australia in the 1970s, the Whitlam government accentuated this with the introduction of free tertiary education. As Ashley Lavalle points out, however, even by 1978, when Whitlam had been out of office only three years, he was already arguing that this reform would not have been possible any later than the early 1970s; the "changed economic circumstances" concomitant with the perceived failure of late modernity would have precluded it.[32] Yet education rewards excellence, not ordinariness. If education is to replace the welfare state as a social panacea, only those who are excellent, or who are judged excellent within the self-reinforcing parameters of the system, can expect social mobility.

One need look no further than J. K. Rowling's Harry Potter series (referenced in *Barracuda*, when "a toy model of Hogwarts" is mentioned) (255) to see the apotheosis of the selective school as an arena for self-definition, in an era theoretically open to the potential merit of all but still committed to hierarchies of excellence.[33] Ronald A. Manzer, speaking of the intersection of "educational regimes" with "Anglo-American democracy", notes that, in New South Wales in the 1960s, "reform shifted the organisation of public secondary schools from tracks defined by occupational classes to ability grouping by subjects".[34] This message of mobility also applied to private schools, which, despite their elite associations,

29 McCann, "Discrepant Cosmopolitanism", 136.
30 Liliana Olmos, Rich Van Heertum and Carlos Alberto Torres, *Educating the Global Citizen in the Shadow of Neoliberalism: Thirty Years of Educational Reform in North America* (Oak Park: Bentham Science Publishers, 2011), 3.
31 Joe Hockey, "The End of the Age of Entitlement", speech to the Institute of Economic Affairs, London, 17 April 2012; published in the *Sydney Morning Herald*, 19 April 2012. http://www.smh.com.au/national/the-end-of-the-age-of-entitlement-20120419-lx8vj.html.
32 Ashley Lavalle, *The Death of Social Democracy: Political Consequences in the 21st Century* (Aldershot: Ashgate, 2008), 61.
33 Donna Tartt, in *The Goldfinch* (New York: Little, Brown, 2014), also uses Harry Potter as an analogue for twenty-first-century male identity when the hero's best friend, Boris, calls him "Potter" amid the paradoxes of twenty-first-century Las Vegas.
34 Ronald A. Manzer, *Educational Regimes and Anglo-American Democracy* (Toronto: University of Toronto Press, 2003), 141.

were seen as aiming to reach out to the underprivileged and deserving. William Empson famously read Thomas Gray's "Elegy Written in a Country Churchyard" as being about the lack of a "scholarship system". If there are "mute inglorious Miltons" in a world that offers scholarships to talented boys and girls, it will be, unlike in Gray's eighteenth-century world, because they have tried and failed, not because they never had a chance.[35]

Or rather, they will be *said* to have tried and failed, for what Tsiolkas makes clear in *Barracuda* is that competition to define excellence creates its own self-justifying rules. Danny's involvement with two institutions in the book – his elite school and the prison – suggests that these two systems have more in common than it might at first seem. Both are intended to sort, to confine, to rank. Both are about winning and losing; the implication is that if you do not fit into the categories of the elite school, in a society in which fortune is bimodally distributed, prison is your only other option. Of course, the elite school as a setting is hardly new to Australian literature. Danny's fall from grace is no more terrifying than that of Laura Rambotham in Henry Handel Richardson's *The Getting of Wisdom* (1910), when she is frozen out by the other girls for making up stories in order to make herself look better. In Richardson's time, however, a general belief in social progress could palliate these specific belittlements by giving hope that they will eventually be redeemed; for Richardson's Laura, the adult world, after school, promises something better. For Tsiolkas' Danny, the neoliberal adult world can only offer more of the same: hypertrophied, self-sanctioned complacency.

Tsiolkas is dissatisfied with institutions – old and new Europe, youth culture, the family in all its various configurations, the elite school – that we are often told define our culture. As James Bradley has commented, for Tsiolkas, fiction is about confronting society with "unpalatable truths, disrupting consensus".[36] Ali Alizadeh's searing poem "Letter to Adam Smith" speaks of the "historically inevitable boredom" of neoliberalism, the way a capitalist utopia creates a "fantasmatic" that is "too harmonious". Only crisis can disturb this. Only "subtraction / can lead to attraction".[37] Disharmony of Tsiolkas' sort forestalls this phantasm of the false fantastic from gelling into irrefutable dogma.

Tsiolkas categorically asserts his Greek identity in *Barracuda*. Danny's mother is Greek, and one of Danny's most pleasant exchanges is with a woman of Greek background named Mila, meaning "apple", with all its connotations of fertility. In a male Anglo world that values competitiveness and excellence above all, both the Greek and the maternal stand out and are difficult for the mainstream to accommodate.

In Tsiolkas' 2008 novel *The Slap*, the slap given by Harry, a Greek-Australian, to the misbehaving young Anglo child Hugo at a barbecue disrupts several assumptions about the contemporary: that people of all ethnic stripes and backgrounds are getting along, and that we can all unite around how wonderful today's children are; that their well-adjusted temperament represents a new utopia, a different and redeemed humanity. The slap is at once emblematic of and resistant to the neoliberal order. It is resistant to neoliberalism because it represents an old-fashioned parenting style, one in which corporal punishment is routine and adult authority unquestioned, recalling the punitive patriarchal regime in Harrower's novels, rather than the more permissive attitude of today, which is represented

---

35 William Empson, *Some Versions of Pastoral* (1935; New York: New Directions, 1974), 4.
36 Ali Alizadeh, "Letter to Adam Smith", published in *Jacket2*, 16 November 2012. http://jacket2.org/poems/poems-ali-alizadeh.
37 James Bradley, "All Fired Up", *Monthly*, November 2013, 44–55.

in the novel by Hugo's parents, Rosie and Gary. The slap can even be seen as an instinctive response to the deliberate disorganisation sown by neoliberalism, a disorganisation used to disguise the arbitrariness of the search for personal excellence and success. Yet Harry's slap is also emblematic of neoliberalism. It symbolises how, for all its rhetoric of freedom and transparency, neoliberalism retains a residual and fiercely enunciated sovereignty. The slap enacts Giorgio Agamben's sense of sovereignty, which entails, as Aihwa Ong puts it, "the exclusion of living beings not recognised as modern humans".[38] That Harry is a self-made entrepreneur drives home the way the slap can be a metaphor for the hidden exercise of violent force by the self-proclaimed winners of society. Compulsion and violence underlie neoliberalism's rhetoric of autonomy. Harry is of Greek descent and his wife is of Serbian background; Tsiolkas does not suggest that being non-Anglo-Celtic automatically means one is subversive or dissident. But mainstream society's reaction to the migrant often is analogous to its reaction to dissident lifestyles or ideologies.

Tsiolkas follows in the vein of many classic Australian novels, both highbrow and lowbrow, in which the migrant is a magnet for trouble. This is as true of Zlinter in Nevil Shute's *The Far Country* (1952) as it is of Himmelfarb in Patrick White's *Riders in the Chariot* (1961), both middle-aged men forced into manual labour in their new country. As a young athlete with a premium education, Danny Kelly at first seems to have avoided this fate, although trouble eventually finds him. The migrant reminds Australians of truths they would prefer to avoid.

But Tsiolkas does not romanticise Europe as a locale of cosmopolitanism and tradition. It is a paradox of settler colonialism that the intellectual elite most likely to resist an unthinking attachment of the country's British or European cultural origins are the likeliest to privilege, in Bourdieu's terms, the "distinction" of travelling to Europe or acting "European".[39] *Dead Europe* contends that the only European tradition still prospering is that of vampirism, as Isaac, the young protagonist who at first hopes serenely to photograph post-1980 Europe, emblematising himself as a member of the new, blessedly post-communist generation, becomes someone who preys on other people's blood. The radiant future is not only haunted but despoiled by the ghosts of the past, and Europe, in a prescient anticipation of the political problems of the mid-2010s, is less revived by the post-communist era than zombified by it. In *Barracuda*, Danny travels to Glasgow, but it proves not to be the solution, as his Scottish boyfriend, Clyde – named with blatant metonymy for the Firth of Clyde on which Glasgow sits – is, in James Bradley's phrase, a "privileged cosmopolitan".[40] Clyde discerns the hypocrisies in Australian professions of egalitarianism. But in dismissing Australia, he is himself wielding his status. Clive, who as a Scotsman could be Danny's fellow subaltern, is instead a snob, one of many in the book who fail to understand Danny because "for them, working at a supermarket was tangential to life" (254).

Clyde has fallen into the "lifestyle" excoriated by Les Murray in his poem of that name: "Once it was unions … now it's no carbohydrates". Clyde channels "all his regret and disappointment" into "snide, bitter attacks on Australia" (434), a country which, for Danny, is home. Danny, the person in the book who suffers most from the inequalities in Australian

---

38   Aihwa Ong, *Neoliberalism as Exception: Mutations in Citizenship and Sovereignty* (Durham: Duke University Press, 2006), 7. This is not Ong's own position, which is quite critical of neoliberalism, but one she summarises.

39   Pierre Bourdieu, *Distinction*, trans. Richard Nice (Cambridge: Harvard University Press, 1987).

40   Bradley, "All Fired Up".

society, nonetheless holds on to a positive idea of Australia. He does not have the social mobility to disidentify with Australia in favour of more cosmopolitan climes. This is reminiscent of Les Murray's posture in "The Suspension of Knock" when he asks, "Where will we hold Australia, / We who have no other country?" Murray, in this poem, indicates that it is all very well to chide white Australians for stealing the land from Indigenous people and disadvantaging their migrant brethren – but where have they to go? Tsiolkas and Murray are admittedly odd poles of comparison due to their generational, political and affective differences. But here they seem of like mind.

For Danny, Australia, like it or not, is home. He does not love it, but he knows he cannot escape from it and this gives him a commitment to it that his more sophisticated peers, who assume they need only travel or migrate to shed Australian problems, do not. It is this paradoxical defence of Australia that frustrated some reviewers, who tried to see the book as a critique of Australian xenophobia and small-mindedness along standard left-of-centre lines. Tsiolkas is no fan of these problems. But, like Murray, he does not think meritocratic elitism alone can solve Australian xenophobia or small-mindedness; indeed, he sees the hegemony of the winners as the root of them. Tsiolkas – gay, Greek, willing to slap the face of public taste – cannot be seen as a conventional tick-the-boxes leftist.

Expatriation is not a solution for Tsiolkas either, as *Dead Europe* makes clear with its acrid portrait of post-1989 Eastern Europe. In *Barracuda*, by setting the diasporic sections in Scotland, a place also struggling to come to terms with a postmodern nationalism, Tsiolkas makes clear that the internationalism of today has not yet categorically supplanted nationalism. Expatriation does not mean sophistication or social justice. For Danny, an Australian face can still inspire affection, despite his disappointment in Australian institutions. Julieanne Lamond comments that Danny "feels uncomfortable about the criticism his left-leaning friends heap upon his country" and mentions his "resistance to the progressive politics of most of his friends and family (and of Tsiolkas himself in his published essays and interviews)".[41]

I would argue, however, that *Barracuda* ultimately opts for the virtues of community, and turns away from a possessive individualism to incarnate solidarity. Danny's swimming coach at the elite school leaves him a small legacy and shared use of his house. Danny does not take the money and run. He uses that legacy to build a community. Danny realises the coach left the money to him, and to a few others, because the coach trusted these people not to use it selfishly. The coach makes a deathbed swerve from encouraging competition to fostering cooperation. Such an ending, which stresses the reliance of human beings upon one another, may risk being called sentimental, but one of the virtues of rancour is that it can inoculate a text from such an accusation. As a rejoinder to the neoliberal "cruel optimism" chronicled by Lauren Berlant, Tsiolkas evinces a sort of kind pessimism, a caring that is both visceral and disillusioned.

Ouyang Yu: Freelance Antagonist of the Complacent

Although he so far has not had Tsiolkas' mainstream success, Ouyang Yu also throws down a rancorous challenge to the twenty-first-century consensus. This is not to say that all other

---

41　Julieanna Lamond, "The Australian Face", *Sydney Review of Books*, November 2013. http://www.sydneyreviewofbooks.com/the-australian-face/.

multicultural Australian writers are meek assimilants into the mainstream. Even writers who might seem middlebrow and media-friendly in their approach – Randa Abdul-Fattah in her multicultural chick-lit, for example, or Merlinda Bobis in her largely realist depictions of the Philippine diaspora – have made clear that they see their work as a critical project. Writers such as these employ popular genres to try to spur awareness of cultural plurality among readers who might otherwise not encounter such a message. Ouyang is less concerned with reaching a wide readership, although this is not to say he is a hermetic writer. John Kinsella has observed that "when the Anglo-Celtic majority does a mea culpa in terms of European colonisation in Australia, it does so to emphasise its own power".[42] In this atmosphere, the consensus will accept a multicultural writer it feels it can control; the mainstream will applaud ethnic voices for contributing to the diversification of society, so long as they play by the mainstream rules.

Ouyang's poem-cycle *The Kingsbury Tales* (2012) looks unromantically at the contemporary Australian scene. "An Aboriginal Tale" shows the speaker meeting an Aboriginal person, "an old lady who I saw get on a train", which prompts a "white lady" to get up and find a spot "more relaxed and comfortable".[43] This leads the speaker to an encounter with an Aboriginal musician who wanted to become a teacher but was turned down because he did not conduct himself "by the book", and did not grow any facial hair. Yet there is no multicultural solidarity here; the speaker and the Aboriginal man lose touch as the Aboriginal musician does not have access to the internet, and the speaker's last recourse is to vow never again to read Xavier Herbert, with his problematic representation of Indigenous people, a gesture at once adamant and futile. This is pure Ouyang: a scoring of existing social conditions and prejudices, and a searing pessimism about any single individual's ability to countervail them other than through small acts of reading, writing and, in this case, not reading.

Also characteristic is the half-gesture towards Anglophone tradition in the title of *The Kingsbury Tales*, which echoes Chaucer. But the collection has a disaffected and intransigent tone, far from Chaucerian rambunctiousness. While upbraiding the intolerance and presumption of white Australian society, the speaker expresses unhappiness with China as well. He wants China to be stronger geopolitically, but also to stand for positive ideals, including the rights of indigenous people.

The speaker of *The Kingsbury Tales* interacts with both Sinophone and Anglophone authority, but is not particularly respectful of either. Furthermore, Ouyang writes in two languages, and maintains residences in both Australia and China. He has translated both his own work and that of others, from English into Chinese and vice versa. With this deep immersion in two languages, one native, one acquired, the very idea of language itself is contingent: if a thing can always be said as well or better in another language, language is freed from adequacy to float towards heedless, impulsive, ad hoc creativity. Normally stable notions of the authorial body and language thus become fungible. This is particularly true given that Chinese and English are two of the world's most widely spoken languages. Ouyang's snarling voice and vigilant, deadpan gaze are in many ways exemplary of Australian writing: he both navigates the currents of transnationalism and stands in the way of them overpowering the individual voice.

---

42   John Kinsella, *Spatial Relations*, Volume 1 (Amsterdam: Rodopi, 2013), 234.
43   Ouyang Yu, *The Kingsbury Tales* (Kingsbury: Otherland, 2012), 371.

In Ouyang's novel *The English Class*, a Chinese truck driver, Jing, looks to learning English as the solution to all his problems.[44] Although Jing – or Gene, as he is later called when he goes to Australia – over-idealises English, the novel genuinely admires his curiosity in attempting an utterly strange mode of communication and seizing it incipiently as his own. Chinese speakers may be learning English as a means to gain prestige and global success, but at least they are learning it, as opposed to the teacher of Jing's class, Mr Wagner, who does not deign to learn a syllable of Chinese. Jing eventually runs off with Wagner's wife, Deirdre, and goes with her to Australia, showing how the second-language learner can abduct the language and spirit it away from its native speakers. Jing eventually feels that he is being, as it were, unfaithful to Chinese in concentrating so much on speaking English: the root etymological sense of translation, after all, is betrayal. The novel plays all this for laughs: although his humour can often be savage, Ouyang is, along with Michael Wilding, Linda Jaivin and David Foster, one of the genuinely comic writers active in Australia today. But the book is also a critical reflection on the role language plays in personal and national identity. Necessarily, the language taught in the book is the very language in which we are reading it. How well do we, the reader, know English? What exactly is *our* English? Where does it come from? Who taught it to us?

Ouyang, of course, is not Jing, a naive learner of English as a personal fillip. Ouyang is a sophisticated, savvy artist and a respected cultural figure in both linguistic spheres. Yet the theme of English as a second language adds extra brio to Ouyang's writing, especially in the descriptive passages, in which a lyrical sprightliness is permitted to rove unchecked, giving a sense both of the exuberance possible in English and how a foreign eye can envision that exuberance differently than someone confined in the language since birth. The book's first two epigraphs, from Rilke and Neruda – the latter of whom, as Ian Campbell has pointed out, has a considerable Indonesian afterlife in terms of influence, and is thus more than usually relelvant to Australia – interject third and fourth languages into the mix.[45] They make the point that the Chinese–English encounter is not just between a migrant and his new country, but part of a wider negotiation among multiple world tongues. But they also give the sense of a new language as a desired, distant other, a horizon whose very remoteness renders it tantalisingly appealing. These vistas, however, cannot just be conquered on a whim: they can only be reached through hard work. Jing's occupation, driving trucks, involves mobility, yet is also prosaic and menial.

In a poem related to *The English Class*, "Bad English", Ouyang depicts a foreigner teaching English in Australia who receives an email from a student apologising for his bad English.[46] Unlike Wagner in *The English Class*, this teacher understands that as he does not speak his students' language, he can hardly reproach them for speaking his badly. The poem tacitly argues, however, that in today's world, there are not really any categorically good and bad Englishes; that the English of the Chinese student is a new kind of English but also communicates and makes real thoughts and emotions. Phrases that are ungrammatical in English, such as "on that day's noon", are highly poetic in a surreal way. Misprisions reveal conceptual fault-lines: "We must uphold human tights" – where the substitution of "tights" for "rights" upbraids Westerners' imposition of a human-

---

44   Ouyang Yu, *The English Class* (Melbourne: Transit Lounge, 2010).

45   Ian Campbell, "Post-Nerudaism in Indonesia: Tracing and Memorializing Neruda in the Dutch East Indies (1930–1932) and Beyond", *Antipodes* 26, no. 2 (2012): 181–88.

46   Ouyang Yu, "Bad English", *Cha* 4 (August 2008). http://www.asiancha.com/content/view/216/124/.

itarian agenda into Chinese life, while slyly insisting that human rights must in fact be upheld. These are mistakes, but they enlarge our field of perception. This is a rejection of perfection. If bad English is also, in its own way, a new English, the world cannot simply and categorically be split between winners and losers.

Ouyang's two major works are *The Eastern Slope Chronicle* (2002) and *Loose: A Wild History* (2008). The latter, a sprawling work that is among the most daring novels published in Australia in the twenty-first century thus far, is set between 1999 and 2001, but utterly abjures euphoric celebration of the millennium and the Sydney Olympics, or any foreshadowing of 9/11.[47] With a complicated spiral structure containing both a progressive narrative and a series of diary-like jottings, *Loose* is fierce in its criticism of both Western complacency and the Chinese government's authoritarianism. The narrator, at once adorable and disconsolate, stays unattached, at the cost of often feeling alienated. *Loose* tells a history away from the mainstream, and far from a Eurocentric axis. Whether describing Beijing high-rises or Melbourne literary gatherings, *Loose* subverts the official cultural narrative of progress. Like *Barracuda*, it is set largely in 2000, the year that was supposed to be the acme of Australian expectation, the consummation of the country's emergence onto the world stage. *Loose* is a sour visitor at the self-congratulatory spree of the millennium.

That Ouyang is so adamantly uncowed by consensus should not obscure that he is a master of the gritty quotidian. Witness this description of Melbourne weather in his most accomplished novel, *The Eastern Slope Chronicle*: "It was a typical Melbourne day. Clouds were rolling over the grey Melbourne sky. Trees outside the window stood still as if frozen. The only living thing was a stray dog that kept running in the front yard."[48] This is a realism of subject matter but not a realism of angle, as the narrator simply refuses to accept that anything he sees is inevitable, or so surprising as to deserve a fuss. Ouyang is not a satirist. Satire presumes a solidity of attack from which somebody of Ouyang's generation would no doubt shy away. Born in 1955, he is of an age to have experienced the horrors of the Cultural Revolution. Yet Ouyang's work speaks from the declared vantage point of the satirist.

Ouyang, as the Asian-American critic Timothy Yu has argued, is as much an Asian Australian as he is a diasporic-Chinese writer.[49] But he is also an example of an Asian-Australian writer who does not look chiefly to the UK or USA but to China; he demonstrates that there can be another Anglophone cosmopolitanism, one with a Sinophone centre. This Sinocentrism does not mean that Ouyang does not draw upon other literary traditions: the lyric asperity of the Kingsbury poems owes a decided debt to the poems of Thomas Hardy, of whom Ouyang is a great admirer. This insistence on plurality has a cost: a writer who refuses to defer to expectations of what he should be risks missing out on canonisation. Although Ouyang Yu is widely regarded, with Brian Castro, as one of the leading Asian Australian authors, he has never developed a popular readership, even though general readers might well find his work enjoyable. Ouyang is not averse to his work being recognised, but he will not cater to institutional tastes. That being said, along with Castro, Ouyang is probably the most academically studied Asian-Australian fiction writer of his generation, followed in the next generation by the Vietnamese-Australian Nam Le, who would certainly be the most well known internationally. Le's sense of

---

47   Ouyang Yu, *Loose: A Wild History* (Kent Town: Wakefield, 2011).
48   Ouyang Yu, *The Eastern Slope Chronicle* (Sydney: Brandl & Schlesinger 2003), 347.
49   Timothy Yu, "On Asian Australian Poetry", *Southerly* 73, no. 1 (2013): 75.

Australia as one destination in a wider global diaspora goes beyond Castro's and Ouyang's acceptance of an Australian element to their work. Ouyang writes from within Australia but castigates Australia for not judging him totally of it. Ouyang's homeland is not, as George Steiner once observed of the Jews, the text, although Brian Castro's might be.[50] Ouyang does not claim a purely literary genealogy, nor does he see his diasporic identity as any more literary than cultural.

Ouyang's attitude has inevitably meant that he has missed out on some acclaim and awards that he might otherwise have enjoyed. The very theme of *The Eastern Slope Chronicles* – that Chinese identity cannot simply be confined for Australian readers into a convenient box – has thwarted his reception. But Ouyang Yu has also thwarted the canonising agencies of millennial world power. He is in the largest sense a dissident, in all the various contexts which he inhabits and addresses.

John Kinsella: Against "The Bloodiest of Values"

John Kinsella attained success at an extraordinarily young age. By the time he was thirty-five he was already known across the world; by the time he was forty, he had obtained significant academic positions in the UK and USA, at Cambridge and Kenyon College respectively, as well as the support of eminencies such as George Steiner and Harold Bloom; by the time he was forty-five, he had composed a body of work equal to that of poets who lived a full life, and then some. Kinsella achieved this by being a conspicuously avant-garde and experimental poet. He shares much with Les Murray, including a feeling for his own rural district and an identification with its people: a sense that locality can be a basis for genuine poetry. Yet Kinsella, although as capable of traditional formal operations as Murray, was far more consciously experimental. In his early years as a poet it was possible to distinguish between a "dark pastoral" aspect to Kinsella – a corroded, disillusioned but nonetheless cohesive lyric voice that savagely and rancorously lamented the erosion and exploitation of the Australian landscape, seen in collections like *The Silo* (1995) and *The Hunt* (1998) – and a more referentially diffuse experimental mode, in dialogue with international Language poetry, exemplified by collections such as *Syzygy* (1993). Since about 2000 or so, this dichotomy has become less sustainable. Kinsella's poems are always animated by a strong lyric impulse, yet are always decentred. They are not prone to balance, nor to telescope the meaning of the verse into a single node. "I cannot take the many paths towards the valley's centre", Kinsella says in "Retired Reservoir", and there is in his poem a refusal to gravitate to a fixed position of authority.[51] In "Strobe: The Road from Toodyay to New Norcia", he describes

---

50   George Steiner, "Our Homeland, the Text", *Salmagundi* 66 (1985): 4–25.
51   John Kinsella, "Retired Reservoir", from *Poems 1980–1994* (South Fremantle: Fremantle Press, 1997) via Australian Poetry Library, http://www.poetrylibrary.edu.au/poets/kinsella-john/retired-reservoir-0217133.

> the road absorbing yet not occluding
>
> dark sunglasses cannot prevent light
>
> destroying direction[52]

The road runs from a wheatbelt market town to the Benedictine monastery famed for its wine, ostensibly out towards the sea and civilisation, but there is no trajectory, only an ambiguous stasis: "The interior sun is a calmative red"; nature is neither a recourse nor an enclosure to be escaped. The same sun that fires also calms. Equally, Kinsella's anger fuels his contemplation, but he renounces the idea of a centre of sapient judgement that was so indispensable to the poetics of A. D. Hope.

Kinsella has not just received recognition in the USA and UK but actively operates as an editor, anthologist and galvanising agent in these countries, as well as writing convincing and idiomatic poems about their landscape (no British poet has written better about the fens of Cambridgeshire than Kinsella has). Yet Kinsella has continued to anchor himself in Western Australia, if anything in recent years strengthening his ties to the state by taking up an academic position at the University of Western Australia. He lives at Jam Tree Gully near Toodyay in the wheatbelt, a region surrounding Perth and standing between it and the outback. This region is fertile yet fragile, economically vital yet socio-politically marginal, ranging topographically from the height of Mount Bakewell to the serpentine valley of the Avon River to the sloping hills of Jam Tree Gully where Kinsella resides. The wheatbelt is rural but on the verge of the urban. It grounds Kinsella's work while providing a side arena in which to roam; Kinsella's poetry, as Tony Hughes-D'Aeth has argued, reveals both the promise and the peril of the contemporary natural world.[53] The wheatbelt for Kinsella is a place of "fault-lines and earthquakes", of "repetition, imprint of incursion, and memory, unwinding daily". It is where "trees blacken / into thin wisps, spinifex fires / and white cockatoos. Strangled / in telegraph wire, hang / dry and upside down".[54] Kinsella relates to the wheatbelt with a threefold respect: for its ecology, with the "drifting sand" that does not "lend itself of description"; for its local inhabitants and their distinct regional history ("just outside York a memorial to an ex- / bikie who became a JP and the best loved / citizen of the community"); and for its Indigenous heritage: "The rainbow begins or ends / on the Wagyl tracks, and there's / nothing romantic about it".

Kinsella is so insistent on this respect that he is willing to discipline himself to make sure his art remains within these criteria. Moreover, Kinsella is frequently blunt in his anger at corporations, greed and white privilege in general. Notwithstanding, there is exhilaration in how he depicts the wheatbelt, a sheer delight in its incongruities and the intimacy of his relation to the land, its shape and story. Speaking in "Quellington Road" of the town of Meckering, which had to relocate itself after an earthquake in 1968, Kin-

---

52 John Kinsella, "Strobe: The Road from Toodyay to New Norcia", from *Full Fathom Five* (South Fremantle: Fremantle Arts Centre Press, 1993) via Australian Poetry Library, http://www.poetrylibrary.edu.au/poets/kinsella-john/ strobe-the-road-from-toodyay-to-new-norcia-0401008.

53 Tony Hughes-D'Aeth, "*Salt Scars*: John Kinsella's *Wheatbelt*", *Australian Literary Studies* 27, no. 2 (2012): 18–31.

54 John Kinsella, "Reflectors: Drive I", in *New Arcadia* (New York: Norton, 2007).

sella writes, "the back-way to Meckering cuts fault-line, earth-rip, roads never thin as they look".[55] It is landscape he knows well: both the landscape of childhood and adulthood; of primordial memory and quotidian life.

If one tendency of Kinsella's poetics of rancour is spite at the object of its critique, another tendency is a sense of implication. The wheatbelt is an interstitial place between Hope's "five teeming sores"; it might not be the full plunge into the interior but it is not simply hugging the coast. In the wheatbelt, Kinsella is implicated (in the etymological sense of "folded in"). Kinsella does not claim to be one with the region's people as Les Murray might. He shies away from the mantle of the region's ambassador to the world as Seamus Heaney sometimes did for the bogs of Northern Ireland. Yet his critique of Australian life is enabled by the way he is half embedded in it. For all of Kinsella's uninhibited polemicism, there is a casual serenity in his poetry that never lets ideology get in the way of observation. Even when its convictions are fiercest, it keeps its eye on what is being depicted, usually a corroded version of what Gerard Manley Hopkins called the "sweet especial rural scene".[56]

Also in "Quellington Road", Kinsella surveys the land and is filled with fury at its misuse by generations of settlers:

> avarice
> has bite where the needle of asphalt runs through rises,
> falls, tamed breakaways, To take a run past
> salt clefts, paddocks to be burnt; less bushland
> than there might be;

There is an ecological agenda here, but also a socioeconomic one: the paddocks and the bushland are victims not just of corrosion, but also of avarice. Kinsella has spoken of his "vegan anarchist" politics. His radical ecological critique also has in mind the institutions of capitalism and global governance themselves. Yet Kinsella is aware that his poetry, published in metropolitan centres by international houses, circulates on the social and cultural currents concomitant if not entirely parallel with those of financial capital. Furthermore, he knows that his own presence upon the land is occasioned by acts of unfairness. Kinsella auto-historicises himself; he reckons, as far as possible, with his own contingency. Thus his rage is one of implication as much as severance, and his polemical fervour is sharpened by his self-questioning:

> Where else am I to home in on? The travel bug
> A dung-eater, a godless transportation where culture
> Is the memory of a road-side stop

55   John Kinsella, "Quellington Road", in New Arcadia (New York: Norton, 2007).
56   Gerard Manley Hopkins, "Binsey Poplars" (1879), Poetry Foundation, http://www.poetryfoundation.org/poem/173655.

Kinsella critiques his own mobility: "these excursions we make / these sightings we keep largely to ourselves" at once elegise and intensify the deterioration they lament. Yet Kinsella is a romantic not so much in subject or in presupposition but in his belief in the possibility of poetry to be meaningful to a wide range of communities beyond a coterie of reviewers. If there is an alternative to the "wells struck where water won't flow / plant machinery touching off no memories" it is in poetry, "the best prayers for human effort I can manage", even if here they are, self-deprecatingly, "desiccated lines to the road". He is talking about poetic lines, but also about the lines on the road. Between voice and subject, enunciation and enunciated, the line is vertiginously thin:

> CY O'Connor,
> State Engineer, went some of the way
> Linking Goldfield with Mundaring Weir,
> Driving water into desert,
> Quenching the thirst of gold diggers,
> Washing the finds[57]

This is neither an encomium to a pioneer, nor vitriolic denunciation, but a tragic awareness of how a benign act for public health – supplying gold miners with water from the Swan–Avon river system – was also an act of violence in dislocating Indigenous people. Kinsella's own artistic representation of the region is both a furtherance of and an atonement for this violence.

Kinsella's most ambitious recent work is *Divine Comedy* (2010). This book has Dantean parallels, but the tercet form is handled nimbly; the length of the canto allows Kinsella to range further than the conventional lyric would, without being epic. Instead of an upward journey of redemption, the order here is Purgatorio, Paradiso, Inferno. The stark differences between heaven, purgatory and hell heighten the range of emotion Kinsella brings to landscape. In "Canto of the Doubled Terraces" Kinsella speaks of poachers trying to profit off the burl of a gum tree, used as finely grained wood for furniture:

> There's a flooded-gum burl
> Idaho burl importers would love to get a hold of,
> the raw materials they plan to buff and polish,
>
> To constitute as souls in the world's most active
> Burl market[58]

"To constitute as souls" is the key phrase: financialisation implies that even the beautiful aesthetic effects of natural intricacy are galvanised by greed; that our contemplative re-

---

57 John Kinsella, "Harmonium", in *Spatial Relations*, Volume 2 (Amsterdam: Rodopi, 2013), 36.
58 John Kinsella, *Divine Comedy* (New York: W. W. Norton & Co., 2008), 111. All subsequent references are to this edition and appear in parentheses in the text.

sponse to them is plagued by a sort of cognitive guilt, something that pains Kinsella as much as anyone as he is so responsive to their beauty. The burl is shaped by nature, yet employed in human shaping, and Kinsella is intrigued by patterns that hover just below consciousness, that violate humanity's rage for order by possessing pattern but not intention:

> The fungus
> Is smooth and grows dully
> And cracks of bark, fragments
>
> Where it anchors
> Is hidden; you imagine it as soft as the bark
> Of York gums entombed by termite mounds: a pulpy
>
> Nexus point: a metamorphic pap.
> The jam tree's is semi-life – a demonology
> Of lush branches, dead branches, death-talking. (60)

This is from the "Purgatorio" section, and the predominant note is one of suspension, a viscous meditation, a world of semi-life whose shape is reinforced by verbal patterning ("pulpy", "point", "pap"; the analogous networks – quasi-rhizomatic – of tomb, nexus, branch). This death-in-life melding is frustrating for the perceiver but it is all that is left of life now, and all that can be left in this place and time. Its pulpy plenitude is vividly contrasted to the severe rhetoric of economic rationalism, as represented by the former federal treasurer, Peter Costello, here pictured by Kinsella as speaking in the first person:

> Welcoming four corners of earth
> Into the living room
> I vacuumed
>
> I strengthened big flashes
> And warning signs, coaled
> Over the differences,
>
> Bet on the bloodiest of values. (29)

Kinsella's treatment of Paradise is the most striking turn in the book. Instead of making Paradise into a second Hell, or merely inverting the affective qualities of Paradise and Hell, Kinsella renders Paradise as genuine a paradise as one is to find, in this part of the world, given the prejudices imposed by Western optics. But the title to Paradise is in question. As Philip Mead observes, "paradise is land stolen from others, the Ballardong Noongar people". Kinsella's Paradise may be, as Mead argues, "ruptured … sideways".[59] Yet even if it were unsullied in its purity it would still be stolen. So, in general, might the pleasures and splendour of the neoliberal era be stolen, appropriated through what Nixon calls "slow violence", abstracted through an economic division in which there is heaven for the few and hell for the many, with no purgatory to split the difference or to offer succour.

The "slow violence" depicted here is everything that Kinsella loathes. To combat it, although he is infused with the environmental sympathies and populist-aesthetic delicacy of a Judith Wright, Kinsella needs the prophetic, satiric rage of an A. D. Hope. There are other sources here. Kinsella is, as of 2015, editing the collected poems of Aboriginal poet Jack Davis, who, like Hope, died in 2000. Addressing the 2014 Perth Poetry Festival, Kinsella ended his speech with these lines from Davis:

> The government is my shepherd,
> I shall not want.
> They let me search in the Aboriginal reserves
> which leads me to many riches
> for taxation's sake.
> Though I wallow in the valley of wealth I will fear no weevil
> because my money is safe in the bank
> vaults of the land,
> and my Government will always comfort me.[60]

This splenetic parody of the twenty-third psalm was written in 1977; today Davis might say not "the government" but "the market", or "what the government privatises". But Davis was prophetic in seeing wealth as the be-all and end-all of the contemporary, the dead centre to which all rational roads travel.

Kinsella's rage, however, does not assume the tone of leadership projected by Davis' voice. Kinsella withholds himself from complicity as far as possible, aware that no one today can do so completely. It was far easier to have Kinsella's radical epistemology in a previous generation, when, for example, the New Zealand poet James K. Baxter could practise an idiosyncratic spiritual ecology, live on a rural commune, and be acclaimed. The era of late modernity prized such a dissenting posture as it seemed the only way to avoid regimentation. Neoliberalism, however, exalts urban dynamism and is sceptical of rural retreats. Furthermore, the claim to unmediated association with the land that Baxter put forth, even though he was sympathetic to Māori land claims and identity, would seem imperialistic now. Kinsella as a landscape poet has had to operate within far more strict protocols – most of them imposed by himself – about how territoriality can be evoked in

---

59   Philip Mead, "Connectivity, Community, and the Question of Literary Universality: Reading Kim Scott's *Chronotope* and John Kinsella's *Commedia*", in *Republics of Letters: Literary Communities in Australia*, ed. Peter Kirkpatrick and Robert Dixon (Sydney: Sydney University Press, 2012), 152.

60   Jack Davis, "Mining Company's Hymn", from *Jagardoo: Poems from Aboriginal Australia* (Sydney: Methuen, 1978). Quoted in John Kinsella, "For Beauty's Sake: Poetry and Activism", keynote address to the Perth Poetry Festival, 2014. http://poetsvegananarchistpacifist.blogspot.com.au/2014/08/for-beautys-sake-poetry-and-activism.html.

language. Kinsella has spoken of his "dramatic shift to the overtly political voice" over the course of the past twenty years, a sharp veering towards the polemical and the angry.[61] Kinsella has attained a rare perspective on questions of land and territory precisely by his blatant willingness to disturb the peace – his own peace, and that of the world consensus.

The Bad Years of J. M. Coetzee

To continue writing after winning the Nobel Prize is rather like being an ex-politician: you do not have to campaign any more and are free to say what you think, limited only by expectations of gravitas. J. M. Coetzee has taken full advantage of this unusual freedom, buttressed by his moving to a new country virtually at the same time as he won the Prize. Coetzee rose to fame as a South African writer, first coming to world awareness with *Life & Times of Michael K* (1983) and *Waiting for the Barbarians* (1980), abstract, modernist parables of a South Africa on the brink of either change or explosion. Later books such as *Foe* (1986) and *The Master of Petersburg* (1994), rewrites of such canonical figures as Defoe and Dostoyevsky, critically reappraise the past in a way familiar in Australian literature in works such as Peter Carey's *Jack Maggs* (1998). Since moving to South Australia in 2002 Coetzee has reinvented himself as an Australian writer, assuming a stance as simultaneous sage and provocateur. Coetzee is the first Nobel Prize winner to in effect establish a new national identity *after* winning the prize (as opposed to writers already living in exile or straddling two national identities, which has happened a few times). Perhaps as human beings live longer and become more mobile and transnational, Coetzee's situation will become more common; but for now, it is an intriguing one-off. Few writers have come into a national situation with as much leverage to criticise existing conditions.

Coetzee has exercised this leverage not just to criticise the neoliberal consensus of contemporary Australia but also his own authorial position, which since *Elizabeth Costello* (2003), his first Australian book, he has teased, performed and improvised upon. He has even defied the expectation of gravitas. His later books are unsettlingly pessimistic and (self-)lacerating. They are not what one would necessarily expect of a writer who has achieved unassailable world stature and acclaim. But Coetzee has seen Australia, like South Africa, as a nation plagued with a past it would prefer not to examine, and in the present falling well below its manifest ideals.

Diary of a Bad Year (2007), like *Dunciad Minor*, is a savage indictment of the times and mores confronted by the writer, which in turn does not exempt his own sensibility, or the stability of the writerly position, from that irony. The book is a general critique of neoliberalism. But Coetzee partially destabilises any predominant authorial voice by featuring three characters – Señor C, a Coetzee-like famous author; Anya, the young woman from the Philippines he employs; and Alan, her businessman lover – and by splitting the story between Señor C's official "Strong Opinions" and his more intimate account of his relationship with Anya.[62] Coetzee's ironisation of his own views in an authorial persona is reminiscent of Hope's questioning of his own neoclassical *auctoritas* using supplementary footnotes and inquisitions. The aim is not to negate the author's own viewpoint but to

---

61 John Kinsella to Nicholas Birns, 27 November 2014.
62 J. M. Coetzee, *Diary of a Bad Year* (New York: Penguin, 2007). All subsequent references are to this edition and appear in parentheses in the text.

ramify it and make it more manoeuvrable. Coetzee sympathises with the prophetic style of late Tolstoy but points out that it did not prevent Tolstoy from being read in a deconstructive manner by the Russian formalists. Morality and aesthetics are not necessarily at loggerheads.

Nor does Coetzee's textual irony prevent him from evincing clear opinions about his adopted country. When Señor C first came to Australia, he admired the way people conducted themselves in their everyday dealings:

> frankly, fairly, with an elusive personal pride and an equally elusive ironic reserve. Now, fifteen years later, I hear the sense of self embodied in that conduct disparaged in many quarters as belonging to an Australia of the past now outmoded … Strange to find oneself missing what one has never had, has never even been part of. Strange to find oneself feeling elegiac about a past one never knew. (118)

It is the "atomistic faith in the market" that brings out the neo in neoliberalism. Neoliberalism is more than a belief that one will improve one's lot in life by "hard work and saving". It is a financialisation of all of human life. Señor C even goes so far as to despair of democracy itself, coming close to the line pursued by contemporary speculative Marxists such as Alain Badiou, that the democratic process cannot be trusted to produce moral leadership. Coetzee's persona is not that of someone who zealously works within the system to change it, for whom the election of a reform-minded leftist will decisively tilt the arrow. The solution is not a restoration of late-modern top-down conformity but a creative, humble, emancipatory individualism, much of the sort Coetzee himself, with necessary idiosyncrasy, practises.

As Paul Giles has noted, many South African critics who previously lauded Coetzee for his parables of oppression and resistance in apartheid-era South Africa have been less than laudatory since his move to Australia.[63] David Attwell is quoted by Giles as speaking of "the light-touch quality" of Coetzee's relation to Australia; Attwell sees Coetzee's Australia-based work as "metafiction".[64] Yet *Diary of a Bad Year* is a plea from an agonised, riven heart, and it is fundamentally political and economic. As Giles relates, Coetzee has distanced himself from the United States.[65] His choice not just of Australia but of Adelaide, by no means the most metropolitan of Australia's cities, represents a move away from the sophisticated centre. Yet Coetzee's Australia is not just a peripheral sanctuary, chosen simply for its distance. Coetzee values Australia, as much for what it once was – the egalitarian society of modernity and late modernity – as for what it is now, just another society reeling from neoliberal excess.

Neoliberalism in *Diary of a Bad Year* is not merely a political tendency, but an all-pervasive climate. The market, as Alan puts it, explicitly citing Nietzsche, is "beyond good and evil". Coetzee, like the contemporary American political philosopher Corey Robin, sees neoliberalism's excesses as an extension of Nietzsche's call for going beyond good and evil.[66] Yet it is questionable whether Nietzsche wished for a dichotomy between winners

---

63   Paul Giles, *Antipodean America: Australasia and the Constitution of US Literature* (New York: Oxford University Press, 2013), 459.

64   Giles, *Antipodean America*, 459.

65   Giles, *Antipodean America*, 461–62.

66   Corey Robin, "Nietzsche's Marginal Children: On Friedrich Hayek", *The Nation*, 27 May 2013.

and losers. In a sense, that is exactly what Nietzsche blamed Christianity for: dividing the world into winners and losers and embracing the losers. Neoliberalism is an inversion of this: it divides the world into winners and losers and embraces the winners. But this is a far more binary vision than anything Nietzsche outlined. Thus even Alan's eidolon of the market has a saving neutrality, as "beyond good and evil" is still more open-ended than a narrow division between winners and losers of the sort from which Danny Kelly suffers in Tsiolkas' novel.

But it is still decisively different from late-modern Australia, which Coetzee is aware of but which he only personally experienced in what turned out to be its dying vestiges. That the early twenty-first-century consensus either ignored or co-opted any certitude of it, is, for Señor C, because an intellectual apparatus marked by a conscious knowledge of its insufficiency is an evolutionary aberration. Señor C is not a "heteronym", designating a persona substantially different from Coetzee. He hovers near to but not coincident with Coetzee's own implied stance, meaning that we can take his opinions seriously, but are aware that, however percipient in their critique, they also perch on the edge of the trough of absurdity into which all they critique has already fallen.

Coetzee's career intersects with Australian literature at an unusual angle not just because of his anterior eminence but because his is a case of South to South migration, even if the South Africa in which he grew up was, like Australia, a white-dominated society, albeit one with different demographics. Such South–South connections have been the Holy Grail of a subversive Australian internationalism, but the magnetic pull of metropolitan hegemony has tended to short-circuit these aspirations. Still, Coetzee – who with the very name of "Señor C" gestures towards Latin America, another part of the Global South – is used to writing, in an abstract sense, from the periphery. As James Ley puts it, Coetzee "has often been moved to reflect on the problems that arise from the distance of the postcolonial artist from the centres of cultural authority".[67] Coetzee has a fundamental scepticism, a lack of credulousness about alternatives, in common with other South African-Australian writers such as John Mateer and Marcelle Freiman. In these writers, there is a place for the negative, or even the blank, as in Freiman's "Seven Ways of Mourning":

> Forgetting is like
> light on sharp edged fences,
> clears spaces between.[68]

Here forgetting, despite the renunciations it entails, is affirmative, and also perhaps inevitable. Rancour – and this must have been a tough pill for the precedent-minded A. D. Hope to swallow – has little place for history; its discontent is too present-at-hand. Rancour, as in Coetzee's critique of neoliberal Australia, may rage at a society that has lost its moorings, but in its own rhetoric jettisons those moorings in order to rage with potential recklessness. Rancour needs to forget or to reduce so as to shake off any last remnants of hope, leaving rage as the only option. In Mateer's "Pinjarra", Indigenous people are too

---

67   James Ley, "I Refuse to Rock and Roll", *Sydney Review of Books*, 19 September 2013. http://www.sydneyreviewofbooks.com/i-refuse-to-rock-and-roll/.
68   Marcelle Freiman, "Seven Ways of Mourning", *Cordite Poetry Review* 46, May 2014. http://cordite.org.au/poetry/notheme3/seven-ways-of-mourning/.

afraid of destruction, too taken up with survival to be spiritual, to find aid in the traditions the white observer assumes they have:

> Down at the site of the battle which was more like a slaughter
> some Nyoongar blokes showed him the crossing
> where, there low over the blackened water,
> they'd seen that fireball hovering white as a blind eye,
> and he'd asked them if they'd tried to call out to those spirits
> and they'd laughed:
> *No way, mate, we were off like a shot!* [69]

The South African-Australian writer tends not to assume white privilege – the active malice, rather than passive complacency, of such assumptions having been proven in their homeland – and also not to be simply Anglophone in aural terms: witness Mateer's interest in Portuguese and Indonesian as potentially "Australian" languages in the broader sense. Yet *Diary of a Bad Year*, despite all its potentially global vectors, is strangely local, not just in its setting, but in its centring around three people whose relationships to one another are constrained. From the poetry of Hope onward, rancorous pessimism makes a stand, assumes a sarcastic local redoubt against global orotundities. Ironically, while the euphoric Australia is the more global one, issues of global import – refugee detention centres, struggles to come to terms with Indigenous dispossession, growing social inequality – are oddly localised, played out within Australian space, as if the world does not want to hear bad news from Australia. Rancour thus shifts from the tacitly right-wing angle occupied by Hope. This is not just because the era of neoliberalism assumes the centre-right as the consensus, much as Hope's era of late modernity assumed the centre-left. More abstractly, pessimism became the more measured option *and* the more empirical one, an attitude local and habited.

Diary of a Bad Year is worried we have lost our moorings. It critiques the "anti-social, antihuman turn" as seen in the introduction of mechanical measurement into horse racing (here Coetzee takes a slight turn in the direction of Gerald Murnane) (75). Coetzee, or his fictional counterpart in his "Strong Opinions", perhaps goes beyond critiquing neoliberalism and casts a quizzical eye on such contemporary academic practices as actor-network theory and distant reading. There is something of the old-fashioned humanist in Señor C's stance, and Alan goes so far as to criticise the book as a "morality play" (7). This old-fashionedness both ironises Señor C slightly – as the reader begins to see the persona as slightly crotchety – and humanises him, as his anger, like that of the speaker of Hope's poems, is a testament not only of bitterness but of inadequacy. Even as the speaker assumes the mantle of prophetic authority, the path of emotion both slows him down and softens him. He is a grumbler, but a grumbler who has chosen the parish over the world, the periphery over the centre. That Señor C's self outside the "Strong Opinions" – perhaps practising weak thought, *pensiero debole*, in Gianni Vattimo's term – seems readier to compromise with the

---

69   John Mateer, "Pinjarra", *Manoa* 18, no. 2 (2006): 21.

world reflects the Achilles heel of rancour: it must assume a hyperbolic rhetorical position in order to resonate.

"The world into which we are born, each of us, is our world," Señor C ruminates. Is it our world to seize, or to acquiesce in? In a perceptual matrix in which "a secret is an item of information" (23) everything becomes referential, awash in a sea of fragmentary irony: we do not know what to take seriously and what to see as persiflage. Where discerning attitudes necessarily turn misanthropic, there is little room for exaltation of a global centre. Señor C exhibits a species pride that "one of us" could write Sibelius' Fifth Symphony (45). This corresponds with a shame that one of us could perpetrate the detention camp of Guantanamo. The twenty-first century is not an improvement over the twentieth – and it is notable that Coetzee chooses an early twentieth-century symphonic work here, one associated with the liberation struggle of a small nation, rather than a more abstract or transnational figure such as Schoenberg or Stravinsky, or one associated with modernist difficulties both technical and ideological, such as Shostakovich. The Sibelius Fifth is stark, forbidding and recalcitrant; its complexity, even if more emotional than intellectual, is hard for the naive listener to puzzle through, as if creative power can still awe us, but can no longer (if it ever could) aid us. The Sibelius Fifth is romantic, but it is a romanticism with only the grandeur left; it is vigorous, but this is a vigour no longer subtended by any sustaining or animating vision, one that refuses to stun, to console or to be wistful. In Sibelius, as ardently national as he was, as much as he epitomised the liberation struggle of Finland from Russian political and Swedish cultural dominance, the national marks a difference but not an essential difference.

Coetzee similarly does not presume upon his own life experience in an essentialist way, preferring instead to interrogate it. Coetzee has lived through the supreme liberation struggle of the late twentieth century in South Africa, but now, in the contemporary sanctuary of neoliberal Adelaide, he still seems to feel the need for some subsidence in the local, even if it is necessarily lacerated with scorn, contempt and disgust at the vulnerability of self and other to the devaluation of all values. Señor C realises that both his physical location and his social situation give him greater insight than the other two characters, Alan and Anya, who are immersed in neoliberalism (Alan to the point of defrauding the eloquent but gullible Señor C) but do not think about it. Their reality is coextensive with their sex lives and their instinctual level of gratification, and they would acquiesce in whatever cultural climate they found themselves in. The alphabetical twinning of Anya and Alan, combined with C not just potentially standing for "Coetzee" but also being two steps on in the alphabet, posits the two lovers as primary, the garrulous, splenetic writer as not only secondary but, true to his initial letter, tertiary, signifying a higher level of ordinality and reflectiveness. Yet Señor C, however dissemblingly removed from experience he is, at least thinks about it, even if he is prone to intellectual arrogance and self-certainty, like a prophetic Amos or a satiric Juvenal without the wind of tradition behind him. To be truly resonant, the oracle of contemporary rancour must admit that tradition in any viable sense has been relinquished, and that local shards of resentment are all that remain upon which to stand. *Diary of a Bad Year* concerns one year in its explicit scope; in its implications it argues that the contemporary is a whole slew of bad years.

Speaking Truth to Piety: Pam Brown and Jennifer Maiden

The subject position rancour presumes is undoubtedly gendered. All the prophets who have books named after them in the Bible are male; so are all the Roman satirists extant. In the era of Pope and Dryden there were some female satirists: Anne Finch, who wrote of "Woman, armed with spleen", and Anne Killegrew, who longed to "speak the truth" as Cassandra does in Greek myth. But they were few and far between.[70] This has changed both because women have a lot to be angry about and because of a shift, presumably caused by the larger and more impersonal scale of modernity, in the target of rancour. Instead of denouncing individual malefactors or a corrupt state of affairs, rancour now stands athwart a consensus. It is now not so much a malcontent guest nursing a grudge from within the party as a gate crasher, uninvited and angry. Pam Brown's poetry profits from its lack of clarity: just enough of the picture is provided for the reader's impression to gel, but not so much so that the author's presence becomes dogmatic or monologic:

> time to lie down again
>
> on the royal Stewart tartan picnic blanket
>
> in the shademottle & so on
>
> the light dark leaf
>
> at the outdoor ecocide ceremony
>
> feeling foul
>
> after completing an atavistic circuit
>
> muddy twigs smoke out the bonfire
>
> in the end nobody wakes you
>
> & you miss whatever you knew
>
> reeking dead frozen fish thawing rotten
>
> you chuck your flux[71]

Lyn McCredden has described Brown as "one of Australia's lesser-known great poets", both "philosophically and technically rich".[72] The idea of rancour as a recalcitrant party guest is here vividly enacted. In the "ecocide ceremony", there is an uncomfortable proximity between the ecological and the ecocidal, as the easy transferability of "just change meadow to paddock" denotes. The "atavistic circuit" could in other circumstances connote a reassuring back-to-nature romp, and the royal tartan blanket an avatar of a rural Highland fling. But these easy solutions are ruled out from the start. All that is left is the individual voice, and this is the characteristic operation of rancour. It retrieves the initiative of individu-

---

70   Anne Finch, Countess of Winchelsea, *Selected Poems*, ed. Denys Thompson (Manchester: Carcanet, 1987), 42; Harriette Andreadis, *Sappho in Early Modern England: Female Same-Sex Literary Erotics, 1550–1714* (Chicago: University of Chicago Press, 2001), 112.

71   Pam Brown, "At 'The-End-of-the-World-as-We-Know-It Retreat'", *Otoliths*, June 2014. http://the-otolith.blogspot.com.au/2014/06/pam-brown.html.

72   Lyn McCredden, "'untranscended / life itself': The Poetry of Pam Brown". *Australian Literary Studies* 22, no. 2 (2005): 217.

alism away from the appropriation of free will by the free market. Rancour reclaims the genuinely personal, albeit in a state of extreme outrage, from the metronomic individualism of free-market economics.

Ecocide can despoil, but a cleaned-up world is that destruction's hellish antipode. In "Pique", Brown viscerally evokes a neoliberal dystopia, a world in which all idiosyncrasy is eliminated, the urban grit of late modernity all washed away so that the centre has been vacated by both people and meaning:

> Pique
>
> no one
>
> on the corner
>
> here
>
> silent,
>
> not spiritual,
>
> the city is empty
>
> antispectacular
>
> & as
>
> deodorised
>
> as heaven
>
> no sleeping boys
> no density
> no belching
> pissing bodies
> no spitting
> in the street
>
> utilitarian –
>
> make one step
>
> another step
>
> follows[73]

"Silent not spiritual": the late-modern deadlock evoked so powerfully in Elizabeth Harrower's fiction might have been thought to be soluble by an eruption of spirituality, even of the parodic sort, as instanced in the crucifixion of Himmelfarb in Patrick White's *Riders in the Chariot*. But this silence is antiseptic, eviscerated; it is what Brown calls "the tedium of the blessed". Against this tedium, one could muster all sorts of polysyllabic critiques gleaned from Continental theorists, from Jacques Ellul through to Bernard Stiegler, but none would pack a punch emotionally: for this one must turn to Brown's com-

---

73   Pam Brown, "Pique", from *50-50* (Adelaide: South Australian Publishing Ventures, 1997), via Australian Poetry Library, http://www.poetrylibrary.edu.au/poets/brown-pam/pique-0280014.

pressed, utterly disillusioned rancour. And utterly disillusioned she is, as neither the past nor intellectual activity brings recourse or respite.

> absorbed
>
> in poetic gesture,
>
> arrivistes paraphrase
>
> biography –
>
> & animate
>
> early C20
>
> heroes & heroines[74]

Nostalgia offers no alternative; remembering a time when things were otherwise provides only empty solace. For a poet like Hope, his own cultivated rage was the only redemptive feature in the frame, but this poet does not offer herself that way out.

Yet rancour also leaves room for declared opposition. In 2005, a couple of years into the war in Iraq, I read Jennifer Maiden's "Costume Jewelry", a poem attacking the then US Secretary of State, Condoleezza Rice, to an audience at New York City's hip Housing Works secondhand bookshop. I had included Maiden in a selection of contemporary Australian poetry in Philip Fried's *Manhattan Review*. The audience was politically left-leaning, the scruffier hipster descendants of the Howards in Harrower's *In Certain Circles*. They were not pro-Bush or pro-war. But one member of the audience found the end of the poem truly outrageous:

> Always the White House was bright as a cake with candles, fiery nothings.
>
> The lights of the White House are blazing cubic zirconia, con dolcezza,
>
> But you're not hungry with terror, you're not starving[75]

The audience member, a young, white male whose clothing denoted vaguely countercultural affectations, objected to the play on Rice's first name in "con dolcezza", a verbal gesture he considered derogatory in a personal sense, maybe even racist, as Rice is African American. He averred that it was not that Rice was not starving that was the problem; it was her policies that were wrong, and many wealthy people had opposed the Iraq War. He was reading Maiden's poem as primarily an attack on certain policies or politics, when in fact it might have been an attack on neoliberalism as such. To be a decision maker in the twenty-first century, someone who decides whether or not to wage war, is to be privileged, and the writer of rancour undermines that privilege in the same way that Pope and Hope undermined the privilege of the poetasters, sycophants, trendies and imposters they disliked. The excess that made even a young hipster man who was politically unsympathetic to Rice object to the ferocity of the poem was precisely the point. The unabated nastiness

---

74   Brown, "Pique", http://www.poetrylibrary.edu.au/poets/brown-pam/pique-0280014.
75   Jennifer Maiden, "Costume Jewellery", in *Friendly Fire* (Artarmon: Giramondo Publishing, 2005).

is what gives Maiden's voice the appalling, unpalatable vigour to burst a desiccated consensus. As Jal Nicholl comments, Maiden's "fascination is not with world historical figures but with their epigones".[76] The same could be said of eighteenth-century satirists such as Pope, and inevitably produces rhetorical excess. Epigones, derivative followers, can only take so much venom, while world-historical figures can absorb venom infinitely.

But the young New Yorker's critique of "Costume Jewelry" did, in a larger sense, signal the limitations of rancour as a mode. Rancour may have a savage, visceral appeal. But its shelf life is short, and satiric anger has seldom been a sustainable mode: its venom is contingent on timeliness; its polemics, if not *ad hominem*, are directed at passing rather than permanent aspects of the human condition. The American critic Brooke Allen, reviewing the essays of Muriel Spark (whose *The Prime of Miss Jean Brodie* we will see influence Eleanor Catton in Chapter 9) quotes Spark as objecting to literature of "sentiment and emotion" (what in the next chapter I will call "concern") and advocating instead "the arts of satire and of ridicule. And I see no other living art form for the future. Because we have come to a moment in history when we are surrounded on all sides and oppressed by the absurd". Allen comments sagely: "Each generation seems to think its own to be uniquely absurd; each has been wrong."[77] This delusion extends to Hope, who thought the "chattering apes" of modernism were sillier than average. It is why the Augustan aspects of his work have paled, and the Orphic ones have had to redeem them. It is why rancour, for all the achievement of the female writers discussed here, is still associated with a male-gendered posture that seeks rhetorical strength through heroic, solitary dissent.

Why then the salience of rancour with respect to Australia? Because the Australian literary condition, as constituted by the world and internalised by Australia, has to promise reassurance in order to overcome marginality. The world does not look to Australia for bad news, or accept bad news from Australia in the way it does from, say, France, from Zola to Sartre to Houellebecq. The world gets, or is willing to receive, so little news from Australia that there is immense pressure for what news does get through to be good news. Rancour allows Australian literature to deflect these expectations.

The danger of this global complacency regarding Australia is especially acute when it comes to Indigenous issues. Anita Heiss, in *Am I Black Enough for You?* defies conventional stereotypes of Aboriginal identity.[78] She travels to world capitals and paints the town red, writes stylishly self-conscious "chick-lit", is glamorous and flirtatious – all while making clear that she is not forsaking an activist agenda. She does a lot of direct community work and sees her other activities as community work by other means. In refusing expectations of what a black woman should be – self-sacrificing, stoic, suffering – Heiss is at once an Indigenous activist and a with-it prognosticator, both Wiradjuri and, through her father, Austrian, but she seeks no consolation in hybridity. Whereas whites often look to non-whites either to preserve an "authentic" version of an imagined pre-neoliberal era, or to embrace the commercial imperative of neoliberalism all the more for not being white, Heiss dwells within consumer society and revels in its pleasures, but is neither bound by it nor takes it too seriously. Although neither satirist nor prophet in the sense of some of the other writers examined in this chapter, Heiss is unafraid to speak truth to power, or to piety. She notes that the "success of Aboriginal authors" – she names some of the most

---

76   Jal Nicholl, "Review of Jennifer Maiden's *Liquid Nitrogen*", *Southerly* 73, no. 1 (2013): 234.
77   Brooke Allen, "The Essays of Slender Means", *The New Criterion*, June 2014, 78.
78   Anita Heiss, *Am I Black Enough for You?* (Sydney: Random House, 2013).

prominent – in "getting French translations of our work is partly because some French people are quite comfortable to slag off the Brits for their own colonial exploits. But to consider their own, well, that's another story".[79] The usual pious Australian attitude to the transnational is gone; in its place there is a frank acknowledgement of the motives of those who embrace Australian Indigenous culture, even if it is unseemly; yet, as in Tsiolkas, there is a certain Australian patriotism, even if it manifests itself in a refusal to see other people as inherently more altruistic than Australians.

Much like Ouyang Yu, who disdains the Asian Australian roles the broader society assigns him while remaining a passionate and much-admired advocate for Asian Australian concerns, Heiss can express such challenging opinions because her activist bona fides are unquestioned. Many of the figures in this chapter have, despite their rancour, also been constructive: Hope as a devoted teacher and mentor; Kinsella in his environmental activism and his fostering of worldwide poetic communities; Brown in her editorial and critical work. To use rancour to see through the ludicrous pageant of life's posturings can be ascetic. But it is not necessarily destructive. Through its ability to challenge consensus, rancour can go beyond critique to offer contemporary Australian writers an alternative to cruel inequality.

---

79   Heiss, *Am I Black Enough for You?*, 281.

6
Failing to Be Separate: Race, Land, Concern

African Nations

In October 1988, I went to the Australian instalment of the "Common Wealth of Letters" series presided over at Yale University by the Jamaican-born Michael Cooke (1934–1990). This was a cornucopia of stimulation, and it was here that I first met Australian scholars and writers such as Kevin Hart, Ivor Indyk, Andrew Taylor and Michael Wilding, who continued to be important reference points as I delved further into the intricacies of books from down under. But the unquestioned star of the conference was Thomas Keneally. Though the film *Schindler's List* (1993), based on his 1982 Booker Prize-winning novel, *Schindler's Ark*, had not yet been made, Keneally was already a world literary celebrity. From my reading of his *Confederates* (1979), I knew him as a writer with an astonishing ability to imagine times and places distant from his own, and to do so with impressive economy.

At the conference dinner, I was fortunate enough to be at Keneally's table. This repast was distinguished by Keneally, in the middle of a voluble discourse, realising that he had not yet touched his main course, a Salisbury steak, and popping the entire thing into his mouth in a gesture of genial, offhanded machismo worthy of Paul Hogan. More seriously, Keneally was addressing the topic that had convulsed Yale over the past year. This was the revelation that Paul de Man, the acclaimed professor of comparative literature and nonpareil of deconstructionists, who had died in 1983, had, during his youth in wartime Belgium, written articles that were collaborationist or pro-Nazi. Keneally spoke wisely of writers who had made mistakes, or ethical lapses, both of the right and of the left. Keneally's own books had been equally critical of Nazi and communist totalitarianisms. His clear-eyed moral witness was a refreshing change from Australian writers such as Katherine Susannah Prichard, Frank Hardy and Eleanor Dark, who, out of an excess of radical zeal, had been frankly toadyish in their attitudes to the Soviet Union, which had proven itself a monstrosity.

Keneally addressed the scandal of de Man's collaborationist wartime journalism from a conceptual angle as well as a political one. He found the speculations about language characteristic of deconstruction to be arcane trivia, comparing deconstruction to the theological differences in the fourth century AD (a comparison first made a few years before by Richard Rorty).[1] In contrast, he spoke of his recent visit to Eritrea, an insurgent area in northeast Africa at that time governed by Ethiopia. Here, a rebel Eritrean army was opposing the malignant Soviet-allied Ethiopian government of Mengistu Halle Mariam. The Mengistu government was responsible for the atrocious famine that had garnered headlines worldwide in the mid-1980s and had inspired, "records, tapes, and performances", as Keneally later put it in his Eritrean novel, *To Asmara* (1989).[2] A year before the dinner, Keneally had written for the *New York Times Magazine* about his visit with the rebels in Eritrea. In his engagement with Eritrea, Keneally was witnessing real hope and real pain, far from what he saw as the academic hair-splitting of deconstruction.

I was aware that the Eritreans, like their Ethiopian suppressors, were Monophysite Christians (or as they prefer to call themselves, "Miaphysite") who separated from the rest of Christianity over theological disputes of the fourth and fifth centuries.[3] I pointed out to Keneally that the Eritreans were descendants of those for whom these arcane theological disputes mattered, my implication being that deconstruction ultimately might also matter. Considering all the other people at the table were scholars of world eminence and I was an unknown 23-year-old who had not yet published a word, Keneally was admirably tolerant of my cheekiness. He aided *Antipodes* many times in the years ahead, once personally sending me two books of his that the journal was unable to obtain from the publisher for review.

Keneally is thus a writer capable of showing concern in matters both large and small. On a more abstract level, in this chapter I address the issue of "concern" as a general affect in contemporary Australian literature. What are the ethics of writers caring about people of different origins and backgrounds? Is this a manifestation of altruism or liberal guilt? In an era when so many philosophers, from Martin Buber to Emmanuel Levinas to Adriana Caverero, have written about the ethics of addressing, speaking for, caring about or presuming upon "the other",[4] and if, as Martha Nussbaum has argued, compassion on an individual level is "a central bridge between the individual and the community",[5] what does the idea of concern, which generalises compassion across communities, mean in moral and affective terms? Does the potential bad faith of feigning concern for others or using that concern to make oneself look good outweigh the benefit of showing concern for the social conditions of other groups? Is even a hypocritical or self-deluding concern better than callous indifference?[6] Is concern inevitably a part of what Ruwen Ogien calls the "non-coercive means" by which prescriptive agents try to move people in directions they have not willed for themselves?[7] Or is concern a solution, albeit a piecemeal one, to problems that emanate from neoliberalism itself?

---

1   Richard Rorty, "Deconstruction and Circumvention", *Critical Inquiry* 11, no. 1 (1984): 22.

2   Thomas Keneally, *To Asmara* (New York: Warner Books, 1989).

3   Gawdat Gabra, *The A to Z of the Coptic Church* (Lanham: Scarecrow Press, 2009), 76.

4   Martin Buber, *I and Thou* (New York: Scribner, 1937); Emmanuel Levinas, *Alterity and Transcendence*, trans. Michael B. Smith (New York: Columbia University Press, 2006); Adriana Caverero, *For More Than One Voice: Towards a Philosophy of Vocal Expression*, trans. Paul Kottman (Stanford: Stanford University Press, 2005).

5   Martha Nussbaum, "Compassion: The Basic Social Emotion", *Social Philosophy and Policy* 13 (1996): 27–38.

6   Bernard Williams, *Moral Luck* (Cambridge: Cambridge University Press, 1982).

7   Ruwen Ogien, "Neutrality Towards Non-Controversial Conceptions of the Good Life", in *Political Neutrality: A Re-evaluation*, eds Alberto Merrill and Daniel Weinstock (New York: Palgrave Macmillan, 2014), 106.

This chapter starts with Keneally in Africa, but I will chiefly consider how white Australian writers have addressed Indigenous Australian issues, concentrating on Kate Grenville, Gail Jones and Alex Miller. I will conclude with an Indigenous writer, Alexis Wright, who in *The Swan Book* (2013) writes from an Aboriginal perspective of the asylum-seeker issue as it has manifested itself in Australian politics since the 2001 *Tampa* crisis. All the above gestures towards social altruism are aspects of what the Canadian theorist Northrop Frye called "the myth of concern", a collective social vision that, through means both social and imaginative, postulates an interest in humankind as a totality, and includes altruism in a sense of the creative.[8] Frye calls concern "the response of the adult citizen to genuine social problems", and contrasts it with anxiety, which depends on a nervousness about protecting ourselves manifested by buttressing ourselves in self-buffeting groups – like Martin in Tsiolkas' *Barracuda* when he castigates Danny Kelly as a loser. The concern–anxiety dichotomy, however, does not neatly align with differences in political or socioeconomic philosophy. It is about a fundamental attitude to the world that might include politics but also supersedes them. Concern is about what cannot be fulfilled at present in legal or formal terms, which is why it is a myth rather than a doctrine. It is speculative more than it is polemical.[9]

Frye stated that once "a myth of concern is recognised as such, it becomes clear that you cannot express its truth without lying". This is because concern is "contradicting accepted truth with something that is going to be made true but isn't true now".[10] When contemporary Australian novelists write about global inequality, racial differences, and the mistreatment of Indigenous people, they are fostering a hope for something not currently true but which they hope to make true; this is precisely why the imagination is needed. The imaginative writer cares about people in a way that it is impossible currently to care through conventional socio-political means. Concern is what remains of a collective horizon once the state is no longer seen as a vehicle to bring us towards that horizon. While all of these writers are aware of the pitfalls of concern, they nonetheless maintain it as the central agent of their affective mission.

Part of the *modus operandi* of concern can be linked to "the relational turn" in 1990s psychological thought, particularly as exemplified in the work of Axel Honneth. Honneth's *The Struggle for Recognition* is subtitled *the moral grammar of social conflicts*, and concern, as a concept, argues just that: that social conflicts have a moral basis and can be regarded ethically as much as polemically, interpersonally as much as ideologically. Honneth's work represents the socialisation of psychoanalysis, which in Freud's era had emphasised the individual ego and its relation to the society, but in the postwar era, with the dominance of the object-relations school, emphasised how inner and outer circumstances mutually and constructively adjusted. Honneth takes this dynamic a step further, seeing the individual's experience as meaningful only in the context of other individuals; individuals constitute one another in relationships of mutual recognition, which "must possess the character

---

8 John Robert Colombo and Jean O'Grady, ed., *The Northrop Frye Quote Book* (Toronto: Dundurn, 2014), 84.

9 Frye is often criticised for being apolitical, but here he was really being speculatively political in ways comparable to such thinkers as Walter Benjamin and Alain Badiou.

10 Colombo and O'Grady, *The Northrop Frye Quote Book*, 85.

of affective approval or encouragement".[11] Importantly, for Honneth, recognition is built upon, but is larger than, Eros, "supplementing libidinal drives with affective".[12]

The Australian novelists of concern have similar insights: in depicting the romantic relationship of Bo Rennie and Annabelle Beck in *Journey to the Stone Country*, Alex Miller makes clear that the erotic is subtended by a deeper connection to land and values, premised on the recognition of both self and other. Annabelle thinks about how she might speak of Bo to her ex-husband in Melbourne: "I knew him as a child. There are connections between us you would not understand. In this place I am becoming myself again."[13] Love is not just Eros, but recognition, concern, an implicated acknowledgement. Analogously, concern is political altruism ramified by the acknowledgement of affect. It is an awakening not just to political inequality but to interpersonal feeling. As Joel Anderson says in his introduction to Honneth, "justice demands more than the fair distribution of material goods", and the "emancipatory struggles" of "marginalised groups" must be situated within a social world that is interactive and affective, not just economic or political.[14] To care about a place there must be some sort of affective tie. It cannot simply be a matter of short-term political or ideological pilgrimage.

It was clear at that Yale dinner that Keneally was aware of the pitfalls of political engagement on the part of writers. The American scholar Paul Hollander, earlier in the 1980s, had written *Political Pilgrims*, featuring intellectuals who had made trips to communist countries and become convinced that these societies represented positive achievements.[15] Earlier in the century, there had been a wave of Anglophone intellectuals who adored or at least tolerated the Nazi regime in Germany. In both cases, these outsiders assumed they could assess the situation in a foreign country and take a political endorsement back to their home countries. Keneally has been aware, unlike the aforementioned political pilgrims, of the dangers of speaking of and for another people. The book that brought him to international fame – *The Chant of Jimmie Blacksmith* (1972), powerfully adapted to film by Fred Schepisi in 1978 – was told from the point of view of its Indigenous protagonist. By 2001, Keneally had reconsidered this, stating that he was wrong to presume he could speak from inside an Indigenous person's experience.[16] By the time of *To Asmara*, Keneally did not funnel any of the narrative through the point of view of African characters and thus avoided accusations of cultural appropriation. Yet his stake in the Eritrean situation was nonetheless open to question. Keneally was in the difficult position of exploring a conflict in which he had sympathies – for the Eritrean rebels, against the Ethiopian government – but which he did not mean to present in a moralistic or propagandistic way. This can be seen in the last line of his novel, attributed not to the protagonist Darcy but to an authorial over-voice: "and all the incidents fail to be separate".[17] If the earlier writers who

---

11   Axel Honneth, *The Struggle for Recognition: The Moral Grammar of Social Conflicts* (London: Polity, 1995), 95.

12   Honneth, *The Struggle for Recognition*, 97.

13   Alex Miller, *Journey to the Stone Country* (Crows Nest: Allen & Unwin, 2002), Kindle edition, location 2704. All subsequent references are to this edition and appear in parentheses in the text.

14   Joel Anderson, translator's introduction to Honneth's *The Struggle for Recognition*, 1.

15   Paul Hollander, *Political Pilgrims: Western Intellectuals in Search of the Good Society* (New Brunswick: Transaction Publishers, 1997).

16   Thomas Keneally, "A New Chant for Jimmie Blacksmith?", *Sydney Morning Herald*, 25–26 August 2001, *Spectrum* 4–5.

17   Keneally, *To Asmara*, 290.

had been naive about the nature of the Nazi or Soviet regimes and trusted too much in the brotherhood of man and soil, Keneally disclaimed what the theorist Louis Althusser termed an expressive causality, a yoking of historical currents. And yet, try as he might to see things cautiously and analytically, the narrator has to grasp for a collective lens, even while aware of the totalising flaw in such a gesture.

While the American edition of the book was titled *To Asmara* (Asmara being the capital of Eritrea, which the rebels hoped to liberate from its Ethiopian occupiers), the British and Australian title was *Towards Asmara*. This was surely intended to be a micro-linguistic distinction, reflecting the fact that American English uses "to" as a directional while British and Australian English might favour "towards". Yet there was also a semantic difference: "to" is more inspirational, even martial, as in "marching to Pretoria" or the cries of "*À Berlin!*" at the end of Zola's *Nana*, whereas "towards" seems more tentative, a setting-out that never quite gets where it is headed. In the book, the rebels do not reach Asmara, but in actual history they did: the Ethiopian government fell and, in 1993, Eritrea was recognised internationally as an independent state under the presidency of Isaias Afewerki, the rebel leader whom Keneally had lionised. Keneally praised Afewerki's concern for education, his respect for the value of each individual, and his promotion of a progressive, humane, business-friendly Africa, while attributing to Afewerki's opponents a desire to see Africa fail. Keneally hoped for an Africa that the West would not have to feel sorry for, an Africa that could avoid white patronage. At the beginning of *To Asmara*, a rock singer who talks with Darcy about the region finds Eritrea uninteresting because he cannot see its people as simply passive agents of compassion and patronage.

Keneally recognised the principle of statehood in Africa, that contemporary Africa is a set of states that exercise sovereignty. Westerners who make cultural or anthropological generalisations about Africa are unconsciously hearkening back to colonial days in denying the importance of African state sovereignty, and in seeing Africans either as an undifferentiated mass of poor people who need Western help, or as an "uncontaminated" people who can teach Westerners alternative wisdom. The phenomenon of "Afropessimism", what Manthia Diawara terms a "fatalistic attitude towards economic and social crisis" in Africa, is but the inversion of an overly utopian and categorical expectation of the African future.[18] Keneally was trying to change that, or to challenge it.

Keneally's hope for Eritrea, alas, ended in disappointment and bitterness. The Eritrean regime got bogged down in a border war with the new Ethiopian government and Afewerki remained in power for twenty years, amid accusations of human-rights violations and political repression. In a 2004 interview, Keneally spoke of Afewerki possessing "purity" and noted that Afewerki did not cultivate a Stalin-like cult of personality; there were "never posters of him anywhere".[19] Keneally further averred, "If he's a tyrant, he's pretty remarkable." Although Keneally makes no bones about criticising the Eritrean leader's repressive policies, there was still a more than sentimental attachment, much as a teacher might still see promise in a former student who has not realised his potential. One should not be too hard on Keneally here, for the mistake he made – hoping an African leader would break the continent's perceived cycle of failure and establish a model state – has been repeated by others, most recently with the independence of South Sudan in 2010, which

18 Manthia Diawara, *In Search of Africa* (Cambridge: Harvard University Press, 2009), 239.
19 Thomas Keneally, interviewed by Mark Corcoran, *Foreign Correspondent*, ABC TV, 25 May 2004. http://www.abc.net.au/foreign/content/2004/s1115693.htm.

excited the same sort of energised partisanship as occurred in Eritrea. In both cases, one suspects Western interest was inspired in part by the Christianity of the rebel regions, and by their proximity to the lands of the Bible (Cush, Punt and Havilah, in what today is the region of Eritrea and South Sudan, are even named in the Biblical account of the Garden of Eden).

Keneally can be said to have written about this region once before, in his 1973 children's book *Moses the Lawgiver*. In addition, there is a traditional Australian tie to the region through the Suez Canal, the British Empire, the two world wars, and the explorations of Alan Moorehead in East Africa. Thus there is a larger point here than just Keneally's endorsement of a leader who ended up disappointing. All of us make mistakes; Western imperialism colours even benign attitudes towards Africa; no intellectual is infallible, certainly not politically. More largely, *To Asmara* is about a search for affective understanding, however partial and foredoomed. At the end of Darcy's narrative, he admits, "We could not share the same table."[20] He is not speaking about the Eritreans but about Anna, a German woman who has witnessed scenes of untold carnage and horror, and is unable to accept Darcy's more detached and touristic attitude, however compassionate his intent. Darcy's perspective reveals the limits of individual compassion. Keneally anticipates critiques of his inevitably partial and inadequate relationship to the material. He realises that the same social concern that animates the altruistic thrust we so often value in fiction might also impede our awareness.[21]

Settler Land Claims: From Sustenance to Fragility

In his next book, *Flying Hero Class*, Keneally contrasted different kinds of subalternity – Palestinian and Aboriginal – by having an Aboriginal dance troupe fly on an aeroplane hijacked by Arab terrorists. In 1991, when the book was published, readers might have seen Palestinians and Aborigines as two populations with legitimate grievances. But they may also have seen Australian Indigenous people, as Keneally tends to, as more "spiritual", as somehow benign and otherworldly, in contrast to the Palestinian political activists striving for national liberation. Twenty years later, scholars such as Steven Salaita have identified similarities between Palestinians and other indigenous groups in Anglophone settler colonies.[22] Rosanne Kennedy has studied trauma and memory in Palestinian contexts in a manner directly applicable to Aboriginal circumstances.[23] International sympathy for

---

20   *To Asmara*, 316.

21   *To Asmara* was nonetheless clairvoyant in its sense both that Eritrean independence was near realisation, and that it mattered; Keneally should be given credit for this prescience. Interestingly, in the following decades Keneally turned more and more away from this sort of "topical" novel. Even a potential example of such a book, such as 2003's *The Tyrant's Novel*, is far more fictionalised and allegorised than his earlier work.

22   Steven Salaita, *The Holy Land in Transit: Colonialism and the Quest for Canaan* (Syracuse: Syracuse University Press, 2006).

23   Rosanne Kennedy, "Humanity's Footprint: Reading *Rings of Saturn* and Palestinian Walks in an Anthropocene Era", *Biography* 35, no. 1 (2012): 170–89. Michael Brull, "A Tale of Two Settler Colonies: Israel and Australia Compared", *Overland* 217 (2014): 53–59, makes a similar point. In Alex Miller's *Journey to the Stone Country*, the point-of-view character, Annabelle, compares relations between Indigenous people and settlers in Australia to those between Palestinians and Israelis, especially in the whites' inability "to be forgiven by the people one lived among".

the Palestinians has risen. Furthermore, the fight for land rights changed perceptions of Indigenous Australians: they were no longer seen as otherworldly exemplars of ancient spirituality, but as political actors who were advocating for their rights, both through Western legal systems and through the traditional frameworks of their own peoples. Yet Keneally's juxtaposition of the Aboriginal and the Palestinian retains some residual provocation. Inevitably, when Westerners think about land and claims to land – and when Western ideas leave traces on Indigenous writers who have had Christian upbringings or read the Bible – the idea of Israel as a promised land underlies these thoughts.

This can be seen very clearly in New Zealand, where the frequently used phrase *tangata whenua* – people of the land – could almost be a calque of the Hebrew *am ha'eres*.[24] The Ratana and Ringatu religions, established by Māori leaders in the nineteenth century, were syncretic faiths that braided traditional Māori spiritual practices with a sense of the Hebraic; today, many Māori personal names are adaptations of Biblical ones. Māori nationalism, in rhetoric, like most Western nationalisms, appropriated the self-identification of the Jews as the chosen people.[25] In Alex Miller's *Journey to the Stone Country* (2002), repeated references to imagined Queensland localities called Nebo and Pisgah bring to mind Mounts Nebo and Pisgah near the Promised Land, which Moses envisioned but never reached. In Alexis Wright's *Carpentaria*, the Rainbow Serpent is depicted as a revered creator-god, but the serpent imagery inevitably also brings to mind the far more destructive serpent in the Bible. There is much crossover in Western and Indigenous ways of talking about land. Thus the history of concern features both Indigenous writers and, with varying degrees of effort and acuity, white writers negotiating these enabling contradictions and using literature to heal the wounds of land that has been stolen and, frequently, arrogantly misused.

Africa, with its legacy of slavery, apartheid and colonisation, can aptly serve as a ground for Australian modes of concern. Gillian Mears' *The Grass Sister* (1995) plays with these African–Australian analogues. Yet for Australian writers the problem of concern is inevitably local, as it has to do with land and claims to the ownership of it. Indeed, what is pertinent about all three forms of affect that I am surveying in these chapters – rancour, concern and idealism – is what a localising effect they have on Australian literature. Hope reads Juvenal and Pope, yet snarls from Canberra at chattering European apes. Tsiolkas' Danny has problems in Australia, but has no place else to go. Concern is inevitably bound up with specifically Australian territory, because it is there that the injustices perpetrated by settlement have to be addressed. Although affect is something psychological, in Australian literature it is a force that tugs back against the transnational. As Eve Kosofsky Sedgwick points out, affect theory gestures to the abstract even as it plausibly operates to "bind one ever more imaginatively and profoundly to the local possibilities of an individual psychology".[26] Australia is a continent and a country, not an individual person. But affect is specific because feelings are specific. If politics and world history take Australian writers abroad, states of feeling tether them to (a revised version of) home.

---

24 I am not suggesting that the second phrase influenced the first, only that they mean the same thing. The Hebrew phrase appears often in the Bible and would have to be translated in Māori as *tangata whenua*.

25 This is seen in the very title of Maurice Shadbolt's 1986 *Season of the Jew*, the first of his Māori Wars trilogy.

26 Eve Kosofsky Sedgwick, *Touching Feeling: Affect, Pedagogy, Performativity* (Durham: Duke University Press, 2003), 106.

Sedgwick also points out that this affective "fold" is often characterised by repetition of the same key concepts, in ways that at once totalise and distract. This can be seen in the role of the land in mid-twentieth-century Australian popular fiction. For settler Australians in the mid-twentieth century, land was the magnetic pull that prevented them from simply soaring away, à la Teresa Hawkins in Stead's *For Love Alone*, to metropolitan sophistication. To be Australian was to feel a tie to the land, and that tie often obviated any other personal goal, fate or preference. In Frederick J. Thwaites' *The Broken Melody* (1930), the hero goes through many travails, finds and loses love and fortune, but has his family's ancestral land to fall back on:

> The cello had a voice, too, a deep, vibrant voice which carried far into the cold night. Thus fate after toying with the human emotions, after being ruthless to the point of extreme cruelty, had in fact relented. Thus one, two, three hundred years later from now a Mason would still be strolling over "Nullabean's" broad acres.[27]

Just seventy years later, however, the tonality of the affect had changed: the Masons may still have possessed their fictional land, but, post-*Mabo*, the ontological and legal question of whether non-Indigenous Australians could "really" own the land was in question. In *The Broken Melody*, land has an affect deeper even than love or art, and is able to fend off the losses incurred in those emotional enterprises; but after *Mabo*, this deep, geological life is suddenly more frangible. There is a large-scale shift away from a view of the land as an inanimate backbone underneath merely temporary feelings. Yet residues of this view remain, even in the rhetorically powerful ending to David Malouf's *Remembering Babylon* (1993). Despite earlier acknowledging that "here the very ground under their feet was strange", the book concludes with the idea that the land can be a source of consolation, albeit a far more gossamer consolation than imagined by Thwaites:

> It glows in fullness till the tide is high and the light almost, but not quite, unbearable, as the moon plucks at our world and all the waters of the earth ache towards it, and the light, running in fast now, reaches the edges of the shore, just so far in its orders, and all the muddy margin of the bay is alive, and in a line of running fire all the outline of the vast continent appears, in touch now with its other life.[28]

For Australian writers of an earlier generation, the "other life" that Malouf speaks of so eloquently was often connected with "atavism". In *The Storm of Time* (1948), the second novel in her *Timeless Land* trilogy, Eleanor Dark uses the adjective "atavistic" repeatedly to describe how Dilboorn, depicted as the daughter of the Eora man Bennilong (sic), is tugged back to an *Ur*-primitivism even after experiencing white manners and mores. In the most popular white depiction of Aboriginal life from this era, Arthur J. Upfield's detective series featuring the half-caste Inspector Napoleon Bonaparte, Bonaparte is depicted as an Aboriginal man with wit, tenacity, charm and unmatched intellectual ability. But Upfield indicates that these traits are part of a conscious self-fashioning on the part of the detective, cultivated to prevent himself from careering back into the bush.

27 Frederick J. Thwaites, *The Broken Melody* (Sydney: Publicity Press, 1930), 256.
28 David Malouf, *Remembering Babylon* (New York: Vintage Books, 1994), 222.

Upfield makes clear that he sees the ratiocinative quality of Bony's detective abilities as at one complementing and counterpoising his Aboriginal identity. Complementing, as Bony's notable abilities as a tracker are matched by his intellectual discernment. Counterpoising, because, as the detective himself says, "I had to conquer greater obstacles than social prejudice. I had to conquer, and still have to conquer, the almost irresistible power of the Australian bush over those who belong to it."[29] A similar "atavistic" tug of the bush at once fuels and imperils Inspector Bonaparte's profession. Upfield's novels are poised on the edge of concern, acknowledging the reverberations of "country", in the Indigenous sense of the word, but still keeping them at a distance.

Upfield's *Death of a Swagman* contains a fascinating scene between Inspector Bonaparte and Mr Jason, the son of the murderer but also a sensitive if impaired young man who, like Bony, has an affection for Rose Marie, the young daughter of the local police sergeant. At one point, Bonaparte and Jason stare at each other in both confrontation and solidarity. The entire dilemma of Australian identity might be boiled down to the fact that their two constituencies – to put it broadly, Indigenous Australians and lower-class whites – have been put at odds when in many ways their interests are the same. Concern can speak to this gap only in a limited way because it is inevitably an upper-class initiative of the privileged, like the Western helpers in Keneally's Eritrea: a cadre of well-intentioned professionals, intellectuals and altruists. Les Murray might level the charge of left-elitism against such a group. Yet concern has to make do with this possible layer of bad faith. It does not have behind it any sort of organic or essential solidarity.

Given the formal kinship between the detective story and the *récit*, as discussed in Chapter 4, Upfield's novels also provide a formal precedent for concern, as the novels of Gail Jones and Alex Miller, shortly to be explored, have the quality of *récits*, in which style matters more than sprawl, stance as much as content. Upfield also provides a precedent for such later novels of concern by having the physical landscape of his novels precisely laid out, and by not only associating Bony with a knowledge of country but also having that knowledge, in terms of tracking and discerning clues upon the landscape, be portable, as the various cases Bony pursues occur in New South Wales, Victoria and Western Australia, as well as in his native Queensland. Upfield acknowledges the specificity of the landscape without making his detective merely a parochial figure who knows his own territory; rather, Bony understands the *idea* of territory. Bony's expertise is tethered to *a* country even when he is not working in his own country (only one of the novels, *An Author Bites the Dust*, is set in the city). Bony has adventures in every Australian state except Tasmania – perhaps reflecting the then widespread belief in the effacement of the Indigenous people in Tasmania after the death of Truganini in the late nineteenth century.

Although Upfield's tales were idealising, he made advances both in presenting Indigenous Australians as intelligent and resourceful (and in Bony's case, more so than most whites), and also in registering that the attitude to possession declared by the fact of settlement and colonisation cannot be an inalienable trait of white Australian identity. There is always another claim, another layer, as is revealed by Bony's knowledge of the land, which helps him to solve innumerable puzzles and quandaries. This is true not just of the Jindyworobaks, the white poets who awkwardly espoused Aboriginal themes, but also of writers such as Colin Thiele, who focused on the animal inhabitants of the land in ways that dislocated anthropocentrism. If, as Martin Harrison's poem "Breakfast", puts it, "to

---

29   Arthur Upfield, *Death of a Swagman* (Sydney: Angus & Robertson, 1980), 24.

conceive a dam's bearing towards human nature requires the same skill as the resolution of any ethically knife-edge, historically many-sided issue", nature and history, with respect to Australia, can crisscross, although not coincide.[30] It is a mistake to imagine that Aborigines before European contact did not alter or manage the land, as Bill Gammage shows in *The Biggest Estate on Earth*.[31] As Marcia Langton asserted in her 2012 Boyer Lectures, there is a potential competition between environmental awareness and Aboriginal participation in the contemporary resource boom.[32] Philip Mead describes Langton's critique of the "meme of the noble savage", a meme that has the potential not only to deny Aboriginal people access to natural resources and the income derived from them, but also to absorb urgent assertions of Aboriginal sovereignty into a more quietist and anodyne acknowledgement of the sanctity of the land.[33] Ecology and Indigenous sovereignty are not necessarily aligned. But, as an initial critique of Eurocentric assumptions, awareness of both ecological crisis and the disinheritance of Indigenous people unsettled assumptions about who owned the land called Australia.

By the 1970s, this uncertainty had worked its way into even mainstream books that did not aspire to take the Indigenous question into account. Although the 1977 publication of Colleen McCullough's *The Thorn Birds* could have been said to augur the more propitious climate in publishing Australian novels in the USA that led to the high-cultural break-through of Peter Carey in the next decade, there has always been embarrassment, in the USA and sometimes elsewhere, about including McCullough in the Australian canon.[34] Examining *The Thorn Birds* in light of this increasingly shaky sense of landed reassurance, however, can be productive. Whereas there will always be a Mason in Thwaites' Nullabean, at McCullough's Drogheda there will not always be a Cleary. The novel ends with the descendants of the Cleary family renouncing their Drogheda estate in western New South Wales. McCullough presents a parable in which white settlers' relation to the land begins in vainglory and ends in futile consolation; in its view of the land, the book is more reminiscent of Faulkner's vision of the American South in *Absalom! Absalom!* than of earlier middlebrow reassurances such as Thwaites'.

No sales would have been lost had McCullough opted for a hearty, there-will-always-be-Clearys-in-Drogheda ending, but instead she went for a bittersweet and melancholy note, providing an early portent of the more self-aware melancholy to be found after *Mabo*. Drogheda – an Irish name meaning "bridge of the ford", epitomising the idea of the transference of European title to Australia – fails. Although Germaine Greer is right to say the novel has "dated horribly" in only making one mention of "half-caste aboriginals",[35] it does metonymically imbibe a sense of the fragility of white claims. It is also infused with a sense

30   Martin Harrison, "Breakfast", Poetry International Rotterdam, www.poetryinternationalweb.net/pi/site/poem/item/786.

31   Bill Gammage, *The Biggest Estate on Earth: How Aborigines Made Australia* (Crows Nest: Allen & Unwin, 2013).

32   Marcia Langton, 2012 Boyer Lectures, *The Quiet Revolution: Indigenous People and the Resources Boom*, November–December 2012. http://www.abc.net.au/radionational/programs/boyerlectures/2012-boyer-lectures/4305696.

33   Philip Mead, "Alexis Wright's Fiction and Sovereignty of the Mind", paper presented at the 2015 Modern Language Association of America Convention, Vancouver, 10 January 2015.

34   Colleen McCullough, *The Thorn Birds* (New York: Harper & Row, 1977).

35   Germaine Greer, "Old Flames: Rereading *The Thorn Birds*", *Guardian*, 10 August 2007. http://theguardian.com/books/2007/aug/11/featuresreviews.guardianreview21.

of melancholy, as instanced in the very image of the self-impaling, titular thorn birds, who after impaling themselves sing beautifully until they die: an early symptom of a diminished white cultural arrogance. So is the character of the Catholic priest, Ralph De Bricassart, who can only reproduce illegitimately and *sub rosa*, perhaps implying that any white possession of the land will never have full formal title. Middlebrow *The Thorn Birds* may have been, but it told a sadder story with regard to whites on the land than many highbrow successes of the next decade. Indeed, the fate of the Clearys foreshadows that of the Bigges of Ranna Station in Alex Miller's *Journey to the Stone Country*; both books describe a formerly dominant white family now wiped out from the land. If there are few direct references to Aborigines in *The Thorn Birds*, there is a resonant sense of the fragility and perishability of settler claims to the land.

Of the Australian books that made it big abroad in the twenty years after *The Thorn Birds*, only *Remembering Babylon* had similar resonance with respect to ideas of whites on the land, although the sales of Malouf's novel, for all its acclaim, were much smaller. Other books tracing the erosion of white entitlement to the land received less notice. John Hooker's *Beyond the Pale* (1998) depicts the British aristocracy's victimisation of Irish working-class settlers who in turn victimise Aborigines, passing on brutality in an endless cycle. The bleak despair of this cycle provides little reassurance, and thus Hooker's fierce and original book proved totally unremarked-upon. David Ireland's *Burn* (1974), featuring the rage against the system of a half-Aboriginal man, is also pertinent here. The last novel by the underrated Elizabeth O'Conner, *Spirit Man* (1980), echoed McCullough's sense of the fragility of white land claims while introducing Aboriginal characters of various dispositions who give a vivid indication of Indigenous presence on the land. But this book did not do well even within Australia and was unheard of abroad.

By the late 1990s, the international viability of the Australian blockbuster of the land was gone. Bryce Courtenay, for example, wrote huge bestsellers throughout the 1990s and 2000s, mainly set in the Australian landscape with big plots and compelling themes of hope and loss. But the only book of his ever published in North America was *The Power of One* (1989), a book set in Courtenay's native South Africa that gained success through word-of-mouth and through its inclusion on high-school reading lists, rather than through reviews in highbrow periodicals. Although Courtenay did mention Indigenous Australians in his books, particularly in *Jessica* (1998), by the 1990s international readers were more alert to the frailty of white land claims.

A faint vestige of the traditional blockbuster of the land was seen perhaps in the success of a book such as Bail's *Eucalyptus*, a far more filtered and artistically conscious novel, or of the decidedly pre-*Mabo* approach to the land of Robyn Davidson's feminist outback travelogue *Tracks* (1980). The latter was described by Paul Sharrad as "complicit" with hegemonic colonialism, but nonetheless paraded its "struggles" with it.[36] After *Mabo*, however, any complicity, even a complicity as self-aware as Davidson's, had little high-cultural cachet. The land could no longer be a sanctuary for white Australian writers.

---

36   Paul Sharrad, "The Post-Colonial Gesture", in *A Talent(ed) Digger*, ed. Hena Maes-Jelinek, Gordon Collier and Geoffrey V. Davis (Amsterdam: Rodopi, 1996), 137.

Something Going to Be Made True: The Novelists of Concern

Kate Grenville is the best-known contemporary Australian novelist of concern worldwide. Grenville emerged in the 1980s with *Lilian's Story* (1985), which told the story of a young girl victimised by her abusive father. *Joan Makes History* (1988) gave the first sign of Grenville's interest in a more ambitious purview, as it spanned many years in the long life of a twentieth-century woman and highlighted the ability of the individual, even the inconspicuous one, to mean, historically. *Dark Places* (1994), published as *Albion's Story* in the USA, delved into the point of view of Lilian's abusive father. The change of title for the American edition was of note, as its foregrounding of a character already known from the previous novel signified that Grenville had a high enough profile in the USA for her books to be marketable to a defined audience, one that saw Grenville primarily as a feminist author.

The Idea of Perfection (1999) was a transitional book for Grenville's career: more philosophical, even tendentious, and also more situated within the local and Australian. Like David Ireland's *The Chosen*, it uses Australian small-town life in a way that is both parabolic and representative. It was with this book that Grenville crossed the boundary between "writer *from* Australia" to "writer *of* Australia". In *The Secret River* (2005) Grenville began her historical Thornhill trilogy, concerned with the first decades of contact between settlers and Indigenous Australians.[37] Notably, as in the cases of Jones and Miller, an interest in what I am calling concern surfaced in the second half of Grenville's career, after she had established herself as a notable world writer. Cultural changes were one reason for this. But another may be that concern, with its reflectiveness and its sense of social interaction, seems to be an affect that surfaces later in a writer's career, when she or he is no longer functioning, in Pierre Bourdieu's terms, as an oblate trying to enter the cultural (and, in the case of Australian writers, often the world-cultural) system, and can focus instead on matters and destinies that are not merely personal but suprapersonal – or matters, in Keneally's wise words, that fail to be separate.

If Carey's *Oscar and Lucinda* launched the first stage of the contemporary Australian historical novel – although its genealogy went back to Patrick White's *A Fringe of Leaves*, if not to *Voss*, and included Randolph Stow's *A Haunted Land* (1956), Jessica Anderson's *The Commandant* (1975) and many novels by Thomas Keneally – it was Kate Grenville's *The Secret River* that launched its second. This stage dealt centrally with Indigenous issues, in ways that White's and Carey's novels had not, although they had included Aboriginal characters or references. It did not repeat Keneally's blunder (as he came to see it) of voicing an Aboriginal perspective: Grenville sees everything through the white characters' points of view, although she seeks to render those points of view problematic. The novel's protagonist, the frontier settler William Thornhill, has two choices as he tries to carve out the land around the Hawkesbury River for settlement: find a *modus vivendi* with the Darug people, or try to extirpate them. The fact that Grenville sketches out the first possibility – the fugitive hope of finding a state of coexistence – marked the breakthrough to this new stage of the historical novel: there was a substantial difference between the elegiac wish that "things might have been otherwise" in another major trilogy written by a white writer about early settlement, Eleanor Dark's *Timeless Land* books of the 1940s, and Grenville's sense of a real possibility of active acknowledgement and interchange between two peoples.

37　Kate Grenville, *The Secret River* (New York: Canongate, 2007).

In the trilogy's next instalment, *The Lieutenant* (2008), set twenty years earlier and only tenuously linked to the other two books, Grenville provides a mode of cultural encounter that has less to do with the usual premises for interchange – war, sex, territory – but is conducted on the level of language and abstract knowledge.[38] The Marine Lieutenant Daniel Rooke (Grenville's fictionalisation of the real William Dawes) embarks with the First Fleet in 1787 and ends up serving as an interpreter as he begins to comprehend the Eora language, as taught to him by the Eora girl Tagaran.

As opposed to the real-life relationship between Dawes and the young Eora woman Patyegarang, who was fifteen years old and whose age led to (uncorroborated) speculation about a sexual relationship, Grenville makes the girl younger and rules out sex as a motive so she can more purely isolate the idea of concern: that is, of cross-cultural understanding conducted for its own sake. This agenda is unapologetically reformist; as Sue Kossew puts it, Grenville wishes "to take the reader out of his/her comfort zone and into a new, uncomfortable space" that can operate as a "way of challenging set ideas and beliefs".[39]

This tendency is liable to be attacked by those who see it as condescending. Grenville attracted criticism not only from the right but also from members of the public intelligentsia such as Inga Clendennin, who criticised the assumption that fictional deviations from history could either improve or testify to the historical record, and from influential Indigenous scholars such as Jeanine Leane (to whose critiques I will return). The historian John Hirst sees Grenville's stance as exemplary of "the liberal imagination", which "does not believe in savagery".[40] In Hirst's reading, the fact that Aborigines are not portrayed as violent reveals a Rousseauistic assumption about the nobility of the "state of nature". Hirst depicts Grenville as a sentimental liberal apologist, perhaps more or less a version of the American novelist Barbara Kingsolver: a writer popular among well-intentioned whites, especially women, for evocations of cultural difference that are at once reparative and anodyne. Such depictions offer, in the philosopher Ruwen Ogien's phrase, "non-controversial conceptions of the good life".[41] On the other hand, however, there is a family resemblance between Grenville's historical trilogy and Kingsolver's work. Grenville is a more literary writer, but her work does, in its sinews, take on some of the issues raised by Hirst.

One could also point out, in response to Hirst's criticism, without sanctifying Indigenous people or denying that they committed violence, that not only were the whites indisputably the aggressors in a strategic sense, but also that anthropologists such as Pierre Clastres have observed differences between statist and non-statist societies. It is not simply a question of indigenous vs non-indigenous peoples: Clastres and others have identified "statist" indigenous societies in the Americas (for example, the Incas) whose state practices were similar to those of European and Asian empires.[42] In Maurice Shadbolt's trilogy about the Māori wars in New Zealand, the Māori are depicted as warriors who wield structures of power and domination in their own defence. Although Australian Aboriginal society was complex, such structures of domination were largely absent. This is not to say that

---

38   Kate Grenville, *The Lieutenant* (New York: Atlantic Monthly Press, 2009).

39   Sue Kossew, *Lighting Dark Places: Essays on Kate Grenville* (Amsterdam: Rodopi, 2010), vii.

40   John Hirst, *Sense and Nonsense in Australian History* (Melbourne: Black Inc., 2009), 86–87.

41   Ogien, in Merrill and Veinstock, *Political Neutrality*, 97.

42   Pierre Clastres, *Society Against the State: Essays in Political Anthropology*, trans. Robert Hurley with Abe Stein (New York: Zone Books, 1989).

Aboriginal people committed no acts of violence, but that they did not have access to state power structures of the sort wielded by the white colonists.

Given the reality of racism and white privilege in Australia, Hirst's insistence on moral equivalence between white and Aboriginal violence seems disingenuous. But the larger issue is that writers of concern have to risk being anodyne or hypocritical. There is always the danger of being judged inauthentic. Rooke's relationship with Tagaran in *The Lieutenant* is tentative, distant, marked by politesse and decorum; they maintain the tactful and respectful distance of academic colleagues, not the heedlessness of unfettered personal encounter. There is also Grenville's temporal distance from her characters; inevitably, she brings to bear a twenty-first-century affect. A similar gap existed between Patrick White and his character Voss, who was based on the explorer Ludwig Leichhardt. Patrick White was a twentieth-century Australian, Cambridge-educated, upper-class, and gay. Ludwig Leichhardt was a nineteenth-century rough-and-tumble German heterosexual who lived a life of action, not of thought. How, we might ask, could White possibly portray such a man?[43] If we grant White aesthetic licence to do so, why not grant the same licence to Grenville? Is the difference that some of her characters are Aboriginal – should Indigenous characters be off-limits for any imaginative representation by white writers? It may well be Hirst, rather than Grenville, who is making an exception for Aborigines. In imagining the early years of contact between British and Indigenous peoples, Grenville might be seen as asserting her right to try to understand, and to possibly get things wrong in the process.

This sense of inviolable intercultural curiosity, even if it is a tentative, unobtainable ideal, suffuses *The Lieutenant*. Rooke's cognitive quest is epistemic as well as affective, knowing as well as feeling. Concern strives to disenthrall human relationships from the customary grooves of power, greed and possession, and to put them on a more abstract level. At the end of Malouf's *Remembering Babylon*, it is not just that the whites who have met Gemmy have been transformed, but that the whites' nature has been transformed, and taken out of conventional heterosexual relationships. Malouf casts a slightly queer light here whereas Grenville, in *The Lieutenant*, keeps sex out of the relationship so as not to trivialise it, while Miller, in *Journey to the Stone Country*, takes the dynamics of an erotic energy and makes them concomitant with debates about acknowledgement and recognition. Concern is all about, as Honneth's relational turn suggests, broadening erotic energies into a larger affective realm of care and mutual knowledge.[44]

The third book of Grenville's trilogy, *Sarah Thornhill* (2012), concentrating on William's daughter, returns to the Hawkesbury and examines how traumatic events have consequences in the next generation.[45] *Sarah Thornhill* has been sharply questioned by Jeanine Leane for its sentimental glossiness, its "colonial affluence", and its sense of the Indigenous issue as merely a place for well-minded whites to show their liberality, without fully acknowledging the deep existential pain and loss suffered by the Indigenous people.[46] In owning up to the past, Leane asks, are whites merely attempting to appropriate it, or

---

43   John Beston states that White is not "much interested in the geographical exploration of the Australian interior" but nonetheless White does represent it. See Beston, *Patrick White within the Western Literary Tradition* (Sydney: Sydney University Press, 2010), 242.

44   Honneth, *The Struggle for Recognition*.

45   Kate Grenville, *Sarah Thornhill* (New York: Grove Press, 2012).

46   Jeanine Leane, "Tracking Our Country in Settler Literature", *Journal of the Association for the Study of Australian Literature (JASAL)* 14, no. 3 (2014). http://openjournals.library.usyd.edu.au/index.php/JASAL/article/view/10039.

to re-annex by contrition what was first attempted by armed aggression? Leane's critique is couched not in terms of historical accuracy, but of rival affect – she substitutes loss and rage for plangent attempts at understanding. Clendinnen, who was more critical of Grenville for deviating from history than for being racially utopian, also saw Grenville's work as potentially too pessimistic about history's ability to construct the past in a determinate and documentable fashion.

Grenville's novels are in many ways the fictional enactment of what Bain Attwood calls the "Aboriginal turn" in Australian historical studies.[47] Attwood characterised the Aboriginal turn as bringing into focus "the burden of the Aboriginal past for the Australian present".[48] The Aboriginal turn, however, quickly received a more colloquial name in the media: "black-armband" history (as Geoffrey Blainey first called it). Debates about Indigenous history dominated the culture sections of the broadsheet Australian press in the 1990s and 2000s. In one of the most dispassionate academic accounts of the controversy, Patrick Brantlinger quoted newspaper columnist Greg Sheridan as criticising the "moral and linguistic overkill" of "left-wing" historians.[49] Black-armband history was decried for its racial critique and its questioning of white ownership of Australia. As Brantlinger puts it, the black-armband debate had potential "legal and political outcomes". It was not just academic rhetoric.

Grenville's willingness to look at the unresolved fissures in the past told the reader that history was not a process that could culminate or be resolved in the present. This nuance features in *Sarah Thornhill*, a book in which a conventional love plot is redefined in light of awareness of the moral lapse of colonisation. This pattern, of melding the social and psychological in a broader canvas of, in Honneth's terms, "recognition", is a practice also participated in by Grenville's fellow novelists of concern, Gail Jones and Alex Miller.

All this tended to be lost in the noisy debate over Grenville's work. The initial *Secret River* controversy provided a fillip to a debate about "black-armband" history that had been underway since the publication of Keith Windschuttle's *The Fabrication of Aboriginal History, Volume One* (2002).[50] This in turn stemmed from debates that had begun with the *Mabo* decision ten years earlier. Technological changes also played a role: as McKenzie Wark has asserted, the early years of the internet saw an eruption of controversies that at once demonstrated the vitality of the online media sphere as an arena of debate and reaffirmed the idea of an Australian national space, however virtual.[51] Indeed, the era of the black-armband debates was, technologically speaking, a borderline one, as it saw both the early abundance of internet reading – and the quantum increase in the audience for Australian debates abroad – as well as perhaps the last years of a robust broadsheet weekend-supplement culture. Ironically, a white Australian hegemony whose arrival on

---

47 Bain Attwood, *Telling the Truth about Aboriginal History* (Crows Nest: Allen & Unwin, 2005), 18.
48 Attwood, *Telling the Truth*, 19.
49 Patrick Brantlinger, "'Black Armband' versus 'White Blindfold' History in Australia", *Victorian Studies* 46, no. 4 (2004): 655–74.
50 Keith Windschuttle, *The Fabrication of Aboriginal History Volume One: Van Diemens Land, 1803–1847* (Sydney: Macleay Press, 2002). Windschuttle's title echoed the subtitle of the first book of Martin Bernal's *Black Athena* trilogy, *The Fabrication of Ancient Greece 1785–1985* (New Brunswick: Rutgers University Press, 1987). It is doubtful Windschuttle, a staunch defender of the West, would sympathise with Bernal's contention that ancient Greece owed much to the anterior achievements of Egypt and Phoenicia.
51 McKenzie Wark, *The Virtual Republic* (Crows Nest: Allen & Unwin, 1997).

the continent had been accompanied by print culture began to unwind in print culture's apparent last period of glory. Grenville's novels came into this discursive field, determined not only by redefinitions of Australian racial identity but by the new discursivity of the internet. As Brigid Rooney asserts, *The Secret River* was received as "an intervention in contemporary debates about Australia's past".[52] Rooney observes that Inga Clendinnen, who famously excoriated the novel, was at first sympathetic to it, but altered her position after the media debate was well underway. These debates often had their own logic, and carried their participants in their train.

These debates were catalysed by the transitional media space of the early 2000s. In the 1970s, cultural debates might be aired in newspapers, but they were unlikely to spread further. Both in Australia and elsewhere, national radio and television networks were designed to address a broad, not necessarily university-educated, public. The spread of the internet in the 1990s allowed a more self-selecting and consciously intellectual quotient of this larger public to tune in to these debates, as Wark suggests. Although they flourished on the internet, however, these debates originated in broadsheet newspapers and print quarterlies. There was a combination of the emergent and the residual in this era, the cutting-edge and the vestigial, which maximised the impact of cultural news. Furthermore, there was a sense of crisis: intellectual stances seemed up in the air in the 1990s, following the fall of the USSR. Meanwhile, the rise of multiculturalism, challenges to traditional gender roles, and, in Australia, Indigenous rights, provided new challenges to a white-dominated consensus. By the mid-2010s, with the very survival of newspapers in peril, the further fragmentation of the reading public, and the personalisation of cyberspace, Wark's "vernacular republic" was splintered. But during that transitional phase of the 1990s and 2000s, these cultural debates could be fruitfully disseminated both in print and on screen.

Similarly, Grenville's trilogy still inhabited what Rooney has described as an "aesthetically conventional" novelistic form.[53] This conventionalism expedites Grenville's affective concern even while fastening it to palatable narrative patterns, and thus is privileged. A similar issue affects Andrew McGahan's *The White Earth* (2004), a book at once about the discovery of Indigenous remains and a story of a young boy growing up. McGahan's book, despite its excursions into what Ken Gelder has termed "the postcolonial Gothic", feels the pressure of integrating Indigenous-related material with customary narrative form.[54] It is hard to rid ameliorative assumptions, no matter how revisionary, of their association with colonial settlement. The coming-of-age novel is too tied into imperial entelechies of betterment to operate as a capacious mode of critique, as welcome as McGahan's attention to the issue of land rights was.[55]

---

52   Brigid Rooney, "Kate Grenville as Public Intellectual", in *Lighting Dark Places: Essays on Kate Grenville*, ed. Sue Kossew (Amsterdam: Rodopi, 2010), 29.
53   Rooney, "Kate Grenville as Public Intellectual", 27.
54   Andrew McGahan, *The White Earth* (New York: Soho Press, 2006); Ken Gelder, "The Postcolonial Gothic", in *The Cambridge Companion to the Modern Gothic*, ed. Jerrold Hogle (Cambridge: Cambridge University Press, 2014), 203–05.
55   See Helen Gilbert and Chris Tiffin, eds., *Burden or Benefit: The Legacies of Benevolence* (Bloomington: Indiana University Press, 2008) for more on the residue of imperial "benevolence". "Benevolence" is something of a cognate term to "concern" as it is used in this volume, although concern is as much a part of a potential solution as it is a part of the problem.

Gail Jones, by contrast, came to the subject of concern as a consciously experimental writer, and also as a literary academic with a theoretical perspective on her own writing and that of others. Jones, born in 1955, grew up and made her early career in Western Australia. She started as a writer of metaphysical short stories, published in the collections *The House of Breathing* (1992) and *Fetish Lives* (1997), that were influenced by her wide reading in feminist and poststructuralist theory as well as in the Anglophone and Western canons. In the 2000s she turned to the novel and was published internationally. From *Black Mirror* (2002) through *Sixty Lights* (2004) and *Dreams of Speaking* (2006), a series of *récits* established Jones as a major Australian novelist. Although they were challenging in form and mode, they were less overtly academic than Jones' short stories, deftly communicating to the reader through limpid implication. They took on transnational, and, in the case of *Sixty Lights*, historical subject matter, and also, like much of Alex Miller's work, dealt with artists and the making of art. *Sorry* (2007) and *Five Bells* (2011), books Jones published after she moved to Australia's east coast to take up a chair at the University of Western Sydney, received international acclaim and found their way onto numerous academic syllabi.

Jones is more interested in our grasp of the material than what the material actually is. Perception matters to Jones as much as cognition, the abstract as much as, or more than, the concrete. Jones is not primarily a political or social novelist, which makes her forays into those areas all the more original and captivating. The very title of *Sorry*, which foreshadowed Prime Minister Kevin Rudd's apology to the Stolen Generations in 2008, performs a complex gesture of reparation (as did the title of the 1997 *Bringing Them Home* report), one which goes beyond novelistic closure. There has always been a sense that the accommodation of indigeneity in the Anglophone novel is a formal, not just thematic, problem: that the novel is so rooted in certain assumptions about land and society that it is incapable of incorporating Indigenous ways of thinking.

Jones' heroine is named Perdita Keene and the imagery of Shakespeare's late plays, with their sense of reparation and community renewal, pervades the novel.[56] Notably, however, it is her mother, Stella, whose denial of the truth represents white Australia's customary "white blindfold" attitude towards Aboriginal issues, and whose recurrent motif of "snow falling softly in the desert" represents white cultural arrogance, who is preoccupied with Shakespeare (19). While *Sorry* enacts late-Shakespearean patterns of recognition and forgiveness, it delinks them from a veneration of Shakespeare, which in this context has the danger of bolstering white self-importance. Thus Shakespearean patterns are at once jettisoned on one level and reaffirmed on the other. Jones' novel involves not only the exoneration of Mary's Aboriginal father as the killer of Stella's, but the recognition that Stella's father, an anthropologist studying Aboriginal life, committed sexual abuse against Mary. The family legend that for Perdita has been a source of identity is poisoned at the source. Indicatively, Western knowledge of Indigenous people, so often culturally mediated through anthropologists, is rotten at the core.

Jones is not indicting all Australian anthropologists, but calling into question previous knowledge, both academic and literary, of the Indigenous: she implies that anthropologists have presumed a virtue they have not earned and do not possess. Thus the novel moves beyond a benign and bland cultural recognition, and beyond a rhetorical guilt (which is ultimately self-affirming and self-congratulatory) to a much more pervasive culpability. If, as

---

56   Gail Jones, *Sorry* (New York: Europa Editions, 2008). All subsequent references are to this edition and appear in parentheses in the text.

Michele McCrea argues, *Sorry* conducts Perdita "from trauma to recovery and from forgetting to remembrance and responsibility", it does so with an acknowledgement of the moral costs that have been incurred.[57] Jones recognises that forgiveness can only be achieved in a projected future, a future that the novel has, it is to be hoped, done its small bit to create.

In an interview with Maria del Pilar Royo Grasa, Jones spoke of the affinity she sees between the production of art – not just her own, but also Indigenous art – and the politics of hope. She expressed a sense that a given body of work is not just valuable in itself, but for the possibility of survival it projects.[58] The poetics of respite that Jones espouses (one thinks in particular of the two "political" characters in *Five Bells*, Catherine and Pei Xing) are not only about healing specific personal injuries or political fissures; they are engaged in an ongoing project of concern. The role of disability in the novel – as exemplified by the deaf and mute Billy Trevor – recalls that of the mute Decima James in Janet Frame's *The Carpathians* (1988); in both novels, portraits of characters who are deprived of conventional communication are used to testify for those generally objectified by conventional, dominant modes of representation.

But generalised goodwill alone will not do the job. Only by acknowledging the depth of guilt can this novel, or any novel, do more than merely say "sorry". Nishant Shahani has spoken of "the politics of reparative return", as part of which a critique (in Shahani's examples, a queer critique) deliberately returns to an origin it knows is brutal and traumatic in order consciously to politicise its present moment.[59] This dark, complicit return, rather than a pastoral sprucing-up of history, is what unfolds in *Sorry*. The novel remains in a self-assigned limbo: it knows it cannot possibly repair the sufferings it has evoked, yet it tries to do as much as it can, through a subtle form of social critique. As Jones reveals in her essay "Sorry-in-the-Sky", she participated in the May 2000 March for Reconciliation across Sydney Harbour Bridge, and the novel *Sorry* is for her a "form of activism". Necessarily, it is indirect, subterranean, tacit rather than focal, told, as Perdita Keene says, "only in a whisper" (3).

Indeed, one of the great appeals, and yet perhaps the most vexatious feature, of concern is its vagueness, its inexactitude. Jones is herself aware of the potential pitfalls of imprecision, which is why she prefers the historically specific trauma theory of Dominick LaCapra to more generalised deconstructive models privileging a more vague disruption and difference; Marc Delrez adduces the trauma theory of Cathy Caruth as an example of the latter, vaguer model.[60] Concern may try to be historical in its account of what it seeks to redress, yet its resulting initiatives are condemned to be inchoate. Concern may forsake the grand syntheses of Enlightenment settler knowledge, but it does not replace them with an alternative analytic precision.

---

57 Michele McCrea, "Collisions of Authority: Nonunitary Narration and Textual Authority in Gail Jones' *Sorry*", in Cassandra Atherton, Rhonda Dredge et al., eds., *The Encounters: Place, Situation, Context Papers – Refereed Proceedings of the 17th Conference of the Australasian Association of Writing Programs* (Canberra: The Australasian Association of Writing Programs, 2012), 2.

58 Maria del Pilar Royo Grasa, "In Conversation with Gail Jones", *JASAL* 12, no. 3 (2012). http://openjournals.library.usyd.edu.au/index.php/JASAL/article/view/9828.

59 Nishant Shahani, *Queer Retrosexualities: The Politics of Reparative Return* (Bethlehem: Lehigh University Press, 2012).

60 Marc Delrez, "Fearful Symmetries: Trauma and 'Settler Envy' in Contemporary Australian Culture", *Miscelánea: A Journal of English and American Studies* 42 (2010): 51–65.

In Keneally's words, concern fails to be separate, even if it renounces a Eurocentric synthesis. Thus it can provide neither an overall grand theory nor a graspable policy solution. It is general, conceptual, influenced by the fluidities and conjectures of the "soft sciences": sociology, anthropology and humanistic psychology, with which its intellectual sources are so intimately, if ambiguously (as shown in the mostly negative sense of anthropology as depicted in *Sorry*), connected. The vagueness of the soft sciences is illuminated by Foucault, in the final section of *The Order of Things*, when he speaks of how the human sciences are bounded by the hard, evidence-based facts of biology and economics but never actually dwell in these fields. Instead, they eddy around helter-skelter in their bounded interrelation.[61] In the novels of Australian concern, this social-scientific vagueness is pulled even further away from the calculable by affect: by grief, shame, repentance, and a sympathy that will always be too belated.

Perdita herself realises that she should have said sorry to Mary much earlier, and that by the time she feels the need to say it, the apology has become stale and superfluous, its enunciation archaic. Something has unquestionably been lost: the prescriptiveness that, say, Keneally felt he could give in his account of Africa, the sense that a particular person or party has the potential to "cure" history, is not available to Jones. No policy prescriptions about how to improve the lives of today's Indigenous people can emerge from Jones' book. The wounds she foregrounds cannot be healed overnight by fiat, repentance or pardon.

Even Jones' exacting self-scrutiny has perils. There is always the danger of bad faith in concern. Les Murray, in his summarising end-of-century verse novel *Fredy Neptune*, enjoins:

> Forgive the Aborigines. *What have I got to forgive?*
> They never hurt me! *For being on our conscience.*[62]

This implies that white concern can become a self-expiating preoccupation, and that people saying "sorry" to the Aborigines in fact resent them for being on white Australians' conscience. But, even if we take Murray's deftly made point, injustices have still been done to Australia's Indigenous people, and literature is not ill motivated in trying to take a leading role in addressing them.

Alex Miller: Landscapes of Concern

In his late-career emergence, Alex Miller resembles such classic novelists as Defoe, Miguel de Cervantes, Theodor Fontane and, more recently, as discussed in Chapter 1, the crop of Australian women writers who emerged in midlife in the 1970s and 1980s.[63] Born in 1936, he published his first novel only in 1988, and made his breakthrough with 1992's *The*

---

61   Michel Foucault, *The Order of Things: An Archaeology of the Human Sciences* (New York: Vintage Books, 1984), 384.
62   Les Murray, *Fredy Neptune* (New York: Farrar, Straus, & Giroux, 2000), 274.
63   Miller playfully gives his late emergence over to Annabelle Küen's shallow husband Steven in *Journey to the Stone Country*, an example of the many inside jokes and self-underminings that make Miller's books so much more than they at first seem.

Ancestor Game, one of the first serious novels to depict Chinese–Australian affective relations and the Chinese experience in Australia. His major sequence, however, can be said to have started even later, with 2000's *Conditions of Faith*. From this novel through 2013's *Coal Creek*, Miller has written a series of artistically self-conscious books that meditate on the legacies of totalitarianism in Europe, the experience of subaltern and colonised peoples, and on the moral consequences of whites' violence towards Indigenous Australians. (As of 2015, Miller was doing research for a new novel set partially in Poland.)

Miller's novels from 2000 to 2013 – *Journey to the Stone Country, Landscape of Farewell, Conditions of Faith, Prochownik's Dream, Lovesong, Autumn Laing* and *Coal Creek* – have been exacting in their awareness of the limits of representation.[64] They exemplify how ideas of concern challenge comfortable attitudes about the nature and mission of fiction. *Journey to the Stone Country*, the highly personal love story of Bo Rennie and Annabelle Beck, is modelled on real individuals and on the experience of the Jangga people in central Queensland. Miller has explicitly acknowledged the real identities of the individuals involved – notable both because one of them is Indigenous and also because of the intimate and personal nature of the story. This is necessarily more confrontational to the reader than the traditional novelistic contract to which most readers are accustomed, which tells the reader that the novel will deal with personal emotions without naming the real individuals who are the sources for those emotions.

Journey to the Stone Country suggests that fiction must acknowledge what Miller calls, with respect to his aims in *Landscapes of Farewell*, "the persistence of violence in human history".[65] This can be seen in *Lovesong*, in which the author-figure, Ken, listens to a story of love and loss among members of the Maghreb diaspora in France, as told to him by a man named John Patterner – a name that is an obvious nod to the idea of the writer as someone who patterns other people's stories and melds them into shape. But Ken too is a "patterner"; he moulds the story to suit his own narrative ends. John Patterner, indeed, is the novel's source of agency, someone who alters his life by marrying the North African woman Sabiha and helping her and her family to run a bakery in Paris.[66] Niki Tulk has suggested that in Miller's fiction, the agency of his characters is sacrificed to "the agency of the storyteller".[67] In fact, Miller reverses two customary ideas about narrative. First, he subverts the idea that the narrative consciousness patterns material reality, and thus is privileged over that reality. Second, Miller upends the Eurocentric assumption that the non-European provides the content, but the European provides the form. It is the European, Patterner, who provides the content; form yields to content and white privilege is, in a sense, ceded, even if not entirely. In foregrounding Ken's retelling of Patterner's story, Miller is not pursuing narrative intricacy or authorial self-consciousness for its own sake, but because people's stories, real or fictional, require permission to be used. Miller acknowledges the dynamic relation of his fiction to its material sources and insists on both the ethical and artistic dimensions of this awareness. What Robert Dixon calls the danger of "easy harmonisation" is avoided.[68]

---

64 Robert Dixon, ed., *The Novels of Alex Miller* (Crows Nest: Allen & Unwin, 2012), 2.

65 Quoted in Robert Dixon, *Alex Miller: The Ruin of Time* (Sydney: Sydney University Press, 2014), 96.

66 Alex Miller, *Lovesong* (Sydney: Allen & Unwin, 2009).

67 Niki Tulk, "My Self, My Country: Robert Dixon's Critical Collection on the Works of Alex Miller", in *Reading across the Pacific* (blog of *Antipodes*), 9 April 2014. http://antipodesjournal.blogspot.com/2014/04/my-self-my-country-robert-dixons.html.

68 Dixon, *Alex Miller*, 100.

Indeed, Coetzee's reading of Tolstoy – prophetic but also hyper-self-conscious – could well be applied to Miller, and Brenda Walker has written compellingly of the Tolstoyan aspect of Miller's fiction.[69] Tolstoy took on, in works like *Hadji Murad*, representational and intercultural questions much like those explored in Miller's fiction. Miller is that rare novelist who believes both in art and in the novel's social mission. One could take up the subjects he has in a more Keneally-like style, as dispatches from the front, incidents of moral witness, but that would lose not just Miller's positive sense of art's capacity to heal wounds, but also his deeply earned sense of the costs of art, of the inevitable character flaws of the artist, of the way art cannot help but distort even as it enlivens.

Of the novels mentioned above, all but *The Ancestor Game* were written after Miller turned sixty. Like Grenville and Jones, he established himself as an acclaimed novelist before turning to matters of concern. Again, this might simply reflect a larger cultural shift towards reconciliation and Indigenous issues after *Mabo* and leading up to Sorry Day. But it might also reveal something about the individual trajectories of these three writers: perhaps concern is a mode for the second half of life, one that emerges in the careers of novelists after their initial literary reputation has been established. Similarly, David Malouf's *Remembering Babylon* moved into the area of concern when the author was approaching sixty. Concern is something one writes into, as it were, rather than writes out of; it is unfinished and self-questioning. Concern pertains not to something that has been true and needs to be expressed, but to something, in Frye's terms, that is "going to be made true" and needs to be striven towards, to be aesthetically "built" as Friedrich Schiller might say.[70] At times concern becomes a kind of being-towards-death: not a second-half-of-life question, but an end-of-life question. We see this in the resonant detail in Kim Scott's *That Deadman Dance* where Wunyeran and Dr Cross, a Noongar man and a white coloniser, establish a friendship based on intellectual affinity, and are, albeit temporarily, buried together. Concern is no country for young men, or young women. It is a product of reflection, retrospection, and even remorse.

In 2013, Alex Miller, in discussing the Australian government's refugee policy, lamented that the fair-minded, compassionate Australia he knew on arriving in Queensland at age sixteen no longer existed.[71] Miller worked as a young stockman in central Queensland in the late 1950s – he would come back to this material in fiction thirty years later, in *Watching the Climbers on the Mountain* (1988) – and became acquainted with the Australian rural working-class in a way Patrick White, who spent a "gap year" as a jackeroo, never was. By the time Miller wrote about this world, however, it was as distant from present-day Australia as were the European, Chinese and Indigenous heritages evoked in Miller's other novels. To write about "ordinary Australians", Miller has to go back in time, to the world he first knew as a migrant from England. This is the world Coetzee says he glimpsed when he arrived many years later, even as it was dying. Miller had a long incubation period as a writer. This late start may have unshackled him from the systemic expectations of what a novelist should do and given him the courage as a novelist to

---

69   Brenda Walker, "Alex Miller and Leo Tolstoy: Australian Storytelling in a European Tradition", in Dixon, ed., *The Novels of Alex Miller*, 42–54.

70   Friedrich Schiller, *On the Aesthetic Education of Man*, trans. Reginald Snell (New York: Dover Books, 2009).

71   Oliver Milman, "Novelist Alex Miller Attacks Australia's 'Cruel and Inhumane' Refugee Treatment", *Guardian Australia*, 27 December 2013. http://www.theguardian.com/world/2013/dec/27/novelist-attacks-cruel-refugee-treatment.

explore intercultural communication: the relationship between an Indigenous man and a white woman in *Journey to the Stone Country*; the relationship between a white man and an Arab woman in *Lovesong*; the depiction of Chinese immigration to Australia in *The Ancestor Game*; and the difficult attempts to render the experience of the visual artist in literary terms in *The Sitters, Prochownik's Dream* and Autumn Laing.

Miller might be criticised for exploring horizons of concern instead of addressing specific political issues. Again, one of concern's vexatious features is its vagueness, its cognitive haziness. But as we have seen with Keneally, there is a danger in hitching one's wagon to the star of a particular country or leader. If a writer puts his or her imaginative energies into endorsing a specific political cause, for better or for worse, he or she may be tainted by that cause. Moreover, even when the cause is morally justified by history – as was the case with Harriet Beecher Stowe's *Uncle Tom's Cabin* – the writer may still be dismissed as being merely a social campaigner rather than an artist. Miller's later works address issues of cultural difference and global inequality without tethering themselves to specific agendas. The writer thus protects both his political independence and the status of his work as self-conscious art.

In *Journey to the Stone Country*, Annabelle Beck is a recently separated middle-aged woman who returns from Melbourne, where she has spent her adulthood, to the central Queensland of her youth, a region scorned by her husband as "culturally a lost cause" and worthy of "no serious attention" (3040). The reader is set up for a story of an alienated urbanite returning to her home country and reclaiming it. But whose land is it, really? Once back in Queensland, Annabelle comes across Bo Rennie, an Aboriginal man whom she knew briefly in their youth, although they were never close friends. The affective tie between the two, however, is deep. Bo says to Annabelle, "We tumbled naked in the water together" (339). Annabelle then thinks that she knows the place and can picture them there together. The repaired or restored memory is secondary, but it also fills an emotional gap. Annabelle and Bo's ensuing love is an emotion at once newly kindled and rekindled. As Robert Dixon indicates, Annabelle's love for Bo is initially laden with exoticism, but this is purged as she comes to know him and his context better.[72] That this middle-aged love is not innocent of bad faith does not staunch its healing power. Equally, as per Axel Honneth's theory of recognition, Annabelle and Bo's love, although sexual, is not reductively libidinal. It opens out to a larger reach of affect; in articulating her feelings for Bo to herself, Annabelle thinks in terms of trust, respect and companionship as much as of the "body's message that love would work" (2512).

Annabelle wonders, when Bo first tells her that they knew each other in childhood, "Could his claim be true?" This claim to shared childhood turf morphs into a larger claim: an assertion of land ownership. While Annabelle's family and the neighbouring Bigges family premised their ownership of the land on the effacement of Indigenous people, Bo's white pastoralist grandfather married a "traditional Jangga woman". He fostered an inclusiveness and heterodoxy that was not only rare for the time but "exceptional" in comparison to Annabelle's conventional grandfather. Bo tells Annabelle, however, that "around Mount Coolon" most people acted in this inclusive, live-and-let-live spirit (340). As with Grenville's work, the reader might be tempted to cry anachronism here: our image of 1950s Queensland is not generally one of racial inclusion. But not only should we give Miller, who was actually there in the 1950s, some credence on this point, but also, more

---

72   Dixon, *Alex Miller*, 100.

importantly, the novel's role in this context is as much to herald what should be as to reflect an attested historical condition. Literature's power to bring hope stems from its being hypothetical; this necessarily involves the possibility that it be inauthentic. Concern, as a mode, risks anachronism and inauthenticity, as well as an overly diffuse general goodwill, in order to reimagine the present and provide alternative futures to those that may seem predestined or inevitable.

This does not mean that Miller is incapable of precision. Indeed, the topography of the book is not only beautifully rendered but precisely limned, from the verandah on Zamia Street in Townsville to the stations of Ranna, Verbena and Haddon Hill. Yet this locality does not imply an organic sense of the land. True, the stone country is Annabelle's mental recourse, a curative ground to which she returns sickened by the false relationships and meretricious trendiness of the city. Miller's novel might therefore seem a tale of pastoral redemption, of the rescue of the damsel in distress from the rapacious city by the timeless land. But Miller is, despite his love of character and landscape, a riddling and intricate chronicler. The book's references to Ludwig Leichhardt, metonymically pointing to the explorer's fictionalisation in *Voss*, acknowledge that the otherness of the Australian landscape has already been encountered by white writers. Miller's is a ruminated, twice-told tale. He does indeed see the land as a home for Annabelle that she lacked in the city; but he also sees it as a source of more material resources. Bo Rennie is involved in the negotiations for the use of the stone country on behalf of the Jangga people, and is not *a priori* opposed to development, although he is horrified by the way the land has been poisoned by previous exploiters. As if to dispel traditional associations of Indigenous people with antidevelopment ideology, Miller has Les Marra, a radical Indigenous activist, be the most vocal advocate for building a dam that would obliterate the Bigges family's Ranna Station.

Indeed, the Bigges family occupies the role ascribed to the Indigenous people in Dark's trilogy: they are a vanishing race, set to be obliterated like the Clearys of Drogheda in McCullough's *The Thorn Birds*. (This sense of the effacement of white settlement is also seen in the ghost town of Mount Coolon.) Unlike the Rennie family, who on their station, Verbena, envisaged the future "as a modest continuation of the past", the Bigges had hoped to spearhead "a landed dynasty according to the old model, a new European aristocracy of the Antipodes" (4548). The Bigges asserted not only control of the land but also sovereignty; they sought to enforce European hierarchies and precedents. In consequence, their estate crumbled. The Rennies, meanwhile, survived by keeping to a middle way, and by fostering a more inclusive relationship with the people of the land. Miller does not see a simple upending of European modes of sovereignty. His level of enthusiasm for Les Marra's activism is discreetly cool. For Miller, Indigenous and Western traditions are different from each other, but not radically so; the unread editions of Edward Gibbon on the shelves of the abandoned station are the white equivalents of Aboriginal memory. If Bo's people have an oracular "language of signs and silence" (1000), so did the ancient Greeks. In a hybrid world, it is hard to untangle tradition and modernity. However, what Bo and Annabelle end up seeking together, in all their compromised, weathered frailty, is a way of life in which recognition depends more on affect than on sovereignty.

If we need to speak in a new way, and the only language we know is the old language, how then may we speak? Ten years later Miller set another novel in central Queensland, this time focusing on a young white man, Bobby Blue. In *Coal Creek* (2013), Bobby Blue is framed and goes to prison for a crime he did not commit.[73] He loves Irie, the daughter of his employer, Daniel Collins, but she does not come to his defence even though she knows the truth. At the end of the novel, Bobby reconciles with Irie but comments, "I do not think that we could speak"; he feels an emotion, he says, "more than I can speak of" (291). In forgiving Irie yet struggling to articulate why, Bobby Blue embodies the major problems both of Australian literature in the first half of the twentieth century – how to speak as an Australian, as the inhabitant of an old land newly settled – and in more recent decades: how can the pain of others be acknowledged without merely buffeting ourselves? How can language be at once a medium for artistry and intricacy and a tool for restorative justice?

"Blue", short for Blewitt, perhaps denotes depression, as well as potentially a kind of primitivism. The character of Blue in Eve Langley's *The Pea-Pickers* (1942) – female yet cross-gendered, migratory yet associated with the land – may also inform the name here. Bobby Blue's stance in the face of his unjust imprisonment – stoic to the point not just of martyrdom but of stupidity – suggests a kind of inarticulacy born of oppression and relegation. When Prince Philip, consort of Queen Elizabeth II, visited Australia in 2002 on a royal tour, he asked if Indigenous people still threw spears at one another. An Australianist of my acquaintance remarked, waggishly, that the Indigenous individual so addressed should have retorted, "Do the British still paint themselves blue?" – garnishing oneself with woad dye having been a practice of the ancient Celts. All peoples, of whatever colour, have at one point in their histories been on the wrong side of cultural encounter, and so often, as in Conrad's *Heart of Darkness* or Clarke's *For the Term of His Natural Life*, references to the ancient Britons have been used to express the relativistic nature of all colonisation or ideas of racial hierarchy. Bobby Blue is white. He is not Indigenous. But as a convict he has, like Indigenous people, experienced a fundamental injustice. He is, as it were, rewarded for this suffering by being granted, by the author and by life, an undisturbed, harmonious relation to the land. At the book's end, Bobby and Irie are "going back to Mount Hay, where we belonged" (287). Bobby's white privilege has been abraded by his own disabilities and through suffering. This broadens the canvas of reconciliation – without denying the categorical difference between the collective victimisation of Indigenous people and that of individual whites – by making concern a hypothetical territory in which all manner of gaps and fissures in understanding transpire.

This is why concern is not just hypocritical white self-pity or a consummately acceptable sentimentalism. Concern can easily be a means of getting out of the predicament it at the same time expresses – as when Stella, the culpable character in *Sorry*, "enjoyed the concern she solicited" (59). Concern, to get out of this trap, has to examine itself meticulously. These novelists of concern distinguish themselves with the scrupulousness with which they all – whether or not they succeed – measure themselves and are aware of the protocols and pitfalls of writing about Indigenous issues. Earlier writers who described Indigenous characters, such as Eleanor Dark and Katharine Susannah Prichard (whose *Coonardoo* was published in 1929), were communists or communist sympathisers who were committed to a teleological view of world history spearheaded by a white power, the Soviet Union. Their accounts of Indigenous culture had a touch of the "vanishing Australia" motif about them.

Jones, in including Pei Xing, survivor of the Cultural Revolution, in *Five Bells*, and Miller, in featuring many refugees from communist countries as well as Australians who have become disillusioned with communism (such as Freddy in *Autumn Laing*), draw a clear distinction between critiques of existing Australian institutions and the grievances

---

73 Alex Miller, *Coal Creek* (Crows Nest: Allen & Unwin, 2013). All subsequent references are to this edition and appear in parentheses in the text.

once aired by communists and others. The leftists Dark and Prichard could assume either that a social safety net existed or that the advanced world was moving towards such a safety net. In the contemporary era, thanks to neoliberalism, a rhetoric of concern that might previously have been only ornamental has had to take up the slack.

Concern between Sacred and Secular

Not all articulations of concern are overtly spiritual, and none of the major white Australian writers of concern – Jones, Miller, Grenville, Malouf – seems particularly to espouse any form of transcendental belief. But concern has its rough equivalent in what Lyn McCredden, among others, has termed "the contemporary sacred": a sense that braids spiritual awareness with a radical reaching-out to the other.[74] McCredden's "contemporary sacred" nimbly circumvents the question of, which sacred? Is it a case of a genuine acknowledgement of Indigenous spirituality complementing traditional Christianity, as occurs in Les Murray's *Buladelah-Taree Holiday Song Cycle*? If, as Elaine Lindsay has argued, scholars have assumed that Australia is "embarrassed by discussion of religious and spiritual views",[75] is this silence somehow equivalent to the relative silence about Indigenous issues in mainstream Australian fiction before *Mabo*? If, as Michael Griffith has argued in his work on the mystical poet Francis Webb, there is a link between Webb's outsider status and his dynamic sense of the sacred, is to seek transcendence a form of rebellion against Australian conventionalities?[76] A radical Christianity exceeding the bounds of both secular progressivism and traditional liturgy, as in the poetry and criticism of Kevin Hart and his complicated engagement with ideas of "negative theology", or the eco-spirituality seen in the work of Judith Wright, John Kinsella and Oodgeroo Noonuccal, could both address this question.[77] McCredden's rendition of the sacred is thus not just a fetishisation of the Indigenous, not just Christianity by other means, but an intermediate, even synthetic compound. It is a sacred that does not insist on purity or organicism, which finds plenitude without needing that plenitude to be anchored in authenticity. In this respect, the almost inherent inauthenticity of concern, its tendency towards bad faith, can be an advantage. Concern makes no claim to total reparation or perfection; it knows that it cannot cure all the wounds it acknowledges, but it nevertheless hopes to treat them.

For concern, heterogeneity and imprecision become assets. Toby Davidson evokes this semi-curative imprecision in "Arrival of the Sunling":

> Little bird, where have you come from?
> Too buoyant for this mottled garden,

---

74   Lyn McCredden, *The Contemporary Sacred* (Adelaide: ATF Press, 2012).
75   Elaine Lindsay, *Rewriting God: Spirituality in Contemporary Australian Women's Fiction* (Amsterdam: Rodopi, 2009), 45.
76   Michael Griffith, *God's Fool: The Life and Poetry of Francis Webb* (Sydney: Angus & Robertson, 1981).
77   Kevin Hart, *The Trespass of the Sign* (New York: Fordham University Press, 2008).

> You must have escaped from a nearby commercial,
> picture perfect, digitally enhanced.
> But there was no hook, no spurious truncation,
> you just glowed ardent yellow[78]

It is not that the songbird is so beautiful as to assert its beauty over the country. It is that the dominant alternative to it seemed so overpowering, until the surprise the songbird represents. The rhetoric of concern often operates as a surprise: surprise that there is still another order of values out there to rival the flattening consensus of self-interest.

In another avian poem, "Black Swan", Davidson associates the distinctive bird of Western Australia with the beliefs of the Nyoongar people:

> *Drip lip-lap*, the salivary silk in flux and retroflex hushes me.
>
> If I actually knew anything about boating I'd tell you the knots of my head:
>
> forget-me-knot, knot natural, half-hitch,
>
> breath we're stitching from ancient infancy,
>
> lambent tapestry, aqua aplomb.
>
> Black cloud. Dear moon with her fragmented fan.[79]

The black swan is linked to the Indigenous idea of the Rainbow Serpent and to an overall sense of heightened perception as signalled by the assonance and paronomasia so abundant in Davidson's language. This is not simply consolation, but an attempt to braid awareness of indigeneity into a heightened understanding. Concern often sets out to be primarily perceptual: its intended work is not necessarily social work. Concern did not set out to be an alternative to neoliberalism, but it has had to assume that role for lack of a better option.

In *The Last Utopia*, Samuel Moyn argues that in the 1970s, progressive thinkers embraced the ideal of "human rights" simply because earlier social utopias had failed and human rights, as a principle, was sufficiently transcendental to fill the gap.[80] Although concern is quite different from human rights as a concept – it focuses on the viability of others, not on the inviolability of individuals – both involve a non-collectivist ideology in place of a collectivist one. The distinction is captured in Winton's *Eyrie* when Keely's post-industrial, ad hoc caring takes the place of his mother Doris' more purposive, late-modern altruism. Yet there are articulations of concern that are not necessarily spiritual, such as Alison Ravenscroft's in *The Postcolonial Eye*,[81] which combines a sense of attention to the integrity of Indigenous cognition and experience with a rigorous critique of spectatorial fetishes or illusions. Analogously, Jennifer Rutherford's *The Gauche Intruder* links a more inclusive moral sense to the attenuation of white privilege in Australia.[82]

---

78   Toby Davidson, *Beast Language* (Wollongong: Five Islands Press, 2013).
79   Davidson, *Beast Language*, 15.
80   Samuel Moyn, *The Last Utopia* (Cambridge: Harvard University Press, 2012).
81   Alison Ravenscroft, *The Postcolonial Eye: White Australian Desire and the Visual Field of Race* (Farnham: Ashgate, 2012).

Concern is so nebulous that it evades the inflexibility and paralysis of late modernity that abetted the rise of neoliberal individualism. In this, concern's ability to accommodate multiple levels of being is paramount. In allowing the contemporary world to register what McCredden calls "luminous moments", concern affirms that interpersonal regard does not have to be characterised by a culling of losers. The imprecision of concern is what enables its affect to unfold.

The Thanatopolitics of Concern: Aboriginal Writing into the Contemporary

Do Indigenous writers themselves explore themes of concern? Concern largely stems from liberal guilt, which in turn comes from white privilege. The writers I have discussed have meticulously tried to disassemble that privilege, but they have had to do that in a way Indigenous authors have not. Frye posited that concern provides a collective solution that lacks Marxist authoritarianism while broadening an ethics of care potentially comparable to that of psychoanalysis. Frye's criticism, however, espoused Jung rather than Freud, partially because Jung seemed to represent a more optimistic and autonomous role for the imagination. Australia's few Jungian-influenced thinkers – David Tacey paramount among them – have articulated a framework of anchored and sensible compassion that complements the reparative ethical aesthetic of writers such as Miller. Whites have had the privilege to be this meditative and reflective. Indigenous people have been in the direct path of racism and oppression. Much Aboriginal writing has of necessity been protest writing: Jack Davis, Oodgeroo, the early Archie Weller and the "Aboriginal" Mudrooroo. Protest literature, as in Davis' poem quoted in the previous chapter, is closer to the affect of rancour than of concern. Yet through the course of their oppression Indigenous Australians, in life and writing, have offered succour to others within and outside their community.

Mudrooroo was the least compromising of polemicists, and although in middle-period works such as *Us Mob* (1995) he seemed to espouse a non-essentialist basis for divisions between white and Indigenous, in general as an essayist he came not to bring peace but a sword. In the 1990s, partially due to the institution of the David Unaipon Award by the University of Queensland Press and the flourishing of Indigenous-run publishers such as Magabala Books, a far wider range of Indigenous writers began to be published, articulating a challenging variety of affects and priorities long present but relatively new to print culture.

Many novels of the 1990s and early 2000s by Indigenous writers, such as Melissa Lucashenko's *Steam Pigs* (1998) and Vivienne Cleven's *Bitin' Back* (2001), are close to the *Bildungsroman* genre, which with its emphasis on individual development precludes the idea of concern, as Gayatri Spivak demonstrates in her classic postcolonial reading of *Jane Eyre*.[83] This is so even if both of the books mentioned above are formally risky, and even though the identities of their protagonists are, as Jeanine Leane puts it, "fractured".[84] As Leane points out, in the Aboriginal *Bildungsroman* collective growth or enlargement

---

82   Jennifer Rutherford, *The Gauche Intruder: Freud, Lacan and the White Australia Fantasy* (Melbourne: Melbourne University Press, 2000).

83   Gayatri Chakravorty Spivak, "Three Women's Texts and a Critique of Imperialism", *Critical Inquiry* 12, no. 1 (Autumn 1985): 235–61.

sometimes lies beneath an individual story, as in John Muk Muk Burke's *Bridge of Triangles*.[85] The traditional *Bildungsroman* protagonist does not face a deep temporal reservoir of debilitating circumstance. But as Leane shows, in a novel such as Tara June Winch's *Swallow the Air* (2006), a protagonist ostensibly too young to have experienced the trauma of the Stolen Generations is nonetheless haunted by it.[86] In books such as these, the main tension is between self and other, whereas concern jettisons the very idea of self – which is why so many novels of concern are either ensemble novels or layered novels, in which one story subtends another. This is not to say that many Indigenous-authored narratives do not show solicitude of one person for another or for a community. Jackie Huggins' *Auntie Rita* (1996) is a consummate portrayal of relations of affection and dependence proceeding from altruism. Bill Neidjie's concern for Kakadu in the Northern Territory, as a lived space, as expressed in books like *Kakadu Man* (1985), is not just narrowly ecological but part of a broader human network of care and connection. Eric Willmot's *Pemulwuy: The Rainbow Warrior* (1989) is an exemplary portrait of altruism as a mode of leadership, as the early freedom fighter against white occupation of coastal New South Wales not only rallies disparate Aboriginal peoples to his cause but even persuades white convicts to join him. *Pemulwuy* indeed comes close to being a novel of concern simply because Pemulwuy has power, or, as a resistance leader, tries to arrogate power to himself. Power is a correlate and prerequisite of concern: if one is powerless, one has no leverage to care for others, a task at the heart of concern's mission.

There are indeed numerous instances of Indigenous characters in novels by Indigenous people caring, looking out for, or helping each other. To again adapt Leane's logic concerning the *Bildungsroman*, mere routine acts of care might be a great achievement for Indigenous people denied the very idea of a natal family or family of origin, considering the agenda of the Stolen Generations was to break up families in the interests of assimilation and eugenic racism. In addition, Leane argues that the Western *Bildungsroman* is based on an individual growing out of his or her community, often leaving a narrow parochial background to search for art, self-realisation, knowledge and sex. The Aboriginal *Bildungsroman*, in contrast, is more centred on the achievement or recuperation of community that racial oppression has tried to shred. In this respect, Kim Scott's portrait in *Benang: From the Heart* (1999) of Ernest Solomon Scat, who attempts to assimilate Indigenous people and obliterate their identity, is the opposite of a figure of concern. The alternative road is represented in the novel by the reparative posture of Scat's part-Nyoongar grandson, Harley, who tries both to reclaim his Indigenous identity and to atone for his grandfather's crimes.

But the senior Scat's sense of governmental power as a means to social improvement does highlight something which must be faced: that concern is frequently conditioned by white privilege and by the exercise of power. As Leane points out, the trajectory of the *Bildungsroman* presumes individual agency, which whites can assume as part of their birth right, but which has a different connotation in Indigenous literature. This is because the rights claims subtending the *Bildungsroman* – which Joseph Slaughter has discussed as tan-

84   Jeanine Leane, "Rites/Rights/Writes of Passage: Identity Construction in Australian Aboriginal Young Adult Fiction", in Belinda Wheeler, ed., *A Companion to Australian Aboriginal Literature* (Rochester: Camden House, 2013), 108.

85   Leane, "Rites/Rights/Writes of Passage", 112.

86   Leane, "Rites/Rights/Writes of Passage", 117.

tamount to that of the cognitive subject in civil society – have historically not been able to be asserted.[87] Analogously, it can be said that Aboriginal Australians have felt, in centuries of historical experience, the timbre of threats that white Australians have felt only recently – of a calamitous upheaval in the natural order as seen in anthropogenic climate change and the erosion of people's sense of security in the face of the massive sociocultural change of the neoliberal explosion. That being said, even the "losers" of the neoliberal era, such as Tsiolkas' Danny or Winton's Keely, are permitted far more agency by the "winners" than whites have historically permitted Indigenous people. They still enjoy white privilege, and the problems of neoliberalism and late modernity are but pinpricks compared to the protracted trauma of occupation, disinheritance, and the arrogant white forecast of Indigenous extinction. And in any case, Indigenous communities are themselves subject to the same effects of neoliberalism as the larger community of the nation.

We can even go deeper and say that not just agency but, in Agamben's terms, life itself is what white Australian literature can assume but which Indigenous literature has to fight for. As Michael Griffiths[88] has argued, Aboriginal people in Australia were subjected to what the African political theorist Achille Mbembe[89] calls necropolitics: both the prospect of literal murder and the assumption that as a people they would either die out or be forcibly assimilated. Necropolitics is an inversion of the idea of biopolitics as proposed by Foucault and Agamben to describe the power and processes by which populations and bodies are managed. Concern tries to be the affective avatar of good biopolitics, or biopolitics which is as benign as possible. It tries for tendance, supervision, or, to use Foucault's term, pastorship. It is an affective successor and *locum tenens* for the gutted mid-century welfare state. It is compassionate and inclusive, but from a position of privilege. Rainer Forst has discerned a problem with "tolerance as an individual virtue": it implies a gracious putting-up-with of flawed people, people about whom a "normatively substantive objection" still exists.[90] As we have seen, this implicit bad faith is also present in concern. But concern tries to *use* its bad faith and its awareness of such as a synthetic catalyst to create internal change. That concern proceeds from privilege thus is not an indictment but a prerequisite. Without power there can be no concern.

One can liken the difference between earlier Indigenous fiction and the works of Alexis Wright, to which I will turn shortly, as similar to the difference between early and late Dickens. Early Dickens features *Bildungsroman*-style protagonists and a fairly straightforward protest against cruel social conditions. Later Dickens involves ensemble casts of characters and more ambiguous constellations of beneficence. Similarly, where earlier Indigenous novels often focused on the fortunes of an individual protagonist, Wright's *Carpentaria* (2006) is notable for its portrayal of an entire community, or really two Indigenous communities among the Waanyi people, the East Side and West Side Pricklebush mobs. There is an emphasis on the totality of the community in its strengths and weaknesses rather than an attempt to single out an exemplary hero who will, like the "talented tenth" of African Americans W. E. B. Du Bois identified, emerge as something between a

---

87   Joseph R. Slaughter, "Enabling Fictions and Novel Subjects: The 'Bildungsroman' and International Human Rights Law", *PMLA* 121, no. 5 (2006): 1405–23.

88   Michael Griffiths, "Unsettling Artifacts: Biopolitics, Cultural Memory, and the Public Sphere in a (Post)Settler Colony", PhD thesis, Rice University, 2013, https://scholarship.rice.edu/handle/1911/71283.

89   Achille Mbembe, "Necropolitics", *Public Culture* 15, no. 1 (2003): 11–40.

90   Rainer Forst, *Toleration in Conflict: Past and Present* (Cambridge: Cambridge University Press, 2013), 18–19.

redeemer and a role model for her people.[91] Indeed, the most likely candidate for this role in *Carpentaria*, Kevin Phantom, has his wonderfully promising mind severely damaged by a mining accident and is disabled. His once-brilliant prospects are ruined. The community's problems will have to be solved more collectively: under the sort of capitalism sustained by the mining company that dominates Carpentaria, no single champion will be permitted to emerge.[92] Phantom's very name illustrates that, in the white world's eyes, the Indigenous people are ghosts, people who in the white-supremacist view of history died out simply because they were consigned to death. Bain Attwood states that the dominant Eurocentric theory of history in settler Australia held that "Aboriginal people had no place in the modern and progressive nation because it was deemed that they were an ancient or even regressive people. Indeed, they were commonly regarded as a dying race."[93]

Wright's novel is suffused with an awareness that the rhetoric of racial death, even if unsuccessful, has a real and brutal impact. The Phantom clan, in its various permutations and often fierce internal divisions are, collectively, survivors not just of necropolitics but also of what Roberto Esposito calls thanatopolitics: presuming the extirpation of people.[94] Necropolitics assumes that the relegated or oppressed will just die; thanatopolitics actively seeks to kill them. Thanatopolitics can operate literally, as in genocide, or metaphorically, as in the consignment of "losers" to insignificance under neoliberalism, via what Nixon calls "slow violence". A palpable mode of slow violence transpired in the Northern Territory intervention in 2007, in which the federal Australian government, just before a national election, intervened to halt what it saw as rampant child abuse in the territory. The intervention was an event of crucial importance to Wright. Indeed, the media coverage when Wright won the Miles Franklin Literary Award for *Carpentaria* in 2007 was eclipsed by the controversy over the intervention, and this event deeply infuses her subsequent novel, *The Swan Book*. In a politics that substitutes death for life, a decisive collective amelioration cannot happen, at least not in the present. In Melissa Lucashenko's *Mullumbimby* (2013), the Bandjalung woman Jo Breen's role as caretaker for the dead reveals an association between regard for the dead and Indigenous advocacy that goes beyond a reverence for forebears. Contemporary Indigenous people are portrayed as using the reality of death as a galvanising premise for care, while white assumptions about Indigenous identity are shown to reflect a tacit white belief in a link between indigeneity and death.[95] In Kim Scott's *That Deadman Dance*, similarly, Bobby Wabalanginy is seen as fundamentally dead in the eyes of the white invaders with whom he vainly seeks to develop ties of affection and collegiality. The verbal leitmotif of Bobby's experience is "rose a whale", a phrase that describes a whale rising as whalers approach, but which also augurs a resilient, natural optimism, standing in dolorous counterpoint to the reality plotted for Bobby by the conquerors. Whales might rise, but in the whites' minds, Bobby's people never will.

91   W. E. B. Du Bois, "The Talented Tenth", in *The Negro Problem: A Series of Articles by Representative Negroes of To-day*, ed. Booker T. Washington (New York: James Pott, 1903), 33–75.
92   Alexis Wright, *Carpentaria* (Artarmon: Giramondo Publishing, 2006). All subsequent references are to this edition and appear in parentheses in the text.
93   Attwood, *Telling the Truth About Aboriginal History*, 15.
94   Roberto Esposito, *Bios: Biopolitics and Philosophy* (Minneapolis: University of Minnesota Press, 2008), 110–13.
95   Melissa Lucashenko, *Mullumbimby* (St Lucia: University of Queensland Press, 2013).

Launching Concern Forward: Alexis Wright's *The Swan Book*

Given that concern is hypothetical, interested in things that are yet to be, speculative fiction may be its most apt genre. Alexis Wright's *The Swan Book* is set late in the twenty-first century. Climate change has engulfed the world, leading scores of refugees to come to Australia. One of these is Bella Donna, a benign old woman from Italy who raises a young Indigenous girl, Oblivion Ethylene. Why does this act of individual care register as concern, while earlier plots involving individual acts of care might not? It has to do with the issue of sovereignty.

The character of Warren Finch, the first Aboriginal prime minister of Australia, has been read, for instance by Jennifer Mills in a 2013 issue of *Overland*, as a fictionalised version of Noel Pearson,[96] the Aboriginal activist from Far North Queensland who in the late 1990s was seen as a potential future prime minister of Australia, presumably from the left side of politics, but in the 2000s emphasised personal responsibility and, as Emma Kowal has argued, saw rights as essentially opposed to responsibilities, with responsibilities proposed as constructive and communitarian and rights seen as a symptom of entitlement.[97] Finch views himself as responsible, and thus a winner; his policies help only those deemed responsible, and thus winners. Finch at once adheres devotedly to the rigid expectations of others and imposes his own rigid expectations on those over whom he gains power. Oblivia is made to marry Finch against her will, putting a Harrower-like allegory of domestic tyranny at the heart of this book about contrasting modes of power. The ethics of concern are affirmed by the exaltation of Oblivia, who cares for others, and also in Finch's death: the Indigenous communities reclaim him, burying him in his ancestral territory and showing his body the concern he did not show for others in life. Finch is not excoriated or turned into a scapegoat; he is depicted as a human being whose life has human value.

In the past generation, "custodianship" has emerged as a term to describe the Indigenous relation to land. Nicholas Jose, in his novel *The Custodians* (1997), depicts custodianship as a process in which, in different ways, both Indigenous and non-Indigenous can engage, and as an attitude that puts stewardship above possession.[98] Custodianship, however, involves not only responsibility but also authority, even if it does not make the claim of ownership and thus sovereignty. It is not merely a duty, a keeping watch of the land, but an active process of care, not only for the land but also for larger Indigenous cultural traditions. The Bangarra Dance Theatre, for instance, in its publicity material for its performance piece *Brolga* (first staged in 2001) says that the company exists for "the care and celebration of Aboriginal and Torres Strait Islander life".[99] *The Swan Book* does not make an absolute, legitimist claim to land on the part of Indigenous people, as if trying to mimic a European nation-state. Instead, it depicts Indigenous people tending and shepherding a commonwealth in which non-Indigenous people who share their values can also gather. This is not just a utopian countercultural community, however. If Oblivia's mind is, as she

---

96   Jennifer Mills, "The Rarest of Birds", *Overland*, 19 September 2013. https://overland.org.au/2013/09/the-rarest-of-birds/.

97   Emma Kowal, "The Subject of Responsibilities: Noel Pearson and Indigenous Disadvantage in Australia", in *Responsibilty*, ed. Ghassan Hage and Robyn Eckersley (Melbourne: Melbourne University Press, 2012), 43–56.

98   Nicholas Jose, *The Custodians* (New York: St Martin's Press, 1998).

99   Bangarra Dance Theatre, "Education Resource: *Brolga*" (Sydney: Bangarra Dance Theatre, 2013). http://bangarra.com.au/wp-content/uploads/2013/07/Brolga_3-4-printable-version-FINAL.pdf.

laments at the book's end, "only a mansion for the stories of extinction", it is a mansion in which "acts of love" have been practised, and where vulnerable animals and people have been sheltered.[100]

The *Mabo* decision was about sovereignty. In New Zealand, the Māori had the 1840 Treaty of Waitangi, which formally acknowledged their stake in the land; even Native American peoples had reservations, which acknowledged their parallel legal status as nations in some form. In Elazar Barkan's view, both of these would be examples of "fictitious legality", legal documents which the white signatories had no intention of following. Yet these documents, operating, in Barkan's terms, within "the formal constraint of the law", create the possibility of a gap between intention and reality; although the white signatories might dishonour them, their hypocrisy would then be foregrounded and could potentially be redressed.[101] In Australia, because the white settlers never felt even tactically compelled to engage in negotiations or mock-negotiations, they did not. Therefore the Indigenous people never ceded sovereignty, and as early as 1981 Aboriginal activists such as Kevin Cook began to speak of the "unceded sovereignty" exercised by the Indigenous people.[102] *Mabo*, not so much in its acknowledgement of substantive land claims, which in themselves did not involve sovereignty, but in abrogating the principle of *terra nullius*, which claimed that nothing before the arrival of Europeans could constitute a legal precedent, raised the spectre of sovereignty. Sovereignty involves self-determination but it also involves the exercise, or at least the discourse of, force.

Inevitably, this force can be perverted. In *The Swan Book*, Warren Finch's political rise proceeds from the Australian state making a formal treaty with the Brolga nation. The Brolga people become an international showcase for faux-utopian human rights, one that holds up a pleasing mirror to neoliberalism and allows its political leaders to hail "the most peaceful era in the existence of the world" (although this utopia is punctured by the disasters consequent on climate change). Elders are "hailed for sitting on their land since the beginning of time" (1539), something that apparently only becomes admirable when whites stop trying to annul sovereignty. *The Swan Book* treats sarcastically the postcolonial instruments of recognition.

When Coetzee moved from South Africa to South Australia, his work took a turn from the postcolonial – reimagining European classics, fashioning allegories of vigilance and brutality – to the biopolitical: that is, to a concern for animal rights and a scepticism about the role of the intellectual in a world suffused by cynicism. In *The Swan Book*, Wright's work has undergone a similar turn: from tales of the land and people themselves to stories in which the flow of refugees is described alongside a luxuriant animality, epitomised by the swans, and a recognition that the matrices of world power are more complex than those that are legibly colonial. Wright and Coetzee share a sense of *Homo sapiens* as an animal, and of the biopolitical as not totally separate from the animal world, yet distinguished from it by those dark necropolitical, thanatopolitical practices of which only humans have so far been shown to be capable.[103]

---

100   Alexis Wright, *The Swan Book* (Artarmon: Giramondo Publishing, 2013). Kindle edition, location 1539. All subsequent references are to this edition and appear in parentheses in the text.
101   Elazar Barkan, *The Guilt of Nations: Restitution and Negotiating* (Baltimore: Johns Hopkins University Press, 2011), 177.
102   Kevin Cook, *Making Change Happen* (Acton: Australian National University Press, 2013), 209.
103   This sentence was helped by comments made by Philip Gourevitch at the Windham Campbell Prize event, New York City, September 19, 2014. Ceridwen Dovey's *Only the Animals* (2014) is another

Thus the totemic animal for Wright's novel is not simply the swan, but the symbol of the swan, with all the significance humans ascribe to it. Like most birds, the swan has lyrical associations. But they are also associated with coursing along on rivers and lakes, and so are associated with the earth. Swans symbolise beauty and indeed in the late nineteenth-century poetry epitomised it, but also beauty in distress. Beauty can be a trivial or distracting adornment; but in the form of the swan, it gestures towards a tragic yet redemptive augury of a meaning beyond what is there on the surface. Warren Finch, of course, has a bird name too, although not as majestic or sonorous a one.

Oblivia's recognition of others, such as refugees and animals, is not so much an act of personal or collective discovery as, as her name suggests, a creative, positive remembering, much as seen in Gail Jones' *Sorry*. If Oblivia is to un-forget herself, it is necessary to engage in the exercise of power, even if it is a very different mode of power than that of Warren Finch.[104] Indigenous people in *The Swan Book* are not simply adorable victims, "beautiful losers" in Leonard Cohen's phrase.[105] They are agents who can wield and dispose of power. It is the exercise of power that is important and from which Wright does not flinch. As Ghassan Hage and Robyn Eckersley have argued, "responsibility" has often been used as a paternalistic, colonial code word, implying that whites can take responsibility for others, but Indigenous people cannot even take responsibility for themselves.[106] Oblivia and to a lesser extent her loved ones take responsibility for themselves and others, and can only do so because they have some power. If one is disempowered there is no way one can express concern. It is only in the wake of the collapse of traditional sovereignty – "all around the world governments fell as quickly as they rose in one extinction event after another" (155) – that concern is a possibility.

Oblivia is plagued by *nostalgie de la boue*, a French term used to represent intellectuals' yearning for a ground with which they feel out of touch, recalling Rousseau and his yearning for a lapsed nature. The phrase literally means "nostalgia for the mud", but it was often used metaphorically, for instance to describe 1960s radicals fascinated by violence and the marginal. But this *nostalgie* is not, in Wright's novel, a yearning for Indigenous Australian land; it is a "virus" that introjects memories of refugees from other places who are exiled from where they have been (114). Oblivia thus accommodates the thought-worlds of other, distressed people. But she also asserts her relation to her own ground; the swamp-world where she and so many others take refuge is not essentialist. Oblivia is not tethered to the ground either materially or cognitively, nor does she yearn for territory as such, but for sovereignty. Her community of concern in *The Swan Book* is made rather than born. Concern, both as Frye originally articulated it and in my own extension of the concept here, is secondary, derived, "imagined" in Benedict Anderson's sense; it is part of *natura naturata* and not *natura naturans*, heterocosmic. Wright's heterological idea of concern finds echo in Ali Alizadeh's and Penelope Pitt-Alizadeh's argument that for contemporary Australian Indigenous writing, an awareness of "the destructive combination of intercon-

---

example, aside from the work of Coetzee, of Australian fiction that responds to questions of modern and contemporary inhumanity by re-examining interspecies relationships and animality.

104   Finch's power combines the governmentality of Sam Pollit with the emphasis on bimodal partition between winners and losers seen in neoliberalism.

105   Leonard Cohen, *Beautiful Losers* (Toronto: McClelland & Stewart, 1968).

106   Ghassan Hage and Robyn Eckersley, eds, *Responsibility* (Melbourne: Melbourne University Press, 2012).

nected factors and forces unleashed by life in an unjust ... society" is more pertinent than identity politics (their example is Charmaine Papertalk-Green).[107]

In *The Swan Book*, it is Finch, the white man's willing puppet, who gets to where he is by articulating an Indigenous identity that is yet legible within the system.[108] After Warren Finch appropriates ideas of Indigenous belonging and uses them to make his leap to power, Oblivia's people are left "for dead" by Finch (3581). Out of this thanatopolitical mire they feel solidarity with "the throngs of banished people wandering aimlessly throughout the world". By becoming symbolically homeless, they discover compassion for others, of whatever background, who are homeless as well. And it is Oblivia, a victim herself, who acts, not the male figures in the community. The men are consumed by rage at Warren Finch, at the same time as they are unwillingly fascinated by him. While they rail against him, it is Oblivia who acts to bring people to safety.

Wright depicts two different modes of Indigenous governmentality: one epitomised by Warren Finch, an Aboriginal man who has triumphed within the system by conventional means; the other epitomised by Oblivia, who sets up a new power formation that is able to fulfil the duty of a state to care for the people under its umbrella. If, as Foucault has pointed out, there are hypocrisies and self-perpetuations in any form of power, as bureaucracy develops its own momentum and its own privilege, at least for the "refugees of every nationality coalesced by flights from the ruined cities" (4284), there is tendance, and some of the refugees will take that succour even if it is inevitably accompanied by the velvet prison of governmentality.

We are back to the important gesture made by Keneally in *To Asmara*, of seeing Africans as organisers of a state and African institutions as state institutions. Similarly, the international recognition of the Brolga nation, although tokenistic and motivated by white complacency, creates the formal outline of a sovereign Indigenous state, an outline that can one day be filled in by reality. As Mala Htun has pointed out, tokenism can be an important force in establishing the conceptual possibility of leadership by formerly subjugated groups.[109] Similarly, material conditions among Indigenous Australians were not much changed by their attainment of formal citizenship in the 1967 referendum, but that event created the rhetoric of enfranchisement, which could be used to highlight the shortcomings of reality, as Wright with consummate causticity does repeatedly in *The Swan Book*. Thus it is compelling that Warren Finch, however failed his politics, is an Aboriginal leader who governs both whites and Aborigines, as the Indigenous community makes clear when it seeks to bury Finch in his own territory. They are reclaiming him from himself. But they also codify their own sovereignty in the act of rebuking and outflanking Finch. Oblivia's swamp commonwealth cares for its people more effectively than Finch's Australia can. Although Finch is the villain of the novel, he possesses his own pathos.

---

107   Ali Alizadeh and Penelope Pitt-Alizadeh, "Metapolitics versus Identity Politics", *Southerly* 73, no. 1 (2013): 71.

108   The idea of the legacy of Australian settlement being allegedly reversed by a single Aboriginal leader, in a kind of false symbolic reparation, seems a nightmare scenario for many Indigenous writers, as seen in Ellen van Neerven's *Heat and Light* (2014) in the character of Tanya Sparkle, a female counterpart to Warren Finch who is the first president of a republican Australia.

109   Mala Htun, "Political Inclusion: Women, Blacks, and Indigenous Peoples", in *Constructing Democratic Governance*, ed. Jorge Domínguez and Michael Shifter, third edition (Baltimore: Johns Hopkins University Press, 2008), 72–96.

Wright's concern incorporates all those distressed and itinerant in the world, an affirmation of the value of all human life. In a world bereft of a constructive statism or of a sense that social equality can be achieved, the imperative to reconcile with the Indigenous people and to take in refugees became correlated with the very possibility of altruism, and in tackling these issues contemporary writers are also tackling something more general. The idea of concern provides a way for literature to be altruistic without being moralistic, to care for others without subjecting them to social control. Concern envisions a world in which inequality might not be cured, but in which reparation is lived out, and incidents still fail to be separate.

7
Australia's International Styles: The Idealisms of Architecture and Mobility

This chapter will discuss idealism in Australian literature, with especial consideration given to the role of artificial structures in promoting idealism. In the work of Frank Moorhouse, the artificial capital of Canberra is linked to a global idealism of international organisations and a realm of perpetual peace. In the work of Gerald Murnane, idealism pertains to imaginary landscapes and the cognitive and ethical power they exert. The chapter concludes with an examination of recent Australian fiction by Michelle de Kretser and Brian Castro that continues this idealism in a more mobile and transnational mode.

Idealism can be defined as the optimism that resists commercialism. As Nicholas Rescher puts it, idealism, in the philosophical sense, is "mind-directed or mind-coordinated" and transcends the material.[1] Twenty-first-century conventional wisdom, dominated by a neoliberalism no less materialistic than classical Marxism, is apt to deride or dismiss it. Nowhere is this more true than in architecture, where the utopian and pedagogic aspirations of modernism are now seen as absurdly lofty paeans to a future that never came about – they are "hymns to yesterday's future", as Margaret Thatcher put it when denouncing the Berlaymont building in Brussels.[2] During the unrest between Sikhs and Hindus in the Punjab in the 1980s, it was routinely noted that the modernist architect Le Corbusier had designed the city of Chandigarh, as if his architecture were somehow to blame for failing to foresee or to prevent the ethnic strife.[3]

In her acclaimed 2013 novel *The Flamethrowers*, the American novelist Rachel Kushner uses the Brazilian capital of Brasilia, designed as a capital by the architects Oscar Niemeyer and Lucio Costa as a metaphor for twentieth-century totalitarian violence ("Brasilia equalled death"). Kushner sees modernist architecture, such as Eero Saarinen's airport terminal building in New York, as "the underside of modernity".[4] The character Sandro believes Brasilia amounts to "a prescriptive lie about progress and utopias".[5] In general in the post-romantic era, literature has been slightly less euphoric about modernity

---

1   Nicholas Rescher, *Studies in Idealism* (Berlin: De Gruyter, 2005), 11.
2   Margaret Thatcher, "Europe's Political Architecture", speech in the Hague, 15 May 1992. www.margaretthatcher.org/document/108296.
3   Stanley Wolpert, *An Introduction to India* (London: Penguin, 2000), 216.
4   Rachel Kushner, *The Flamethrowers* (New York: Scribner, 2013), 372.
5   Kushner, *The Flamethrowers*, 366.

than other genres or disciplines. Dickens scorned the Crystal Palace, as did William Morris.[6] Much of canonical modernism seemingly lamented technological modernity.[7]

Although the architect of Australia's own modernist capital, Walter Burley Griffin, was not a modernist in the same vein as Le Corbusier – he respected earlier vocabularies, while still revolutionising urban life in the habitats he designed – his architecture participated in the broader modern challenge to traditional concepts of design and space.[8] If Canberra attracted no less a traditionalist than A. D. Hope and no less an environmentalist than Judith Wright, that was due to academic and career happenstance; surely the grain of these poets' work pointed towards a more organic location, whether rural or urban. Although reconsiderations of cultural modernism have palliated any melodramatic gap between literature and technology, this has not extended to the technological by-product of the artificial capital.[9]

How provocative, then, that one of the more sustained efforts at genuine idealism in contemporary Australian literature – Frank Moorhouse's Edith Campbell Berry trilogy – set its final instalment, *Cold Light* (2011), in Canberra.[10] In this novel, Edith, who had formerly worked for the idealistic if doomed League of Nations, goes home to Australia to help actualise the stillborn vision of Griffin. Canberra is unquestionably Australia's Brasilia, even if it is far less doctrinaire-modernist in architectural terms than the South American city, so it is pertinent that Moorhouse does not see the capital as yesterday's future, or as a prescriptive utopian lie. Moorhouse views Canberra as a poignant unfinished project that still beckons in challenge to contemporary Australians.

The artificial capital exists in settler colonies for perhaps two and a half reasons. Most European countries have grown around a discrete capital for centuries, whether as "imagined communities" (as Benedict Anderson puts it), through nationalising violence, or through the presence in a certain city of a ruling house. Settler colonies, conversely, are often the amalgamation of several different initial settlements. The major cities of those different initial settlements develop rivalries that have to be mediated by establishing a third city (Montréal / Toronto / Ottawa; Sydney / Melbourne / Canberra; Boston / Richmond / Washington DC; Rio de Janeiro / São Paulo / Brasilia). Australia here is more like Canada or Brazil than the USA. In the USA, since as early as 1880, every city other than New York has been provincial in literary terms, whereas in the other settler countries both of the original major cities continue to exert a national cultural pull. The artificial capital as a concept is wholly different from the renovation of an existing city – such as that led by Baron Haussmann in the Paris of Napoleon III, so memorably lamented by Baudelaire and chronicled by Walter Benjamin. Building new buildings and demolishing old ones may

---

6   Philip Landon, "Great Exhibitions: Nature and Disciplinary Spectacle in the Victorian Novel", PhD thesis, University of Rochester, New York, 1995; Martin J. Wiener, *English Culture and the Decline of the Industrial Spirit, 1850–1980*, second edition (Cambridge: Cambridge University Press, 2005), 69.

7   Sara Danius, *The Senses of Modernism: Technology, Culture, and Aesthetics* (Ithaca: Cornell University Press, 2002), 39. Danius speaks of the "founding myth of modernism" as the "split between the technological and the aesthetic".

8   Walter Burley Griffin also designed another municipality in Australia, the Sydney suburb of Castlecrag; this much smaller design fit in organically with the existing landscape much more than did Canberra, and might well be more esteemed by today's standards.

9   Todd Avery, in *Radio Modernism, Literature, Ethics, and the BBC, 1922–1938* (Aldershot: Ashgate, 2006), 54. Avery points out Virginia Woolf's interaction with broadcast mass media.

10   Frank Moorhouse, *Cold Light* (Milsons Point: Random House, 2011). All subsequent references are to this edition and appear in parentheses in the text.

change the visual scene of an existing city, but the new buildings inherit the accumulated cultural prestige and centrality of the old. In countries such as India and China the situation is slightly different, as those cities that have attracted the greatest attention for their cosmopolitanism – Mumbai and Shanghai are not the capitals, but the capitals are also, in relative terms, old, established cities with layers of cultural heritage.[11] The artificial capital, conversely, starts out anew, with no accumulated prestige but an association with the government that, in terms of the city's cultural capital, is at best a double-edged sword. Settler colonies take this risk because they want to mediate arguments between competing factions. They may also want to embrace the land that they are in, not just to hug the coasts but to advance boldly into the interior. Canberra, of course, is not that far inland, which leaves room for even more utopian visions, such as the eidolon of an Inner Australia in Gerald Murnane's *The Plains*, or the quixotic quest of Patrick White's Voss to consummate his spiritual vision in the outback. But the choice of Canberra's location was still a gesture towards a move away from the coasts, as was Brasilia more concertedly. Mustafa Kemal Atatürk's relocation of the Turkish capital from Istanbul to Ankara, a city further inland and without European historical associations, is another pertinent example.

Other nations have tried and failed to build such a capital. In April 1986, Argentina under the presidency of Raúl Alfonsín considered moving its capital to the more southern interior city of Viedma, the goal again being to get away from the coasts. By then, however, the fissures in such an idea were more apparent. It was seen as a diversionary tactic from the nation's legacy of past misrule and, as Carolina Rocha puts it, as testimony to the "failure" of Argentina to fulfil its promise to replace "the barbarian tribes by civilised and productive" European culture.[12] In the twenty-first century, Argentina again considered moving its capital, this time to the more centrally located city of Santiago del Estero, but this idea received heavy opposition; it was denounced by the Harvard academic Filipe Campante as an "isolated, planned refuge".[13] Sometimes, the idea of an artificial capital can be dystopian rather than utopian. The Burmese military junta's move of the capital from Yangon to Naypyidaw, calculated to limit the government's vulnerability to protest and dissent, is an example.[14] Australian literature contains a terrifying example of the susceptibility of architecture to authoritarian exploitation in Peter Carey's short story "Kristu-Du", in which a Western architect is hired by an African dictator to design a capital that is also a slaughterhouse.[15]

Even in democratic societies, artificial capitals can be burdened by the privilege of government. It is easier for populists to campaign against a monolithic "Canberra" or "Washington" than it would be to campaign against Sydney or New York. Artificial capitals separate government from the rest of society. Whereas the young man from the provinces in a novel by Stendhal or Balzac or Flaubert can come to Paris to pursue both political and literary ambitions, in settler societies with artificial capitals the two career paths are kept separate: one has to choose. Nick Carraway and Jay Gatsby can come from the Midwest to

11   On Mumbai, see Arjun Appadurai, "Cosmopolitanism from Below: Some Ethical lessons from the Slums of Mumbai", *The Salon* 4 (2011), 32–43; on Shanghai, see Lynn Pan, "Of Shanghai and Chinese Cosmopolitanism", *Asian Ethnicity* 10, no. 3 (2009): 217–24.

12   Carolina Rocha, *Masculinities in Argentine Popular Cinema* (London: Palgrave Macmillan, 2012), 57.

13   Filipe Campante, "Rural Capitals, Big Time Problems", *New York Times*, 10 September 2014, A27.

14   Diane Zahler, *Than Shwe's Burma* (Minneapolis: Twenty-First Century Books, 2010), 68.

15   Nicholas Birns, "'A Dazzled Eye': 'Kristu-Du' and the Architecture of Tyranny", in Andreas Gaile, ed., *Fabulating Beauty: Perspectives on the Fiction of Peter Carey* (Amsterdam: Rodopi, 2005), 101–14.

the East and plumb the depths of high society; if they had wanted to scale the heights of government, they would have had to go to a different city. The artificial capital separates government from the nation's cultural centre, rendering it impossible for writers to access governmental figures who might otherwise bestow patronage or prestige, as would have occurred in renaissance Florence or the Paris of the *belle époque*. If the Medici had been in a different city than Michelangelo, but still governing the polity where he worked, the support of his art would have diminished. Had Paris not been the governmental and cultural capital of France, the plots of books like Flaubert's *Sentimental Education* would not be feasible.

This makes the topography of settler-colony novels very different from that described in Franco Moretti's *Atlas of the European Novel*. If, as Moretti puts it, the "lack of a clear national centre" produces a "sort of irresolute wandering", it becomes even more complicated in settler-colony literatures, in whose lands there is a defined national capital, but that capital is not the first or the second or even the third city in the country.[16] The separate founding of the various Australian colonies, the rivalry between Sydney and Melbourne, and the consequent construction of Canberra have prevented Australia from having this unitary centre. In Nicholas Jose's *The Custodians*, a novel consciously modelled on *The Great Gatsby*, several contemporaries from Adelaide rove widely in the larger world – some to Sydney, some to New York, but none to the centre of political power. There is no single magnetic drawing-point, no defined centre. This clutters up the literary map, and renders moot a firm distinction between the metropolitan and the provincial.

The utopian urge of the artificial capital also has, within Australia, a distinctly dystopian underside. The very idea of the Europeans embracing a new land and migrating inward is an affront to the Indigenous people and to their custodianship of the land. The building of Canberra may have taken the Australian government further into the interior of the continent, but it only further derogated the Ngunnawal people who had been historically associated with the land. The idea of idealism is problematic in settler colonies because of this, and there is an inevitable point at which idealistic writing must deal with themes of concern. Murnane figures the limit of this idealism in his story "Land Deal", in which Australian settler history is a nightmare from which Indigenous dreamers struggle to awake.

The two writers active in the twenty-first century mentioned so far in this chapter, Moorhouse and Murnane, will, along with Brian Castro, be its focus. Both Murnane and Moorhouse are rather unconventional idealists. Moorhouse made his name as an irreverent satirist, Murnane as an idiosyncratic but rigorous metafictionist. Neither is associated with the left in conventional terms. Moorhouse is often seen as a libertarian, albeit one with atavistic Labor sympathies. Murnane has stayed as far from public political posturing as is possible for an Australian writer to do. Both writers might easily be associated with one of the potential drawbacks of idealism: its traditional alignment with what George Kateb has termed "antidemocratic individualism", which sees the idealistic figure as valuable because he stands out above the crowd.[17] But Murnane and Moorhouse are idealist in not being bound by the material of being non-realist. They are not tethered to a reductive

---

16 Franco Moretti, *Atlas of the European Novel* (London: Verso Books, 1999), 66.

17 George Kateb, *The Inner Ocean: Individualism and Democratic Culture* (Ithaca: Cornell University Press, 1992), 153.

idea of things as they are. This is very different from any sense of head-in-the-clouds optimism or an elitist disdain of the given. Their idealism is a fundamentally democratic one.

The artificial capital, for all the dark aspects mentioned above, exemplifies this democratic idealism. But it does so curiously and unpredictably. Because it is usually inland, with a less developed cultural infrastructure than the older and larger cities it has replaced, the artificial capital is often less cosmopolitan and diverse than the longer-established cities. Compared to Rio and Sydney, Brasilia and Canberra seem provincial company towns, lacking the layers of historical architecture so brilliantly evoked by the Polish-descended Melbourne writer Antoni Jach in his experimental novel about Paris, *The Layers of the City*.[18] The artificial capital has the deracination of the transnational without its glamour; it is poorly positioned to accumulate cultural capital in an age that wants sophistication, not utopianism.

The artificial capital is but one of many possibilities of contemporary urban manifestations that do not fit the neoliberal script. If Canberra sits at one end of the transnational spectrum, Western Sydney sits at the other. Michael Mohammed Ahmad describes the Western Suburbs as Australia's "most densely populated region, and specifically, the most diverse region, with the largest populations of people from Aboriginal, migrant and refugee backgrounds". Ahmad proposes that Western Sydney is the "kind of Australia that we all imagine and hear about, and that we constantly say is worth celebrating, but one that is heavily underrepresented when I watch television, read books, go to theatres, or attend arts festivals".[19] This underrepresentation also pertains to how Australian culture is represented overseas, always under the mantle of globalisation, but not in light of the communities where people of diverse backgrounds actually live. What the international model of globalisation wants is a sheen of exoticism, sweetened by the allure of the economically privileged; neoliberalism is more than willing to accept multiculturalism if that multiculturalism is economically successful. As discussed in Chapter 5, the most challenging multicultural Australian writers resist this consensus, which is at once anodyne and cynical. For all its transnationalism, neoliberalism shrinks from reaching out to places like Western Sydney, where the ideal of cultural hybridity, even if hardly utopian, is lived out. As Lachlan Brown, writing of Macquarie Fields in Sydney's southwest, puts it:

> we're not in Vaucluse or near some beach
> where they film iconic Australian TV. You
> know that within these cul-de-sacs you
> have to earn any hint of breath or change. You
> have to pay with sweat, with grease on
> a two-stroke, with teeth set like wire cutters,
> ready to meet the fenced-edge of the landscape.[20]

---

18   Antoni Jach, *The Layers of the City* (Melbourne: Hodder Headline, 1999).
19   Michael Mohammed Ahmed, "Western Sydney Deserves to be Written About", *Guardian Australia*, 18 July 2013. http://www.theguardian.com/commentisfree/2013/jul/18/western-sydney-representation-community.
20   Lachlan Brown, "Poem for a Film", *Limited Cities* (Artarmon: Giramondo Publishing, 2013), 13.

Vaucluse features in both Harrower's *In Certain Circles* and White's *The Hanging Garden*, and seems almost paradigmatic of late modernity. The representative Australia of the neoliberal era, meanwhile, is to be found in cosmopolitan, commercially buzzing metropolises, not in working-class, multi-ethnic communities. One could here compare the Newcastle of Greg Bogaerts' *Black Diamonds and Dust* (2005), even if the latter is not set in the present. Both Brown and Bogaerts describe gritty urban spaces that have difficulty being seen among the hyper-capitalist urban sheen of neoliberalism.

Moorhouse's Artificial Capital

Moorhouse's Canberra, although different again from the inland urban settings described by Ahmed, Bogaerts and Brown, with its utopian qualities and its bustling dynamic cultural producers, poses as much of a challenge to the neoliberal ideal of the glistening metropolis as Western Sydney does with its grittiness. It may be, fundamentally, that there is something suburban about artificial capitals, and something artificial about suburbia; this makes them abject in relation to the glistening metropolis. The artificial capital thus becomes an interstitial place. Like other such places, such as the suburbs of Western Sydney, and Steven Carroll's suburban locales in his Glenroy series, these places reveal fissures in the corporate urban space. Even the left often lauds corporate urban space. Saskia Sassen, a scholar widely seen as being part of the radical vanguard, stresses in her oft-cited *The Global City* three time-honoured, teeming metropolises: New York, London and Tokyo. Of these, only Tokyo has a whiff of artificiality, as it was not the capital of Japan until the Meiji Restoration in 1868.[21] Sassen sees urban space as the dynamic hub of large, long-inhabited metropolises. The futuristic yet quasi-organic urban aesthetic Sassen is promulgating is the contemporary equivalent to what Robin Boyd, in his 1960 book *The Australian Ugliness*, decried as "featurism" – the love of adornment for its own sake, the assumption that a pluralism of possibilities for design and living is equivalent to a true dynamism.[22] Neoliberal urbanism postulated itself as an antidote to suburban featurism, but ended up becoming an aesthetic similarly constraining and stereotypical. A neoliberal exaltation of laissez-faire urban dynamism, represented by entrepreneurial and creative energies, can lead to a cynicism about such presumed fixities as government and bureaucracy, and idealism about the creative destruction of unfettered capitalism. Yet there are places where "featurism", for all its flaws, can become more interpretively interesting: when it is not endorsed by the consensus or not ratifying already existing inequalities of power. I would argue that midcentury Canberra, as represented by Moorhouse, is one of them,

Thus there are modes of cosmopolitanism which are slighted because they are seen as too artificial or too suburban, but in reality they evade the consensus. Their cosmopolitanism veers off the straight and narrow; it is not comfortably energised and neoliberal. In the first two books of his Edith Campbell Berry trilogy, Moorhouse chronicles the history of the League of Nations, an institution that was decidedly utopian in its cosmopolitanism. It has since been stigmatised in the USA for its failure to prevent World War II (the United States, after spurring the League's formation, ended up refusing to join).[23] Although this

---

21   Saskia Sassen, *The Global City: London, New York, Tokyo* (Princeton: Princeton University Press, 1992).

22   Robin Boyd, *The Australian Ugliness* (1960; Sydney: Text Publishing, 2010).

stigma no doubt limited the American success of the first of Moorhouse's Edith novels, *Grand Days* (1993), the book nonetheless did well in the USA, garnering a particularly perceptive review in *The New Republic* by Michael Heyward (later publisher of the Text Classics series), a rare instance of an American publication inviting an Australian rather than a British critic to review a major Australian novel.[24] After the calamity of 9/11, there was a growing interest among the American reading public in international organisations and global cooperation. When on 14 October 2001 a teaser of the upcoming week's *New York Times Book Review* mentioned that there would be a review of a book about the League of Nations, one naturally assumed it would be the second instalment of Moorhouse's series, which had earlier that year won the 2001 Miles Franklin Literary Award (an honour denied him for the first book as it was deemed not to be sufficiently "Australian", despite its Australian protagonist). But no; it was a history by John Milton Cooper. *Dark Palace* (2001) went unreviewed in the *New York Times*, and in most other places in North America. The opportunity for the USA to understand how Australian writers might see world order faded.

Moorhouse's trilogy also considers "artificial capital" in a different sense: the League's cultural capital, in Bourdieu's sense, was never accepted by nations and their politicians. Two factors were at work here. The League of Nations had accumulated the same sort of stigma that modern architecture eventually would; people from both the left and the right saw it as a utopian folly. Even its more durable successor, the United Nations, would eventually be seen as a disappointment by many. (The UN was chronicled by the expatriate Australian Shirley Hazzard in both fiction and nonfiction: *People in Glass Houses* and *Defeat of an Ideal*. Hazzard excoriates the bureaucratic tedium of the United Nations and the way it became the de facto instrument of the Great Powers.[25]) The League's major flaw was the fact that, because of American non-participation, it became the de facto vehicle of the two remaining dominant powers, Britain and France.

Yet as Hazzard makes plain in *Defeat of an Ideal*, an ideal can be defeated without being invalidated. The League of Nations represented the ideal, not just of international cooperation but also of the potential self-determination of nations in all parts of the world. Although the League's mandate system in one sense perpetuated colonialism, it also anticipated the future independence of countries such as Iraq and Namibia. Inevitably the League failed its own promise, even before the rise of the totalitarian impulses so acridly reflected in Christina Stead's fiction made its very idea impossible. Brazil left the League when it was not made a permanent member of the Executive Council, and the mandates were prolonged and defined in such a way that they became little more than colonies by another name. But the principle of a different sort of internationalism was, as Peter Holquist has argued, at least aired, even if it remains unfulfilled to this day.[26] (Moorhouse began his trilogy at a time, at the end of the Cold War, when many hoped that the international order might be made fairer.)

---

23   Thomas A. Bailey, *Woodrow Wilson and the Great Betrayal* (New York: Times Books, 1963).

24   Michael Heyward, "*Grand Days*, by Frank Moorhouse", in *The New Republic*, 1 August 1994, 43–45.

25   Shirley Hazzard, *People in Glass Houses* (New York: Knopf, 1967) and *Defeat of an Ideal* (New York: Little, Brown and Company, 1973).

26   Peter Holquist, "The Origin of the Concept of Crimes against Humanity", lecture, Janey Program of the New School, 12 December 2014.

There is an Australian international idealism, beyond simply "winning" and being economically successful, and beyond gaining notice for work well done: a desire to make the world better, to strive for a world not yet dead. This goes back to the 1890s, when Australia was well ahead of the world in terms of women's suffrage, labour rights and democratic governance.[27] The twentieth century saw this Australian determination to build an ideal or better society exported abroad. The consummate expression of this was the work of H. V. Evatt to secure a greater voice for smaller countries. Later Australian writers on international affairs such as Coral Bell have continued this tradition of advocating for a multipolar world, even if, as time went on, the arguments were made more in realist than in idealist terms.[28] Australians continued to look to the wider world not only to make their own fortune, but also to contribute meaningfully to making the world better. This idealism is apt to be lost in a world market that has emphasised the commercial success of Australian fiction more than its literary merit. Terry Smith has commented similarly on the role of Biennials and other special exhibitions in the world art market. By institutionalising the exceptional, such events encourage a bimodal categorisation of artists into the successful and the unsuccessful, elevating hype over enduring achievement.[29] Such has been the Australian situation in the world literary market.

Frank Moorhouse was born in 1938 and gained fame in the 1970s as part of a new irreverence and informality in Australian writing. Initially, his work was associated with that of the novelist and academic Michael Wilding, as well as with the critic Brian Kiernan, as part of another vector of the "Andersonian" tradition of Sydney libertarianism. In his early work, Moorhouse displayed an internationalist irreverence, and wrote mainly short stories as well as longer but not organically unified sequences, which he termed "discontinuous narratives".[30] It was somewhat surprising, then, to see Moorhouse turn, in the 1990s, to *Grand Days*, the first of three lengthy books concerning twentieth-century diplomacy and government service. Although Moorhouse's style is more sprightly and comical than Stead's, like Stead he describes a young woman entering the cosmopolitan world and navigating complicated sexual relationships. The foremost of these is Edith's relationship with Ambrose Westwood, a cross-dressing British diplomat whose presence queers the trilogy, shifting it away from the sterile sexlessness often (perhaps misleadingly) associated with the bureaucratic corridors of modern power. Edith and Ambrose's sexual escapades operate formally as a leavening of both the high serious and the bittersweet idealism that might otherwise characterise a series about the League of Nations. The books avoid both the earnestness of the pacifist novels of Henri Barbusse and Romain Rolland, and the social chronicle of Upton Sinclair's Lanny Budd novels or the later work of John Dos Passos.

The sexual experimentation in the books also inflects their depiction of bureaucracy. Far from George Orwell's *Nineteen Eighty-Four* and its sense of bureaucracy as incipiently

---

27   William Pember Reeves, an early New Zealand reformist politician, talked of the "absence of any sort of alarm, fervid advocacy, or strong repugnance" in the passage of women's suffrage for all of Australia. This sort of gradual, orderly progress is just what Moorhouse is pointing to in his trilogy. See Reeves, *State Experiments in Australia and New Zealand* (1902; Cambridge: Cambridge University Press, 2011), 103–104.

28   Coral Bell, *Crises in Australian Diplomacy* (Canberra: Australian National University Press, 1973).

29   Terry Smith, *Thinking Contemporary Curating* (New York: Independent Curators International, 2012), 86–92.

30   Quoted in Peter Pierce, *The Country of Lost Children: An Australian Anxiety* (Cambridge: Cambridge University Press, 1999), 125.

totalitarian, Moorhouse sees the League's proliferation of agencies and bureaus as a cornucopia of experimental forms. What attracts him about bureaucracy is just what repels most of those who have denounced it: it is not especially political or ideological. Instead, it provides a vehicle for both routine and improvisation. Far from being deadly and monotonous, there is a ludic aspect to the interplay of bureaucracy that plays into the muted but persistent counterfactual element in Moorhouse's trilogy. (Not every historical datum he mentions, such as Azerbaijan being a member of the League, is reliably true.) Bureaucracy exemplifies the practice, not the theory, of governance. It is the material expression of idealism: altruistic, goal-driven, but not dogmatic or charismatic. In *Cold Light*, Edith's brother and his partner are depicted as communists, and the charismatic but ideologically corrupt communist organisation is contrasted with the Canberra bureaucracy.

Of course, bureaucracy is no utopia, and contains its own dangers. Importantly, Edith works for the International Atomic Energy Agency and visits Israel, both entities that are idealistic yet associated with potential domination or destruction. Despite this threat, what Delia Falconer calls Moorhouse's delight in the "less obvious machinery of political engagement – meetings, lunches, minute taking, memos and, above all, negotiation"[31] – has the potential to be boring, and this is why most authors, if faced with this subject matter, would satirise it. Yet, although there are many comic moments in *Grand Days*, Moorhouse takes his governmental processes seriously. In *Grand Days*, as an epilogue to the book's diplomatic intrigue and sexual hijinks, Moorhouse provides a short panegyric to the first-stage copying machine employed by the League, which reproduced paper for bureaucratic needs to an unprecedented extent. Whereas a late-modern writer would have scorned bureaucracy for trammelling individual freedom and agency, Moorhouse sees it as a symptom of a range of possibilities emancipated from crude political motives. Although the action of Moorhouse's series is basically set in the first half of the century, he brings to it a contemporary sensibility. He celebrates personal freedom but does not express the cynicism about large-scale social action, such as the League, that is routine under neoliberalism.

Edith is demeaned and slighted in her government work, but this is due to misogyny, and to the infighting that is the peril of any sort of organisational work; the problems with her job are not presented as symptomatic of a problem with the idea of statist government itself. Although sexually libertarian, Edith's values include a positive role for governmental and supragovernmental organisations. Moorhouse is one of the few novelists to depict such a politics. (David Foster Wallace came close in his posthumously published *The Pale King* (2011), but his early death made it impossible to complete that vision.) In both his idealism and his defence of bureaucracy, Moorhouse is conscious of going against the grain. The despair at the end of *Grand Days*, when present-day *Genevois* have no idea of Aristide Briand, the great peacemaker, is a reaction to the unseasonable nature of an ideal that in another age might have been, or might yet be, a resounding success.

Government bureaucracy is so unromantic that Moorhouse knows he is being irreverent by romanticising it, and by lacing it with sexual and social transgression. Moorhouse is idealistic but not smugly so, and indeed the reader always wonders when the curtain will be pulled down and the entire tableau revealed as an outrageous parody. The books verge on, but never quite attain, the comedy that readers of Moorhouse's earlier

---

31   Delia Falconer, "Grand Vision of Frank Moorhouse", *Weekend Australian*, 26–27 November 2011, 18–19.

"discontinuous narratives" have come to expect. Moorhouse takes bureaucracy and government seriously because he intuits that, although they are ostensibly at the centre of things, in the minds of most they are on the margin. Edith thinks that "the isolation from the world, and even the isolation from Australia at large, gave them an intense observer status about the wider world" (159).

Why set the third volume in Canberra? It may be Moorhouse's rejoinder to the accusation that the first book was not sufficiently "Australian". But Canberra, as an artificial capital, is strangely both within and outside the Australian national space. Although certain modernist architectural icons have been lionised in Australian literature (as in Frank Cash's 1920 *Parables of the Sydney Harbour Bridge*), more often than not Australian literature has foregrounded the natural landscape. Even Jørn Utzon's Sydney Opera House, as portrayed by the contemporary poet Louis Armand, is seemingly liminal:

c.1970 le repos
du modèle
(vivisection of
the nude, industrial:
sub-
cutaneous geometries
proliferate
towards incompletion)[32]

Modernist architects of a later generation than Walter Burley Griffin, such as Harry Seidler, made much of Sydney's streetscape seem as prefabricated and rectilinear as any other twentieth-century metropolis. As Erika Esau and Jill Julius Matthews have observed, Australia embraced modern architectural styles, mostly proceeding from the USA.[33] But this is not what the world seems to expect from Australia, and it is not what most Australian literature has presented to the world. At the tail end of the late-modern period and in the early days of neoliberalism, Australian modern architecture frequently got a bad press. Craig McGregor, writing in 1985 for the *New York Times*, welcomed the return of a more "vernacular" Australian architecture:

In architecture there has been a clear move away from Bauhaus principles, and architects are designing bush vernacular houses of galvanised iron and timber, as well as preserving old city districts and facades and indulging in an eclectic historicism that extends to the nation's new Parliament House in Canberra – designed by an American postmodernist, Romaldo Giurgola.[34]

32 Louis Armand, "Utzon", from *Calyx: 30 Contemporary Australian Poets*, edited by Michael Brennan (Sydney: Paper Bark Press, 2000).
33 Erika Esau, *Images of the Pacific Rim: Australia & California 1850–1935* (Sydney: Power Publications, 2010); Jill Julius Matthews, *Dance Hall & Picture Palace: Sydney's Romance with Modernity* (Sydney: Currency Press, 2005).
34 Craig McGregor, "Australian Writing Today: Riding off in All Directions", *New York Times Book Review*, 19 May 1985, 3, 40.

That the new Parliament House, by the twenty-first century, seemed as typically 1980s as an early MTV video, illustrates the problem with "eclectic historicism": in any of the arts, the creations of one generation will be eclectically historicised by the next. McGregor wrote three years too early to be aware of Carey's *Oscar and Lucinda*, in which the idea of constructing a glass church in the late-nineteenth-century Australian bush figured the Gothic revivalism of architects such as William Butterfield, George Gilbert Scott and Viollet-le-Duc, as, with respect to Australia, just as much an external imposition as the modernist architecture of Seidler and Utzon. But it also illustrates that, in 1985, an eclectic historicism was seen as the solution for an Australia in which modernism was not just an introduced species, but was fundamentally alien. With respect to Australia, the International Style of architecture, and cosmopolitan modernism in general, seem so incongruous as to be a portent of disaster. Even the instinctually modernist John Kinsella expresses this in his early poem "Dematerialising the Poisoned Pastoral":

> Beneath the picture subterranean streams overflow,
> Underwriting patches of poison bush they'd see
> The whole flock stone dead on the spread, blue as blue Venus
> In a deeply blue light, blue as the International Klein Blue sea
> Beside which the locals spend their holidays.[35]

Kinsella, however, injects a note of the natural – the very ocean is described in terms of a colour which was artificially concocted by the Swiss painter Yves Klein as a gesture of deracination. Moorhouse's international-bureaucratic cold light – echoed by other writers on Canberra such as Paul Daley, who repeatedly uses the words "bureaucratic" and "artificial" in what is generally an admiring portrait of the capital – may be disruptive to more organic norms of Australian habitation. But it is not finally foreign to an Australian sensibility. This directly contradicts the assumptions of McGregor's article, which also spoke of "a swing back to representation" in Australian painting. The point is not whether or not this was true. Anne Stephen's copious presentation in *Modern Times* of the manifold influences of modernist abstraction in Australian design might lead us to think otherwise.[36] The point is that it was said to an audience that wanted to hear it, that associated Australian works with sprawling representational bravado, not cerebral, metafictive introversion. McGregor's portrait of Australian art fed so readily into what the audience already desired to believe to be true.

In July 2014, I overheard a conversation between a young couple walking along Anzac Parade in Canberra. As they passed by the Anzac Park West building, a modernist building devoted completely to housing government offices, the female of the couple said to the male, "Oh, I love the International Style". This was said in a tone of enthusiasm but also faint defiance, with a sense that the International Style was now, like Kushner's vision of Brasilia, seen as passé, as a token of the faded twentieth century. Moorhouse's portrait of Edith Campbell Berry is similarly defiant, although even at the height of modernism Edith

---

35   John Kinsella, *The Hunt* (Fremantle: Fremantle Arts Centre Press, 1998).
36   Ann Stephen, *Modern Times: The Untold Story of Modernism in Australia* (Melbourne: Melbourne University Press, 2008).

is a wayward and maverick character who, as a middle-aged woman in *Cold Light*, does not find an adequate outlet for her talents in mid-century Canberra. This is due not only to misogyny but also to self-limitation. Both Edith and Canberra are caught in the contradiction of their own aspirations. Australia wanted a modernist capital, but not too much of one; it wanted an artificial, twentieth-century city but not to spend too much money on it, or to have it be too daring. Walter Burley Griffin's dream, at once methodical and mystical, of a city that would integrate governmental and civil life and be both systematic and liveable, was never fulfilled, and the city remains half-built, if that. Moorhouse's plangent frustration about this, however, is not an exercise in Australian nationalism. It is a mistake to attribute Edith's eventual, and understandable, dissatisfaction with Ambrose as husband to his allegorically functioning as a figure for a British imperial authority, an authority both effete and residual. The appeal of Canberra for Moorhouse is that it stands for an Australia not just national but international, not just emergent but visionary, even if Canberra's achievement is truncated and unfinished.

Like Switzerland and like bureaucracy generally, there is a neutrality about Canberra that other writers would excoriate in favour of the pungency of committed partisanship, but which Moorhouse likes for its abstraction and indeterminacy. As with the League of Nations, Moorhouse's depiction of Canberra is of a dream at once rooted in modernity but incompatible with it. Nicholas Jose sums it up well when he says that, for Moorhouse, Canberra is the "ideal flawed subject, with a double time scale of the transient individuals who make it and the impersonal institutional memory it carries beyond the life of any one person".[37] That Canberra is built on circles rather than on a rectilinear grid, and that it separates its civil and governmental precincts by a great artificial lake, gives a mysticism to its rationalism that is apt for Moorhouse's grave yet witty narrative mode. Edith wages a quixotic battle not to have the lake named "Lake Burley Griffin". She points out that "Griffin", not "Burley Griffin", was the architect's surname; his wife, his partner in planning Canberra, was Marion Mahony Griffin – her name did not contain "Burley". If the lake is to be named after Walter alone, it should be "Lake Walter Burley Griffin". As a woman, Edith identifies with Marion's underappreciation; as a bureaucrat, she values exactitude. Moorhouse's idealism is modern, not romantic, and eschews vagueness.

Edith also manages to purge residual romanticism in herself. She first comes to Canberra hoping to work in foreign affairs, to change the world, and, despite her *a priori* optimism about what is possible in office work – which Moorhouse seemingly shares – finds herself shunted to a minor bureaucratic niche. Canberra may be the centre of political power in Australia, and of Australia's engagement in foreign affairs. But Edith is denied this global reach (although *Cold Light* entertainingly derives much of its tension from Cold War skulduggery and the drama surrounding Australian government attempts to ban the Communist Party). She has her energies redirected – misdirected – into the merely local. She comes to realise, however, that creating a modern city, one which can give substance to internationalist ideals, is just as important, and far less precedented, than the work she initially hoped to do. It is a genuinely modern adventure, and Edith senses the thrill of it even though it is literally and figuratively incomplete, and even though its relationship to

---

37   Sara Dowse, Subhash Jaireth and Nicholas Jose, "Three Past and Present Canberrans Respond to Moorhouse's Account of the Nation's Capital" (review of *Cold Light*), *Meanjin* website, May 2012. http://meanjin.com.au/articles/post/cold-light/.

twentieth-century reality is still only sketchy, much like the political cartoons by Emery Kelen that Moorhouse so admires.

Although its ideals may not have been realised, Canberra's local variation on the International Style can yet provide a respite, a perch from which to observe the rest of Australia and the world from a different angle. Canberra is a place to which Edith, after her internationalist education in Geneva, can come home. It is easy for an Australian to migrate abroad; much harder to return (a theme explored in Joan London's *Gilgamesh* (2001), which also features a heroine named Edith).[38] The very shortfall of ideals that characterises Canberra is what, in Moorhouse's vision, makes the city sustainable and exemplary; the city's very artificiality prompts its denizens to strive more actively and independently for a fresh vision of what community might be, unencumbered by inherited assumptions. If it is still uncertain, after all the compromises and disappointments recorded in *Cold Light*, what Canberra stands for, there is at least the hope that it stands for something.

Gerald Murnane and Australian Idealism

If Moorhouse depicts an urban landscape characterised by a surprising hope, the landscapes of the novels of Gerald Murnane seem at first far more abstract and unpeopled. Murnane, in biographical terms, is a parochial figure. Born in 1939, one year after Moorhouse, Murnane has never left Australia, and has never visited Queensland, the Northern Territory or Western Australia. He has visited Sydney several times, once in a brief attempt to train for the priesthood, the other two times for academic symposia. He went once to Tasmania – a landscape of immense symbolic importance to him, especially in the bravura short story "The Interior of Gaaldine" – a story once thought by Murnane and by his readers to be the conclusion of his published oeuvre. He is overwhelmingly associated with Victoria, the state of his birth, and lived for many years in the Melbourne suburb of Macleod. After the death of his wife Catherine in 2009, he moved to Goroke, in the western part of the state; he now occasionally goes over the border to South Australia to attend race meetings in Bordertown or, once, to read at the Adelaide Festival. Goroke is just over a hundred kilometres from Penola, a small town in eastern South Australia where the early twentieth-century lyric poet John Shaw Neilson was born. This apposition is pertinent, as both Murnane and Neilson are at once vernacular and abstract; they are of the common people and fruitfully sourced in specific places, even as their works speak to the mind and to the soul. Like Neilson, who said that life:

> Would be dismal with all the fine pearls of the crown of a king;
>
> But I can talk plainly to you, you little blue flower of the spring![39]

Murnane is not an ornate writer. He is grounded, simple, and severe. Yet, also like Nielson, he reaches for the difficult, for effects attained only through a concentration on the personal and on images that, real or imagined, resonate deeply with the author.

---

38   Joan London, *Gilgamesh* (Sydney: Vintage, 2001).
39   John Shaw Neilson, "To a Blue Flower" (1911), Australian Poetry Library.
http://www.poetrylibrary.edu.au/poets/neilson-john-shaw/to-a-blue-flower-0037009.

The publisher Ivor Indyk, whose Giramondo Publishing rescued Murnane from relative obscurity and has made him a highly regarded, worldwide figure (Murnane's name is frequently mentioned in speculation about the Nobel Prize), has described Murnane as the epitome of "the Provincial Imagination".[40] Yet Murnane is also one of the most international of Australian writers. Even his first two, fairly realistic novels, *Tamarisk Row* (1974) and *A Lifetime on Clouds* (1976), have lengthy moments of reverie that floats elsewhere: Palestine and Egypt in the first, a lengthy fantasia on America in the second. With *The Plains* (1982), Murnane permanently jettisoned realism; indeed, the book was published by Norstrilia Press, a firm specialising in science fiction whose name, taken from the science fiction of Cordwainer Smith, punned on Australia and was the name of a planet, projected as a remote descendant of Australia; the firm also published Thomas Pynchon.

The Plains is the story of a young filmmaker who is hired by the grandees of a fictional "Inner Australia" that exists on broad grasslands of the sort that do exist in Australia but only intermittently; they are considerably expanded in Murnane's visionary imagination, as the novel's narrator seeks in essence an Australian equivalent of the Great Plains of the United States. The narrator yearns to extrapolate from the plains an ultimate meaning, even as his imaginative ambitions coalesce with his romantic desires: he tries to impress a young woman by surreptitiously placing a book in a library, hoping she may read it. Although there is disagreement among the Plainsmen about the meaning of the plains – members of the Horizonites faction exult in the texture of the plains, while the Haremen are local-colourists who strive for grassland *costumbrismo* – all believe that there is such a meaning.[41]

The Plains meditates upon the Australian search for national identity and has a pronounced internal geography. It is not simply full of nebulous landscapes of the mind. What Murnane describes as the principal goals of the Horizonites, "to push back the limits of pasturage into regions too long neglected", and the Haremen, with their "realistic plans for closer settlement" (35), might be allegories for the literary duel between Patrick White and A. D. Hope, or between the Jindyworobak poets and James McAuley: between romanticism and classicism. Murnane is an aesthetically excellent writer with abstract, theoretical concerns, as Borges and Calvino were; but they were men who were also deeply, if not always wisely, imbricated in the politics, including the literary politics, of their own times.

In the thirteen years after *The Plains*, Murnane produced three masterful books of short fiction, *Landscape with Landscape* (1985), *Velvet Waters* (1990) and *Emerald Blue* (1995), none of which has been published internationally. Many international readers will not know Murnane until these three books, or a selected or collected short fiction, ideally edited by the author himself, are available. But Murnane's generally agreed upon major work is the novel *Inland* (1988). While *The Plains* is programmatic and abstract, *Inland* is vividly specific, even if these specificities are ruthlessly spliced between fiction and reality, moving as it does between landscapes such as that between the Moonee Ponds Creek and the Merri Creek, which Murnane knows intimately, and the Sio and Sarvez rivers in Hun-

---

40   Ivor Indyk, "Gerald Murnane and the Provincial Imagination", paper presented at the Writing and Society Research Centre, Western Sydney University, 2014. http://tiny.cc/indyk_2014.
41   Gerald Murnane, *The Plains* (New York: George Braziller, 1985), 35. All subsequent references are to this edition and appear in parentheses in the text.

gary, which he knows only through imagination. It is *Inland* rather than *The Plains* that set the paradigm for his future work.

After *Emerald Blue*, Murnane fell silent for nearly a decade. Many thought that the hauntingly tentative litany of jockeys, horses and racing-silks that characterised "The Interior of Gaaldine", the last story of *Emerald Blue*, would be his final aesthetic testament. It was well known that the published works were but a small portion of a far larger canon of mainly unpublished work, and that Murnane did all sorts of writing: epistolary correspondence, highly personal and idiosyncratic notes on horse racing, forms of diary and memoir. Murnane's insightful and moving memoir *Something for the Pain* (2015) gives the reader some sense of what this material is like, as does Murnane's description of his archive, published in 2013 in the international journal *Music & Literature*.[42]

Murnane's oeuvre also got a second wind from a seminar organised by his first and cardinal critic, Imre Salusinszky, at the University of Newcastle in 2001, at which Indyk, who as editor of *Southerly* had edited a symposium on Murnane's work in 1995, was present. Indyk not only reissued Murnane's two earliest novels but encouraged Murnane to write further. Within a few years Murnane published three more novels, *Barley Patch* (2009), *A History of Books* (2012) and *A Million Windows* (2014), and the essay collection *Invisible Yet Enduring Lilacs* (2006). These reached a far wider international audience thanks to three developments. One was the rise in popularity of ebooks (which Giramondo, like Text, wisely allowed to be released directly into the international market, defying the conventional wisdom of the past, when the tendency had been to wait for an overseas publisher to buy rights to the book before allowing it to reach their particular market). The other was the fact that Dalkey Archive Press, the leading avant-garde publisher in the USA, picked up *Barley Patch* and *Inland* in the early 2010s. There had previously been two American editions of *The Plains*, neither of which had made a huge impact, although the second, published by New Issues Press in Michigan and introduced by the American poet Andrew Zawacki, remained in print. And, thirdly, J. M. Coetzee, who was by that time Murnane's fellow Australian, published a lengthy and appreciative essay on Murnane's work in the *New York Review of Books* in late 2012, concentrating especially on *Inland*.[43]

Although Murnane has found an international readership, he should not be stripped of the core of his imaginative framework. Without Murnane's Australian dimension, *The Plains* would be a dry and abstract parable. That it is not is demonstrated by the novel's awareness of social class. Much is made of the contrast between the wealth of the landowners who employ the young man and the young man's own bohemian penury. The Plainsmen are able to speculate on philosophical questions because they have the leisure to do so. In conceiving a society abstract enough to pursue its own dream, Murnane is not simply wishing away the society that produced him. But few, other than Indyk, have valued this provincial aspect of Murnane – the way that, as he himself concedes, he is an ordinary Australian male of his generation whose background, bearing and attitudes make him the sort of humane, tolerant, unpretentious person that Coetzee admired among the Australians he first met. Murnane commented at the 2014 Melbourne Writers' Festival, "I

---

42   Gerald Murnane, "The Three Archives of Gerald Murnane", *Music & Literature* 3, 2013.
http://www.musicandliterature.org/features/2013/11/11/the-three-archives-of-gerald-murnane.
43   J. M. Coetzee, "The Quest for the Girl from Bendigo Street", *New York Review of Books*, 20 December 2012, 60–62.

didn't feel any need to grow a beard or wear a beret, no offence to anyone here who does."[44] He did not self-consciously seek out literary pretention. In addition, it is easy to misunderstand *The Plains* as more of a riddle than it is because Murnane did not originally conceive this material as standing on its own, but as part of a far more ambitious and complex work called *The Only Adam*.[45] This book presumably would have cavorted on the interstices between fiction and reality the way Murnane's later, major work has done.

In 2011, I wrote an article for Dalkey Archive's in-house journal, *Context*, in which I proposed that Murnane is at once the most and the least Australian of writers. This article was quoted on Chad Post's popular and erudite *Three Percent* blog, but Post only quoted the statement about Murnane being the "least Australian" of writers, suggesting that being avant-garde made a writer less Australian.[46] Writers from other countries are not often discussed in these terms. Yes, there are special cases such as Kafka, who, as Deleuze and Guattari famously pointed out, lived as a minority in an undefined national situation. But with writers more securely anchored in a particular national identity, like Dostoyevsky or even Proust, it is possible to consider their national identity without detracting from their aesthetic achievement. In other words, to say that Proust is the least French of writers does not make him more of an aesthete or a metafictionist.

When Indyk speaks of Murnane's provincial imagination, he is not arguing that Murnane is parochial or minor; indeed, he sees him as one of the most daring and imaginative writers currently writing. But Indyk suggests that, as with other great writers, an appreciation of the local is necessary to understand his transnational importance, just as it is to understand writers from Joyce to Lermontov, from Faulkner to Mann. Locality and transnationalism are often in poignant counterpoint, as the local is frequently the base of lived experience, while the transnational is necessary for that experience to be disseminated.[47] In speaking of *Inland*, Coetzee labelled Murnane a "radical idealist", someone who exalts (as another South African writer, Olive Schreiner, put it) dream life over real life.[48] Coetzee, however, is not classifying Murnane as socially evasive. As James Ley has said, a "wrestle with idealism" is "one of the unifying features of [Coetzee's own] work".[49] Coetzee sees Murnane's idealism as a catalysing purity, a quality that explodes banality. It is not for nothing that, in medieval scholastic philosophy, the long-time anchor of Roman Catholic speculative thought, idealism was tantamount to realism – as opposed to nominalism. Murnane's Catholic background, inculcated in the 1950s, has stayed with him conceptually even after being unhesitatingly jettisoned dogmatically. Coetzee says: "His fictional personages or 'image-persons' (*characters* is a term Murnane does not use) have their existence in a world much like the world of myth, purer, simpler, and *more real* than the world from which they take their origin".[50] Against those who would see Murnane as a dreamer

---

44   Quoted by Beth Driscoll, "Gerard Murnane at the Melbourne Writers' Festival", Storify, 22 August 2015. https://storify.com/Beth_driscoll/gerald-murnane-at-the-melbourne-writers-festival-2.

45   Gerald Murnane, "The Breathing Author", in Pardeep Trikha, ed., *Delphic Intimations: Dialogues with Australian Writers and Critics* (New Delhi: Sarup & Sons, 2007), 100–21.

46   Chad Post, "Context #23 [Back!]", *Three Percent* blog, 3 November 2011. www.rochester.edu/College/translation/threepercent/index.php?id=3704.

47   See Amitav Ghosh, "The Testimony of My Grandfather's Bookcase", *Kunapip: A Journal of Post-Colonial Writing* 19, no. 3 (1997): 2–13.

48   Coetzee, "The Quest for the Girl from Bendigo Street", 60–62.

49   James Ley, "I Refuse to Rock and Roll", *Sydney Review of Books*, 19 March 2013. http://www.sydneyreviewofbooks.com/i-refuse-to-rock-and-roll/.

who deals with aesthetic castles in the air, Coetzee sees Murnane as renouncing the real world because it is not good enough or true enough to be really real.[50]

These ambiguities in Murnane's relationship with the referential have begun to be seen the more his fiction received sustained consideration. Emmett Stinson comments that Murnane is "altogether different from the various postmodern practitioners of metafiction – such as John Barth, John Fowles, Italo Calvino, B. S. Johnson and Robert Coover – to whom he has frequently been compared".[51] Whereas these authors, according to Stinson, act as if fictional characters are as real as real people, Murnane presumes that neither is real, that both are gestures made towards a vanishing point of imagination. Stinson bases this on comments made by the narrator of Murnane's 2014 novella, *A Million Windows*, that he does not like self-referential fiction.[52] Although the narrator plausibly speaks for Murnane, and although Murnane is not susceptible to a formalist separation between implied author and breathing author, there is a chance that there is iterative irony here. As in the poetry of Wallace Stevens, even the most complex aesthetic declarations and renunciations cannot be taken straightforwardly in Murnane. On another level, it could be argued that all of these authors mentioned by Stinson (Murnane's narrator mentions only Calvino) had convictions about reality. Fowles actually possesses, somewhat like Alex Miller, a Tolstoyan, realist aesthetics alongside his game playing. Calvino was a convinced leftist. Barth points as much to regionalism and to morality as to metafiction. Each of these writers as a writer has a soul, even if not an obvious or stereotypical one. Geordie Williamson wisely speaks of Murnane's combination of "obdurate literalism and visionary pitch".[53] International critics celebrate the latter, but the former is just as crucial an ingredient of Murnane's achievement.

Murnane's Million Windows

Bodies may or may not have souls. What is indisputable in Murnane's world is that houses do. Although Murnane's interest in actually existing architecture is nowhere near as pronounced as Moorhouse's, architecture is not insignificant in his work. Williamson speaks of Murnane evoking architecture "oddly yet profoundly".[54] There are the houses of the magnates in *The Plains*. There is the haunting image of the second-story window in *Barley Patch* – which in that novel comes to embody consciousness or reflectiveness, the very idea of there being a surplus or perceptual mystery to life, "the observer from an upper room" indicating perspective but not omniscience, perceptual privilege but not totality; every angle brings with it an obscurity, a vanishing point.

Finally there is the metaphor of the house of fiction having "a million windows", borrowed from Henry James for Murnane's 2014 novella of that title. If Canberra is an inland capital, Murnane's "Inner Australia" is an Australia liberated from the coasts and their, as

50   Coetzee, "The Quest for the Girl from Bendigo Street", 60–62.
51   Emmett Stinson, "Remote Viewing", *Sydney Review of Books*, 2 September 2015. http://www.sydneyreviewofbooks.com/million-windows-gerald-murnane/.
52   Gerald Murnane, *A Million Windows* (Artarmon: Giramondo Publishing, 2014). Kindle edition, location 406. All subsequent references are to this edition and appear in parentheses in the text.
53   Geordie Williamson, *The Burning Library: Our Great Novelists Lost and Found* (Melbourne: Text Publishing, 2012), 198.
54   Williamson, *The Burning Library*, 10.

Hope would say, five teeming sores. But it is not an unhoused Australia, and it is not try-ing to escape from Australia itself. Murnane does not seek to deny or repudiate the world as it is, but to be free of rigid codifications, and to let in randomness, chance and conjec-ture. Coetzee's recognises the importance of love in *Inland*, and the point is apposite here. The title of Coetzee's article in the *New York Review of Books* was "The Quest for the Girl from Bendigo Street", a reference to the second half of *Inland*,[55] in which an adult male narrator tries to find the address of the girl he "liked" as a boy, a girl he knows as "the girl from Bendigo Street". He tries to get the address from another girl, whom he knew at school and for whom he did not have romantic feelings; this second girl is called "the girl from Bendigo". Bendigo Street is in Melbourne; Bendigo is a mid-sized city ninety minutes' drive north-west of Melbourne. The metonymic apposition of Bendigo and Bendigo Street links the idealism of pure unyielding love affirmed across decades with the other idealism of going beyond the material and direct. We cannot assume that something is more present imaginatively because it is more present materially. This is a logic that would lead people to reject artificial capitals – perhaps, by extension, Calvino's "invisible cities" – in favour of traditional cities because of the former's thinner and deliberately engineered levels of ref-erence. Coetzee's thoughtful reading of Murnane links irreverence towards the reality of the real with an ability to love, to cherish, and to care.

This tie between imaginative idealism and affective altruism is opposed to the real world. It argues that no reality can be fully satisfactory. Now, a neoliberal utopia is to be preferred to a fascist or Stalinist one. It could be that neoliberalism is an auspicious con-stellation that brought economic opportunity to millions around the world, variegated our cultural alternatives, and brought us material plenty without the stricture of government control. Even if that were true, however, neoliberalism runs up against the same hurdle as every ideology: it can never be as good as it claims to be. To hail any ideology unequivo-cally as an unalloyed good is to relinquish the sort of horizon that allows what Keats called "negative capability", and what Bill Ashcroft reframed as "horizonal capacity"[56] (Neolib-eralism, with its reductive vision of winners and losers and its definition of man as *homo economicus*, encourages us to jettison this longer view and take the foreground only). To accept neoliberalism's claim that it offers a pluralistic plenitude is to mistake its surface for depths. This is the "cruel optimism" Lauren Berlant speaks of that asks us to accept the in-completely or only superficially good in place of the ultimate good.[57] Cruel optimism asks us to circumscribe our aspirations to the material, to the immediately beneficial and to the instantly discernible; it tells us to forsake image-life and image-reality simply because they are neither calculable nor measurable.

Murnane's idealism is in part a rejection of "dun-coloured realism", but it is also more than that. His books also resist a simple postcolonial reading that sees Australia as merely reacting to the British legacy. To argue for an approach to Australian literary studies that does not see everything in terms of British colonialism is not to gainsay either the rele-vance of postcolonial theory or the residual role of colonial governmentality. Nor should it discourage comparative studies across the English-speaking world, as seen today in such

---

55   Gerald Murnane, *Inland* (Melbourne: William Heinemann, 1988), 214.

56   Bill Ashcroft, "The Horizontal Sublime", *Antipodes: A North American Journal of Australian Literature* 19, no. 2 (2005): 141–51; John Keats, letter of 21 December 1817, www.mrbauld.com/negcap.html.

57   Lauren Berlant, *Cruel Optimism* (Durham: Duke University Press, 2011).

cases as Hari Kunzru's and Teju Cole's championing of Murnane and Colm Tóibín's of Christos Tsiolkas.[58]

Murnane broadens this internationalism into a truly multipolar globalism. In Murnane, it is not Britain, or even Murnane's ancestral Ireland, that is the "other" of Australia, but Hungary, Paraguay (troping on the New Australia adventure as did Stead in *Letty Fox*), Romania, the United States, in the title story of *Emerald Blue*, the "Helvetia" or Switzerland, so differently explored by Moorhouse's. Very little in the world is entirely foreign to Murnane.

It would be easy to see his interest in Hungary, as some have done, as a *Mitteleuropäisch* high-aestheticism. But Murnane is not only conscious of the 1956 Revolution – as the Hungarians call it, the *Forradolom*, many refugees from which came to Australia – but aware of the status of the Magyar language as a Finno-Ugric language related to tongues spoken in inner Asia and injecting a quasi-Asian element into the heart of Europe. Murnane, however, is not at all representing the real Hungary or the real Hungarians. For him, Hungary is forever a landscape of the mind. But that there are real Hungarians and a real Hungary do matter to him; his learning of the language and his translation and appreciation of Hungarian writers such as Gyula Illyés, Attila Jószef and Sándor Márai have made that clear. That Jószef was, in his own idiosyncratic way, a proletarian writer, and that there is a highly populist aspect to Illyés, suggest that these connections stem from a deep identification on Murnane's part with the people of Hungary. The Hungarian element, as well as the importance to Murnane of the Catholic milieu in Victoria in the 1950s, strongly influenced by recent European migrants, makes his work, if not literally migrant fiction, not totally distant from the work of such writers as Peter Skrzynecki, Arnold Zable and Rosa Capiello.

The idea of the Hungarian in Murnane operates as a foreign voice within the mind, a tendency not quite decisively other but that evades the same. An analogue to this can be glimpsed in the haunting episode in *A Million Windows*, when the narrator, in late adolescence, sees "a dark-haired girl" of a similar age on a train. She might almost be the prototype of "the girl from Bendigo Street". The "young woman hardly more than a girl" (a locution used repeatedly in *A Million Windows*, as if to acknowledge that the young woman involved is an adult, even though the affective realm might try to define her more securely as a child) sees the narrator's name on his schoolbook (480). He has written it in bold letters precisely in order to capture her attention. For Murnane, inestimable yearning is combined with the stipulation that the beloved be "difficult of access". He is far keener to have her learn his name than to learn hers. Yet at one point she unexpectedly, and perhaps semi-intentionally, lets the narrator see her first name, which seems to be the exotic Dathar:

> He did not need to consult any books of girls' names to know that no girl-child in the
> English-speaking part of the world had ever been named *Dathar*, although he sometimes

---

58   Hari Kunzru, quoted in "The Best Holiday Reads", *Observer*, 14 July 2013, http://www.theguardian.com/books/2013/jul/14/best-holiday-reads-2013. Teju Cole, "Teju Cole's Top 10 Novels of Solitude", *Guardian*, 24 August 2011, http://www.theguardian.com/books/2011/aug/24/teju-cole-top-10-novels-solitude. Colm Toibin, interviewed by Malcolm Knox, *Sydney Morning Herald*, 15 May 2010, http://www.smh.com.au/entertainment/books/the-interview-colm-toibin-20100514-v3m4.html.

thought her mother might have belonged to some or another dark-haired Slavic minority group in whose language *Dathar* meant fair of face or *blessed by fortune*. (700)

He eventually finds out, when he actually speaks to her a year later, that her name is not Dathar but the more mundane Darlene. The episode illustrates that the exotic is but the mundane differently regarded; "the drab of the everyday, so to call them, are mere signs of another order of things" (645). The theoretical locutions here, "signs" as in semiotics, "order of things" as in Foucault's translated title, are interesting even though Murnane claims to be indifferent to theory.

The epigraph to *Inland* is a quotation from Paul Éluard: "there is another world, but it is in this one". In Murnane's work, the transcendent is summoned and then held, suspended, in what Harald Fawkner, a Swedish academic and a superbly incisive reader of Murnane, contends is multivariant immanence: a dense, elusive, yet still palpable affectivity (a word Fawkner himself used with respect to Murnane).[59] The line from Éluard implies that there is a world of art, but it is feeling. (The same line from Éluard, by the way, appears in White's *The Solid Mandala*, his most searing Sarsaparilla novel, filled with savage social and psychological subversion.) Murnane does not find the material world sufficient as an object of representation, but he is not seeking merely to divert or to elevate his reader from the material world, but to recognise its immanent fissures and contradictions.

The Dathar episode evokes a cherished ideal, never fully to be realised. Edith Campbell Berry's dreams of Canberra are similar: although she yearns for them to be achieved, they are ideals that are not really intended to be fulfilled. Murnane's writing has surprising continuity with other Australian writing. The next generation of writers influenced by or taught by Murnane during his years as a lecturer in writing at Deakin University includes Christopher Cyrill, Tim Richards, David Musgrave and Tom Cho, all writers of self-conscious playfulness and melancholy. One can further contextualise Murnane. In *A Million Windows*, the narrator says his fiction is an example of Australia's leading novelistic export: historical fiction. The narrator mentions that he has read a historical novel about the Vendée rebellion (1216) (a historical episode we will encounter again, in Peter Carey's *Parrot and Olivier*, in Chapter 8) as well as Richard Blackmore's *Lorna Doone*, the only book known to have been read by another maverick from Victoria, Ned Kelly.[60] Lorna Doone and the Vendean book are regionalist novels: novels of a given place or time, the obverse of metafictive, but also books that speak back to a metropolitan consensus.

Murnane's "chief character" (a winsome phrase often used by him, expressing both agency and contingency) expresses certain preferences about the fiction he would like to read, and explains certain facets of the fiction they are writing or would like to write. But, as the phrase "a million windows" indicates, he does not laud only one kind of book. Nor is Murnane indifferent to society, even if he is hardly a conventional advocacy novelist. The emphasis on plains and grasslands in his novels, even if they are often plains of words and rhetoric, does have a real environmental significance, as Lawrence Buell, one of the lead-

---

59 Harald Fawkner, *Grasses That Have No Fields: From Gerald Murnane's* Inland *to a Philosophy of Isogonic Constitution* (Stockholm: Stockholm University, 2006).

60 Delia Falconer's story "The Republic of Love" includes a sentence about Ned Kelly, as viewed through the consciousness of Mary Hearn, that is downright Murnanean in tone: "He said he thought of going to America, that free land, where he would race steam locomotives on a piebald horse across the plains". In Delia Falconer, ed., *The Penguin Book of the Road* (Melbourne: Penguin, 2012), 328.

ing American ecocritical scholars, has pointed out.[61] In *A Million Windows* the narrator speaks of his fascination with the Native American man Ishi. In the early twentieth century, Ishi was claimed to be the last Native American living in the wild by the American anthropologists Theodora and Alfred Kroeber. Murnane imagines a female counterpart to Ishi; together the pair would constitute the "last of their people on earth" (1915). "Land Deal" had already established Murnane's awareness of the urgency of Indigenous issues. These are not Murnane's main subject as a writer. He does not, as writers such as Grenville, Miller and Jones do, profoundly explore themes of reconciliation. But the mantle of concern, of restorative justice, is not absent from his work. In *A Million Windows* Murnane gently satirises his traditional Labor-voting family, who see the Liberals as "the party of the oppressors" (1216). The narrator's parents are horrified to learn that their son is using a Liberal ladies' lending library. Their left-leaning politics, however, are not recanted, or ironised.

If there is no real but only a visible, no material but an ideal, then there can be as many ideals as there are perceivers. One cannot assert a radical subjectivity and then posit it as the only mode of perception. Murnane fosters deep attention on the object of perception, even if that object is not presumed to be real. Murnane's representation of women has been either lauded as idealistically Petrarchan or attacked for putting women on a pedestal.[62] There is a tradition in Australian fiction of male writers associating the ideal – in both the conceptual and affective senses – with the vanishing woman as symbol of irresolution and indefinition. This is seen in Liam Davison's *The White Woman* (1994) and Michael Meehan's *The Salt of Broken Tears* (1999),[63] and as far back as Christopher Brennan's Lilith poems in the early twentieth century. The Indigenous poet Peter Minter captures this feeling of melancholy aftermath:

> I hear faint words when flung above their signature below
> An echo of my buoyancy
> In ink or what remains in undertow.[64]

Language becomes an effect of experience always already lost, which we can love but never retrieve. With these and with Murnane's image of the occulted beloved we have a figure of the lost object of desire to match that of the lost child made famous by paintings of the Heidelberg School and by Peter Pierce's monograph on the subject.[65] Idealism can be an acknowledgement of what has been lost. In Kim Scott's *That Deadman Dance*, Bobby

---

61   Lawrence Buell, "Antipodal Propinquities: Environmental (Mis)Perceptions in Australian and American Literary History", Robert Dixon and Nicholas Birns, eds, in *Reading Across the Pacific: Australia–United States Intellectual Histories* (Sydney: Sydney University Press, 2010), 3–22.
62   Sue Gillett, "Gerald Murnane's *The Plains*: A Convenient Source of Metaphors", *Ariel* 26, no. 2 (1995): 25–39; Nathanael O'Reilly, " 'Whoever observed her': The Male Gaze in Gerald Murnane's *The Plains*", paper presented to the 2014 ASAL Conference, University of Sydney, 12 July 2014.
63   Liam Davison, *The White Woman* (St Lucia: University of Queensland Press, 1995); Michael Meehan, *The Salt of Broken Tears* (New York: Arcade, 2001).
64   Peter Minter, "From *Incognita*, Book One", *Jacket2*, 24 January 2012. http://jacket2.org/poems/poems-peter-minter.
65   Peter Pierce, *The Country of Lost Children: An Australian Anxiety* (Melbourne: Cambridge University Press, 1999).

Wabalanginy's arc of values, as opposed to the actual events that happen to him, motivate him to work for the *convivencia* of whites and Aborigines. This is foiled, in Scott's narrative, by white arrogance and colonial inflexibility. But Scott strenuously posits this supple idealism as a mode for present and future. Between the extremes of idealism as a policy and idealism as a conceptual category there is idealism as an affect – the belief in a life lived forward in an international style of Australian hope.

Streets and Gardens: Brian Castro and the Architecture of Mobility

Brian Castro was born in 1950 in Hong Kong and moved to Australia in 1961. He is of Portuguese, Chinese and British descent, and has written of the African chicken available in the former Portuguese dependency of Macau as an epitome of the hybridity his own life also represents.[66] Castro, as of 2015, holds a named chair at the University of Adelaide, and, although his work is underrated in the USA and UK, he has become an increasingly canonical Australian author in continental Europe, as well as in China. Castro is comparable to Bail and Murnane in rejecting conventional ideas of referentiality.

If Moorhouse and Murnane, in very different ways, display the architecture of idealism, Brian Castro's oeuvre emphasises another sort of non-normative building space: the architecture of mobility. Castro's novels are often about migrants, or juxtapose people from different backgrounds; more crucially, they also depict landscapes that are in flux, or highly dependent on the angle of the perceiver. *After China* (1992) has as its protagonist a Chinese architect who, like Gail Jones' Pei Xing in *Five Bells*, migrates to Australia in the aftermath of the Cultural Revolution. Most stories about architecture either describe architects and their visions (such as Carey's "Kristu-Du"), or the consequence of built environments (such as *Cold Light* and, in a different sense, *The Plains*). *After China*, however, considers both: the action of the story, involving the architect's relationship with an unnamed female writer, takes place in a hotel he has himself designed. This hotel is a transitional space, something like what Marc Augé calls a "non-place".[67] Both characters have experienced trauma and suffering, and a non-place thus peculiarly suits them, as a post-traumatic space of reparation.

In the architect's hotel, Castro seeks a hybridity that escapes consensus and even permanent monumental status. What Bernadette Brennan terms the novel's "denial of linear time" challenges ideas of fixed space.[68] It is not what Castro's characters find but what they pursue that matters. In *The Garden Book* (2005), however, to search for the ideal requires that the point from which the search starts is already complex. The heroine of the novel has a distinct origin – the Dandenong Ranges of Victoria – but she is half-Chinese by descent and identifies with her Chinese as much as her Australian heritage. Her name – Swan Hay – sounds like it comes out of an allegorical Australian pastoral utopia, but it is in fact Shuang He. Castro confounds our ideas of home. And, although home is more than a house, the architecture of mobility is used in *The Garden Book* to elicit the interstitial spaces between deracination and belonging.

---

66   Brian Castro, *Looking for Estrellita* (St Lucia: University of Queensland Press, 1998), 225.

67   Marc Augé, *Non-Places: An Introduction to Supermodernity* (London: Verso Books, 2009).

68   Bernadette Brennan, *Brian Castro's Fiction: The Seductive Play of Language* (Amherst: Cambria Press, 2012), 78.

Swan Hay is not a first- or second-generation migrant; her father, Baba, a famed professor, muses that for "years, before the turn of the century, my father, grandfather and their people went back and forth freely between Australia and China".[69] Yet in the eyes of white Australian society, these Chinese people were not encouraged to call Australia home. Baba remembers a "large group of us living in the shadows beneath these brooding hills. Then came the restrictions. No freehold land, no bank loans, our labour boycotted" (228). As Swan tries to find a home she blossoms into an experimental, internationally renowned poet, but as with Edith in the Moorhouse trilogy she must challenge stereotypes of gender and culture in order to do this. The man she marries, Darcy Damon, could be a classic Harrower husband: initially appealing, with clear force of will and an interest in books, he is ultimately a tyrant. The man who becomes most important to Swan, Jasper Zenlin (an odd combination of "Zen" and "Lenin") has more in common with Edith's Ambrose Woodward: he accepts and encourages her ambitions and is accommodating to her agency.

Jasper is also an architect, but unlike many fictional architects, he does not have ambitions to surpass the human scale. He not only, to cite the title of one of his treatises, insists on keeping the art in architecture, but, through his relationship with Swan, becomes interested in "the architecture of disappointment" (186). As in Edith's relationship with Ambrose, a person who is "logical and rational, by predisposition", is driven to be "ridiculous and illogical" by his "infatuation" with Swan (186). It is Jasper who encourages Swan to write poetry and who helps her to achieve international acclaim.

Castro's next novel, *Street to Street* (2012), is an even more explicit portrait of an idealist, this time the great Australian poet Christopher Brennan (1870–1932). Brennan was at once a quintessential embodiment of the cosmopolitan society of his day and a misfit within it. Notably, within the space of a few years, both of Australia's major cosmopolitan poetic voices, Brennan and Kenneth Slessor, had significant novelistic afterlives, Slessor in Gail Jones' *Five Bells* and Brennan in *Street to Street*. Although *Five Bells* is not "about" Slessor the way *Street to Street* is "about" Brennan, the title and the book's focus on Sydney Harbour do much to broadcast Slessor to readers who may be unfamiliar with his work. *Street to Street*, similarly, is at once a tribute to Brennan and an introduction to him. Both Jones and Castro insist on the continued relevance of these poets. Slessor and Brennan are both emblematic of colonial modernity, in that they participated in and exemplified the emergent idioms of their day – symbolism and modernism – but did not receive credit for it internationally. Castro and Jones, as contemporary Australian fiction-makers of an innovative mien, seek a usable aesthetic past in their poetic predecessors while vindicating them in an international arena.

Street to Street is as much reverie as narrative. But it is also a portrait and a polemic. Brennan, although his poetry is sufficiently modern to fit into the global project of his era, is sharply rebuked by a bourgeois and conformist Sydney for daring to be a dissenter and bohemian. Although one might expect an academic career to suit such an introspective and imaginative person perfectly, the department of comparative literature at Sydney University is conservative; the chief professor tells Brennan to "get a haircut and buy a proper hat".[70] The dilemmas of an imaginative soul in a world determined to deny imagination are also seen in the book's contemporary strand. This deals with Brendan Costa,

---

69   Brian Castro, *The Garden Book* (Atarmon: Giramondo Publishing, 2005). All subsequent references are to this edition and appear in parentheses in the text.
70   Brian Castro, *Street to Street* (Atarmon: Giramondo Publishing, 2012), 78.

a modern-day academic. Costa bears some resemblance to Castro, and shares his initials, which in turn are the inversion of Christopher Brennan's. Costa is having an affair with a young Dutch woman, Saskia. This allows Castro to bring in Dutch realist art as a rooted counterpoint to the wandering quality of Brennan's Sydney streetwalking. As well, Costa's feelings for Saskia parallel Brennan's obsession with the feminine ideal, represented in his poems by a figure named Lilith, dimly reflecting the poet's late-in-life mistress, Violet Singer. As in Murnane's work, where the quest for the girl from Bendigo Street leads the narrator through a complex imagined landscape, so in Castro love and yearning lead the way through the architecture of mobility in modern Sydney and contemporary Amsterdam. Although, as Brennan muses, "lovers do not write the best love verses" (86), the presence of love and its potential loss prevents Castro's descriptions of urban landscapes from becoming eulogies for contemporary urban dynamism. The architecture of mobility generates artistic achievement, but also commemorates and even occasions loss.

Can Architecture Travel?

We have seen how architecture can represent national or transnational ideals. But can architecture do this in an era when people and even institutions are so relentlessly on the move? The architecture of mobility is more flexible and ingenious than the architecture of idealism. It is able to produce non-places such as Augé describes while also designating places with reinvigorated meaning. In the era of non-place, even the place becomes a premise for speculation about how it can be relativised. In Murray Bail's *The Pages* (2008), a sheep station deep in the country provides an arena for a contest between the claims of philosophy and psychology, as if the paradox of a built domicile on a "trouser-khaki dryness stained with trees. With shadows ink spilt" is the fitting instance for this conceptual clash.[71] Romy Ash's *Floundering* (2012), the taut, contemporary story of Loretta, a failed mother who abducts the sons she previously abandoned and takes them west across the Nullarbor Plain, embodies this clash in personality and landscape.[72] *Floundering* is as emblematic of the architecture of mobility as *The Pages* is of contemplative life. Motifs of autonomy and transitivity prevail in Ash's book; the protagonist's car is even personified as "Bert", suggesting that mobility is so important it has to be affectively embodied. *Floundering*'s final line is "I stare out through the glass blurred by dust. The highway stretches black and liquid into the sky" (202), and the novel is galvanised by a sense of escape and possibility characteristic of neoliberalism far less available in the more constricted days of late modernity. But, inevitably, the escape offered by travel in Ash's book is illusory.

Of course, ultimately a novel of any sophistication will not promise liberation merely through journeying. This is seen in Tony Birch's *Blood* (2012), in which Indigenous children fend for themselves in the absence of an effective parental structure, and the city is no improvement over the country.[73] In "Sound", the last story in Ellen van Neerven's David Unaipon Award-winning *Heat and Light* (2014), the Aboriginal narrator, Jodie, looks for her brother David, who has been sheltered by a white woman named Sarah.[74] In Sarah's

---

71   Murray Bail, *The Pages* (London: Harvill Secker, 2008), 126.

72   Romy Ash, *Floundering* (Melbourne: Text Publishing, 2012).

73   Tony Birch, *Blood* (St Lucia: University of Queensland Press, 2012).

74   Ellen van Neerven, *Heat and Light* (St Lucia: University of Queensland Press, 2014).

house, Jodie at once finds an unexpected erotic relationship and a sense of the ambiguity of the house as a place of refuge. Domesticity is not as domestic as it used to be, and the architecture of mobility may be all that we have. There should not be too reductive an opposition between stasis and mobility. Steven Carroll's *The Art of the Engine Driver* (2001), the first in his Glenroy series, uses trains and cars to delineate a time now passed, the novel's end "tolling the end of an era".[75] In Carroll, cars and trains are vehicles for secrets, for hidden identities. Ash, however, uses mobility to outline the contemporary: a condition of mobility and transparency where affect, if it can manifest itself, must do so on the move.

In *Floundering*, the connection between the two architectures is resonantly evoked when Tom finds, in the back seat of the car, "a bit of Coke as hot as tea" (17). Coke in autos, as opposed to tea in middle-class suburban houses, should indicate that contemporary mobility is associated with prosperity, but the comparative advantage is all lost. Ash captures how Australia has changed since the time of Edith Campbell Berry. Moorhouse's heroine dreamt of a cosmopolitanism that is now at our fingertips. In *Floundering*, Mongolian lamb is available, a token of a superficial gastronomic sophistication, a far more cosmopolitan repast than the "bananas and onion and sausages" (17) eaten at a representative moment in *The Long Prospect*. Yet this availability of exotic Asian food does not prevent Loretta from casually uttering an anti-Asian ethnic slur. Similarly, *Floundering* takes place outside of the psychological landscape of suburban limitation, amid prodigious kangaroos and stunning red cliffs jutting above beaches, but the characters cannot therefore escape those limitations. Indeed, Ash's great achievement is to portray such iconic vistas of Australian nature as, affectively speaking, "non-places" in the sense in which Augé speaks of supermarkets or airports: meaningless, transactive places that cannot provide serenity or restorative virtue. The image of the public bathroom in *Floundering*, that banal corollary of travel, embodies this. The architecture of mobility has its virtues, but its glamour is no more durable than that of the architecture of idealism.

Michelle de Kretser's *Questions of Travel* (2012) similarly tries to deromanticise travel; however, it has a larger agenda.[76] Like Castro, de Kretser seeks not just to introduce Asian and Asian-Australian experience into the Australian literary mainstream, but also to complicate the dichotomy between home and elsewhere. The novel's two main characters, Ravi Mendis from Sri Lanka and Laura Fraser from Australia, seem to be travelling along opposite trajectories. Ravi is fleeing the civil unrest in his homeland for refuge in Australia while Laura, lucky enough to inherit money, seeks the glamour and sophistication of overseas travel. Laura works for a publisher of guide books, run by a family marked by complacency and spurious philanthropy (not unlike the Howards in Harrower's *In Certain Circles*). The novel is concerned throughout with a pitfall in the idea of cosmopolitanism. Its epigraph quotes E. M. Forster: "Under cosmopolitanism, if it comes, we shall receive no help from the earth. Trees and meadows and mountains will only be a spectacle ..." Although Forster was influenced by a Paterian aestheticism, the quotation also reflected the ambition, seen in Niemeyer's Brasilia and Le Corbusier's Chandigarh – although not in Griffin's Canberra – to transcend the mundane and the local. In de Kretser's time, the Promethean altruism

75   Steven Carroll, *The Art of the Engine Driver* (Pymble: Fourth Estate, 2001). Carroll's other Glenroy novels are *The Gift of Speed* (2004), *The Time We Have Taken* (2007), *Spirit of Progress* (2011) and *Forever Young* (2015).

76   Michelle de Kretser, *Questions of Travel* (Crows Nest: Allen & Unwin, 2012).

that once led to the architecture of idealism has yielded to a more professionalised world of NGOs (such as the one Ravi's doomed wife works for) and cultivated tourists. De Kretser's second epigraph, from the Canadian-born American poet Elizabeth Bishop's "Questions of Travel", makes one think of Bishop's line from the villanelle "One Art": "I lost two cities, lovely ones". Within the architecture of mobility, if one home is lost, another can all too easily be found simply by the exercise of financial or cultural capital.[77] This is a world in which, as Dominic Pettman observes:

> while relatively privileged diasporic peoples and expatriates crave some kind of surrogate or symbolic "home", those far more neglected victims of globally regulated capital are prepared to risk anything and everything to *get away* from home – and then, when caught, to *avoid being sent back* home.[78]

Although Ravi Mendis is an individual with a life of his own, and although Laura Fraser is not simply a synecdoche for contemporary Australia, but a sensitive and caring woman with her own problems and travails, de Kretser makes clear that Ravi's travel is the second sort described by Pettman, while Laura's travel is merely the first.

In this world, architecture is no longer the architecture of idealism. The Ramsey guide book firm is headquartered in "a former knitwear factory in Chippendale" (226), the sort of place that Harrower's Felix Shaw or Patrick White's Mordecai Himmelfarb might have worked, now gentrified and turned into office space for the service economy; the building's industrial use is now so far away as to seem, in Margaret Thatcher's phrase about the Berlaymont, yesterday's future. But *Questions of Travel* also presents a more interstitial view of the architecture of mobility, one that can destabilise congealed and privilege expectations. The town where Ravi grows up just outside of Colombo has colonial churches laden with a "baroque flourish" (7), which confounds tourists seeking the purely exotic, not third-rate copies of images they have already seen. The novel's harrowing denouement – in which Nimal Corea, a Sri Lankan-born web designer now living in Australia, sees Sydney mansions briefly illuminated and then abruptly lose power on the day of the devastating 2004 tsunami – highlights the role architecture can play in inequality. In this regard a more transitive and mobile view of architecture can bridge the gap between the privileged and the victimised. Architecture can travel. But, while the architecture of mobility might seem poised to upset hierarchies, its actual deployment often seals them.

Mobility, in de Kretser's view, tacitly needs to be pried away from an idea of winning. In her *Journals*, Antigone Kefala notes the way assumptions of success turn a deaf ear to genuine diversity:

> Everyone discussing work, new positions, possibilities. Yet it seemed that none of them had heard someone with a different accent for some time. They were listening to me politely, with an increased amount of attention, so that the air became charged while I spoke.[79]

---

77 Elizabeth Bishop, "One Art", from *The Complete Poems 1926-1979* (New York: Farrar, Straus & Giroux, 1983), via the Poetry Foundation. www.poetryfoundation.org/poem/176996.
78 Dominic Pettman, *Love and Other Technologies: Retrofitting Eros for the Information Age* (Stanford: Stanford University Press, 2006), 191.

Contemporary prosperity hails cultural diversity in the abstract but, when it actually encounters it, often treats it with suspicion. The need to divorce "the desirable" or "the excellent" from "the successful", to make sure that, unlike in the world of Tsiolkas' *Barracuda*, in which only the winners are desirable, there are other desirables than mere success, is seen in Claire Corbett's speculative-fiction novel *When We Have Wings* (2011), set in a fantasy world in which human beings acquire wings via massive surgical and prosthetic intervention, which elucidates the difference between those who soar while thinking of others and those whose wings are simply appurtenances of self-aggrandisement. Throughout the book, two narrators, Peri, a female champion flier, and Zeke, a male detective, exchange attitudes to flying. Zeke wonders whether he wanted his son Thomas to fly – to have wings – simply to "set himself up for life" or to "make him a success".[80] *When We Have Wings* ends with the sense that transcendence must mean more than simply prevailing. The wings of the characters provide embodiment as well as exhilaration; idealism is expressed by the firmness of architecture. This is seen in another speculative novel, James Bradley's *Clade* (2015), which like de Kretser's book describes an ecocatastrophe.[81] In the near future, climate change devastates not just the land itself but also architectural structures, including a seemingly secure beach house in Bondi. The novel focuses on a married couple, Adam and Ellie, and their teenage daughter, Summer. Summer's friend Meera, rebellious but charismatic, breaks into houses and spurns politics. Her destructiveness is not just non-idealistic but seemingly intentionally *anti*-idealistic. At the end of the book, one of the survivors of the global catastrophe, Bo, has a "reassuring solidity" about him as he engages in a "reconstruction project".[82] The association of natural disasters with anarchy, and with anti-architecturalism, is clear. Planned environments can be utopian. But they can also act as sanctuaries in which the affect of idealism can persist. In this context, modern architecture, with its ideal and interstitial relationship to lived reality, shows that it can be more than merely yesterday's future. The planners' make-believe of the artificial capital, like the writers' make-believe of fiction, can render sustainable cities in which we can move beyond a division between winners and losers.

Affect as Antidote

The three modes of affect discussed in this chapter – rancour, concern, and idealism – are the literary solutions this book proposes to the problems of neoliberalism. Of course, these three are not the only affects, just the ones most pertinent to this book's argument. The affect theorists cited at the beginning of Chapter 5 discuss alternative affects, as well as the discursive operations of affect itself. But my aim in this book is to show that states of feeling can offer an answer and an antidote to the hierarchies and reductions of neoliberalism, and to neoliberalism's putative division of the world into winners and losers. This is probably as strong a riposte to neoliberalism as we can expect from literature or from literary

79   Quoted in Ivor Indyk, "The Journals of Antigone Kefala", in Vrasidas Karalis and Helen Nickas, eds, *Antigone Kefala: A Writer's Journey* (Melbourne: Owl Publishing, 2014), 231.
80   Claire Corbett, *When We Have Wings* (Crows Nest: Allen & Unwin, 2011), 457.
81   James Bradley, *Clade* (Melbourne: Penguin, 2015).
82   Bradley, *Clade*, 231.

criticism. As tempting as it might be to attempt a more polemical or prescriptive response, that is best left to public policy makers.

A deeper danger, and one to which literary criticism has historically been intermittently subject, is of nostalgia, a wish for the way things were, or might have been. If the welfare-state structures of late modernity had survived, the inequalities of neoliberalism would have been avoided. But those structures collapsed, and, as my analysis of the work of Christina Stead and Elizabeth Harrower has shown, there was much in them that was static, repressive and patriarchal. That these two writers were committed leftists, albeit of different stripes, makes their critique all the more compelling. The last outcome their books solicit would be a resurgence of free-market capitalism. Yet the predicament of late modernity they describe was burst by just such a resurgence.

Australia cannot go back to late modernity today because late modernity's elevation of the white male is unacceptable, because late modernity was too confining, and because humanity, and the world, have changed too much. The way forward is through the states of feeling whose expression neoliberalism has encouraged, but whose emotional depth challenges the flattening and monetising of neoliberalism's Darwinian, monochromatic anthropology, its sense that the agenda of mankind is naught but getting and spending. It is through the vehicle of emotion that, in the preceding three chapters, writers not explicitly political, like Alex Miller, Gail Jones and Gerald Murnane, can have a tacit politics as much as writers such as John Kinsella, Ouyang Yu and Michelle de Kretser, whose political thrust is far more manifest. Affect also provides a way for spiritual themes, in their various avatars of fury, compassion, and hope, to be paired with literary analysis without, on the one hand, elevating any particular religious dogma or, on the other, melting into a blandly pluralistic soup.

Literature engages with politics and history. But it is also distinct from them. It unfolds itself imaginatively, as more of an apparition than a proposal, and thus generates emotions in the reader. To lean too much on these emotions, however, or to simplify them, would lead to sentimentality. It is because rancour, concern and idealism are such contradictory and self-conscious emotions that they do not succumb to self-pity. Yet, in the strength of their purpose and their confidence in their arduously achieved convictions, they lead the way forward.

Australian Literature in the World Market

8

Australian Abroad: Peter Carey's Inside Course

This chapter will discuss the later work of Peter Carey, arguing that it is far more politically progressive and formally daring than critics have assumed, and suggesting that Carey's extensive engagement with the United States – as aspiration, foil and enemy – speaks to the heart of how contemporary Australian fiction can challenge the banalities of neoliberalism. In this, Carey's first novel of the twenty-first century is exemplary.

Ned Kelly after Joyce and Freud

When Carey wrote a novel about Ned Kelly (published in 2000 as *True History of the Kelly Gang*) it was a case of one Australian icon writing about another. It was quite daring, as, despite efforts by Robert Drewe, Douglas Stewart and others, no Australian novelist (as opposed to historians such as Manning Clark) had so confidently taken on the historical episode of Kelly and his gang of bush outlaws. This gap in Australian literature was especially striking given Sidney Nolan had depicted Kelly with such originality and aptitude in his series of paintings on the theme. (Carey saw Nolan's paintings at the Metropolitan Museum in New York in 1994, while he was working on *The Unusual Life of Tristan Smith*.)

True History of the Kelly Gang was spectacularly successful: it won Carey his second Booker Prize and was acclaimed as at once a stirring tale and a masterpiece of narrative voice. It was read as both an anti-colonial book and as a continuation of Carey's interest in fictive documents and forged history. Carey's iteration of Kelly's voice is tangible, vernacular, and limited. Although far more articulate than Bobby Blue in Alex Miller's *Coal Creek*, Kelly also struggles with language, lacking the words fully to express himself, but developing an engaging verbal idiom that can passionately and pointedly relate his grievances and hopes:

> At dusk I saddled the cart horse a quiet old mare named Bessie I set Mary and her sick baby on her back this were no way to be either a mother or an outlaw but we had vowed never to be parted from each another. As the moon shone on the King Valley we begun to poke slowly up a spur on the western side of the King after the ridge were attained we proceeded south towards the mountains I were always in front leading Bessie by a rope

but this were scratchy country & a great ordeal for Mary who would be no horsewoman even on McBain's rich river flats.[1]

Carey's Kelly is brilliantly observant and descriptive, but ungrammatical; totally rational in thought process but unpunctuated by any normative markers; a proud outlaw but a reluctant warrior; and, as I will discuss below, a man who cares for and is sympathetic to the women in his life. Kelly's voice is more than just "authentic". It has strengths despite its weaknesses; it is not so much inadequate as an alternative form of adequacy. Where does Carey get this language? Necessarily, from the Jerilderie Letter, a document dictated if not written by Kelly and read by Carey in adolescence. It was influential on Carey's style from the beginning.[2] The Jerilderie Letter has a similar incongruous combination of eloquence and illiteracy, exclusion and confidence, something which Carey's own style tries to embody as seen in the following passage from the novel:

> there was some brush fencing where the post and rail was taking down and on this I threw big cowardly Hall on his belly I straddled him and rolled both spurs into his thighs he roared like a big calf attacked by dogs and shifted several yards of the fence I got his hands at the back of his neck and tried to make him let the revolver go but he stuck to it like grim death to a dead volunteer he called fo rassistance to a man named Cohan and Barnett Lewis, Thompson Jewell, two blacksmiths who was looking on I dare not strike any of them as I was bound to keep the peace or I could have spread those curs like dung in a paddock they got ropes tied my hands and feet and Hall beat me over the head. (168)

There are clear differences between the novel's voice and the Jerilderie Letter: the letter's style is much more paratactic and annalistic in mode, lacking the introspection and descriptiveness of Carey's Kelly. But Carey's hypothetical idiom is a plausible extrapolation of the letter's. Carey has pointedly said that he observed an Irish quality in Kelly's voice, and associated it not only with the Irish oral tradition already extant in Australian culture, such as in the ballad of "The Wild Colonial Boy", but with the quintessentially modernist style of James Joyce.[3] Carey's voicing of Kelly, as Alex McDermott put it in his introduction to a 2001 edition of the Jerilderie Letter, "prefigures the ambition of modernist literature to make the written and spoken words indivisible, as exemplified in James Joyce's *Ulysses*".[4] In Carey's rendition, there is a convergence of linguistic inventiveness and oral proliferation, as Ned Kelly both experiences his own travails and imaginatively amplifies them even as they are occurring. Graham Huggan suggests that Carey's Kelly may reflect a vestigial white privilege, "an oppositional history that disguises other more significant oppositional histories".[5] Yet the novel realistically depicts Chinese people living in rural Victoria, and

---

1   Peter Carey, *True History of the Kelly Gang* (New York: Random House, 2001), 282. All subsequent references are to this edition and appear in parentheses in the text.

2   The best exploration of the novel's relation to the letter is Paul Eggert, "The Bushranger's Voice: Peter Carey's *True History of the Kelly Gang* (2000) and Ned Kelly's Jerilderie Letter (1879)", *College Literature* 34, no. 3 (2007): 120–39.

3   Carey spoke of the Jerilderie Letter's resemblance to the language of Joyce in an interview at the State Library of Victoria in 2013. Tamsin Channing, "Peter Carey and the Jerilderie Letter", *Dome Centenary* blog, 16 August 2013. http://exhibitions.slv.vic.gov.au/dome100/dome-blogs/blog/peter-carey-and-jerilderie-letter.

4   Alex McDermott, editor's introduction to *The Jerilderie Letter* (London: Faber & Faber, 2001), xxix.

Ned's proto-Joyceanism makes him an aesthetic as well as an ethnic rebel. The verbal performance in the book is not about Carey as a writer but about Ned Kelly as a writer. Carey's humility and grace enable him to present Kelly's imagination as, however stunted and limited by circumstances, a powerful expressive vehicle. Carey conjures a Kelly who, in spite of what the system says is the truth, is capable of voicing his own.

There is an element of pastiche in the book, deriving from a series of allusions to Rolf Boldrewood's 1888 *Robbery Under Arms*, with its bushranger-protagonist and male argot, and to Joseph Furphy's 1903 *Such Is Life*, with its sense of modernity, its (adjectival) energy, and characters who sound the depths of cognitive experience even in their remote Riverina location (Carey also alludes to the Riverina in the name of Wodonga Townes, the left-wing tycoon in his 2014 novel *Amnesia*). Boldrewood's novel was first serialised just after the Kelly saga unfolded and Furphy's is set not far from Kelly country. Both books seemed even more rebellious after the introduction of censorship regarding plays and films about bushrangers, widely known as the "Bushranger Ban". The bush in this era was associated with insurgency.

With *True History of the Kelly Gang*, Carey brought the flavour and achievement of these vernacular Australian writers, generally known only within Australia, into a field of transnational cultural production. In doing so, he insisted on the modernity of Furphy, Boldrewood, and Kelly himself. The late colonialism of the Kelly era and the high modernism of Joyce were not temporally very far apart. Yet a combination of spatial distance and snobbish and/or ignorant derogation of the antipodes meant there had seemed to many a vast gulf between them. Carey's narrative bridges this gap and, more crucially, posits the modern as the intersection of Kelly's colonial experience and Carey's own contemporary articulation of that experience. Again, Nolan's paintings provided a precedent to this, emphasising the abstract qualities of Kelly's homemade armour against a typification of the Australian landscape.

If the exclusion of Australian literature from standard accounts of international modernism has had to do with the assumption that the default mode of Australian representation was realism, Nolan's Kelly posited an Australia that was always already abstract. The point is that Ned Kelly as referent is not just colonial but also modern, in both a positive and negative way, and that Peter Carey in being historical is talking about conditions that have persisted. If, as Bruno Latour opined, "we have never been modern", then Carey is not necessarily "rewriting" history, even when he seems to be doing so.[6] Jonathan Miller's phrase "writing science fiction of the past" is pertinent here.[7] Besides, it only takes a look at Ned Kelly's armour to see the medievalism in it, as Louise D'Arcens has recently pointed out.[8] All histories gesture to even deeper histories. Just because something is in the past does not mean it has ceased to affect the present.

So far so obvious. More speculatively, however, another aspect of Ned Kelly warrants attention: his relationship with his mother. It might be easy, as with Sam in *The Man Who*

5   Graham Huggan, "Cultural Memory in Postcolonial Fiction: the Uses and Abuses of Ned Kelly", *Australian Literary Studies* 20, no. 3 (2000), 65.

6   Bruno Latour, *We Have Never Been Modern*, trans. Catherine Porter (Cambridge: Harvard University Press), 1993.

7   Nicholas Birns, "Science Fiction of the Past: Peter Carey in Greenwich Village", *New York Stories* 3 (2000): 10–13.

8   Louise D'Arcens, *Old Songs in the Timeless Land: Medievalism in Australian Literature 1840–1910* (Nedlands: University of Western Australian Press, 2011).

Loved Children, to see this presence of parental rule as an allusion to the residual potency of British colonialism. The postcolonial interpretation is all the more tempting because when Carey began work on the novel, the 1999 republic referendum in Australia was yet to be held. Many observers were predicting that Australia would vote for a republic in 1999, host the Sydney Olympics in 2000, and then perhaps be rewarded another Nobel Prize for literature in time for the centenary of federation in 2001. Although the likeliest winner of this speculative Nobel was Les Murray, Carey was also considered a strong candidate. In the end, the only element of this envisioned trifecta to come to pass was the Olympics, which provoked an international interest in Sydney that Carey addressed in his ingenious and playful account of his re-engagement with the city in *Thirty Days in Sydney* (2002). But the very premise of the speculation showed the danger of relying on narratives of emergence from colonialism: they make the colonial legacy, which is undeniably an important factor in Australian literature, the *only* factor.

In terms of reading Ned Kelly's relationship with his mother in Carey's novel, the earlier methodology of Freudian psychoanalysis might be as interesting as the postcolonial reading rendered in exemplary fashion by Huggan. In the novel, Ned's mother insinuates Kelly into life as a bushranger by apprenticing him to her. Kelly's idealisation of his mother is a motivating force behind his behaviour. It bars him from successfully integrating into society. Carey shares with Christina Stead an ability to affirm social ideals while also permitting real critiques of those ideals. Even though Carey presents Kelly as a man who, although a rebel, did not intend to be hurtful, we are meant to understand Kelly's fixation on his mother as disabling. This is reminiscent of James Billington's argument in his study of nineteenth-century revolution, *Fire in the Minds of Men*, that much of the ideological energy of nineteenth-century radicals and anarchists was fuelled by sexual frustration.[9]

Carey, however, is *not* using Kelly's emotional entanglement with his mother to mock him. The book at once paints a heroic portrait of Kelly while seeing him as vulnerable. It is no accident that in trying to understand Kelly's behaviour, Carey turns to Freud rather than to Marx, even though Marx might be thought a better fit for a political insurgent. The Marxist tradition, however, has always been hostile to the rural peasantry, from the French Vendée of the 1790s (mentioned in Carey's *Parrot and Olivier in America*) onward, and the closest global analogy to Kelly may be more recent Latin American insurgents such as Subcomandante Marcos and the Zapatistas, or the rebels of Canudos, led by Antonio Conselheiro in the 1890s. The latter was documented by the Brazilian journalist Euclides da Cunha in his *Rebellion in the Backlands* (1902), and his book informed Mario Vargas Llosa's acclaimed novel *The War of the End of the World* (1981) much as the Jerilderie Letter, and the novels of Furphy and Boldrewood, informed Carey's. But the Canudos rebellion, although rural and poor in origin, was religiously motivated in a way Kelly's was not. Kelly's rebellion was much more a quest for the fair go and for social justice; any residual Catholicism had been long forgotten (Carey has observed that the same was true in his family). The word "fair" is a leitmotif in the novel, occurring over thirty times in a myriad of uses. Another index of the novel's cry for fairness is Carey's ventilation of Kelly's real-life reading of Blackmore's *Lorna Doone*, which literary critics might see as a historical romance but which Kelly, percipiently, saw as the story of how a man who perceives himself as ordinary, unspectacular and marginalised, the country-dweller John Ridd, nonetheless won the day in both private and public realms over far more entitled adversaries.

---

9   James H. Billington, *Fire in the Minds of Men* (New York: Basic Books, 1980).

The modernity of the novel, however, is not just political and stylistic but also psychological. Joyce is present in the novel's textual mediation of its content but so, less obviously, is Freud. Psychoanalysis as a method first made news by its positing of roadblocks to a stable, secure self, but the actual point of Freud's working techniques, as reframed by later commentators such as Paul Ricoeur and Adam Phillips, is to point out that these roadblocks can be dissolved and that the talking cure is a gradualist amelioration of them.[10] As W. H. Auden put it in his elegy for Freud, the Viennese psychoanalyst "hoped to improve a little by living".[11] Psychoanalysis is seen by Auden as being as palliative as it is subversive, sounding the darkness ultimately to ballast the light, sourcing the irrational so as to succour "Eros, builder of cities". In its combination of individual agency, clinical expertise and belief in systemic power, Freudianism was an ideology of modernity, one which, to Christina Stead's resentment, many believed spoke to the modern condition more than Marxism.

Carey is living in the twenty-first century and often writing about the nineteenth. But his sensibility gestated in the twentieth. Contemporary writers who set a book in the nineteenth century are sometimes assumed to be nostalgic for a road not taken, as though, despite the failures of the twentieth century, the nineteenth century could still provide a source of optimism. Especially given the association of "the short twentieth century", in Eric Hobsbawm's phrase, with Soviet communism, a recourse to the nineteenth century could be seen as a tacit form of post-communism, a regeneration of liberal optimism avoiding the tragedy of the modern, as well as its critique of bourgeois society.[12] Kelly's circumstances and grievances are colonial, but both the author and the reader encounter them through a modern filter, a filter replete with both the aesthetic experimentation and the social tragedy with which the twentieth century is indelibly associated. Carey's Kelly is both a product and an example of colonial modernity. Robert Dixon defines colonial modernity as taking issue with "the assumption that modernity is first invented in the metropolitan centre and then exported to the colonial peripheries, which are always, by definition, belated".[13] In writing a historical novel of colonial modernity, Carey is showing the world that Australia was as modern as anywhere else when the world was first becoming modern. It is widely recognised that settler colonies such as Australia, New Zealand and Canada had achieved stable governments and prosperous societies by the end of the nineteenth century. But the intellectual consensus tends to remain doubtful that their culture was sufficiently cutting-edge to be relevant to discussions of modernity, especially when modernity is conceived not just as progress, but as a kind of crisis.

There is a distinct sense of crisis throughout *True History of the Kelly Gang*, however. Ned's convict father is dead, and Ned goes to prison in his early teens. By the time he is released his mother, Ellen Quinn Kelly, has married an American named George King, who instructs Ned in the art of bushranging but whose usurpation of Ned's father's role wounds the young man and inflames his more general resentment of class privilege. When

---

10   Paul Ricoeur, *Freud and Philosophy* (New Haven: Yale University Press, 1977); Adam Phillips, *Becoming Freud: The Making of a Psychoanalyst* (New Haven: Yale University Press, 2014).

11   W. H. Auden, "In Memory of Sigmund Freud", from *Another Time* (New York: Random House, 1940), via Poets.org. www.poets.org/poetsorg/poem/memory-sigmund-freud.

12   Eric Hobsbawm, *The Age of Extremes: The Short Twentieth Century, 1914–1991* (New York: Vintage, 1994).

13   Robert Dixon, *Photography, Early Cinema, and Colonial Modernity: Frank Hurley's Synchronized Lecture Entertainments* (London: Anthem Press, 2013), xxiii.

Kelly's mother is jailed, the state, like Claudius in *Hamlet*, takes over the role of Oedipal usurper. Thus Kelly's resentment against the state is not just political and jurisprudential, but also psychosexual. Kelly is haunted by the loss of his mother, first to King and then to the state, and this comes out in the inchoate rage that lands him in progressively more trouble in Wangaratta and Glenrowan. His triumphs and tragedies are modern ones into which psychoanalytic methods lend insight.

Putting Ned "on the couch" in Freudian terms is not to undercut him but to treat him with particular respect as a herald of twentieth-century humanity whose pathologies can be addressed by psychoanalytic methods. If Christina Stead's Sam Pollit, or any of the male villains of Elizabeth Harrower's novels, were treatable by psychoanalysis, they would not be at once so abject and so pathological. When Clemency James in Harrower's *The Catherine Wheel* thinks of her relationships with Christian and Rollo, she reflects that these men are far more depraved than a "normal, intelligent neurotic" such as herself.[14] This exemplifies the anthropological assumptions of post-Freudian humanity – that to have a mother fixation, as Carey's Ned does, is a problem, but one that is clinically treatable. (Similarly, there is a popular Freudianism in Nolan's Kelly paintings, as Kelly's self-manifestation is equivalent to a visual rendering of unconscious energies.) The problems of the characters in Stead's and Harrower's novels are gripping because they are insoluble by psychoanalytic means, whereas Ned's problems would be very differently evaluated were he not so disempowered. The psychological problems are barely visible to the first-time reader as they are, to use the popular phrase, "First World problems", and Ned is distinctly a part of the settler-colony "Second World", as defined a generation ago by Stephen Slemon.[15] Ned Kelly may be a criminal in the eyes of the colonial legal system, but he is not authoritarian like Stead's and Harrower's men. Had he lived in the late-modern milieu of mid-twentieth-century Australia, he might well have been a typical, if more boisterous than average, modern citizen. Certainly he would seem downright normal compared to, say, Waldo in Patrick White's *The Solid Mandala*, if the two were to bump into each other in Pitt Street Mall.

Kelly, however, is trapped in the Victorian in two senses. He is writing in 1879, twenty years before Australia will become a self-governing nation. Ned's life is firmly set in the colony of Victoria, although the physical proximity of the Kelly country to New South Wales gives it a liminality that can also be seen in Furphy's Riverina in *Such Is Life*. Kelly country is a border district. That Victoria in Ned's context applies to a place as well as to a time, to the polity under whose laws he is unjustly tried as well as to the queen who epitomises those laws, makes us see that if the source of Ned's maladjustment is psychological to the small degree it is not socioeconomic, the ways in which he is misperceived are spatio-temporal. Ned is both back in time and distant from the metropolitan. It is for this that he writes a long confession, an apologia to his unseen daughter.

That the daughter is in San Francisco alludes to the transpacific connections already evident in the Kelly era.[16] These can be seen in the American characters in Rolf Boldrewood's novels, not just *Robbery Under Arms*, which features an American card game

---

14   Elizabeth Harrower, *The Catherine Wheel* (Text Publishing: Melbourne, 2014), 185. On Freud as representative of "modern singularity", see Bruno Bosteels, *Marx and Freud in Latin America* (London: Veros, 2012), 159.

15   Stephen Slemon, "Unsettling the Empire: Resistance Theory for the Second World", *World Literatures Written in English* (1990): 30–42.

16   The standard book on this is Erika Esau, *Images of the Pacific Rim: Australia and California, 1850–1935* (Sydney: Power Publications, 2010).

and American characters, but also in *The Miner's Right* (1891), in which many of the diggers are either American or have passed through the United States. These connections increased after 1898, when American naval power moved into the western Pacific. The role of the American consul in Ada Cambridge's *Thirty Years in Australia* also bespeaks a growing American diplomatic and economic interest in Australia. The invention of a daughter for Kelly gives the bushranger a future dimension in both space and time, one that the coercive governmental response to his self-assertion has forbidden him.

Why a daughter and not a son? A son, in Kelly's situation, would only carry on the Oedipal scenario already staged by the absence of his father, his veneration of his mother, and his resentment of King (in a Freudian reading, this would be a stand-in for Oedipal resentment felt towards his real father for possessing his mother).[17] A son might cast Kelly in the role of Laius rather than Oedipus, but the psychosexual skirmishes would continue. A daughter offers a way out of all that, while also perpetuating the presence of the feminine already latent in the Kelly story by the presence of Kate Kelly, Ned's sister, who was a highly effective member of Ned's outlaw gang. Kate Kelly has appeared in a number of Australian literary works, among them Jean Bedford's *Sister Kate* (1982).

Carey also invents Mary Hearn, Ned's beloved, who bears his daughter. Has Carey perhaps invented Mary to indicate that Ned's psychosexual, Oedipal aspects did not preclude him from forming a mature and passionate attachment with a woman? Mary injects some gender parity into bush rebellion, and leavens the homosocial milieu in which the biographical Ned largely moved. Carey uses the relationship with Mary Hearn to show that Kelly lives a tragic life but has potential for psychological growth; he is not calcified into authoritarianism like Sam Pollit. It is this potential that makes him not just a pitiable loser but, in Bourdieu's terms, a loser who wins. In Sidney Nolan's paintings Kelly was a loser who became modernist, which in the twentieth century, was, in aesthetic terms, winning. Similarly, subjecting Kelly to psychoanalysis claims him for modernity. As Perry Meisel says, both literary modernity and psychoanalysis are structured by "antithetical and schismatic traditions".[18] Carey's Kelly is a bush-grown, rambunctious version of these schismatic antithetical traditions.

Freudian theory can also help us to understand the novel's relationship to its source material, both the Jerilderie Letter and Kelly's own life, and the larger context of nineteenth-century Australian popular culture, lore, history and fiction which Carey is at once plundering and salvaging for the international reader. If the historical novel is defined precisely by its relationship with its source material, then psychoanalysis, which relates affective identities to *psychic* source material, figures the relation of symptom to source.[19] A psychoanalytic understanding of the book helps the reader to understand why Kelly became a legend and why it matters, and why Kelly's life, although sad and even pathetic, was not a waste. Kelly had the potential to live a constructive life, and, although a ruffian and an outlaw, was neither a terrorist nor an authoritarian. The adjustment psychoanalysis made to democratic individualism is to include the potential as well as the realised aspects of constructive life. A Freudian Australia, one in which flawed individuals in need of

17   Ernest Jones, *Hamlet and Oedipus* (New York: W. W. Norton & Co., 1949), is the *locus classicus* of Oedipal analyses in literature.

18   Perry Meisel, *The Literary Freud* (London: Routledge, 2007), 17.

19   Ángel Rama, "La guerra del fin del mundo: una obra maestra del fanatismo artístico", *Eco* 246 (1982): 600–64.

fundamental repair are nonetheless welcomed as citizens and participants in the community, is a democratic, possibly egalitarian Australia, in which Ned Kelly's dream of fairness has at least a scintilla of plausibility.

One could, however, argue that to champion Kelly at this late date – after the rise of multiculturalism and Indigenous rights, and at a time when the refugee crisis was becoming a ground of contention in Australian politics – is to privilege whiteness, to substitute a white dissident for non-white dissidence. Yet Carey's Kelly is a bridge between white, privileged Australia and a more culturally heterodox model. A modern reformism that refuses to yield to a contemporary radicalism, that stays in a comfortable mid-twentieth century cocoon of the liberalism of white privilege and does not acknowledge contemporary issues of race and identity, becomes retrograde. But a contemporary radicalism that is unable to track its genealogy back through modern reformism is in danger of becoming boutique dissent in a neoliberal polity. Carey's Kelly is shut out in his Australia the way Indigenous people, refugees and detainees are today. The character of Kelly ties these derogated subjects to a tradition of rebellion and resistance, and to a humane individualism guaranteed by the acknowledgement of sentient will, both avowed and wayward, in Freud's work.

The contemporary era, having largely eliminated psychoanalysis and talk therapy in favour of an emphasis on prescription drugs to cure mental ailments, denies this wayward but humane sentience. As Danny in *Barracuda* finds out, in the twenty-first century one is only a winner or a loser. In the era of neoliberalism, as *The Unusual Life of Tristan Smith* shows brilliantly, Kelly's only way to be successful would be to play a simulated version of himself, to join the circus and exhibit himself to the metropolis between colonial failure and contemporary spectacle. Modernity provided a middle way of normally neurotic pathos between extremes of success and failure. It is Kelly's Freudian vulnerabilities that render his tragic heroism particularly modern.

Global Carey, Subversive Carey

Even before *True History of the Kelly Gang* cemented Carey's global stature, he was the Australian author to make the largest impact on the world stage. This is true even though Patrick White won the Nobel and even though, as David Carter has argued, many other writers, from Henry Handel Richardson to Eleanor Dark and Jon Cleary, had moments when they seemed to be poised to make this sort of breakthrough.[20] But it was Carey's work, in the reputation-making *Illywhacker* and the Booker Prize-winning *Oscar and Lucinda*, that solicited a permanent world audience for Australian literature, and rescued it from being dismissed as marginalia or curio.

Carey was in the right place at the right time. A few months before *Illywhacker* was published in the USA, in the fall of 1985, the *New York Times* ran a lengthy piece by the Australian journalist and cultural commentator Craig McGregor, one of the most substantive essays on Australian literature that had ever run in a major American periodical. McGregor argued that Australian literature had "performed a series of comings of age", and spoke of the "sheer bigness" of the arts in Australia.[21] McGregor's approach was decidedly

---

20 David Carter, "Transpacific or Transatlantic Traffic? Australian Books and American Publishers", in *Reading across the Pacific*, eds Robert Dixon and Nicholas Birns (Sydney: Sydney University Press, 2011): 339–59.

pop (possibly marking the only time that Men at Work and Air Supply have been mentioned in association with Australian literary culture). Although he advocated radicalism in the arts, this was radicalism of a political, not a formal, stripe. Thus a template was sketched for the kind of Australian novel that might be successful abroad: ambitious, politically radical in a vaguely optimistic way, full of life but also outrageously inventive. That Carey's *Illywhacker* fit the bill so nicely was a tribute to the vigour of that engaging novel – but in the 1980s, thanks to the Australian film boom, the growing ease of travel and communications, and the waning of Cold War certainties, such a writer was almost bound to emerge.

Another candidate for the role might have been Rodney Hall, widely published internationally and on the verge, by the 1980s, of being seen as the Australian equivalent of Gabriel García Márquez. Paul Giles speaks of the appeal, for Americans, after the success of Salman Rushdie's *Midnight's Children*, of Carey's "ludic picaresque" style; the characterisation could just as well have been made of Hall's *Just Relations* (1982).[22] Another in the running was Blanche D'Alpuget, strongly backed by the then-influential New York editor Robert Asahina. D'Alpuget's *Turtle Beach* (1981), in a weird instance of precognitive coincidence, was reviewed widely just after Australia momentarily burst into the news after the election of Prime Minister Bob Hawke, whom D'Alpuget later married. *Turtle Beach* involved Australia with Asian themes, while also offering the Australian perspective on the world as a refreshing and invigorating one, showing how an Australian transnationalism might complement or contradict rather than simply reproduce an American one. Glenda Adams' *Dancing On Coral* (1987) intertwined Australia, America, Pacific island peoples and Sixties radicalism in a dynamic and intellectually demanding way. But neither Hall nor D'Alpuget nor Adams, nor any of the many other Australian writers active in the 1980s, broke through in the USA the way Peter Carey was about to.

Carey's novels have not only received positive reviews in the major Anglophone outlets for high-literary book reviewing such as the *Times Literary Supplement*, the *New Yorker* and the *New York Times Book Review*, eliciting deep and insightful criticism from first-rate critics such as Galen Strawson, John Updike and Frank Kermode. He has also been blessed with many fine academic critics, including Andreas Gaile, Anthony J. Hassall, Sue Ryan-Fazilleau and Bruce Woodcock.[23] Yet there has also been a second stream of Carey criticism, beginning with Karen Lamb's 1992 book *Peter Carey and the Genesis of Fame*, that has seen his work more as publishing phenomenon than art.[24] Graeme Turner, in a far more sophisticated fashion than Lamb, has spoken of Carey as a literary celebrity who, even though he lives abroad, lends identity to the nation.[25] Carey has been both privileged

---

21   Craig McGregor, "Australian Writing Today: Riding Off in All Directions", *New York Times Book Review*, 19 May 1985, 1.

22   Paul Giles, *Antipodean America: Australasia and the Constitution of US Literature* (New York: Oxford University Press, 2014), 432.

23   Anthony Hassall, *Dancing on Hot Macadam: Peter Carey's Fiction* (St Lucia: University of Queensland Press, 1998); Bruce Woodcock, *Peter Carey* (Manchester: Manchester University Press, 1996); Andreas Gaile, *Fabulating Beauty: Perspectives on the Fiction of Peter Carey* (Amsterdam: Rodopi, 2005); Sue Ryan-Fazilleau, "Bob's Dreaming: Playing with Reader Expectations in Peter Carey's *Oscar and Lucinda*", *Rocky Mountain Review of Language and Literature* 59, no. 1 (2005): 11–30.

24   Karen Lamb, *Peter Carey and the Genesis of Fame* (Sydney: Angus & Robertson, 1992).

25   Graeme Turner, "Nationalising the Author: The Celebrity of Peter Carey", *Australian Literary Studies* 16, no. 2 (1993): 131–39.

and punished for his success, which is particularly odd given his success was more or less on par with that of other authors of his generation – Julian Barnes, Richard Ford, Martin Amis, Ian McEwan – who have not been seen by critics as totally under the aegis of their own good literary fortune as Carey has been. This was compounded by Carey living in the USA since 1989. There has long been a certain anti-Americanism in Australian letters, running alongside an at times heedless enthusiasm for current American trends. An expatriate who moved to Britain, like Peter Porter, might seem in danger of becoming irrelevant to Australian literature – McGregor, describing Porter's work as "sophisticated" and "structured", made him seem very nearly that. But he would not be seen to have "sold out" the way an Australian writer who moved to America might be.[26]

Australian cultural taste has long seen success in the USA as a barometer of merit. Yet Carey's immense popularity on the American scene, and his taking up permanent residence in New York, was apparently too much of a good thing for the more sensitive among the Australian commentariat, or perhaps more justly the precariat of that commentariat. As early as 1996, Bruce Woodcock spoke of a "Carey backlash in some Australian circles".[27] Carey has been punished for his success in a way that not only is an unbecoming instance of tall poppy syndrome but also bespeaks little faith in the potential for the literary pie to grow. This unfortunate posture was also brutally negligent of Carey's tireless attempts to promote the work of other Australian writers in the United States, and to acknowledge great masters of the past such as Patrick White and Xavier Herbert, whose *Poor Fellow, My Country*, for all its flaws, is a special favourite of Carey's.

Carey was envied for his sheer marketability. Some japed that, as a former advertising man, he knew how to promote his own books. This sort of comment reflected a highly unsophisticated view of how writers make their way in the world. Bryce Courtenay was also an advertising man turned writer, who aimed at a far more popular audience than did Carey and achieved it – in Australia. In the USA, only one of Courtenay's books has been published, and with less commercial and critical success than the average Carey novel. A background in advertising does not guarantee success, and success in one country does not mean success everywhere.

Carey's concerns from 1990 onward mirrored and sagaciously anticipated those of other major contemporary Australian writers: a sense of historical trauma; of Australia's highly compromised legacy of racism and hypocrisy; and of the status of fiction itself in a milieu where a naive realism was no longer possible. In addition, from the Aboriginal characters in *Oscar and Lucinda* to the Chinese in *True History of the Kelly Gang* to the Malay elements in *My Life as a Fake*, Carey has represented Australia beyond whiteness.

Carey similarly extends the representation of America in the Australian novel. Australian writers old enough to fight in World War II – the contemporaries of American GIs like Herbert Jaffa, who as an American serviceman was stationed in Bacchus Marsh, Victoria, in 1942, the year before Carey was born there – admired America not just as a wartime ally but as a place of freedom far from the oppressive colonial residue of Australia, a sentiment visible in David Rowbotham's 2002 *Poems for America*. Yet for Carey, the United States has been far more the villain than the hero.[28] The dystopia of "The Fat Man

---

26 McGregor, "Australian Writing Today", 1.
27 Woodcock, *Peter Carey*, 162.
28 This was recognised as early as Graeme Turner's first article on Carey, "American Dreaming: The Fictions of Peter Carey", *Australian Literary Studies*, 12, no. 4 (1986): 431–41.

in History" (1974) is impossible without the dark spectre of an American-fostered future dictatorship.

Even more directly, "American Dreams", a short story collected in the 1974 volume *The Fat Man in History*, sees America as a metaphor for iconic, gratifying wish-fulfilment. And in *Bliss* (1981), the opposite of the refuge that Harry Joy finds with Honey Barbara is the bleak, greed-ridden metropolitan landscape of the very New York where Carey would one day dwell. Indeed, if one were to read the early work of Peter Carey, rife with smouldering criticisms of the American presence abroad and the American way of life, and then the depiction of America in Gerald Murnane's *A Lifetime on Clouds* – as a land of splendid if exalted dreams – one might pick Murnane as the writer more likely to migrate to the USA. That Murnane has never left Australia at all and that Carey has lived in and been productive and popular in New York for a quarter of a century shows both that one cannot extrapolate life from writing, and that Carey's depiction of America is a curious kind of investment, what Paul Giles calls a "principled deracination".[29] It is not one of outright opposition, or of capitulation. It is a fine-grained challenge. Carey infiltrates the USA, not antagonistically, but with a determination to maintain his foreign eye.

Like Tristan Smith, Carey gravitated to the centre of an empire he loathed. Unlike the sometimes-hapless Tristan, however, Carey had the skill and the wit overtly to attack the American right whose actions he saw as so malevolent and so destructive of American idealism – an idealism Carey has made clear he admires. The best rebuke to those who see Carey as a mere exporter of Australia is that to be an exporter one must be an exponent, and Carey has not only been critical of Australia but has taken the contemporary world as his subject. Paul Giles observes, in response to Hassall's work on Carey, that there is a tendency to see Carey as "one-dimensional", as a simple relayer of Australia to the world.[30] Carey is something more than that: a global writer of global scope responding to an age of global crisis.

Unofficially but palpably, critical opinion has tended to discriminate between "global Carey" and "subversive Carey". Global Carey includes works like *Illywhacker, Oscar and Lucinda* and *True History of the Kelly Gang*: books that win prizes and are accepted abroad as iconic renditions of Australian life and imagination. Subversive Carey includes the early short stories with their dystopian metafiction, matched only in Australian literature by John A. Scott's *St Clair* (1984); and *The Unusual Life of Tristan Smith*, with its conscious roots in postcolonial theory as represented by Homi K. Bhabha and the Australian critics Bill Ashcroft, Gareth Griffiths and Helen Tiffin, and its portrayal of an artificial Pacific fantasy world. Once these rubrics are established it is easy to divide Carey's books into these two categories: *Jack Maggs* (1997), with its exploration of the Australian margins of Dickens' life and writing, is global Carey because of Dickens' own popular celebrity; *The Tax Inspector* (1991) is subversive Carey because neither the Catchprices nor Maria Takis is particularly likeable, and the overall tone of the novel is dark. Carey is prone to throw his implied audience off-course, to prevent them from getting too anchored in a comfort zone. If, as some have argued, he "fails to solve the problems of realism and fabulism", he could be seen as deploying realism and fabulism against each other, to forestall an overly crystallised version of either.[31]

---

29 Giles, *Antipodean America*, 444.
30 Giles, *Antipodean America*, 446.
31 Woodcock, *Peter Carey*, 161.

From *The Unusual Life of Tristan Smith* onward, Carey provides a series of portraits of artists. Tristan himself, clown and spy, combines metafiction and *testimonio* in multiple ways, most importantly in that he tells the entire narrative to his audience, a Voorstand jury, as he is on trial. Tristan is speaking to the enemy, the people who – and we can see a foreshadowing of Kelly here – killed his mother, at once assailing them and appealing to them. Paradox about the metropolitan pervades *Tristan Smith*. Saarlim is the most powerful city in the world, yet it is dilapidated and badly maintained, and its inhabitants, although privileged in wealth, are often misshapen, gross in form, and both vulnerable and vulgar, as in the case of Peggy Kram, a stand-in for a certain kind of American lay reader. The Franciscan Free Church started off as a combination of Calvinist austerity and romantic nature-worship, but has become an exploitative peddler of simulacra. Dissent has become normative and controlling. But none of this critique would be possible if Tristan had never gone to the centre: his willingness to confront the centre at its core makes him a true dissident. Carey is anchored in New York like a dagger at the very heart of the establishment.

Carey in the Twenty-First Century

The very titles of the three novels that followed *True History of the Kelly Gang* – *My Life as a Fake* (2003), *Theft* (2006) and *His Illegal Self* (2008) – reveal Carey's concern with inauthenticity, appropriation, and not being what one seems to be or thinks one is. This concern even came into Carey's nonfiction in this period, as is evident in the subtitle of *Thirty Days in Sydney: A Wildly Distorted Account*, and in the title of his 2005 book on Japan, *Wrong about Japan*. As with Ned Kelly and his armour, Butcher Bones in *Theft* is a home-grown modernist, a congenial Aussie swindler writing his way into modernity by hoaxing it. If modernist art is suffused with irony and inauthenticity, then Australia will not be left behind, but will "forge" its way in: "forge" in the double sense of faking and making.

This is where Carey's world is very different from that of modernism. There was a tradition in modernism of *Kunstlerschuld*, artist-guilt (as sketched in Martin Seymour-Smith's history of modern world literature).[32] Writers such as André Gide, in *Les Faux-Monnayeurs* (*The Counterfeiters*, 1925), pondered the inauthenticity of art, much as does *My Life as a Fake*, while the first great American postmodern novel, William Gaddis' *The Recognitions* (1955), is all about the forgery of artwork, much as *Theft* is. Gide and Gaddis, however, describe characters who forge and fake in an effort to be losers who win, whereas the only possible reason to forge in the contemporary era is for money – to be a winner who wins. Neoliberal forgers are just entrepreneurs by other means.

By the beginning of the twenty-first century, the corporate world had embraced self-reference. So much of finance had to do with making up figures and results and did not pretend to correspond to any reality. What Emily Apter has termed "paranoid globalism" – the sense that everything is interconnected, that the world is even smaller than it in fact is – led to a sense of at least mock total awareness of everything that was going on.[33] The literary world had become commoditised. Modernist forgers may have simulated art for

---

32 Martin Seymour-Smith, *The New Guide to Modern World Literature* (London: Macmillan, 1985), 644, 875.

the sake of money but art and money were separate enough for forgery to seem not only criminal but conceptually audacious, as art and money were so diametrically opposed. The postmodern works of Barbara Kruger, Jenny Holzer and Jeff Koons, however, often deliberately represented commodity fetishism, which was no longer suppressed for the sake of rarefied Art. Thus to say that art was fake was no longer to expose it or to question it. It was to tell everybody something he or she already knew and felt cynically indifferent about.[34]

Theft periodises fakery. The motifs of the mechanical Golem and mechanical Charlie Chaplin, as contemplated by the character Leo Stein, evoke the traumas of twentieth-century history and the Holocaust, as if to say that the period after modernity can only simulate these sorts of traumas. That Butcher Bones is released from Long Bay prison in 1980, one of the possible foundation-years for the neoliberal era, alludes to the possibility of the intertwining of fakery with the financialisation of the public sphere. Taking up this theme would have pulled the novel towards more contemporary relevance. In *Parrot and Olivier in America*, Carey was later to prove that he was consummately able to make these contemporary parallels: so why not here?

One of the keys to *Theft*, and – even though it is not directly about forgery or art – *His Illegal Self* concerns the relationship of modernism to Australia: put bluntly, there was not thought to be one. The Ern Malley hoax, the animating crux of *Theft*, was notable because it represented both an attempt to parody modernism in Australia, and, in the view of critics from Paul Kane to Michael Heyward, a surreptitious, *malgré lui* manifestation of that same modernism, one possibly outdoing in aesthetic achievement the "actual" poems of James McAuley and Harold Stewart.[35] That Carey has his Ern Malley figure, Bob McCorkle, literally come to life is but a dramatisation of the idea that the Ern Malley poems were interesting poems even if their creators had not intended them to be. The book is a warning that aesthetic eidolons may become material realities, and peripheries may be able to write back to centres in more than name only.

Carey used the theme of the hoax at a time of widespread fascination with the topic. In the controversies surrounding B. Wongar, Mudrooroo and Helen Demidenko, authors claimed to be, or believed they were, what they were not: Indigenous Australian, Ukrainian-Australian. Paul Genoni attributes this preoccupation to a 1990s concern with establishing identity.[36] But, equally, the interest might exude from a sense of the fragility of identity. In Ern Malley's case, the phantom conjured by the hoax was that of an Australian modernism. This was a modernism that Max Harris, the avant-garde editor who was hoaxed by Malley because the hoax fit his poetic enthusiasms, wanted. It was one that James McAuley and Harold Stewart in no way wanted. But somehow, in the form of the Malley poems, they gave a forced and agonising birth to it. Carey's novel operates in the wake of this nearly stillborn modernism.

The Ern Malley topic thus figured a perceived crisis within Australian literature: that it did not have enough of a modernism; it had a postmodernism, as Carey's work

---

33   Emily Apter, *Against World Literature: On the Politics of Untranslatability* (London: Verso Books, 2014), 71.
34   Robert Dixon, "Peter Carey's and Ray Lawler's *Bliss*: Fiction, Film and Power", *Studies in Australasian Cinema* 3, no. 3 (2010): 279–94. Dixon uses the art of Andy Warhol to examine the issues of inauthenticity and audience awareness to which Carey's work gestures.
35   Paul Kane, *Australian Poetry: Romanticism and Negativity* (Cambridge: Cambridge University Press, 1996), 141–42; Michael Heyward, *The Ern Malley Affair* (St Lucia: University of Queensland Press, 1993).
36   Paul Genoni, "From the Nineties to the Noughties", *Westerly* 59, no. 2 (2014): 190.

demonstrated, but not a modernism. The title of C. K. Stead's 1979 essay on New Zealand poetry, "From Wystan to Carlos", was notable not so much because, in saying New Zealand poets had shifted from being influenced by W. H. Auden to being influenced by William Carlos Williams, it suggested a shift from British to American precedents but because Williams, born in 1883, was a full generation older than Auden, born in 1907. Thus for antipodean poets suddenly to embrace modernism of the sort found in Williams meant they were going backwards in time.[37] It could be argued that part of the exclusionary and elitist aspects of modernism lay in its exclusion of literatures such as the Australian: that modernism simply canonised a few writers resident in or on the fringes of the metropolitan who conformed to certain experimental or avant-garde norms, and ignored the rest. Or, to put it another way, that Australian late modernity, as figured consummately in Patrick White's Sarsaparilla novels and in the fiction of Elizabeth Harrower, was ignored by non-Australians because it embodied all of the restraints and paralyses of the modern period without any of its rebellions and insurgencies. The iconoclasm of the 1960s is what has led to the decade being described (borrowing from Hobsbawm) as a "very short twentieth century", a decade that epitomised in miniature the self-assertion of the century as a whole.[38]

His Illegal Self is about a group of radicals on the run in Queensland in the 1970s (as is widely known, Carey himself lived in a hippie commune at Bellingen on the north coast of New South Wales at a slightly later date). The upheaval of the 1960s reached Australia somewhat belatedly: Gough Whitlam was not elected until 1972 and, as David McCooey has argued, the poetic generation of '68 in Australia could just as well be termed the generation of '79; it was only by the end of the 1970s that they had written their career-establishing work.[39] Moreover, there were no Australian equivalents of terrorist groups such as the Weather Underground and the Symbionese Liberation Army, and anti-Vietnam War activity only began on a large scale in Australia in 1970, when the war was beginning to wind down. In writing about Vietnam-era American radicalism in His Illegal Self, Carey was writing about what he had missed. Carey draws upon his Bellingen experience and attempts to write himself into the American setting by making references in the novel to such upstate New York communities as Jeffersonville and Poughkeepsie, places in the hinterland of New York's metropolitan area which Carey knows now but which someone living in Australia at the time would not have known about.

His Illegal Self is haunted by an inherent unease. James Bradley commented that it seemed to him Carey's "least successful novel by some distance".[40] In addition, novels with similar themes, written by Philip Roth, Susan Choi, Sigrid Nuñez, Dana Spiotta and Jonathan Lethem garnered more attention in the USA because of their surer grasp of the psychic and imaginative territory.[41]

37   C. K. Stead, "From Wystan to Carlos: Modern and Modernism in Recent New Zealand Poetry", Islands 5, no. 7 (1979): 467–86. Stead himself, in Book Self: The Reader as Writer and the Writer as Critic (Auckland: Auckland University Press, 2008), noted what he called this "strange irony".

38   Nicholas Birns, "The System Cannot Withstand Close Scrutiny: 1966, the Hopkins Conference, and the Anomalous Rise of Theory", Modern Language Quarterly 75, no. 3 (2014): 327–54.

39   David McCooey, "Contemporary Poetry: Across Party Lines", in The Cambridge Companion to Australian Literature, ed. Elizabeth Webby (Cambridge: Cambridge University Press, 2000), 158–82.

40   James Bradley, "Once Upon a Time in America", Weekend Australian, 31 October–1 November 2009, 22–23.

The chief character of *His Illegal Self* is an American woman, Anna Xenos – the surname denoting, obviously, "stranger" – who has taken the name Dial, short for "Dialectic". She takes care of her lover's child, a little boy known as Jay or Che, after the Latin American guerrilla leader. Carey's depiction of Dial, not the boy's natural mother but his mostly responsible caretaker, adds to his portrait galleries of parenthood, real and surrogate, and, more generally, of caring and what might be called a familiar version of "concern". One of Carey's early stories was entitled "Do You Love Me?" In his later books, a recurring question is "Do you care about me? Does my survival and comfort matter to you?" That Carey tells half the book from the viewpoint of the child is bravura, not so much because of the audacity of an adult simulating a child's voice, but because Carey was already an adult during the period depicted. The asymmetries of a sensitive child-narrator can stand for other outsider perspectives – such as the Australian.

Parrot and Olivier: Ingenious Social Hope

Parrot and Olivier in America (2009) is an exciting and exacting book, a novel at once historical and contemporary. With it, Carey revealed himself as a diarist of the present who uses history and fantasy as his preferred means of notation. He not only delves into the archive, but also uses the archive as an idiolect of expression, turning it into, in a Wittgensteinian sense, a language-game that embodies meaning that may have been otherwise conceivable, but not otherwise articulable.[42]

Parrot and Olivier in America contrasts in alternate chapters the *hauteur* of Paris and the incipient democratic chants of the American experiment. Olivier de Garmont, an expatriate French aristocrat somewhat modelled on Alexis de Tocqueville, at first seems somebody so fussy and vulnerable as hardly to be able to interact with a hustling, vibrant frontier society. This comes through in the style of Olivier's chapters, which is accomplished but not expressive. That at book's end we see that there is some merit in Olivier amounts to a recognition that his aristocratic pretensions do bring with them value, or at least panache.

Carey's ability to accept asymmetries is shown not only in his multi-faceted portrait of Olivier, but also in the more discrete and historically situated aspects of the book. Some of the cameos of contemporary figures are outstanding, such as that of Washington Irving, "a lawyer and comic novelist of some renown" (188).[43] In a way this sort of legerdemain is most impressive when done with real people, but in Carey's novel, spearheaded by one character based loosely on a real person and another entirely made up (albeit with stock elements), there is a pleasing sense of the novelist using history to create a distinct fictional world, distinct from the present time and from other fictional worlds but also distinct from

---

41   A. L. McCann explored 1970s European terrorism in Australian terms in *Subtopia* (Melbourne: Vulgar Press, 2005).

42   Peter Carey, *Parrot and Olivier in America* (New York: Alfred A. Knopf, 2010). All subsequent references are to this edition and appear in parentheses in the text.

43   Parrot rears his head far less loudly than Olivier, but the accumulated wisdom of his practical encounters across three continents makes his optimism both weathered and achievable. Olivier's sweeping lens re-enacts inequalities of the past, but Parrot's overt mimicry offers glimpses of a vista of an ampler future, providing what Les Murray, in "Noonday Axeman", termed "a human breach in the silence".

the very history from which it draws its pulse. *Parrot and Olivier in America* is the product of enormous diligence, but its sources dance and pack an integrated cumulative punch. Carey attends to every nuance for its own sake, and this attention to detail, exemplifying, to use Coleridge's word, the "esemplastic" aspect of Carey's imagination, is in full gear in this novel.

Carey has commented that, while many Americans romanticise Tocqueville as the outsider discerning enough to praise American democracy, there are indeed many snobbish and condescending moments in his treatment of the United States, many of them cogent, as in the monotony de Tocqueville observes across the country,[44] a sameness more recently described by the Australian historian Bruce Grant as "the absence of surprise".[45] But the book is a fantasia on de Tocqueville, not a commentary on him. Olivier also hints at earlier French visitors to America, such as Citizen Genêt (in marrying the local aristocrat) and Hector St John de Crèvecoeur (in settling down on an American homestead). Olivier is largely without Tocqueville's genuine idealism. He is much more a figure of reaction, somebody whose family is too conservative to thrive in France even under the moderate July monarchy, never to be mistaken for the Terror. Parrot's relation of parodic servitude to both "Lord Migraine" (i.e. Olivier) and the Marquis de Tilbot makes him a jaded but surprisingly bright-eyed backspring against Olivier's fear of American tumult and levelling.

There is also a third level of New World identity in this book, what we might call the Australian. Before he meets up with Olivier, John "Parrot" Lariat goes to New South Wales at age twelve aboard a convict ship. There, he marries an Irish woman. Parrot is at home everywhere: in Australia, in America, and even – or especially – in Paris, where he marries Mathilde, with whom he has a warm and supportive relationship of the sort Olivier can never attain. Despite being the model for Delacroix's painting of liberty leading the masses, Mathilde is less idealistic and more cynical than Parrot, but they both have an inability to interact with people of a higher class without becoming captivated or overtaken by them. It is not just that Parrot is more successfully American than the arrogant and cavalier Olivier; in many ways he is more successfully French. His very nickname, "Parrot", or Perroquet in French, refers to the abundance of these birds in Australia, as well as the idea of the parrot as a mimic, as Parrot Larritt successfully ingratiates himself with all manner of authorities and superiors, only to show the reader that he is never entirely within their grasp. Birds are an important motif in the novel: they are migratory, beautiful, but also full of violence. Algernon Watkins, Parrot's employer, a forger like Butcher Bones and an etcher of birds, is a clear calque of John James Audubon, who himself was rumoured to be the rescued and anonymous Louis XVII, the boy Dauphin who in fact died young. In this book, nobody is what they seem, and Parrot's ability to parrot is, paradoxically, what maintains his authenticity, even as the free-to-say-what-he-wants Olivier is hamstrung by his own sense of privilege and authority.

Another Australian referent in the book is the role of the Tombs prison in Manhattan, where "everything is suffocating hot", and the emphasis on the prison in Olivier's sociological study of America (167). This reminds us not just of de Tocqueville's own writings on prisons, but also that American prisons in this era were one of Foucault's principal

---

44   "An interview with Peter Carey", Book Browse website, https://www.bookbrowse.com/ author_interviews/full/index.cfm/author_number/556/peter-carey.

45   Bruce Grant, *A Furious Hunger: America in the 21st Century* (Melbourne: Melbourne University Press, 1999), 120.

sources in *Discipline and Punish*.[46] The Tombs was a prison in a former colony; Australia was an entire prison colony unto itself, and anything Carey says about penology inherently resonates on an Australian plane. In a very distant but unmistakeable way, *Parrot and Olivier in America* is a convict novel, and the United States it depicts is reminded that its rhetoric of freedom necessarily entails a considerable number of prisons. America in the novel is at once a respite from the hierarchies of Olivier's natal France, and a kinder, gentler continuation of them by other means, despite the Americans' "enthusiasm for self-congratulation" that they have effaced aristocracy entirely (161). Beyond this dichotomy, there is a vision of Australia as a place where the excluded might aspire to a genuinely egalitarian society, less money-centred than the American, but are inhibited from putting it into practice by a hierarchy as cruel as ever existed in Europe.

This Australian shadow hovers over the protagonists' desire to find both personal and social happiness in the New World. Olivier's eventually unhappy relationship with Miss Amelia Godefroy is indicative of this. It is also a clear example of Carey's ingenious referentiality. Carey uses names as tactical code, as witness his deployment of his own maternal family name, Warriner, in *Jack Maggs*. Godeffroy, with two f's, is a small town in upstate New York. There is plausible reason to believe that Carey knows it, given the mentions of Jeffersonville and Poughkeepsie, both about an hour's drive from Godeffroy, in *His Illegal Self*. Amelia Godefroy, however, comes from Connecticut, not upstate New York, and this provides the perfect referent for the intrusion of commerce into pastoral utopia: the coast of Connecticut is lamented as "the most shocking monument to avarice one could ever have witnessed, its ancient forests gone, smashed down and carted off for profit" (144). Any American beauty is ephemeral and perishable, and likely as not to be pulverised by the inchoate desire of the mob.

Amelia represents the America that has melodramatically renounced rank and hierarchy in name only to yearn for them in actuality; she presents a vista not so far from that of Danny Kelly's school in Tsiolkas' *Barracuda*. Interestingly, however, there is another layer to Amelia. Godeffroy, the town, is named after railroad executive Adolphus Godeffroy.[47] But there was also a German businessman of that era, Johann Cesar Godeffroy, who did lucrative trade in the South Pacific, and who helped to finance collections of Australian ichthyologic paintings.[48] Whether or not Carey knew of Johann Christoph Godeffroy, the name itself is diasporic. A Godeffroy, like an Oliver and even a Larritt, does not come to North America except through diaspora. The surname Godeffroy is Huguenot, and so ended up both in Germany and in the USA because of persecution by the French Catholic establishment. The USA, Prussia and South Africa would not have been the same without the Huguenots, which itself is a lesson in the variability of the benignity of historical outcomes, and there is the same implicit contrast between New York and Dutch-ruled South Africa as there was in *The Unusual Life of Tristan Smith*, where Carey's dystopian hegemonic country of Voorstand is equal parts contemporary New York and apartheid-era South Africa.[49]

---

46   Michel Foucault, *Discipline and Punish*, trans., Alan Sheridan (New York: Pantheon, 1975).
47   Brian J. Lewis, *Deerpark* (Mount Pleasant: Arcadia, 2002), 12.
48   Brian Saunders, *Discovery of Australia's Fishes: A History of Australian Ichthyology to 1930* (Collingwood: CSIRO Publishing, 2012), 94.
49   Douglas Glover, in "Australia on My Mind", *Chicago Tribune*, 19 February 1995, 5, refers to the "odd cross" between the USA and South Africa in *The Unusual Life of Tristan Smith*.

That Godefroy's name has a South Pacific connection may be a happy accident, but once referents become diasporic they have a better than average chance of being Australian; Carey distils a sense of the Australian that operates suggestively even when it is only thinly articulated on the literal level. It is palpable, yet not insistent; it demands to be heard, yet is not stridently nationalist. Analogously, Parrot and Olivier weave themselves around each other, as in their contrasting marriages (Olivier at least at one point to an Anglo woman, albeit one with a Huguenot surname; Parrot to a Frenchwoman, Mathilde).

Parrot's final speech, however, both decisively differentiates him from Olivier and is a clarion call to awareness:

> Look, it is daylight. There are no sans-culottes, nor will there ever be again. There is no tyranny in America, nor ever could be. Your horrid visions concerning fur traders are groundless. The great ignoramus will not be elected. The illiterate will never rule. (381)

He ends the book with a peroration in his character's future, but about his own present:

> America does not need either leadership or deep-laid plans or great efforts, but liberty and still more liberty. The reason for this is that no one yet has any interest in abusing liberty. But wait, monsieur. It may take a century but *le fou viendra*. (337)

The America Carey saw after 1990 could hardly have corresponded to these utopian visions. In some ways, Carey's political trajectory and context is like that of Les Murray in reverse. Murray criticised a late modern, elitist, *bien-pensant* left-wing ascendancy (like the Howards in Harrower's *In Certain Circles*), but then his work confronts and is received by an at least somewhat different neoliberal ascendancy. Carey has said that he was attracted to New York because it was full of people who, like him, "carried two places in their heart, the land of their childhood and their chosen home". Immigrants to America "did not come all this way, as one of them said to me, 'to stay the way I were'", and neither do the societies to which people migrate stay the same.[50]

Parrot's exuberant salutation to Olivier at the end of the book carries a bitter aftertaste of dramatic irony: we know that the idiot will be elected, class disparities will overtake egalitarianism, America will end up being more "European", in terms of inequality, than it ever hoped or feared. Carey is very attentive to class and to the danger of class inequality in this novel, indeed more so than many Marxist theorists such as Alain Badiou, for whom, as Thomas Piketty remarks in the final footnote of *Capital in the Twenty-First Century*, "questions of capital and of class inequality are of only moderate interest".[51]

Amnesia: Trauma and Anamnesis

Amnesia (2014) traces the US–Australia relationship over a trajectory of seventy years, its hinge being the 1975 dismissal of Prime Minister Gough Whitlam. Some might suspect here that Carey is holding on to grievances from his youth, and that he is romanticising

---

50 James Bradley, "Once Upon a Time in America", *Australian*, 31 October 2009.
51 Thomas Piketty, *Capital in the Twenty-First Century*, trans. Arthur Goldhammer (Cambridge: Harvard University Press, 2014), 655.

the cultural position of Australian dissent. But one of the most compelling aspects of *Amnesia* is the imperfect status of its moral protagonists: Felix Moore, from whose point of view the first part of the novel is told, is Carey severely *manqué* (like Carey, he hails from Bacchus Marsh, Victoria). It is almost as if Carey is poking fun at those people who try to see his narrators as stand-ins for himself, for Moore is not Carey. Carey, although an admirer of Xavier Herbert's *Poor Fellow My Country*, judged that Herbert was too close to his fictional stand-in, Jeremy Delacy, and Carey shies away from this mistake, always interposing an ironic distance between his own authorship and his narrators, even those who may resemble him. Moore is an "unlovely old scoundrel", a veteran writer in his seventies with little but sheer endurance to show for it.[52] His best-known work, *Barbie and the Deadheads* (134), is a rather slight satire. Most of his work has been polemical – and forgettable – journalism.

Moore's career has been neither brilliant nor particularly honourable. Wodonga "Woody" Townes is a shady left-wing billionaire, a "collector of first editions" but "most of all, a property developer", (22) an eidolon of Les Murray's darkest nightmares about what the combination of financial entitlement and left-wing views might generate but also, the novel makes clear, someone who could not have risen to the top anywhere but Australia. Gaby, the epitome of the next generation (born on the very day, 11 November 1975, that Gough Whitlam was dismissed) is willing to make moral compromises in pursuit of her ideological aims, yet is passionately moral. Although Frederic Matovic, her Julian Assange-like collaborator, is sinister in more than one sense of the word, Carey, through Gaby, celebrates the liberating political potential of cyberspace. In the 1990s the pessimistically inclined might have suspected that cyberspace would come to see the same hegemony that controlled other media spaces. By the 2010s, however, a disjunctive and subversive vision of cyberspace had arisen, one in which freedom, even at great moral peril, could be obtained for Gaby's generation.

Carey remains vitally engaged not just with the material facts of the Australian condition in the twenty-first century but with the cultural themes and preoccupations that have arisen from them. The name of the character Gaby Baillieux in *Amnesia* possibly alludes to the former Victorian state premier of that name, who was himself from a prominent Melbourne family, a reference visible to Australians but almost totally invisible to global readers. This is a textbook instance of subversive Carey and global Carey being tethered together. In *Amnesia*, Carey is exploring ground similar to writers younger than he is, writers who still live in Australia, and writers of different heritages.

In exploring the hacker psychology of Gaby, Carey tries as hard as he can to understand the psychology of the younger generation, and to envision cyberspace as a place where the bimodalities of neoliberalism are complicated or burst apart entirely. Gaby is decisively contrasted to the previous generation:

> He had been born in the previous geologic age while Gaby was born in the Anthropocene age and easily saw that the enemy was not one nation-state but a cloud of companies, corporations, contractors, statutory bodies whose survival meant the degradation of water, air, soil, life itself. (366)

---

52   Peter Carey, *Amnesia* (London: Faber and Faber, 2014), 151. All subsequent references are to this edition and appear in parentheses in the text.

This passage, quoted by Andrew Motion in his review of the novel in the *Guardian*,[53] is an explicit engagement with the periodisation that is at the centre of my argument in this book, although I have used the terms "late modernity" and "neoliberalism" for what Carey calls "the geological age" and "the Anthropocene" (366). As much as a misfire as *His Illegal Self* may have been, its experiment in representing a younger mentality pays off in the depiction of Gaby in *Amnesia*. Gaby is a younger member of Generation X, someone who heard Rickie Lee Jones songs as a toddler and played computer games as a preteen. Carey extends his reach to the next generation not just to keep up with the times but also to fill out his depiction of the moral history of his own generation by acknowledging its consequences for the next. *Amnesia*'s ties to Carey's Australian youth and to the political wounds of the late twentieth century notwithstanding, it is a novel that fully addresses and comes to terms with twenty-first-century Australia.

Amnesia gives a panoply of Australia over the last several decades. Rozelle in Sydney is tawdry and bohemian; Monash University in the 1970s a "sea of mud that had been a market garden" (29). The book covers much of the Australian landscape, from "the oil-slicked water of the Brisbane River" (81) to the "pretty red flowers with yellow hearts" (157) along the Hawkesbury. The novel's temporal coverage is also wide. Moore had known Gaby's mother, Celine Baillieux, at university in the 1970s, and the story stretches back to World War II and to the experiences of Celine's mother and her staunch Methodist grandmother. The novel thus gives four generations of an Australian family – and takes us back to the mid-twentieth century. Celine is conceived during World War II when her mother, Doris, is raped by an American; during Celine's undergraduate days at Monash University she mentions this when the issue of Vietnam-era anti-Americanism comes up. One of Celine's contemporaries claims that American troops did not even serve in New Guinea during World War II. Carey, who was born in 1943, goes back to high modernity to understand the traumatic roots of the Australian–American relationship, which originated in a heroic moment of solidarity before, like the Franciscan Free Church of Voorstand in *The Unusual Life of Tristan Smith*, it all got simulacral.

The French ancestry of Celine's family recalls the French elements in *Parrot and Olivier in America* and *The Unusual Life of Tristan Smith*. But the name "Celine" is also a reminder of one of the collaborationist and modernist Louis-Ferdinand Céline – one of the century's great writers, who succumbed to the allure of totalitarian politics – and so links contemporary Australian traumas to past European ones. The contemporary Australia presented so panoramically in *Amnesia* is dark and troubled above all by political menace. The issue of "freeing boat people from Australian custody" (5) is mentioned in the book's early pages. Many readers in the USA would be unaware of the asylum-seeker issue in Australia, but Carey remains attuned to Australian media space, and is out to make his polemical mark on the twenty-first-century Australian scene.

After a few years of relative neglect of Carey by Australian academics, who, as Paul Giles observes, regarded him with "so much suspicion"[54], a new wave of graduate students now seems to be reversing that trend, and beginning to do the sort of historicist and archival work on Carey that needs to be done to take Carey studies beyond plot summary

---

53   Andrew Motion, "*Amnesia*: Turbo-Charged Hypernenergetic", *Guardian*, 30 October 2014.
http://www.theguardian.com/books/2014/oct/30/amnesia-peter-carey-review-turbo-charged.
54   Giles, *Antipodean America*, 438.

style appreciation.[55] Nonetheless, there remains a mistaken general impression that the most interesting thing about Carey is his American success.

Yet, paradoxically, the Australian writer who has most vigorously fomented an intelligent, critical anti-Americanism is Carey himself. Carey, like Patrick White, was furious at the circumstances of Gough Whitlam's dismissal from office, and blamed the entire affair on the USA. In a 2014 interview with Melbourne bookseller Mark Rubbo, Carey said, discussing *Amnesia*, that deep opposition to American foreign policy had long been part of his literary vision:

> I wanted to explore the complicated relationship between Australia and the US. Many serious writers (John Pilger in *A Secret Country* being one of them) have pieced together the circumstances of the Whitlam dismissal in 1975 and concluded that our government was brought down by a complex storm system in which the CIA played an active role. The right has devoted forty years to labelling these views as "conspiracist" and "phony", a view much repeated in certain parts of the media, which (for those not old enough to remember) took an active part in the overthrow. These voices continue to insist that it is mad and unimaginable that our powerful ally interfered in Australia's internal affairs.[56]

As it happened, *Amnesia*'s Australian release coincided with Gough Whitlam's death, giving the novel an uncanny currency; Carey seemed a sort of literary mourner-in-chief for Whitlam, and the book's allegations of amnesia provided an occasion for anamnesis, a longer-range remembering. Chapter 25 of *Amnesia* narrates the events surrounding the end of the Whitlam government. Carey endorses the controversial version of history promulgated by John Pilger, who holds that American intelligence services were directly responsible for Whitlam's overthrow.[57] Marshall Green, the American ambassador to Indonesia in 1965, to Cambodia in 1970, and to Australia in 1975, is seen melodramatically by Carey as the "coup-master" (136), although some might argue that Green's appointment was intended to be an honourable but low-key post, a kind of quasi-retirement.[58] Whitlam himself, as shown in his 1977 speech to the Australian parliament, adamantly believed there had been CIA intervention. In a cruel irony worthy of Orwell or Foucault, the only arena in which this wound can be exhibited to a global audience is an American one. Carey envisions the USA as a crypt of secrets, and much of the drama of his fiction comes from exploring its labyrinthine corridors. By seeing the USA, rather than Britain, as the country with which Australia is most problematically engaged, Carey goes beyond the postcolonial paradigm of liberation and self-assertion through which he has so often been analysed.

Richard Flanagan, in a 2015 address to the PEN World Voices Festival in New York, imagined a dystopian 2050 in which the USA had broken up and the corporate entities of Facebook, Google and Apple were all-powerful.[59] Seeing this future scenario as the logical

---

55 I am thinking of work by Claire Corbett, Lydia Saleh Rofail and Kevyan Allahari, among others
56 Peter Carey, interviewed by Mark Rubbo, Readings blog, 6 October 2014.
http://www.readings.com.au/news/mark-rubbo-interviews-peter-carey.
57 John Pilger, *A Secret Country* (Sydney: Random House, 1982).
58 Carey (or Felix Moore, who may or may not be reliable) also slightly fudges the Pakistani origins of Tirath Khemlani, the broker involved in securing the Arab petrodollar loans that the Whitlam government sought to keep itself alive.
59 Richard Flanagan, address to the 2015 PEN World Voices Festival, New York, 4 May 2015.
https://youtu.be/C9nMfNQMiSE.

outcome of changes in the world polity since 1980, Flanagan took just as politically radical a line as does Carey in *Amnesia*, but suggested that the state, even the American state, is withering away, to be replaced by the purely corporate entities of neoliberalism. Carey, on the other hand, sees the state power of the United States as continuing on from the late modernity of his youth to the neoliberal era of his maturity, and sees the structures of sovereignty as being ballasted rather than eroded by the free market. Whereas Flanagan, in his speech, saw the internet as a potential means of mega-corporate surveillance, Carey, through the character of Gaby Baillieux, sees cyberspace as an arena in which to outfox the forces of state authority.

Amnesia promises no liberation, and does not complacently portray Gaby's generation curing the pathologies of her elders. That would be the path of least resistance for somebody of Carey's generation to take: trusting that the kids will make it all right. Gaby is a force for hope. But she is wild and unconsoling; she seems more likely to bring an apocalyptic day of wrath than a harmonious resolution. But *Amnesia* shows a world of multiple forces, in which the dominant powers are challenged by imperfect figures on the margins. It is a world that tries to make us forget its origins, and to jettison dissent by promulgating "the Great Amnesia" (5). This is why the anamnesis – the remembrance – not just of the Whitlam era but also of World War II is so urgent in the book. *Amnesia* is the dystopian sequel to Parrot's pastoral imaginings in his final peroration. The future will not bring equality and justice, but inequality and frenetic moral turbulence, a milieu, as Gaby thinks of the Melbourne suburb of Parkville, that is "smudgy. Layer to layer" (149). Carey's inside track insists on even evident moral polarities being close-up and proximate, so that the reader can discern and imaginatively wrestle with them.

Looking Back, Looking Forward

In the light of the neoliberal dystopia seen in *Amnesia*, Parrot's final speech in *Parrot and Olivier in America* takes on a new valence. His words are prophetic of the erosion of a modern idea of equality that in his day was just coalescing, but which was already in danger from those who wished to heighten, or restore, inequality. As even the Australian Treasury notes, "income distribution in Australia has become more unequal over the last thirty years".[60] Carey is not writing about an exclusively American problem; it is an Australian one as well. Carey, in this passage, is engaging in elegiac mockery, as precisely what Parrot says will never come to pass now has. Yet there is a sense in which Carey means Parrot's words to be read more generously. The ignoramus, after all, is also Andrew Jackson, representative of the democracy that Parrot is seeking. One gets the sense that, for Carey, Olivier is forever tarnished by his association with political reaction, which brings up difficult issues of how the historical novel itself can resist this tug towards reaction. Like Parrot and Olivier, today's writers and readers will one day be judged by a future they will never know. This may be the animating dynamic of fiction: it explores problems that will remain unsolvable during the writer's lifetime. Neither Olivier's condescending idealism nor Parrot's subversive irony wins out completely; no single viewpoint can. That is why the

---

60   Michael Fletcher and Ben Guttmann, "Income Inequality in Australia", in *Economic Roundup* 2. Canberra: Treasury of Australia, 2013.

counter-neoliberal affects of concern, rancour and idealism can be manifested side-by-side and have similar reverberations, if by different means.

Felix Moore in *Amnesia* says that our "sole responsibility to our ancestors is to give birth to them as they gave birth to us" (88). In this spirit, in *Parrot and Olivier in America* Carey returns to the divergence between America and Australia. For it is not true that these two English-speaking countries have only discovered each other since World War II. An early incarnation of the US–Australian relationship can be seen in the first Australian nationalism, that of the 1850s. This was the nationalism seen in Victoria's goldfields and in the "fiction fields" described by the first Australian literary critic, Frederick Sinnett, in the work of "the farthing poet", Richard Hengist Horne, in the miners' resistance at the Eureka Stockade and in the chronicling of that resistance by the Italian migrant Raffaello Carboni. Significantly, Felix Moore in *Amnesia* has a complete signed set of Manning Clark's multi-volume *History of Australia*, and Carey's late work gestures to the entire sweep of settler Australian history. The Australian era evoked indirectly by *Parrot and Olivier in America* is chronologically slightly later than its American setting, but temperamentally quite similar: it is the Australia of the early part of the fourth volume of Clark's history, *The Earth Abideth Forever*, which covers the 1850s to the 1880s. This was the Australia of Daniel Henry De-niehy and his early republicanism, the Australia that Herman Melville might have visited if the tides had carried him that way, the Australia of Louisa Atkinson, whose *Gertrude the Emigrant* (1857) combined spirituality and romance with feminism and a strikingly precise observation of nature worthy of her contemporary, Thoreau. This is a period too early and too colonial to form the crucible of a rousing Australian nationalism, as would later emerge with the *Bulletin* school of the 1890s. The individual Australian colonies still had very separate identities. But the tyranny of distance loomed too large for there to be concerted control from London, or for Australia to feel entirely a part of a British Empire. Queen Victoria was not proclaimed Empress of India until 1876; the Suez Canal, which made the logistical integration of Australia possible, was not operational until the 1860s. At the midpoint of the nineteenth century, what the New Zealand historian James Belich has called the "recolonial" effect of subsequent decades had not really begun to kick in.[61] In this era, Australia was free to look out across the Pacific rather than back towards Europe. When conditions changed, Atkinson fell out of tune with the time and became diminished as a novelist, as in 1864's *Myra*, which is set in England and lacks the perceptiveness of her earlier fiction. From a twenty-first-century perspective, Atkinson is an imperfect writer, not just stylistically but also in her assumptions about race and settler entitlement, assumptions found in most of her white Australian contemporaries. The nineteenth century, in both the USA and Australia, was a time of white privilege and almost instinctual racism, attitudes to which Atkinson's work succumbs, as do many of the most liberal and advanced white thinkers of that era. Despite the equivalent aura of white privilege around such plucky and underestimated protagonists as Parrot Larritt, Carey in *Parrot and Olivier in America* is alluding to the liberal optimism of the USA and Australia of that era as a residual possibility.

But Carey's book is far more overtly centred in America, before the rise of the great corporate trusts in the USA, before the Gilded Age and its rampant inequality, when the country was full of a sense of nourishing possibility. To understand the kind of proto-Australian imaginary Carey is gesturing at here we must gaze more intently at both this

---

61   James Belich, *Paradise Reforged: A History of the New Zealanders* (London: Penguin, 2002).

period and the way it has re-emerged in recent literary study, as the academics who evoke this period are part of the same project in which, albeit from totally different antecedents and with substantially different audiences, Carey's project also participates. The literature of this era in Australian history has attracted scholars of the calibre of Ken Stewart, Meg Tasker and Elizabeth Webby. But it found one of its most devoted students in Victor Crittenden (1925–2014), the foundation librarian of the University of Canberra, the publisher of Mulini Press, and the editor of the journal *Legacy*. Crittenden included 1890s writers in *Legacy*, but generally emphasised earlier, pre-nationalist, pre-Suez writers. At the centre of his vision was Louisa Atkinson, for whose life and work Crittenden had a particular affection. Crittenden was, in the words of his colleague Andrew Clarke, an autodidact. He dropped out of school at fourteen and returned to university later, garnering advanced degrees in engineering and librarianship. Crittenden's combination of amateurism and practicality has a scrappiness, an idiosyncratic quality reminiscent of Carey's awkward and ungainly heroes, waging an individual, valiant and quixotic struggle against forces more standardising and more privileged than they, but nonetheless managing to make their voices heard. Crittenden helps us to see what a Carey hero is: a distinct person trying, in oddness and quirkiness, to make an impact on a world far more cruel and uncaring than he is. The engaged enthusiasm of Crittenden testifies to a resilience much like that which Carey attributes to nineteenth-century America and Australia. If de Tocqueville embodied an America in which both the fruits and the perils of a levelling democracy seemed within reach, writers like Carboni and Atkinson represented the closest thing to a Tocquevillian Australia, an Australia, despite the brutality of colonial governance, of an incipient spirit of self-assertion. Parrot Larritt, as rendered by Carey, has the virtues of this lapsed America and this fugitive Australia: a gumption, a willingness to tackle the problems at hand, and an ambition focused on experiencing life to its fullest rather than simply accumulating the spoils of "winning". Like the wounded but inquisitive Freudian humanity of modernity, this global but pre-imperial nineteenth-century individualism represents an imperfect but valiant alternative to market forces, a spirit of greater generosity.

The global yet pre-imperial Australia represented by this spirit may now be in abeyance. But it is not yet dead, and may lurk in unexpected corners. To see this, we need to take a brief look at a contemporary Australian who, like Carey, desires to be seen as both an Australian and a world figure, both a home-grown progressive and a cosmopolitan eminence. Bob Carr was premier of New South Wales for ten years (1995–2005) and then foreign minister in the Gillard and second Rudd governments (2012–2013). In his memoir *Diary of a Foreign Minister*, he records a visit to New York, where he met with the former secretary of state Henry Kissinger ("my greatest friend and supporter"), the former first lady of New York State Happy Rockefeller (now deceased), and the ABC television broadcaster Barbara Walters, among others.[62] Carr describes this trip more or less in the manner (to use Bourdieu's terminology) of the oblate's pilgrimage to the metropolis, a recapitulation of the picaresque progress made by Letty Fox and Carey's own Tristan Smith. Carr's experience in New York, as he records it in his published diary, embodies the basic situation of a Carey hero: coming face to face with the mighty by simply going his own way, he is both exhilarated and somewhat bemused. In the cosmopolitan contemporary arena, a gifted person from a peripheral culture can have intimate access to the centre. That Carr

---

62 Bob Carr, *Diary of a Foreign Minister* (Sydney: University of New South Wales Press, 2014), 10–11.

was in his mid-sixties when he made this momentous pilgrimage shows the great age of all his distinguished interlocutors, all of whom were at least octogenarians.

For some readers, Carr's account of his trip might prompt disappointment. In New York, Carr sought out people who, however extraordinary, were not currently making policy, had no particular relevance to Australia, and did not represent New York even in their own generation, much less in mine or my students'. Since Carr's portfolio was Foreign Affairs and Trade, he could have met with entrepreneurs or corporate leaders. His amateur enthusiasm for high culture has its virtues, and he is unusually literate for a politician, but in this instance it seemed to lead him to people who were already famous, rather than to those who had the potential to be famous in ten years' time. Moreover, Carr could apparently find no younger people in New York who shared his values and his cultural sophistication.

The first oversight might reflect a wish for an uninflected arrival in the metropolis, a desire to see the Northern Hemisphere centres as stable and unaffected by neoliberalism. Perhaps Carr was yearning for an essential New York, one that Kissinger, Rockefeller and Walters represented. Perhaps Carr looked at younger people in New York and decided that they all represented various shades of neoliberalism, opportunism and self-interest; Kissinger, Rockefeller and Walters, in contrast, might have appeared as vestigial representatives of late modernity – of a world that, however affluent and conformist, was not relentlessly financialised and capitalised. Carr may have been seeking, in reverse, what I sought in Australia in 1985, what Coetzee glimpsed in an Australia he never fully got to see, and what Carey sensed in an America not yet irretrievably changed: a country where everything was not yet dead; today's version of pastoral.

Peter Carey's vision of America, after *Parrot and Olivier in America*, is far more tough-minded. But Carr's pilgrimage to New York, with its mixture of nostalgia and veneration, delusion and panache, shows that a transnational voyage – whether by an Australian to New York, or a New Yorker to Australia – is never free from the threats of mischance, anachronism, and insufficient information; this is the cost of pursuing a largely personal vision. There are as many Australias and New Yorks as there are mentalities and temporalities. Carey's awareness of this range of possibilities, and his rigorous self-interrogation, underpin the merit and acuity of his later work. He faces America as it has existed in his lifetime, even though it contains much that is dispiriting. Perhaps Carey felt, like Tristan Smith, or like Teresa Hawkins in Christina Stead's *For Love Alone*, that he had come to the centre in order to speak. Whatever his reasons, he took on the behemoth from within. Through an ingenious and unflinching oeuvre, he has done so with integrity and honour.

9
History Made Present: Hannah Kent and Eleanor Catton

Hannah Kent: An Australian Iceland?

This book began with an account of my own efforts as a scholar, in 1985, to understand Australia. It will end by examining the work of two writers born in that same year, 1985, both young women from the antipodes who exploded onto the world literary scene in 2013. Hannah Kent and Eleanor Catton are very different writers who, in *Burial Rites* (2013) and *The Luminaries* (2013), wrote books very varied in setting and tone. Kent's is dark and mournful, set on the other side of the world from Australia. Catton's is expansive and high-spirited, set in nineteenth-century New Zealand. But these two writers are comparable not only as authors born in the era of neoliberalism, and therefore taking its consequences as a given, but as examples of how novels from the antipodes unfold not just across the globe but within the temporal space of today. Both have operated from early in their careers in transnational arenas, taking advantage of international networks well disposed to youth and innovation, and not hamstrung by constraints of genre or national tradition.

Critics such as Rita Felski, Stephen Best and Sharon Marcus have warned against "symptomatic" or "deep" readings of literary works, readings that privilege a hidden "ultimate" meaning over what is superficially apparent.[1] Such readings are often ideological: feminist, Marxist, Freudian, and so on. Just as it is easy, once you are a feminist or a Freudian or a Marxist, to seek out books that lend themselves to an ideological reading, so it is easy, if one is an Australianist literary critic, to see "Australia" in nearly anything, particularly when the writer is Australian. My analysis of Stead's *Letty Fox* in Chapter 2 is an example of such a reading. Similarly, in a 2013 interview, Kent linked her book's Icelandic setting to her Australian homeland: "I see a certain connection to Australians' attitude and relationship towards our natural landscape: We too live in a country that can be simultaneously beautiful and hostile."[2] Unlike Catton, who has consciously put her fiction, at

---

1 Rita Felsic, *The Uses of Literature* (Oxford: Wiley-Blackwell, 2008); Stephen Best and Sharon Marcus, "Surface Reading: An Introduction", *Representations* 108, no. 1 (2009): 1–21.

least *The Luminaries*, in a postcolonial context, Kent has tended to resort to the affective in locating the intention of her work.

Burial Rites is set in Iceland in 1829, where a reluctant farming family has been coerced into housing a female prisoner who has been condemned to death, Agnes Magnusdottir.[3] One strand of the narrative describes what happens after this compelled quartering; it deals with Agnes' confinement in the family's farmhouse as she awaits her demise and seeks, with the aid of a sympathetic priest, to come to terms with it. The other is told in flashbacks by Agnes to Tóti, the priest who listens to her. That Iceland, Christian Europe's first colony, was colonised by Viking "barbarians", casts light on what has been called Australia's "settler/invader culture" and its tenuous claims to enlightenment.[4] The remoteness of both Agnes' time and, even further back, Iceland's initial settlement, bespeaks, on Kent's part, of a Greenblatt-like desire to speak with the dead, which, as with Greenblatt himself, may well be driven by a sense that the existing order is haunted by unacknowledged demons. The victimisation of women (exemplified by Agnes), the inefficacy of conventional religion (as seen in Tóti), and the procedural limitation of constituted authority (as seen in Jón Jónsson, the farmstead father), are familiar themes for readers of Australian fiction. The theme of imprisonment resonates with the Australian convict tradition. As Sarah Anderson points out, medieval Iceland did not have a royal court even though it was governed by a kingdom, and neither of course did Australia.[5] Iceland and Australia both emerged as active participants in world diplomacy in the wake of World War II and the increased American role in the world; an alliance with the USA during the Cold War was an important part of both countries' histories. And of course, the Icelandic language is related to English, and courses in Icelandic and Old Norse were often a part of traditional English literature degrees, a tradition derived from Oxford and Cambridge.

Although *Burial Rites* has not garnered the international success of Catton's *The Luminaries*, inevitably Kent's early acclaim tends to occlude what is actually in the book. As Les Murray put it in "Lifestyle", in "the tall cities" the "world is not made of atoms / world is made of careers".[6] While it is always useful to understand a writer's professional approach to authorship, an excessive emphasis on a writer's career is as limiting as a purely formalist emphasis on content. Even works that adamantly declare their independence of the cash nexus, such as Wordsworth and Coleridge's *Lyrical Ballads*, are, as Thomas Pfau has shown, implicated in it.[7] Alexander Welsh, writing on Dickens, and Svetlana Alpers, writing on Rembrandt, have shown the role played by economic pressures in the creation of these artists' greatest works.[8] But, even in the case of frankly commercial writers such as Nevil Shute and Bryce Courtenay, there is something to be said for attending to plots, characters,

---

2   Quoted in Randy Dotinga, "'*Burial Rites* Author Hannah Kent Finds Mystery in Iceland", *Christian Science Monitor*, 29 November 2013. http://www.csmonitor.com/Books/chapter-and-verse/2013/1129/Burial-Rites-author-Hannah-Kent-finds-mystery-in-Iceland.

3   Hannah Kent, *Burial Rites* (Boston: Little, Brown, 2013). All subsequent references are to this edition and appear in parentheses in the text.

4   See Nicholas Birns, *Barbarian Memory: The Legacy of Early Medieval History in Early Modern Literature* (New York: Palgrave Macmillan, 2013).

5   Sarah Anderson, "The Lack of a Court in Medieval Icelandic Narrative", paper presented at the 2015 Modern Language Association of America Convention, Vancouver, 10 January 2015.

6   Les Murray, *The Biplane Houses* (London: Macmillan, 2006), 65.

7   Pfau refers to Wordsworth's poetry as "cultural commodity and instrument" and the product of "an articulate middle-class agency". See Thomas Pfau, *Wordsworth's Profession: Form, Class, and the Logic of Early Romantic Cultural Production* (Stanford: Stanford University Press, 1997), 180.

themes and symbols, just as one would in a highbrow novel. It is no less one-eyed to see books as purely commercial than it is to see them as purely aesthetic; the interpretive always lies somewhere in between.

Kent's novel raises fascinating interpretive issues. First of all, Iceland – unlike Greenland – does not have indigenous people.[9] There was no permanent population in Iceland in 874 when the Europeans came. It is rare that a habitable country has no people. Although Iceland offers Kent the chance to portray a harsh, rigid, parochial, misogynistic and authoritarian settler culture in an ecological atmosphere at once beautiful, unusual and fragile, it does not, unlike Australia, raise questions about the treatment and rights of indigenous people. Iceland's settlement by the Vikings places it in opposition to the first known contact between Europeans and indigenous people in Greenland and the North American mainland. Annette Kolodny has argued that this paradigmatic encounter in Greenland was subversive of established paradigms in that it was difficult for the Vikings to posit themselves as more advanced than their native Greenlandic counterparts.[10] Iceland thus serves as a reminder of the West's fragile hold on its own claims to civilisation, a paradox observed in Alex Jones' *Morris in Iceland* (2008) when Jones, a scholar of Indigenous Australian languages, describes William Morris' Icelandic sojourn with a clear awareness of other European pilgrimages to remote lands such as Australia.[11] Bev Braune, in her experimental project *Skulvadhi Ulfr* (2001), which uses the Viking as an analogue for migratory movements across the Atlantic, including the Black Atlantic, as well as for experimental form itself, does something similar.[12]

Furthermore, the Vikings were not securely Christian at the time of their foraging and exploring in the North Atlantic. In Kent's Iceland, Christianity, however long established in institutional terms, still seems something of an overlay. The island's residual pagan past is palpable. There are echoes of the Icelandic sagas, which embody the tension between a still-robust paganism and the wave of Christianisation that swept over all of Scandinavia at the beginning of the eleventh century, and which the seemingly unrepresentative charity and humility of the priest, Tóti, to whom Agnes confesses her crimes, reveals as only superficially regnant in the early nineteenth.

Any novel by a non-Icelander set in Iceland belongs to the genre the Canadian critic T. D. MacLulich called "the Northern", an equivalent of the Western, in which a wild frontier casts a consoling pastoral light even on the harshest narrative material.[13] The Northern was a mode by which Canada could define its identity; Kent performs the reverse, projecting outward into another space. The Northern is also consciously not "Southern", and the genre evades Latin America, Africa and Asia as possible subjects. This is slightly

8   Alexander Welsh, *From Copyright to Copperfield: The Identity of Dickens* (Cambridge: Harvard University Press, 1987); and Svetlana Alpers, *Rembrandt's Enterprise: The Studio and the Market* (Chicago: University of Chicago Press, 1995).
9   Annette Kolodny, *In Search of First Contact: The Vikings of Vinland, the Peoples of the Dawnland, and the Anglo-American Anxiety of Discovery* (Durham: Duke University Press, 2012).
10   The Australian Old Norse scholar Geraldine Barnes notes the resemblance of discourse regarding indigenous people in Greenland and Vinland to contemporary Australian debates, and registers the absence in Iceland of such, in *Viking America: The First Millennium* (Woodbridge: Boydell & Brewer, 2001), 22.
11   Alex Jones, *Morris in Iceland* (Sydney: Puncher & Wattmann, 2008).
12   Bev Braune, "The Determination of Maps", *Antipodes* 15, no. 2 (2001): 75.
13   T. D. MacLulich, "The Alien Role: Farley Mowat's Northern Pastorals", *Studies in Canadian Literature* 2, no. 2 (1977): 226–33.

paradoxical in an Australian context, as Australia's north is the tropics, and Jon Stratton has argued that Australia's Northern Territory is the "least real" area of Australia, the most laden with exoticism and the imaginary.[14] Furthermore, there is no direct demographic relationship between Iceland and Australia: if Kent were from Canada, which has a migrant Icelandic population, her interest would seem more organic. Australia does not have such an Icelandic presence, although Jeremy Stoljar's 1992 book *My First Mistake*, with its portrayal of an Icelandic migrant to Australia, comes close.[15]

Part of the resonance of Iceland lies in its very remoteness. Fridrik Thor Fridriksson's 1995 film *Cold Fever* portrays the efforts of a Japanese man to mourn his parents, who have died in a plane crash in Iceland. The country's remoteness also figured in its role in the post-2008 Global Financial Crisis, when Iceland's rapid privatisation made it vulnerable to the near-collapse of the worldwide banking system. The 2014 Icelandic musical *Revolution in the Elbow of Ragnar Agnarsson Furniture Painter* satirises this incongruity; Iceland's distance from the rest of the world made the financial crisis there more drastic and visible. Like Australia's, Iceland's exposure to neoliberalism was particularly drastic because there had previously been a culture of solidarity, a solidarity born of a stark environment and the conformity imposed on the population by colonisation. The institution of the *badstofa* – the collective bed in which Agnes has to sleep during her imposed sojourn with the farm family – is emblematic of this dark side of solidarity. In the *badstofa*, individuals sleep in separate enclosures within one large wooden frame. It is a symbol in Kent's book for the nonexistence of privacy and personal liberty. Anyone who attempts to be an individual is reminded of her vulnerability and her contingency; she is reduced to what Giorgio Agamben has famously termed "bare life". The solidarity that emerges among people living in a cold, forbidding landscape is calcified into a culture of exposure and humiliation.

In the cases of both Iceland and Australia, a free-market outlook had the undeniable appeal of unleashing individual energy and creating social winners of a sort that had not previously predominated. In the Iceland of *Burial Rites*, everyone is poor, but there are still winners and losers, and even in death Agnes is marginalised and misunderstood. Now, the stories of the losers can be told. Yet the division the world makes between winners and losers is more emphatic than ever. Kent, in telling the story of Agnes, provides on one level a contrast to today's more humane methods of punishment and on another a prehistory of the brutality of now. Paradoxically, the novel, while telling the story of a loser, is itself a winner, as Kent succeeds precisely where Agnes failed. This is part of the novel's pathos, as the very act of speaking for Agnes is – unavoidably; there is no possible way Kent could have done otherwise – an act of privileging the voice that speaks for her,

The global success possible to Kent is an index of this division, although that is hardly Kent's fault. Lynda Ng, in her analysis of the transnational subject matter and success of Antoni Jach, Evelyn Juers and Anna Funder, says that the international success of these writers suggests that Australia's multicultural and multi-ethnic population can "choose … to inherit the world".[16] Ng provides an eloquent statement of what Australian writers can achieve if they embrace all of the connections and networks now available to them.

14   Jon Stratton, "Deconstructing the Territory", *Cultural Studies* 3, no. 1 (1989): 38.

15   Jeremy Stoljar, *My First Mistake* (Roseville: Simon & Schuster, 1992).

16   Lynda Ng, "Inheriting the World: German Exiles, Napoleon's Campaign in Egypt, and Australian National Identity", in *Scenes of Reading: Is Australian Literature a World Literature?*, eds Robert Dixon and Brigid Rooney (North Melbourne: Australian Scholarly Publishing, 2013), 166.

But what of readers outside Australia? How do they process this Australian transnational inheritance? Is Australia like a hub airport, where Icelandic material changes planes on its way to the metropolis? Or is Australia a producer of substitutes for other national literatures, a vendor of simulacra like those produced in the Sirkus of Peter Carey's *The Unusual Life of Tristan Smith*? Transnationalism succeeds precisely by propagating the subject of the national, returning to what Timothy Brennan called "the national longing for form"; the nation is propagated internationally even as those very international connections supersede it. But in Kent's case, unlike in the case of Salman Rushdie and his relationship to India and Pakistan, Iceland is incontestably not her own nation.

Yet Kent cannot be accused of simply exploiting exotic material, or of swooping into a region to which she has no ties. As a teenager, Kent spent a year in Iceland as an exchange student, and her sense of the landscape is vivid and earned. Moreover, although *Burial Rites* is based on actual historical events, her take on them is highly revisionary. That the novel takes place in Iceland, rather than in Denmark, the colonial administrator, is notable. The Danish state's officials as depicted in the novel make clear that this is done for two reasons. One is economic: the price of bringing the condemned to Denmark would be too high, and Kent is amusing throughout on how the state, so cruel to this victimised if not entirely innocent young woman, is also risibly cheap, avoiding cost overruns even as it tries to maintain its supremacy. Hunavatn District Commissioner Bjorn Blondal finds the price quoted by the local blacksmith for the manufacture of the axe with which Agnes is to be killed to be excessive. An axe is imported from Copenhagen but ends up costing twice as much; the parsimonious plans of the colonial government are foiled. Thus not only the injustice but also the incompetence of the state is revealed (82).

Yet the Danish colonial regime, although ill equipped, knows what it is doing. In quartering the doomed Agnes on the farm family, it is not only saving money but also reminding the family that they too are controlled by the state, even though they have committed no crime. All citizens are potential subjects of surveillance and Agnes' public execution reminds the entire community that it is under state control and better remember it. There is also a sense that all of Iceland, including the colonial administrators who have been sent there, are second-rate. The imputation of subservience and mediocrity onto the subject population is a function of the administration's projection of its own inadequacy.

It is against this background that we understand why Agnes sought out the man who led her to commit her crime, Natan Ketilsson. Natan is an attractive young farmer, one of the few individuals in the book to display a creative spark. He writes poetry and encourages the sundry women in his life to do so too. The anonymity, conformity and deference that underlie such institutions as the *badstofa* are repulsive to Natan, and he tried to escape them, adopting the surname of Lyngdahl (traditionally most Icelanders do not have surnames at all, only patronymics). Nineteenth-century Iceland is puritanically Lutheran, still warding off a residual paganism and distantly conscious of the revolutionary and romantic stirrings in Europe and America (President Franklin D. Roosevelt, after all, claimed that Iceland was part of North America, in trying to defend it from Germany). In this context, Natan is an outsider, and the rhyme of "Natan" with "Satan" was frequently used in popular doggerel about him, both during and after his lifetime (87). A cross between Lord Byron and Charles Manson, Natan was so charismatic that he became a dark star; he attracted all the attention, leaving Agnes to obscurity while he, although castigated, achieved a posthumous local celebrity. The Agnes the narrative portrays is anything but that. Well past thirty, illegitimate, poor, superfluous, she is seen as guilty in Natan's murder even though ultimately it was Natan who led Agnes to believe that he loved her. Natan toys with Agnes, but, inevitably, deserts her for a younger, more beautiful woman. This fuels Agnes and a spurned lover of the other woman to collaborate in Natan's killing, Yet the killing, as Kent depicts it, is not totally intentional: it is manslaughter, not murder. Agnes is not only disadvantaged by the system, and thus the ideal person to serve as a scapegoat. She is also caught between two conflicting modes of domination: the bureaucracy of the state and the dark romanticism of Natan.

The novel's canvas would be totally dark were it not for the priest, Tóti. The Canadian poet Steven Heighton, who reviewed the book in the *New York Times*, found Tóti "a stereotype: meek, callow, indecisive and given to pious, predictable counsel".[17] This misses the point, however, that between bad bureaucracy and bad Byronism, Tóti is the only disinterested person in the book, and he attends to Agnes in subtle duality, giving her both the interest and disinterest she needs. Tóti cares about her, but he knows he cannot save her. He desires at least to tend to her soul. Agnes asks for Tóti to be brought to her as a spiritual counsellor in the one act of autonomy she is allowed in the entire book. She asks for this particular priest because she remembers that he did her a good turn when travelling in perilous conditions, something which Tóti, to his embarrassment, does not remember; he sees her as just another member of, to use the contemporary locution, the precariat. Tóti seeks to grow as a result of hearing Agnes' story, but he knows that any sort of redemptive narrative is limited. Agnes will inevitably be killed. Indeed, his powerlessness makes him the best moral witness to the situation.

Unlike Natan, whose appeal is charismatic and erotic, Tóti's appeal is spiritual and consolatory. Although Agnes cannot make up the damage caused by her misplaced pursuit of Natan, she can, in her honesty to and reliance upon Tóti, model a different sort of relationship, one marked by concern rather than appetite. Through Tóti, Agnes indicates to the state that it, too, might show concern instead of institutional callousness. But the state is deaf, and has the surveillance of the entire community, not just the chastisement of Agnes, on its mind. Tóti is reminiscent of the clerical figure that often crops up in Australian convict novels, such as Mr North in Clarke's *For the Term of His Natural Life*. Tóti is ineffectual, not, unlike the alcoholic Mr North, because he has any visible moral flaws but because he cannot countermand the authority of the state; he can speak truth to power, but no one will listen.

In her foreword to the recent anthology *Sight Lines* (2014), Kent disclaims any redemptive or world-improving power for literature but states that literature "questions. It doubts. It plumbs the depths of the human heart and surfaces with both beauty and the ugliness that lurks in unexpected corners".[18] If the role of the state reveals ugliness where there should at least be the simulacrum of justice, Tóti's witnessing – again given his integrity by the way he can only provide very limited help – is one of the book's unexpected beauties. Kent, however, is not claiming a reductively aesthetic disinterestedness. With respect to the historical record, *Burial Rites* is a subversive and paradigm-changing book. The story of Agnes and Natan is famous in Icelandic folklore, and Kent learned of it during her stay in the country. But in Iceland, all the fame has accrued to Natan, at once culprit and victim, and little to Agnes, at once scapegoat and perpetrator. Kent has restored

---

17   Steven Heighton, "Fire and Ice", *The New York Times*, 27 September 2013, BR17.
18   Hannah Kent, foreword to *Sight Lines: 2014 UTS Writers' Anthology*, ed. Kate Adams et al. (Sydney: Xoum, 2014), 3.

Agnes to centrality in the story. Kent's delineation of colonial governmentality, the interstitial practices of colonial discipline beneath the overt frames of political administration, demonstrates that patriarchy, gender hierarchy and misogyny are perhaps their last vestige. It is interesting that the notoriety of Agnes' execution is that it was the *last* execution in Iceland. Were people so appalled by her suffering that there was social reform? Or did the state simply decide to put on a velvet rather than an iron glove? Foucault's famous remark, in *Discipline and Punish*, that the reform of the prison system was coextensive with the prison system itself might be pertinent here. Even if one takes the first, more inspirational view, a woman had to die in order for the state to reform; a narrative of progress, of emergence from brutality, was only possible over a dead female body. Another Australian book in a totally different genre – the fantasy novel *Hades' Daughter* by Sara Douglass – illustrates the same point.[19] This is a historical fantasy of the ancient world, set a hundred years after the fall of Troy, about the mythical Trojan migration to Britain. Like *Burial Rites*, Douglass' novel is about a colony in which women are treated brutally, and both novels implicitly evoke the settler origins of Australia and its antecedents in previous European conquests and mythologies of conquest. There is a connection between the subordination of women and empire, as if a structure in which women are controlled were a prerequisite for other manifestations of authority.

Burial Rites tries to bring justice and dignity to victims of past cruelty and prejudice. Yet the past cannot endlessly be mined for the purposes of the present, or the very distinction between present and past that makes the retrieval of the past interesting will fade. The idea that the present is rational and the past irrational, that the present represents enlightenment and the past injustice, will be upended. Just as fossil fuels cannot be our main source of energy forever, there is a danger that we will exhaust the past – that we will run out of reserves to draw on. Bain Attwood has commented that in the 1970s, a prominent historian predicted "the death of the past", but, as of 2005, when Attwood was writing, there was a worldwide "growth of public interest" in history.[20] Attwood commends this as an interest in previously suppressed stories such as those of Indigenous Australians. History can mean asking new questions of the past on behalf of the present. But an interest in history can also mean an uncritical yielding to past authority. And the literary surge of history and the historical novel, however many striking works it has produced, can only last so long and yield so much. The stark and grave eloquence of Kent's superb book, traumatic on the level of plot, is just as traumatic on the interpretive level, as it figures a crisis of history itself and its use in fiction. As the Western Australian poet Ian Reid puts it:

> High seas are on the move again – not sudden
> Stormy surges, but a slow deepening flood
> That laps now at new levels of old lives.[21]

History can matter in the present, and in Kent's novel it certainly does. But the way it matters might well be highly disturbing, bereft of the costume-drama reassurance that the

---

19   Sara Douglass, *Hades' Daughter* (New York: Tor Books, 2002).
20   Bain Attwood, *Telling the Truth about Aboriginal History* (Crows Nest: Allen & Unwin, 2005), 11.
21   Ian Reid, "The Shifting Shore", *Antipodes* 7, no. 2 (December 1993): 101–102.

neoliberal consensus often seeks in the historical novel, to anneal the disruption of the present. The way Kent makes history present renders this annealing impossible.

Eleanor Catton: New Zealand's Rehearsal

Some readers will feel disconcerted by this book on contemporary Australian literature closing with a discussion of a New Zealand writer, so before we proceed to our analysis of the superb and provocative work of Eleanor Catton I wish to offer a rationale for this inclusion. Even if Australians and New Zealanders know themselves to be different because of their very different histories, they also experienced similar colonial regimes and were the subject of similar geostrategic positioning. Contemporary literary institutions such as the Man Booker Prize group the nations together in listing the regions eligible to win the award. Most global readers who encounter Australian literature will, like I did in the 1980s, encounter New Zealand at the same time. Inevitably, the two nations have often shared writers, such as Eve Langley, Henry Lawson, Ruth Park, Ronald Hugh Morrieson, Stephen Oliver and Douglas Stewart, all of whom spent time on both sides of the Tasman. Moreover, the 2012 meeting of the Association for the Study of Australian Literature was held in Wellington, and New Zealand scholars such as Lydia Wevers and Philip Steer have participated in Australian literary-academic life.

Even if my inclusion of a New Zealand writer in a discussion of contemporary Australian literature is a gross misunderstanding by a deluded outsider (I do not believe it is, but I understand some readers may see it that way), what Lacanian psychoanalysis calls *méconnaissance*, or creative misrecognition, might be the cost of global access to Australian literature.[22] Globalisation brings instantaneous communication but not necessarily instantaneous understanding. To transnational readers, Australia and New Zealand – Australasia – are widely seen as part of the Anglophone South Pacific, much as transnational readers see Cuba and Argentina as part of Latin America, or Estonia and Bulgaria as part of Eastern Europe. In all cases, this may be misrecognition, and I would argue that the latter examples represent a greater misrecognition than the case of Australia and New Zealand, which are linked not just by language and colonial history but also by sport, popular culture and trade. But transnationalism is no less free of misrecognition than any other human relational state, such as politics or sex. Neoliberalism and its unimpeded markets may allow information to travel more quickly. But attitudes in different areas are still out of joint, remaining resistant to conformity of understanding. Part of a national literature becoming transnational is its becoming subject to these arbitrary but at times consequential misunderstandings. Sometimes these misunderstandings can yield useful insights. For instance, while it has been a struggle for Australia internally to see itself as part of the Asia-Pacific region, global readers, since World War II, have been prone to see Australia in an Asian context.

Pre-eminently, however, the reason Eleanor Catton is included in this book is that her work – both her fiction and her public commentary – has lashed out against the cruel inequalities of neoliberalism in a way no Australian writer has, and in a way (thanks to the cultural proximities mentioned above) that is highly resonant for Australia. The dismay

---

22   David Evans, *An Introductory Dictionary of Lacanian Psychoanalysis* (London: Routledge, 1996), 112.

some Australian writers might feel at seeing a New Zealand writer included here is part of the pain of globalisation, sorrows that are concomitant with its pleasures.

When Eleanor Catton's *The Luminaries*, a massive book of well over 800 pages, won the Man Booker Prize in 2013 it carried all before it, making news in a way that no book from the antipodes had since Peter Carey's early days. Catton may be said to have succeeded in being transnational with respect to earlier writers in her own national literature, while still providing international readers with a sense of New Zealand. Catton's work harks back not to the various nation-building New Zealand modernists of the twentieth century – Frank Sargeson, Allen Curnow, and in her own highly idiosyncratic way Janet Frame – but to an earlier New Zealand, before the political hegemony of the left was established under Richard John Seddon and William Pember Reeves (himself a somewhat lyrical, if stiff, poet) in the 1890s, with what Reeves himself called "state experiments", the visionary policies of social welfare and women's suffrage for which New Zealand became famous.[23] Instead, *The Luminaries* harks back, not only in temporal setting but in emphasis, to the era of the pro-capitalist premier Sir Julius Vogel (himself a novelist, of a science-fictional bent), to the free-market prehistory of a socialist and late-modern New Zealand. Equally, *The Luminaries* can be seen as following in the footsteps of Jane Stafford and Mark Williams in *Māoriland*, with their revaluation of the pre-nationalist period from 1872 to 1914, in contrast to the usual New Zealand nationalist privileging of late-modernism.[24]

The Luminaries, however, is not polemical in its view of history. Catton's first book, *The Rehearsal* (2008), is contemporary in setting and is not set recognisably in New Zealand. That book addresses competition, performance and meritocracy. *The Luminaries*, historical and set recognisably in New Zealand, emphasises money and its attainment, and sees happy endings in individual rather than collective terms. It is as if Catton needed to go back to the 1860s to portray a recognisably liberal New Zealand, a mirror for that of a contemporary New Zealand in which New Zealand's modern welfare state has been fractured by an inequality that threatens to promote what Max Rashbrooke calls "segregation" in society.[25] The previous Booker Prize winner from New Zealand – Keri Hulme's 1985 *The Bone People* – was associated with the coming to power of David Lange's Labour government in New Zealand, with its refusal to accept nuclear-armed US ships and its arrest of the French saboteurs who bombed the environmentalist boat the *Rainbow Warrior*. Intriguingly, *The Bone People*, for all it puts relations with the indigenous people at the forefront of its concerns, is also set on the west coast of the South Island, a comparatively conflict-free zone in New Zealand history compared to the North Island, where extensive warfare between Pakeha and Māori occurred in the nineteenth century (as depicted in Maurice Shadbolt's New Zealand Wars trilogy).[26]

Shadbolt's trilogy did quite well in the United States, and his peculiar combination of economy and historical breadth proved enticing for the world market. In general, however, the writing of twentieth-century New Zealand, with its emphasis on the struggle for national self-definition, as seen in the poetry of mid-century writers such as Charles

---

23   William Pember Reeves, *State Experiments in Australia and New Zealand* (1902; Cambridge: Cambridge University Press, 2011).
24   Jane Stafford and Mark Williams, *Māoriland: New Zealand Literature 1872 to 1914* (Wellington: Victoria University Press, 2007).
25   Max Rashbrooke, *Inequality: A New Zealand Crisis* (Wellington: Bridget Williams Books, 2011), 15.
26   I am grateful to Philip Steer for discussion on this point.

Brasch, James K. Baxter and the earlier Allen Curnow, had little international appeal. Janet Frame did, but her work was radically extra-territorial. For over twenty years, the poet Bill Manhire's writing program at Victoria University of Wellington has produced writers such as Elizabeth Knox and Emily Perkins, who received worldwide distribution and at times seemed poised for worldwide success but never quite secured it.

In a sense, *The Luminaries*' success had been gestating for years. As early as 1993, the popularity of Jane Campion's film *The Piano* brought alive the New Zealand landscape as a locale both exotic and familiar. Since the early 2000s, people in New York and London publishing had been telling me that the Australian "wave" was probably over, and that New Zealand would be the next big thing. In 2012, New Zealand was a "featured nation" at the Frankfurt Book Fair. Catton was the fulfilment of a series of anterior prophecies.

This might infuriate people who remember the succour the young and struggling Janet Frame found in the humble shed of her mentor, the established author Frank Sargeson, and the other austerities of the twentieth-century writing scene. Yet if the neoliberal era stresses cosmopolitan networks and distribution methods, the resourceful writer not only uses these but can critically reflect on them. *The Rehearsal* critiques the way young adults are made to complete and to alter their personalities in order to prevail at what should be a creative, artistic exercise. *The Luminaires* ultimately offers love, not money, as the solution. Neoliberalism often insists on the need to repeal the twentieth century and instead looks back to a happier and freer nineteenth century. *The Luminaries*, which harshly critiques the workings of money in the nineteenth century, blatantly subverts this paradigm.

Equally, the collapse of the twentieth-century socialist model of New Zealand, along with New Zealand's emergence as a global tourist destination by dint of Peter Jackson's film adaptation of J. R. R. Tolkien's *The Lord of the Rings* being filmed there (2001–2003), marked new opportunities. Islands have traditionally played a subversive role, both literally and metaphorically, as explored in the theory of Gilles Deleuze and the critical work of Elizabeth DeLoughrey and the Australians Suvendrini Perera and Elizabeth McMahon.[27] Australia itself has moved from emphasising the solidity of its continental status – which contributed to the demand for fictional heft – to its littoral and liminal qualities, as seen particularly in Alexis Wright's use of the sea in *Carpentaria* and de Kretser's use of the sea in *Questions of Travel*. Thus the success of *The Luminaries*, like that of *Burial Rites,* should not be complained about or resented; it should be explored for its transgressive potential. In January 2015, Catton eloquently criticised neoliberalism, not only in New Zealand but in Australia and Canada, as "profit-obsessed, very shallow, very money-hungry".[28] These remarks led Catton to be attacked by right-wing radio hosts as unpatriotic. They seemed shocked that someone who had sold so well would dare to bite the hand that fed her. A previous Booker winner, Arundhati Roy, had provoked a similar reaction when she turned to political activism. That Catton portrays a capitalistic, pre-socialist economy in *The Luminaries* is at the very least provocatively double-sided.

---

27   Gilles Deleuze, *Desert Islands and Other Texts 1953–1974*, trans. David Lapoujade and Mike Taormina (New York: Semiotexte, 2004); Elizabeth DeLoughrey, *Routes and Roots: Navigating Pacific Island Literatures* (Honolulu: University of Hawai'i Press, 2007); Suvendrini Perera, *Australia and the Insular Imagination: Beaches, Borders, Boats, and Bodies* (New York: Palgrave Macmillan, 2009); David Brooks and Elizabeth McMahon, eds, *Southerly* 72, no. 3 (2012).
28   Quoted in Michael Field, "Eleanor Catton's Problem with New Zealand", stuff.co.nz, 28 January 2015.

The success of the Tolkien films surely if circuitously helped that of the film version of Witi Ihimaera's *The Whale Rider* (2002). Moreover, the books produced by alumni of Manhire's MA program have often had a fantastic element; C. K. Stead described Elizabeth Knox's *Black Oxen* (2001) – a book Stead rightly saw as a tremendous achievement – as "Harry Potter for the bigs".[29] Although lacking overt fantasy, *The Luminaries*, with its ingenious complicated plot and its creation of a vivid, autonomous world within its pages, can be read within this tradition, in which New Zealand fiction is linked with the cultural capital of internationally successful fantasy.

Rehearsing for Recognition

Yet this is not true of Catton's first novel, 2008's *The Rehearsal*. A masterpiece of voice and structure, it is set among a community of young men and women in their late teenage years, musical and dramatic performers who are rehearsing for plays and concerts. Necessarily, there is also an allegorical sense of the late teenage years as a rehearsal for life, although it is a rehearsal that is often richer in its tensions and ramifications than the real thing. The golden boy who returns to the drama institute to show how he has made good says "drama school makes you never congeal. You never set or crust over. Every possibility is kept open – it must be kept open".[30]

The striving of the young people in *The Rehearsal* is not just their own, but that of their parents. One of the teachers mimics the thinking of these pushy parents: "On its own, my life is ordinary and worthless and nothing. But if my daughter is rich in experience and rich in opportunity, then people will come to pity me: the smallness of my life and my options will not be *incapacity*, it will be *sacrifice*." (18) Thus the striving and competitiveness in this novel is not just an attribute of the younger generation, but something imposed or at least abetted by the elder generation. In pushing their daughters to be winners, these mothers are making a final attempt to be losers who win. This is why any critique of neoliberalism must take into account late modernity as well: the way the system – in this case the neoliberal system – co-opts any potential challenges. In this it resembles modern governmentality as dissected by Orwell and Foucault.

This is glimpsed by the boy who, in *The Rehearsal*, complains that "nobody says anything terrible at all" about the school the young performers attend; "nobody gives the finger as they walk out the door". The protagonist of the novel, Stanley, responds that "it's a prestigious school. I guess people just really feel strongly about that." (40) People have so much of a stake in the system that they cannot criticise it. To question it would be to endanger their own status. Yet Stanley's sense of ordinariness, his indifference to his situation's high stakes, makes him the most balanced and sensitive character. To be humane in *The Rehearsal*, one has to be insulated to a degree from what is going on. Without this insulation, one might career around, motivated only by the thrill of risk. The teenage Julia observes that a teacher sleeping with his student is exciting because of the risk it entails; it involves "the possibility that you might lose" (50). This is reminiscent of the

---

29   C. K. Stead, *Kin of Place: Essays on Twenty New Zealand Writers* (Auckland: Auckland University Press, 2002), 373.

30   Eleanor Catton, *The Rehearsal* (2008; Boston: Back Bay, 2011), 23. All subsequent references are to this edition and appear in parentheses in the text.

allure of extreme sex in Winton's *Breath*, and of the spectre of sublimity and disaster that neoliberalism in general affords.

Unlike *The Luminaries*, with its highly specific setting in nineteenth-century New Zealand, *The Rehearsal* is set very vaguely "now" and in an unnamed English-speaking country. Many of the adults in the novel are either not named at all or referred to mainly by their occupations, as if their jobs are what define them. An exception is Mr Saladin, the teacher who sleeps with one of his students. In a novel so denuded of proper names, a foreign name, reminding us of a great Arab leader of the past, stands out. Moreover, there is the inevitable association with Saddam Hussein, who likened himself so frequently to Saladin in the years before the book was published. Mr Saladin is both an outsider and potentially a megalomaniac.

The female saxophone teacher who replaces the fired Mr Saladin is mostly called The Saxophone Teacher, although, in a detail missed by most reviewers, her actual name is indeed given: Mrs Jean Critchley (43). This name alludes to Miss Jean Brodie in Muriel Spark's 1961 novel *The Prime of Miss Jean Brodie*, a teacher who attaches herself to her female students in a way that is both inspirational and excessive. We are meant to realise that even though The Saxophone Teacher seems a more benign, less rapacious figure than Mr Saladin, and less ideologically partisan than the crypto-fascist Jean Brodie, she is manipulative and over-invested in her students, and possibly has erotic interest in her female charges, or at least an interest in their erotic lives.

The Rehearsal is highly recursive, as the students are auditioning for a play based on an accusation of sexual harassment made by a student, Victoria, against Mr Saladin. Meanwhile Victoria's sister, Isolde, is manipulated by The Saxophone Teacher into a romantic relationship with Julia, a fellow pupil who has questioned the school's handling of Victoria's relationship with Mr Saladin. Yet the relationship with Julia expands Isolde's horizons, and helps her to understand what her sister is experiencing.

But The Saxophone Teacher's intervention is not benign. The Saxophone Teacher substitutes diagnosis for decorum in her relationships with her students, prying into their lives instead of merely encouraging their aptitudes. The girls' school, Abbey Grange, is described as delivering a "forcible public fracture of their ego-mold in the interest of rebuilding a more versatile self" (177). The novel's dominant schematic is that of the rehearsal as a rehearsal for life, not just for art; under neoliberalism, society demands that young people go through this rehearsal before they enter the world. As the rewards are potentially unlimited, so is the competition.

As in Tsiolkas' *Barracuda*, society turns to the selective school as an alleged model of meritocracy, when in fact it embodies the age's accelerating inequality. Like the school Danny Kelly attends in *Barracuda* – a boys-only school referred to in an invidious gender-reversal as Cunts College[31] – Abbey Grange is a single-sex school. This might remove the distraction of heterosexual sex, but it also means the only real peer relationships at the school involve a struggle for social status. The relationship between Julia and Isolde, although it is the result of manipulation by The Saxophone Teacher, is at least partially owned by the young girls themselves; it allows them to imagine a different type of value amid the disheartening competition.

Although the novel is titled *The Rehearsal*, not *The Audition*, much of the story pertains to securing roles and performing them well, and the competitiveness of the students

---

31 Christos Tsiolkas, *Barracuda* (Crows Nest: Allen & Unwen, 2013), 9.

could be seen as a preview for the competitiveness of life under neoliberalism. This accords with Australian works I have already analysed, such as *Barracuda*, and some that I have not, such as Peter Goldsworthy's *Maestro* (1989) and Lally Katz's play *The Eisteddfod* (2004), both of which show how society excites the competitiveness of young people in an age that treats artistic ability as another means of filtering winners from losers.

The resulting inhumanity is exemplified by Stanley's father when, in a cruel joke, he urges Stanley to take out "a million-dollar insurance policy" on the student he considers most likely to die (33). Vulnerability is commoditised, reduced to a calculable risk. In Stanley's father's fantasy, the hypothetical suicide of a child is treated as just another vagary of what Ulrich Beck called risk society.[32] Catton chronicles how contemporary adolescent life is hypercompetitive, and how this is exploited by a society that is forever searching for any sort of advantage in status.

Stanley lacks the personal turmoil exhibited by Isolde, his closest female counterpart. Around Stanley, however, our estimations of the other characters swirl. Mr Saladin is somewhat exonerated by the end of the book. There seems to have been a consensual element in his nonetheless unpardonable relationship with Victoria, and there is a slight suggestion that he may be the victim of political correctness. The fact that Mr Saladin is punished for his prurience while The Saxophone Teacher is not introduces a tacit critique of feminism, as in David Mamet's *Oleanna* and Zoe Heller's *Notes on a Scandal*. But, just as Christina Stead's pre-feminism attracted many feminist exegetes, so Catton's post-feminism speaks to the very sense of possibilities, of an expanded configuration of power and of knowledge, that feminism engendered.

New Zealand itself has historically provided a stage for rehearsals. It was among the first nations to embrace political modernity: giving the vote to women, adopting social welfare policies, and fostering a commitment to egalitarianism even in the late 1890s, when most of the world still held to laissez-faire policies. In the 1980s, New Zealand once again showed the way, but this time in a different direction, towards deregulation and free markets. Leigh Davis, a leading New Zealand avant-garde poet, in the mid-1980s became a merchant banker.[33] The leftist, anti-nuclear policies of the Lange Labour government coincided with a pro-free-market economic stance epitomised by the "Rogernomics" of the government's finance minister, Roger Douglas. All these developments disencumbered the rise of neoliberalism from party politics or even ideology, rendering visible the paradoxes of neoliberalism and how it infused an entire period rather than a particular political grouping. *The Rehearsal* shows the consequences of that paradox in the lives and personal choices of the children of the next generation.

Astrological Affections and an Improvised Town: Reading *The Luminaries*

Catton's second novel continues her emphasis on group improvisation. Hokitika, the gold mining community on the west coast of the South Island in which *The Luminaries* is set, is an improvised town, a community generated at short notice and with little advance plan-

---

32   Both the father–son dynamic and the emphasis on teenage death are reminiscent of the suicide of Brett White in Steve Toltz's *A Fraction of the Whole* (London: Hamish Hamilton, 2008).

33   Jane Stafford and Mark Williams, *The Auckland University Press Anthology of New Zealand Literature* (Auckland: Auckland University Press, 2013), 1079.

ning. It is kind of a dress rehearsal, or a performance with a great deal of spontaneity (as Australia of course had its own gold rush, earlier than New Zealand's, an Australian component inevitably obtrudes on this novel, especially given the villain Carver's convict past "in the Cockatoo Island Penitentiary").[34] Hokitika is an agglomeration of aspirants, escapees and nondescripts. It is the obverse of the artificial capital of Canberra as examined in Chapter 7: Hokitika was not built slowly, according to a blueprint, and designed as an ideal of public service, but is a ramshackle scaffolding for extracting minerals from the ground. If this sudden community seems neoliberal in its dedication to money, Catton's point is that there is also a residually "settled" quality even in that improvisation. This settled quality bends forward to the peaceable quality of twentieth-century, socialist-egalitarian New Zealand. Catton, indeed, refers to the New Zealand gold rush as "strangely civilised".[35]

In postcolonial writing, the historical novel frequently had a privileged role, as with Salman Rushdie's *Midnight's Children* (1981) and Chinua Achebe's *Things Fall Apart* (1958). Historical fiction was a site of resistance, a place where histories ignored or travestied by imperial narratives could reassert themselves. The Canadian novelist Rudy Wiebe's *The Temptation of Big Bear* (1973) recorded the resistance of the Cree against their white oppressors; Margaret Atwood's poem "Marrying the Hangman" demonstrated the oppression of women within an already repressive colonial society. It was a Canadian, Linda Hutcheon, who theorised "historiographic metafiction" as a genre that is able to "situate itself within historical discourse without surrendering its autonomy as fiction".[36] By 1998, however, Wayne Johnston's *Colony of Unrequited Dreams*, a historical novel lamenting Newfoundland's decision to join Canada in 1949 – a "Northeastern" novel, to extend MacLulich's "Northern" category – was hailed by Luc Sante in the *New York Times Book Review*, who said of the novel's Newfoundland setting:

> Like few places these days, it seems remote, even exotic in a chilly way, and it's likely you haven't been there. It therefore can assert itself as a setting to the point of claiming a character role: a vast, desolate mystery hovering just over our northeast flank.[37]

The historical novel set in a remote place and time, once a force of resistance, was in danger of becoming a means of commodification. Stephen Muecke, for instance, saw Peter Carey's penchant for the nineteenth century as evidence of a "conservative attitude to literature".[38]

It was in this environment that one of the most internationally successful Australian historical novels, Roger McDonald's *Mr Darwin's Shooter* (1998), was published. It tells the story of Syms Covington, the cabin boy with Darwin on the HMS *Beagle* whose religious beliefs put him at odds with Darwin's evolutionary views. In reviewing the novel, Pearl Bowman noted that, in the 1950s, the consensus had

34 Eleanor Catton, *The Luminaries* (Boston: Little, Brown and Company, 2014), 745. All subsequent references are to this edition and appear in parentheses in the text.
35 Quoted in Lorien Kite, "Interview with Booker Prize-winning Eleanor Catton", *Financial Times*, 18 October 2013. http://tiny.cc/catton_2013.
36 Linda Hutcheon, *A Poetics of Postmodernism: History, Theory, Fiction* (London: Routledge, 1988), 105–23.
37 Luc Sante, "O Canada!", *New York Times Book Review*, 25 July 1999, 6.
38 Stephen Muecke, "Wide Open Spaces: Horizontal Readings of Australian Literature", *New Literatures Review* 16 (1988): 117.

viewed Marx and Freud as the major forces, with Darwin mostly a good collector and classifier. Today it is likely that Darwin would be viewed as the greatest influence, who redefined the human race's past and place in the universe, and provided a challenge to religious beliefs that even the most outspoken heretic never achieved.[39]

It was not just that Darwin's reputation had gone up, but that Freud's and Marx's had gone down. Marx came down, obviously, because of the collapse of communism; it took the Global Financial Crisis of 2008 to bring him back slightly, via the work of Alain Badiou and Jacques Rancière. Freud had only Slavoj Zizek to offer his reputation similar theoretical help, rendering Peter Carey's rehabilitation of Freud through Ned Kelly, as discussed in Chapter 8, all the more timely. Freud's reputation fell thanks to a more subtle range of factors, from psychologists turning to prescription medication over talk therapy as a way to solve individuals' problems to attacks on Freud, ostensibly from the left, that served the interests of the right by eliminating any irrationalism in the human spirit and making mankind into simply *Homo economicus*. Darwin, on the other hand, was associated with the survival of the fittest. Indeed, much of neoliberal anthropology was simply a revived Social Darwinism, even if, at its more compassionate edges, it redefined that fight for survival as what Honneth termed the struggle for recognition, making it less biological and more attidunal, no longer about the survival of the fittest but the comparative social advantage of the fittest.

Yet, even so, McDonald's novel was not seen as an uncritical, progressive celebration of Darwinian thought. McDonald's portrait of Covington as a man of religious faith appalled by what he has helped Darwin to assert is laden with an ambiguous sympathy for Covington as a believer, as McDonald acknowledged.[40] If one sees Darwinism as a precursor to neoliberal selfishness, one can see the spirituality of Covington as palliating the exploitative excesses of neoliberalism. But if one sees Darwin as an emblem of progress – the one progressive figure left standing after the statues of Marx and Freud had been hurled to the ground – the affirmation of Covington's religiosity functions as a tribute to the vestigial. Historical fictions, in this light, are histories of the present as well as the past, far from affirming a residual sovereignty. John Marx describes the historical novel as a "prehistory for globalisation that is also an origin story for … global meritocracy".[41] Catton's novel, with its emphasis on money, luck and individual autonomy, and its setting amid a resource boom at the peak of nineteenth-century laissez-faire capitalism, could be such an origin story.

The plot organisation of *The Luminaries* is reminiscent of Edwardian novels and of genre fiction. The group of collaborators who oscillate between sinister and benign ends is reminiscent both of G. K. Chesterton's *The Man Who Was Thursday* (1908) and Agatha Christie's quasi-parody of Chesterton, *The Seven Dials Mystery* (1929). Catton has admitted to reading Agatha Christie and quoted Chesterton extensively on her Twitter feed in August 2014, so it is plausible to suggest that these are conscious intertextualities.[42] Both Christie's and Chesterton's novels have to do with secret conspiracies, yet totally upend

---

39   Pearl Bowman, "The Timeless Conflict between Science and Religion Finds New Meaning in *Mr Darwin's Shooter*", *Antipodes* 13, no. 1 (1999): 43–45.

40   Roger McDonald, *Mr Darwin's Shooter* (New York: Atlantic Monthly Press, 1998), 6.

41   John Marx, *Geopolitics and the Anglophone Novel* (Cambridge: Cambridge University Press, 2012), 169.

42   Eleanor Catton, interviewed by Matt Bialostocki, Unity Books blog, 21 April 2013. www.unitybooks.co.nz/interviews/eleanor-catton/. A line on page 364 of *The Luminaries*, asserting that

the reader's initial evaluation of the characters. Catton similarly offers a series of surprises in her plot, not just with respect to who was where and did what but as to the essential moral qualities of the major characters. There is mobility and indeterminacy in these rapid permutations and inversions – a sense that destinies are not fixed for anyone. That the politician Alistair Lauderback, who turns out to be the villain of the book, thinks (wrongly) that Francis Carver, the villain of the book, was Crosbie Wells' brother – the son of the same mother, just as Lauderback himself and Wells are, actually, the sons of the same father – indicates the close apposition between the respectable and the disrespectable, the heroic and the contumacious, that such an improvised locality as Hokitika can disgorge. Indeed, much of the novel's moral drama lies in its exposure of the hypocrisy of those who might be thought to represent ideals, such as Reverend Devlin, who conceals secret financial documents between the pages of the Old and New Testaments in his Bible, and the virtue of those who might be thought corrupt, such as the opium-taking whore, Anna Wetherell.

A Kaleidoscopic Cast

The business tycoon Dick Mannering is just the sort of entrepreneurial figure that could be, but often is not, represented in contemporary fiction, for reasons ranging from Forrester's logic that neoliberalism does not want itself actively represented, to a tendency to depict a more diffuse sense of power, as in Winton's *Eyrie*. But the narrative, although it does not make Mannering a villain, puts him on a par with everyone else in the kaleidoscopic cast in that he is a creature of the stars, or a plaything of happenstance. Even if there is "no charity in a gold town" (696), the novel ultimately breaks through to a realisation of the insufficiency of greed as a human motive. But it does so subtly. Rather than being either lionised or demonised, Mannering and his wealth are simply part of the picture, and his financial strength does not overpower the moral strength of others in the ensemble. As the Chinese indentured labourer and gold miner Quee Long says, "All the prestige and the profit belong to the whoremonger, not to the whore" (324). Catton can hardly be said to have written a paean to capitalism. This is both because her sympathies are clearly otherwise and because *The Luminaries* has a complicated structure that does not privilege any one voice. That so much of the first part of the book is devoted to one-on-one encounters between two people, in which characters both reveal and conceal themselves, adds to this effect of potentially infinite recombination. Quee Long measures everything by "a private standard of perfection" (258). This is a standard that potentially commands all the characters, but which no one else but Quee Long can ever know. Desire for money operates as a major motivation in the book, but it is asymmetrical and variegated. Catton does not reduce her characters to a uniform *Homo economicus*, but explores what John Scheckter calls "multiple systems of analysis and evaluation" beyond the merely financial.[43]

Lydia Wells, the opportunistic widow of the slain Crosbie, whose gold is the pivot about which the novel revolves, puts eloquently the novel's unwillingness to endorse unfettered liberty as the solution to the vexations of the human condition: "I find it very wonderful that you should protest a life of virtue and austerity, in favour of – what did you call them – 'freedoms'. Freedoms to do what exactly?" (560). Lydia goes on to defend

---

"heavenly relation is composed of wheels in motion, tilting axes, turning dials", may well allude to the idea of "seven dials" in Christie's book.

43   John Scheckter, "The Pleasures of Structural Uncertainty", *Antipodes*, 28, no. 1 (2014): 237.

Victorian proprieties, which the novel in part subverts, as if to say that true liberty will combine nineteenth-century economics and twenty-first-century mores. Yet the novel elevates an interdependent individualism over both authoritarian deference and narcissistic self-aggrandisement. *The Luminaries* has an important nonfictional source, acknowledged by Catton, in Stevan Eldred-Grigg, who has bucked the majority New Zealand tradition by writing of the rich and the gentry, which could be seen as both violating twentieth-century statist egalitarianism and calling attention to the inequalities it did not smooth out. But Eldred-Grigg's *Diggers, Hatters, Whores* is a much more linear book than Catton's.[44] It no doubt gave her a sense of the possible inventory of characters, yet is quite different in tonality and shape to *The Luminaries*. Eldred-Grigg's book does, however, share with *The Luminaries* an irreverence towards the New Zealand tradition of literary self-effacement and national self-scrutiny.

The Luminaries has been called a neo-Victorian novel.[45] Before the modernist privileging of the *récit*, and in a time of frequent serialisation, narratives were longer, and most major Victorian novels are indeed long and plot-driven, as is Catton's. Yet a comparison with the early twentieth-century detective story, as considered in relation to Chesterton and Christie above, may be more illuminating than a strictly Victorian connection. Catton makes Stead's idea of the "many-charactered novel" look like the most bare-bones *testimonio* by comparison. Critics have likened *The Luminaries* to Wilkie Collins' *The Moonstone* (1868) – the multiple points of view, the complicated plot, the opium theme. But Collins, although he played with the reader's expectations, was not nearly as metafictive as Catton is, and *The Luminaries* represents the integration of the self-consciousness of *Tristram Shandy* into a nineteenth-century formal realism that, even in sensation writers such as Collins, Rhoda Broughton and Mary Elizabeth Braddon, rejected any obvious foregrounding of authorial presence. The novel's ensemble cast, not clearly divided into major and minor characters, is a hallmark of the twentieth-century detective story, much more so than of Victorian fiction. The book's temporal setting is Victorian, but its affective life-situation cannot be neatly pigeonholed. Catton has said that she avoids novels that claim to represent New Zealand as a whole,[46] and *The Luminaries* is not a totalising, magic-realist blockbuster as was Carey's *Illywhacker*, Ireland's *The Chosen* or Hall's *Just Relations*. *The Luminaries*, for all its size, is concentrated.

Catton features a multicultural cast, including not one but two Chinese characters who are deliberately antithetical to the insidious opium-peddling stereotype of Victorian fiction. Catton's Chinese characters can be seen as a fulfilment of the promise of earlier characters, such as the Chinese camp chef Cheon in Jeannie Gunn's *We of the Never-Never* (1903), who contained elements of both racial caricature and three-dimensional portrait. There is also the character of Te Rau Tauwhare, a Māori *pounamu* (greenstone) aficionado, the Jew Benjamin Löwenthal and the Scandinavian Harald Nilssen. Even the minister, Devlin, has an Irish name, although he is Protestant. There is an additional historical touch in Löwenthal's background, as he is said to be from the former kingdom of Hanover, which

---

44   Stevan Eldred-Grigg, *Diggers, Hatters, Whores* (Auckland: Random House New Zealand, 2014).
45   Kirby-Jane Hallum, " 'As Far Away from England as Any Man Could Be': *The Luminaries* as *Sensation Sequel*", *Journal of Victorian Culture Online* 19, no. 1 (2014). http://blogs.tandf.co.uk/jvc/2014/04/28/as-far-away-from-england-as-any-man-could-be-the-luminaries-as-sensation-sequel/.
46   Quoted in Anna Wallis, "Catton Makes a Good Point", *Wanganui Chronicle*, 30 January 2015, http://www.nzherald.co.nz/wanganui-chronicle/opinion/news/article.cfm?c_id=1503423&objectid=11394045.

was absorbed by Prussia in 1866 (315). Hanover was associated with the British royal family, and only passed out of British dominion when Queen Victoria took the throne, because Hanoverian sovereignty required male succession. Its absorption by Prussia foreshadowed later tensions between Britain and Germany, and Löwenthal's emigration as a result of these events anticipates the far greater diaspora of the 1930s under Nazism. Several times in the book, Catton drops hints like these to show the reader that her sense of history is not innocent; the book is not simply a light-hearted romp but understands the ethical consequences of historical events.

Writing in the *Pittsburgh Post-Gazette*, Julie Hakim Azzma noted that:

> The novel silences its Chinese and Māori characters, prohibiting the Europeans from learning their stories. The Chinese man's words aren't translated into English; the Māori isn't invited to testify in court. For … Catton, history is at once a voice and a silence.[47]

Yet the untranslated Bible verses in Māori, read by Reverend Devlin, are a challenge to readers not from New Zealand. Reverend Devlin's realisation that he should not cavil at the Bible being translated into Māori, as his own Bible is also a translation, serves to remind the reader that literacy migrated to the West from other languages and cultures and may migrate again. The Māori Tauwhare delivers the decisive blow to the villain Carver. Emery Staines buries the missing gold in Māori land. These plot developments position indigeneity as a force that can withstand and anneal the ultimately trivial contestations of capitalism. It is not a spiritual fullness, perhaps, but an ethical horizon consistent with the thematic of concern I discussed in Chapter 6 with respect to Gail Jones, Alex Miller and Alexis Wright. The structural parallels between *pounamu* and gold, as commodities at once comparable and incomparable, reveal a level of engagement with Māori themes in the work that is more than superficial multiculturalism.

As for the Chinese characters, Catton introduces two, Quee Long and Ah Sook, and she makes Westerners' inability to tell them apart a linchpin of the plot. It is not anachronistic to depict Chinese people in New Zealand in this period. As in the United States and Australia, the first people of the Chinese diaspora came during the gold rushes. Restrictive and discriminatory government policies, and paranoia about an Asian invasion, kept the numbers in all three countries below what they might have been, but it was the beginning of a migration that the White Australia Policy could not staunch. Often, twenty-first-century students are told that multiculturalism, for good or ill, is a present-day development. It is good for them to see, in Catton's book, that it has a longer history. Catton's depiction of the two Chinese men is thus neither anachronistic nor politically correct. In the most literal sense it is a history lesson.

Gold and Love

The gender politics of *The Luminaries* were not much commented on in reviews, but are worth considering. The key image of the book is of the missing gold being sewn into Anna Wetherell's dresses. That the gold has to be concealed in a woman's clothing rep-

---

47   Julie Hakim Azzam, "*The Luminaries*: A Literary Gold Rush", *Pittsburgh Post-Gazette*, 1 December 2013. http://www.post-gazette.com/ae/book-reviews/2013/12/01/A-literary-gold-rush/stories/ 201312010015.

resents a notable overturning of gender hierarchies. Furthermore, the world of the book is decidedly, even disturbingly, male-dominated. There are really only two major female characters, Lydia Wells and Anna Wetherell. Yet there are so many nearly interchangeable men, all defined by their professions, somewhat like the adults in *The Rehearsal*. Some of this has to do with the book's sources in Chestertonian conspiracy and the highly homosocial world of that sort of plot. Kirsty Gunn was wrong to say that *The Rehearsal* was about a group of teenage girls.[48] Yet, with the exception of Anna and Lydia, *The Luminaries* is about blokes. Catton even gives her own astrological sign, Libra (she was born on 24 September, 1985), to a man and, at that, an inconspicuous and not all that positively portrayed one, Harald Nilsson. This forestalls any possibility for the reader to identify an authorial surrogate in the book.

Anna reflects at one point, "A woman fallen has no future; a man risen has no past" (825). That *The Luminaries* does indeed give Anna a future shows how Catton is, without flinching from historical reality, giving her characters a utopian space. This space is utopian even, and perhaps especially, in twenty-first-century terms; it is a space in which they can find respite from the forces of the market, which values men and women's futures so differently. Furthermore, in a historical novel this gendering of temporality, of past and future, has that much more valence. Emery's willingness to exonerate Anna Wetherell of both the charges against her and the social stigma of her past has an egalitarian effect. It permits Anna to exercise her legal rights as a citizen and not to be preyed upon by a society that has designated her a loser.

The Luminaries is not only compassionate towards the victims of such potential derogations, but actively encourages and solicits their agency, at least within their various astrologically prescribed fates. The haunting series of letters written by the illegitimate Crosbie Wells to his legitimate half-brother Lauderbeck, which never receive a response yet are kept immaculately by their recipient, signifies some sort of failed communication or missed appointment, undergirded by structural hierarchies about who is valuable and who is not. That Lauderbeck comes to regret his indifference when he sees what he presumes is Crosbie's dead body provides, if not the actuality or the sentimentality of reconciliation, at least a conceptual affirmation of such, one which does not accept the severance of socially acceptable and unacceptable as a given. That Crosbie himself genuinely vowed to reform (as seen in his final letter to Lauderbeck), and that it is Te Rau Tauwhare who kills Carver, in an act of spiritual retribution, puts the novel's values on the side of the Māori and not of the Anglo-capitalists. The literal and metaphorical resurrection of Emery Staines through his altruistic gesture on behalf of Anna is also a resurrection of a sort of social possibility. Anna and Emery make sacrifices for each other that are not driven by avarice or hope of gain. *The Luminaries* does not say that greed is good.

Why then, despite the popularity of the novel, is there an undercurrent of doubt about its merits among some readers? The doyen of New Zealand men of letters, C. K. Stead, writing for an international audience in the *Financial Times*, summed this feeling up when he said, "The history of literary fiction in the twentieth century was a struggle, never entirely successful, to escape from this kind of writing."[49] In this view, the modernist com-

---

48 Kirsty Gunn, "*The Luminaries* by Eleanor Catton", *Guardian*, 11 September 2013. http://theguardian.com/books/2013/sep/11/luminaries-leanor-catton-review.
49 C. K. Stead, "*The Luminaries* by Eleanor Catton", *Financial Times*, 6 September 2013. http://tiny.cc/stead_2013.

mitment to austere, self-aware *récits* represented a high-water mark in artistic control that is being abandoned by the younger generation with its heedless indulgence in pop culture and recycling. Yet one could counter that modernism, like any period, had to end sometime, and the paralysis of late modernity in the work of Christina Stead and Harrower indicates why. Furthermore, as C. K. Stead himself observes, the modernist rejection of "this kind of writing" was "never entirely successful". The major Australian writers of the mid-twentieth century – Christina Stead, Patrick White and Xavier Herbert – did not escape from conventional narrative. Yet Randolph Stow's work was possibly inhibited by an excessive adhesion to modernist mandates that kept his books short, spare and symbolic. The same could be said of another Western Australian writer, Peter Cowan. In New Zealand, the two best prose writers of this era, Janet Frame and Frank Sargeson, stuck to modernist conventions, albeit imbuing them with far riskier sexualities and mentalities than the male, heterosexual norm presumed by such modernist writers as William Faulkner, James Joyce and Joseph Conrad.

C. K. Stead's preferred model of high-modernist elitism had its costs. Twentieth-century writers such as Tolkien and Christie and even Chesterton, all alluded to or evoked in varying ways by *The Luminaries*, were underrated in their lifetimes because they were best-selling, sought to entertain, or were not doctrinally aligned with Bloomsbury and other high-modern cliques.[50] If the floodgates of quality are now burst too wide open, it is because the synchronic paralysis of late modernity dammed them in too much. To play on Harrower's titles, the watch tower was too vigilant, the long prospect too distant; inevitably, the objects of surveillance asserted themselves. Catton's generation believes that one can be both impure and high-literary; C. K. Stead's that to be high-literary a threshold of purity is needed. The answer, as with the economic policies of late modernity and neoliberalism, is somewhere in between. But it is the apposition that is interesting.

The concept of the "systems novel", first mentioned by Thomas LeClair in his 1988 book on Don DeLillo, is relevant to Catton's work, and may be a way to wring *The Luminaries* out of the debate over the historical novel cited above.[51] Catton synthesises the patterned, game-playing novel with the realist-psychological novel. Her employment of Martin Buber's "I and Thou" philosophy plays out in the way the characters in the novel ultimately affirm ideals of sacrifice and idealism seen in Buber's call for thoroughgoing commitment to the other.[52] This affirmation is seen in Te Rua Tauwhare's *pounamu*, Anna and Emery's love, and in Lauderbeck's realisation of his love for his half-brother Crosbie and his appreciation of Crosbie's renunciation of covetousness and embrace of a more humanistic way of life. Some might see the emplacement of Buber's "I and Thou" theme, with its call for profound, committed interpersonal engagement, in such an arcade of ingenuities as a dilution, as if personal depth were being outsourced. But in suggesting that we should care about and love one another, *The Luminaries* avoids sentimentality and didacticism by lacing its message through complex imaginative structures.

---

50 Nicholas Birns and Margaret Boe Birns, "Agatha Christie: Modern and Modernist", in *The Cunning Craft: Original Essays on Detective Fiction and Contemporary Literary Theory*, eds Ronald G. Walker and June Frazer (Macomb: Western Illinois University, 1990), 120–34.
51 Tom LeClair, *In The Loop: Don DeLillo and the Systems Novel* (Urbana: University of Illinois Press, 1988).
52 Martin Buber, *I and Thou*, translated by Robin Gregor Smith (New York: Scribner, 2000).

C. K. Stead, despite gently poking at some of modernism's vulnerable points – such as its cosiness with fascism, in his 2001 novella *The Secret History of Modernism* – is in essence a defender of modernism. Yet if *The Luminaries* is not modernist in Stead's sense of the term, neither is it ephemeral fluff. It is a serious meditation on chance, fate and action. The name of the barque *Godspeed*, whose wreck is one of the principal surprises in the narrative, combines luck and destiny. Its catastrophe expresses the surprises life has in store even for those entities whose course seems prefigured. The novel is full of narrative surprises. The enunciating characters do not necessarily turn out to be the main characters. For the latecomer Walter Moody, the entire book is a rehearsal. *The Luminaries* is lengthy and about money at its beginning; brief and about love at its end. A smaller, more meaningful book is hidden within a larger, more diffuse one.

C. K. Stead dismisses the astrological structure of *The Luminaries* in a sentence. But the astrological frame, by suggesting that each character's actions and decisions are determined by the time when they happened to be born, in its denial of agency, its insistence that much of human character and life is forewritten, and in the inherent difficulty its understanding imposes, is an important corrective to the unremitting voluntarism of the neoliberal mind. The astrological frame at the novel's heart, the way each character's motives and psychology are systematically linked to their astrological sign, anchors the book. Astrology may seem to be trivial: a parlour game at best, a fetish at worst. A 1984 special issue of *Partisan Review* devoted to contemporary theory invoked Stanley Fish's term "off the wall" to argue that a Christian or a psychoanalytic reading of Jane Austen would be "on the wall", an astrological one "off the wall".[53] Only the small remaining band of Jungian psychoanalytic critics took astrology seriously as an interpretive mode.[54] But Catton's foregrounding of astrology enables her to be at once mainstream and non-Western. Astrology, with its fatalistic, non-messianic tincture and Babylonian origin, is, like paganism in Kent's *Burial Rites*, a reminder of the presence of the non-normative and the only semi-Western. In its intricate yet (to outsiders) arbitrary patterns, astrology has an element of the stochastic that can make it seem modern and experimental.

The way astrology is deployed in the novel also suggests a tacit relationship to the idea of history. The horoscope begins with Aries, the oncoming (Northern Hemisphere) of spring, and ends with Pisces, the very last of winter's cold. "What was glimpsed in Aquarius – what was envisioned, believed in, prophesied, predicted, doubted, and forewarned is made, in Pisces, manifest" (531). Pisces, in late February and early March, comes after Aquarius, in late January and early February. But, as Catton well knows, in the overall cycle of the zodiac entailed by the precession of the equinoxes, Aries precedes Pisces, which in turns precedes Aquarius – as the world learned in the 1960s, when hippies and new-age mystics spoke of the Age of Aquarius as the dawning of a more enlightened age. Catton sets her book in the last vestiges of the Age of Pisces (said to be roughly from the time of Christ to 2000). On the micro level, time goes forward; on the macro level, backward. Catton's intricate structure, as much as it makes reading the book a kind of role-playing game, circuitously yields provocative intellectual value. Of course, the entire scheme is built around the Northern Hemisphere sky and seasons; by setting the novel in New Zealand, Catton critiques and redeploys these norms. The stars are not the same everywhere.

---

53   Sanford Levinson, "Law: On Dworkin, Kennedy, and Ely", *The Partisan Review* 52, no. 1 (1984): 253.
54   Karen Hamaker-Zondag, *Psychological Astrology* (New York: Weiser, 1990).

The very idea of "The Luminaries" suggests neoliberalism's potential to bring inefficiencies to light. Yet the way the characters aligned with the seven planets, who are generally more important, offset the characters aligned with the twelve astrological signs, who are generally more minor, lends a sense of counterpoint to this ghastly clarity: a pluralistic insistence that no one ideology or cultural formation will carry the day. The planets move, unlike the stars, and have names, such as Venus, that allegorise concrete human characteristics. Astrology may also testify to non-European influences the novel will not notably appropriate but can inconspicuously and subtly mine. If astrology is no more equivalent to Māori cosmology than gold is to *pounamu*, at least the apposition, both inadequate and suggestive, is there. Astrology's appeal is that it is precisely, at this point in time, no longer what Felski, Marcus and Best would call symptomatic: it goes deeper than the surface.

When we first meet Walter Moody, he is an inexperienced whelp, what Pierre Bourdieu termed an oblate, somebody seeking to enter the system, and in this case to make substantial income on the goldfields. Although he is an Englishman travelling in New Zealand, in structural terms he resembles the scores of young antipodeans, both authors and the characters in their books, who have gone to the metropolitan worlds of the Northern Hemisphere to make their progress, or, as it were, luck. Catton describes him as "not superstitious", not because he is jaded but because he is inexperienced: he has assumed, as a default mode, a superficial canniness, a trust in "suspicion, cynicism, probability" (18). In the course of the book, Moody not only discovers a more spiritual aspect to life, but also acknowledges that his involvement with the other conspirators leads him to be "associated? Involved? Entangled?" – the tentativeness provided by the question marks is key here – with forces, animate and inanimate, beyond his own personal aspirations (350). For the characters in *The Luminaires* as in Eleanor Catton's own career, the world is made of more than just careers. Walter Moody goes from the goldfields to prospecting upon what the 1850s Australian critic Frederick Sinnett called the fiction fields.[55] For those determined not to like Catton's novel, the enveloping of Walter in a larger affective network may be but a tantalising game. But to those looking to what *The Luminaries* can offer rather than what it lacks, the book's occult aspects might be a token of a future far beyond winners and losers.

The first step towards this future, however, is to own up to what we face, not to deny it. One of Australia's least polemical but most humane poets, Vivian Smith, Tasmanian-born but long resident in Sydney, has said this with exemplary integrity:

> I've always tried to make the best of things,
> To find a diet in a can of worms.
> The bleakest introspection haunts my days
> But there's no way I'd ever let you know it.
> Trees are stressed and nibbled to the quick
> in this old suburb not far up the line.

---

55   Frederick Sinnett, "The Fiction Fields of Australia", *Journal of Australasia* 1 (July–December 1856), 97–105, 199–208. http://tiny.cc/sinnett.

> The experts say this time of drought will pass
> churches waiting with their prayers for rain.[56]

Smith calls his poem "In Dürftiger Zeit", meaning "fallow time" in German. Writing in 2007, at the age of seventy-four, Smith seems convinced that these years are indeed a fallow time in Australian life, with the very earth in peril and any response seemingly ineffectual. The only token of hope here is the enunciation itself. Here we have a voice that tapers rancour with concern. Beneath the poem's bitter surface, there is an abiding idealism. Moreover, as evidenced in the sophistication of the title and language, there is a conviction that transnationalism and cosmopolitanism do not mean selling out to the market. Instead, they are the possible channels for a more humane and considerate ethic. A transnational and cosmopolitan outlook can yet resist a flattening of value into economics, or a surrender to a reductive consensus. Smith's poem conveys a history of the present that, as in the novels of Kent and Catton, points us to the hope of a world not yet dead.

---

56 Vivan Smith, "October 2007: In Dürftiger Zeit", from *Remembrance of Things: Here, There and Elsewhere* (Artarmon: Giramondo Publishing, 2012).

Afterword: Sly Change

In May 2015 I learned in quick succession of the deaths of two fine Australian poets, Syd Harrex and J. S. Harry. I never met either writer, although I did engage in correspondence by surface mail with Harry, who always signed herself "Jann Harry". Her opulent, generous poems will always be a part of me, even if I never met their author in person. Although I am fortunate to have met many of the Australian writers I have studied, there are many I have not met and will now never meet. Had I not gone to Australia, I would never have met Gerald Murnane; on the other hand Peter Carey came to me, as it were, in the city where I live. Until we had lunch at Songjiang University in Shanghai in July 2015, I had not met Ouyang Yu in person, but, from 1999 onward, I have exchanged more emails with him than with many close family members. Transnationalism does not mean that all is easy or symmetrical, or that communication is entirely unimpeded. The Australia one loves is always dying, always skipping away before us. Harrex's poem "August Front" not only makes this elegiac point but also tacitly challenges the Northern Hemisphere reader to see August as cold and stormy:

> Across the gulf, sly change
> Whiting out the sky.
> Warm airs retreat to die
> In the quarried sea-sawn age.[1]

Neoliberalism in the past generation can be seen as a form of sly change, an atmospheric convulsion – real, not metaphorical, in the case of climate change – that shakes up our awareness of where we are. But imaginative literature can counter that change, not by retreating into stability but by pivoting on instability, and by observing in the patient, sensitive, calculating way that Harrex does with such poise.

Transnationalism alters the terms under which we see literary works as transnational. In 1934, the British composer and musicologist Constant Lambert (son of the Australian painter George Washington Lambert) spoke of the possibility of "an absorption of national

---

1 Syd Harrex, "August Front", in *Inside Out* (Kent Town: Wakefield Press, 1991), 23.

feeling in intellectually self-supporting form" that could resist both vulgar nationalism and an emaciated internationalism.[2] This may have been right then, and even today there are writers of great national importance whose work has not yet successfully travelled beyond their own countries' borders. But the old understanding of the transnational as a measure of success and of the national as a kind of second-rate achievement can be no more. In terms of sales and reviews, Eleanor Catton's success has dwarfed Hannah Kent's. But this does not mean that Catton is more transnational than Kent. Not only is Kent, in her first novel, transnational in subject but her work has travelled and been published in just as many locales as Catton's, albeit on a smaller scale. Whereas in Lambert's time the national stage was a kind of intermediate level between total inadequacy and splashing success, today that idea of the national as cordoning sanctuary has gone – as far as at least academic discourse is concerned – the way of the global middle class itself, into hurtling oblivion, as the world is polarised between rich and poor, success and failure. As anyone who has passed a border control can attest, the national still exists. But academia has decreed that, as opposed to the local or transnational, the national is no longer chic or trendy the way it was in previous generations, such as the era when organisations such as ASAL were founded. To eliminate the national as a middle level between local and transnational risks just this sort of melodramatic polarising.

Neoliberalism, indeed, is melodramatic in its sharp division of people into rich and poor, and it tempts its critics to respond in kind by positing a melodramatic division between evil corporations and virtuous hackers, and other such binaries. This is a trap that this book has tried to avoid, and which Australian writers themselves have tried to avoid. Winton and Tsiolkas, in particular, are exemplary in showing the effects of neoliberalism on a broad range of people. Even Eleanor Catton, the sharpest critic of neoliberalism included in this book, couches her critique not in shrill polemics but in ingenious narrative structures. The authors analysed in this book are of different generations, regions, heritages and philosophies. Yet they share a willingness to name the issues of the contemporary, to confront them, and to do so subtly and insightfully, militantly if necessary but craftily and self-critically when prudent.

I do not wish to make the argument that literature can or should be a privileged mode of resistance to neoliberal inequality. Certainly, in my view, literature is no more so than, say, music or art or, as argued in Chapter 7, architecture, or even the valor inherent in daily acts of living. These daily acts, in their affect and altruism, can contend that contemporary life can be about more than self-fulfilment and the exercise of individual rights. The British political thinker John Gray, a proponent of neoliberalism in the 1980s who later turned drastically against it, has said that

> contemporary theories of rights are designed to close down political discourse. In the United States ... the authority of rights has been used to shield the workings of the free market from public scrutiny and political challenge.[3]

An ideology of rights has been used to confer legitimacy on a novel successor to American social democracy.

---

2   Constant Lambert, *Music Ho! A Study of Music in Decline* (London: Faber & Faber, 1934), 183.
3   John Gray, *False Dawn* (New York: Free Press, 2000), 109.

By restoring interpersonal responsibilities to their place alongside individual rights, the writers in this book challenge the self-aggrandising assumptions of neoliberalism. In all their idiosyncratic and tetchy abundance, they are committed to a purpose beyond self-gratification and entertainment, aware of urgent social and political issues yet not strident, extremist or overly preoccupied with passing fads. I may have been mistaken or deluded in seeing Australia, in the 1980s, as an antidote to all that vexed me about my own country and situation. But Australia, in the end, did not let me down, and Australian writers of today have not let their time down. With ingenuity and emotion, they have opened up the contemporary to the possibility of future sly change.

Works Cited

Ackland, Michael. "Hedging on Destiny: History and Its Marxist Dimension in the Early Fiction of Christina Stead". *Ariel: A Review of International English Literature* 41, no. 1 (2010): 91–109.

——. "Realigning Christina Stead: A 'Red Stead'". *Overland* 192 (2008): 49–53.

Agamben, Giorgio. *Homo Sacer*. Translated by Daniel Heller-Roazen. Stanford: Stanford University Press, 1998.

Alizadeh, Ali. "Letter to Adam Smith". *Jacket2*, 16 November 2012. http://jacket2.org/poems/poems-ali-alizadeh.

Alizadeh, Ali and Penelope Pitt-Alizadeh. "Metapolitics versus Identity Politics". *Southerly* 73, no. 1 (2013): 57–74.

Allen, Brooke. "The Essays of Slender Means". *New Criterion*, June 2014, 78.

Alpers, Svetlana. *Rembrandt's Enterprise: The Studio and the Market*. Chicago: University of Chicago Press, 1995.

Anderson, Sarah. "The Lack of a Court in Medieval Icelandic Narrative". Paper presented at the 2015 Modern Language Association of America Convention. Vancouver, 10 January 2015.

Andreadis, Harriette. *Sappho in Early Modern England: Female Same-Sex Literary Erotics, 1550–1714*. Chicago: University of Chicago Press, 2001.

Andrews, Chris. *Roberto Bolaño's Fiction: An Expanding Universe*. New York: Columbia University Press, 2014.

Appadurai, Arjun. "Cosmopolitanism from Below: Some Ethical Lessons from the Slums of Mumbai". *Salon* 4 (2011): 32–43.

——, ed. *Globalization*. Durham: Duke University Press, 2002.

Apter, Emily. *Against World Literature: On the Politics of Untranslatability*. London: Verso Books, 2014.

——. *The Translation Zone: Towards a New Comparative Literature*. Princeton: Princeton University Press, 2005.

Arac, Jonathan. *Impure Worlds: The Institution of Literature in the Age of the Novel*. New York: Fordham University Press, 2010.

Arendt, Hannah. *The Human Condition*. Chicago: University of Chicago Press, 1958.

Armand, Louis. "Utzon". In *Calyx: 30 Contemporary Australian Poets*, edited by Michael Brennan, 32–34. Sydney: Paper Bark Press, 2000.

Arrighi, Giovanni. "Globalisation and Historical Macrosociology". In *Sociology for the Twenty-First Century: Continuities and Cutting Edges*, edited by Janet M. Abu-Lughod, 117–33. Chicago: University of Chicago Press, 1999.

Ash, Romy. *Floundering*. Melbourne: Text Publishing, 2012.

Ashcroft, Bill. "The Horizonal Sublime". *Antipodes: A North American Journal of Australian Literature* 19, no. 2 (2005): 141–51.

Attwood, Bain. *Telling the Truth about Aboriginal History*. Crows Nest: Allen & Unwin, 2005.

Auden, W. H. *Another Time*. New York: Random House, 1940.

——. *Collected Poems*. Edited by Edward Mendelson. New York: Random House, 2007.

Augé, Marc. *Non-Places: An Introduction to Supermodernity*. London: Verso Books, 2009.

Avery, Todd. *Radio Modernism, Literature, Ethics, and the BBC, 1922–1938*. Aldershot: Ashgate, 2006.

Azzam, Julie Hakim. "*The Luminaries*: A Literary Gold Rush". *Pittsburgh Post-Gazette*, 1 December 2013.

Bail, Murray. *Eucalyptus*. London: Harvill, 1998.

——. *The Pages*. London: Harvill Secker, 2008.

Bailey, Thomas A. *Woodrow Wilson and the Great Betrayal*. New York: Times Books, 1963.

Bangarra Dance Theatre. "Education Resource: *Brolga*". Sydney: Bangarra Dance Theatre, 2013. http://bangarra.com.au/wp-content/uploads/2013/07/Brolga_3-4-printable-version-FINAL.pdf.

Barkan, Elazar. *The Guilt of Nations: Restitution and Negotiating*. Baltimore: Johns Hopkins University Press, 2011.

Barnes, Geraldine. *Viking America: The First Millennium*. Woodbridge: Boydell & Brewer, 2001.

Barta, Tony. "Discourses of Genocide in Germany and Australia: A Linked History". *Aboriginal History* 25 (2001): 37–56.

Bauman, Zygmunt. *Liquid Modernity*. Cambridge: Polity Press, 2000.

Bean, Kellie. *Post-Backlash Feminism: Women and the Media Since Reagan–Bush*. Jefferson: McFarland & Company Inc., 2007.

Beck, Ulrich. *World at Risk*. Cambridge: Polity Press, 2009.

Belich, James. *Paradise Reforged: A History of the New Zealanders*. London: Penguin, 2002.

Bell, Coral. *Crises in Australian Diplomacy*. Canberra: Australian National University Press, 1973.

Bennett, James C. *The Anglosphere Challenge: Why the English-Speaking Nations Will Lead the Way in the Twenty-First Century*. Lexington: Rowman and Littlefield, 2007.

Berberich, Christine, ed. *Place, Memory, Affect*. Lanham: Rowman & Littlefield, 2015.

Berlant, Lauren. *Cruel Optimism*. Durham: Duke University Press, 2011.

Best, Stephen and Sharon Marcus. "Surface Reading: An Introduction". *Representations* 108, no. 1 (2009): 1–21.

Beston, John. *Patrick White within the Western Literary Tradition*. Sydney: Sydney University Press, 2010

Bevir, Mark. "Governance and Governmentality after Neoliberalism". *Policy and Politics* 39, no. 4 (2011): 457–71.

Billington, James H. *Fire in the Minds of Men*. New York: Basic Books, 1980.

Birch, Tony. *Blood*. St Lucia: University of Queensland Press, 2012.

Bird, David. *Nazi Dreamtime: Australian Enthusiasts for Hitler's Germany*. London: Anthem Press, 2014.

Bird, Delys, Robert Dixon and Christopher Lee. *Authority and Influence: Australian Literary Criticism 1950–2000*. St Lucia: University of Queensland Press, 2001.

Birns, Nicholas. *Barbarian Memory: The Legacy of Early Medieval History in Early Modern Literature*. New York: Palgrave Macmillan, 2013.

——. "'A Dazzled Eye': 'Kristu-Du' and the Architecture of Tyranny". In *Fabulating Beauty: Perspectives on the Fiction of Peter Carey*, edited by Andreas Gaile, 101–14. Amsterdam: Rodopi, 2005.

——. "Missed Appointments: Convergences and Disjunctures in Reading Australia Across the Pacific". In *Reading Across the Pacific: Australia–United States Intellectual Histories*, edited by Nicholas Birns and Robert Dixon, 91–103. Sydney: Sydney University Press, 2010.

——. "A Not Completely Pointless Beauty: *Breath*, Exceptionality and Neoliberalism". In *Tim Winton: Critical Essays*, edited by Lyn McCredden and Nathanael O'Reilly, 263–82. Nedlands: University of Western Australia Press, 2014.

——. "Pre-*Mabo* Popular Song: Icehouse Releases 'Great Southern Land'". In *Telling Stories: Australian Life and Literature 1935–2012*, edited by Tanya Dalziell and Paul Genoni, 392–97. Melbourne: Monash University Press, 2013.

——. "Science Fiction of the Past: Peter Carey in Greenwich Village". *New York Stories* 3 (2000): 10–13.

——. "The System Cannot Withstand Close Scrutiny: 1966, the Hopkins Conference, and the Anomalous Rise of Theory". *Modern Language Quarterly* 75, no. 3 (2014): 327–54.

Bishop, Elizabeth. *The Complete Poems 1926-1979*. New York: Farrar, Straus & Giroux, 1983.

Blaber, Ron. "The Populist Imaginary in David Ireland's *The Unknown Industrial Prisoner* and *The Chosen*". *Journal of the Association for the Study of Australian Literature (JASAL)* 5 (2006): 58–71. http://openjournals.library.usyd.edu.au/index.php/JASAL/article/view/10038.

Blanton, C. D., Colleen Lye and Kent Puckett, eds. *Representations – Special Issue: Financialisation and the Culture Industry* 126 (2014): 1–8.

Bloom, Harold, ed. *Hart Crane*. New York: Chelsea House, 2009.

Bloom, Harold. *How to Read and Why*. New York: Scribner, 2000.

Blyth, Catherine. "A Heartfelt Story of Disillusion and Salvation Fails to Soar". *Telegraph*, 18 June 2014. http://www.telegraph.co.uk/culture/books/bookreviews/10894457/Eyrie-by-Tim-Winton-review-overextended-and-underdeveloped.html.

Bolaño, Roberto. *2666*. Translated by Natasha Wimmer. New York: Farrar, Straus & Giroux, 2008.

Bolt, Andrew. "The Great Unread Australian Novel". Andrew Bolt blog, 2 December 2006. http://blogs.news.com.au/couriermail/andrewbolt/index.php/couriermail/comments/the_great_unread_australian_novel/.

Bourdieu, Pierre. *Distinction*. Translated by Richard Nice. Cambridge: Harvard University Press, 1987.

——. *The Field of Cultural Production*. Edited by Randal Johnson. New York: Columbia University Press, 1994.

Boutang, Yann Moulier. *Cognitive Capitalism*. Cambridge: Polity Press, 2012.

Bowman, Pearl. "The Timeless Conflict between Science and Religion Finds New Meaning in *Mr Darwin's Shooter*". *Antipodes* 13, no. 1 (1999): 43–45.

Boyce, Frank Cottrell. "*A Fraction of the Whole* by Steve Toltz". *Guardian*, 21 June 2008. http://www.theguardian.com/books/2008/jun/21/saturdayreviewsfeatres.guardianreview28.

Boyd, Robin. *The Australian Ugliness*. Sydney: Text Publishing, 2010.

Bradley, James. "All Fired Up". *Monthly*, November 2013, 44–45.

——. "Once Upon a Time in America". *Australian*, 31 October 2009, 25.

——. *Clade*. Melbourne: Penguin, 2015.

Brantlinger, Patrick. "'Black Armband' versus 'White Blindfold' History in Australia". *Victorian Studies* 46, no. 4 (2004): 655–74.

Brennan, Bernadette. *Brian Castro's Fiction: The Seductive Play of Language*. Amherst: Cambria Press, 2012.

Brennan, Timothy. "The National Longing for Form". In *Nation and Narration*, edited by Homi Bhabha, 44–70. London: Routledge, 1990.

Brenner, Neil. "Berlin's Transformations: Postmodern, Postfordist ... or Neoliberal?", *International Journal of Urban and Regional Research* 26, no. 3 (2002): 635–42.

Brooks, David. *Bobos in Paradise: The New Upper Class and How They Got There*. New York: Simon and Schuster, 2000.

Brooks, David and Elizabeth McMahon, eds. *Southerly* 72, no. 3 (2012), *Islands and Archipelagoes*.

Brown, Lachlan. *Limited Cities*. Artarmon: Giramondo Publishing, 2013.

Brown, Pam. *50-50*. Adelaide: South Australian Publishing Ventures, 1997.

——. "At 'The-End-of-the-World-as-We-Know-It Retreat'". *Otoliths*, June 2014. http://the-otolith.blogspot.com.au/2014/06/pam-brown.html.

Brown, Rosellen. "Travels in the Quirky Latitudes". *New York Times*, 22 November 1987. http://www.nytimes.com/1987/11/22/books/travels-in-the-quirky-latitudes.html.

Brull, Michael. "A Tale of Two Settler Colonies: Israel and Australia Compared". *Overland* 217 (2014): 53–59.

Buber, Martin. *I and Thou*. New York: Scribner, 1937.

Works Cited

Buckridge, Patrick. "Greatness in Australian Literature in the 1930s and 1940s: Novels by Dark and Barnard Eldershaw". *Australian Literary Studies* 17, no. 1 (1995): 29–37.

Buell, Lawrence. "Antipodal Propinquities: Environmental (Mis)Perceptions in Australian and American Literary History". In *Reading Across the Pacific: Australia–United States Intellectual Histories*, edited by Robert Dixon and Nicholas Birns, 3–22. Sydney: Sydney University Press, 2010.

Bull, Malcolm. *Anti-Nietzsche*. London: Verso Books, 2011.

Cambridge, Ada. *Thirty Years in Australia*. Sydney: Sydney University Press, 2006.

Campante, Filipe. "Rural Capitals, Big Time Problems". *New York Times*, 10 September 2014, A27.

Campbell, Ian. "Post-Nerudaism in Indonesia: Tracing and Memorializing Neruda in the Dutch East Indies (1930–1932) and Beyond". *Antipodes* 26, no. 2 (2012): 181–88.

Capp, Fiona. *Gotland*. Sydney: Fourth Estate, 2013.

Carey, Peter. *Amnesia*. London: Faber and Faber, 2014.

——. *His Illegal Self*. New York: Alfred A. Knopf, 2007.

——. Interviewed by Mark Rubbo. Readings blog, 6 October 2014. http://www.readings.com.au/news/mark-rubbo-interviews-peter-carey.

——. *My Life as a Fake*. New York: Vintage, 2005.

——. *Parrot and Olivier in America*. New York: Alfred A. Knopf, 2010.

——. *Theft*. New York: Alfred A. Knopf, 2006.

——. *True History of the Kelly Gang*. New York: Random House, 2001.

——. *The Unusual Life of Tristan Smtih*. New York: Alfred A. Knopf, 1995

Carr, Bob. *Diary of a Foreign Minister*. Sydney: University of New South Wales Press, 2014.

Carroll, Steven. *The Art of the Engine Driver*. Pymble: Fourth Estate, 2001.

——. *Forever Young*. Sydney: Fourth Estate, 2015.

——. *The Gift of Speed*. Pymble: Fourth Estate, 2004.

——. *Spirit of Progress*. Sydney: Fourth Estate, 2011.

——. *The Time We Have Taken*. Pymble: Fourth Estate, 2007.

Carter, David. "Transpacific or Transatlantic Traffic? Australian Books and American Publishers". In *Reading Across the Pacific*, edited by Robert Dixon and Nicholas Birns, 339–59. Sydney: Sydney University Press, 2011.

Caryl, Christian. *Strange Rebels: 1979 and the Birth of the 21st Century*. New York: Basic Books, 2013.

Casanova, Pascale. *The World Republic of Letters*. Translated by M. B. Debevoise. Cambridge: Harvard University Press, 2007.

Castro, Brian. *The Garden Book*. Atarmon: Giramondo Publishing, 2005.

——. *Street to Street*. Atarmon: Giramondo Publishing, 2012.

Catton, Eleanor. Interviewed by Matt Bialostocki, Unity Books blog, 21 April 2013. www.unitybooks.co.nz/interviews/eleanor-catton/.

——. *The Luminaries*. Boston: Little, Brown and Company, 2014.

——. *The Rehearsal*. Boston: Back Bay, 2011.

Caverero, Adriana. *For More Than One Voice: Towards a Philosophy of Vocal Expression*. Translated by Paul Kottman. Stanford: Stanford University Press, 2005.

Chakrabarty, Dipesh. "The Climate of History: Four Theses". *Critical Inquiry* 35, no. 2 (2009): 197–222.

Channing, Tamsin. "Peter Carey and the Jerilderie Letter". Dome Centenary blog, 16 August 2013. http://exhibitions.slv.vic.gov.au/dome100/dome-blogs/blog/peter-carey-and-jerilderie-letter.

Christensen, Jerome. "From Rhetoric to Corporate Populism: A Romantic Critique of the Academy in an Age of High Gossip". *Critical Inquiry* 16, no. 2 (1990): 438–65.

Clark, Katerina. *Stalinism, Cosmopolitanism, and the Evolution of Soviet Culture, 1931–1941* Cambridge: Harvard University Press, 2011.

Clark, Timothy. "Nature, Post-Nature". In *The Cambridge Companion to Literature and the Environment*, edited by Louise Westling, 75–89. New York: Cambridge University Press, 2010.

Clastres, Pierre. *Society Against the State*. Translated by Robert Hurley and Abe Stein. New York: Zone, 1989.

Works Cited

Coetzee, J. M. *Diary of a Bad Year*. New York: Penguin, 2007.

——. "The Quest for the Girl from Bendigo Street". *New York Review of Books*, 20 December 2012, 60–62.

Cohen, Leonard. *Beautiful Losers*. Toronto: McClelland and Stewart, 1968.

Colombo, John Robert and Jean O'Grady, eds. *The Northrop Frye Quote Book*. Toronto: Dundurn, 2014.

Cook, Kevin. *Making Change Happen*. Acton: Australian National University Press, 2013.

Cooppan, Vilashini. *Worlds Within: National Narratives and Global Connections in Postcolonial Writing*. Redwood City: Stanford University Press, 2009.

Corbett, Claire. *When We Have Wings*. Crows Nest: Allen & Unwin, 2011.

Craven, Peter. "Murray Bail: The Homemade Modernist Finds a Heart". *Heat* 9 (1998): 75–91.

Dailey, Hamish. *The Postcolonial Historical Novel: Realism, Allegory and the Representation of Contested Pasts*. New York: Palgrave Macmillan, 2014.

Dale, Leigh. *The Enchantment of English: Professing English Literatures in Australian Universities*. Sydney: Sydney University Press, 2012.

Danius, Sara. *The Senses of Modernism: Technology, Culture, and Aesthetics*. Ithaca: Cornell University Press, 2002.

D'Arcens, Louise. *Old Songs in a Timeless Land: Medievalism in Australia*. Nedlands: University of Western Australia Press, 2013.

Darling, Robert. *A. D. Hope*. Boston: Twayne Publishers, 1997.

Davidson, Adam. "Welcome to the Failure Age!" *New York Times Magazine*, 21 November 2014, MM40.

Davidson, Toby. *Beast Language*. Wollongong: Five Islands Press, 2013.

Davis, Jack. "Mining Company's Hymn". From *Jagardoo: Poems from Aboriginal Australia*. Sydney: Methuen, 1978.

Davis, Mark. "The Decline of the Literary Paradigm in Australian Publishing". In *Making Books: Contemporary Australian Publishing*, edited by David Carter and Anne Galligan, 116–31. St Lucia: University of Queensland Press, 2007.

De Castro, Juan E. *The Spaces of Latin American Literature*. New York: Palgrave Macmillan, 2008.

de Kretser, Michelle. *Questions of Travel*. Crows Nest: Allen & Unwin, 2012.

——. "*The Watch Tower* by Elizabeth Harrower". *Monthly*, June 2012, 63.

Deleuze, Gilles. *Desert Islands and Other Texts 1953–1974*. Translated by David Lapoujade and Mike Taormina. New York: Semiotexte, 2004.

DeLoughrey, Elizabeth. *Routes and Roots: Navigating Pacific Island Literatures*. Honolulu: University of Hawai'i Press, 2007.

Delrez, Marc. "Fearful Symmetries: Trauma and 'Settler Envy' in Contemporary Australian Culture". *Miscelánea: A Journal of English and American Studies* 42 (2010): 51–65.

Derrida, Jacques. "Force of Law". *Cardozo Law Review* 11, nos. 5–6 (1990): 963–73.

Dessaix, Robert. "An Interview with Harold Bloom". *Australian Book Review* 169 (April 1995): 17–20.

Diawara, Manthia. *In Search of Africa*. Cambridge: Harvard University Press, 2009.

Dirda, Michael. "Book World: Elizabeth Harrower's *The Watch Tower*". *Washington Post*, 19 June 2013. http://tiny.cc/dirda_2013.

Dixon, Robert. *Alex Miller: The Ruin of Time*. Sydney: Sydney University Press, 2014.

——. "Australian Fiction and the World Republic of Letters, 1890–1950". In *The Cambridge History of Australian Literature*, edited by Peter Pierce, 223–54. Melbourne: Cambridge University Press, 2009.

——. "Closing the Can of Worms: Enactments of Justice in *Bleak House*, *The Mystery of a Hansom Cab* and *The Tax Inspector*". *Westerly* 37, no. 4 (1992): 37–45.

——. *The Novels of Alex Miller*. Crows Nest: Allen & Unwin, 2012.

——. "Peter Carey's and Ray Lawler's *Bliss*: Fiction, Film and Power". *Studies in Australasian Cinema* 3, no. 3 (2010): 279–94.

——. *Photography, Early Cinema, and Colonial Modernity: Frank Hurley's Synchronized Lecture Entertainments*. London: Anthem Press, 2013.

——. "Tim Winton, *Cloudstreet* and the Field of Australian Literature". *Westerly* 50 (2005): 240–60.

Dotinga, Randy. "'*Burial Rites* Author Hannah Kent Finds Mystery in Iceland". *The Christian Science Monitor*, 29 November 2013. http://www.csmonitor.com/Books/chapter-and-verse/2013/1129/Burial-Rites-author-Hannah-Kent-finds-mystery-in-Iceland.

Douglass, Sara. *Hades' Daughter*. New York: Tor Books, 2002.

Dowse, Sara, Subhash Jaireth and Nicholas Jose. "Three Past and Present Canberrans Respond to Moorhouse's Account of the Capital" (review of *Cold Light*). *Meanjin* website, May 2012. http://meanjin.com.au/articles/post/cold-light/.

Du Bois, W. E. B. "The Talented Tenth". In *The Negro Problem: A Series of Articles by Representative Negroes of To-day*, edited by Booker T. Washington, 33–75. New York: James Pott, 1903.

Duchene, Anne. "Victors of Love". *Times Literary Supplement*, 8 September 1978, 985.

During, Simon. *Exit Capitalism: Literary Culture, Theory, and Post-Secular Modernity*. London: Routledge, 2009.

——. "From the Subaltern to the Precariat". *Boundary 2* 42:2 (2015): 57–84.

Eagleton, Terry. *How to Read Literature*. New Haven: Yale University Press, 2013.

Eder, Richard. "Wary and Unsettled in Their Ghost-ridden Land". *New York Times*, 5 July 2000. http://www.nytimes.com/2000/07/05/books/books-of-the-times-wary-and-unsettled-in-their-ghost-ridden-land.html.

Eggert, Paul. "The Bushranger's Voice: Peter Carey's *True History of the Kelly Gang* (2000) and Ned Kelly's Jerilderie Letter (1879)". *College Literature* 34, no. 3 (2007): 120–39.

Eldred-Grigg, Stevan. *Diggers, Hatters, Whores*. Auckland: Random House New Zealand, 2014.

Elliott, Robert. *The Power of Satire*. Princeton: Princeton University Press, 1972.

Empson, William. *Some Versions of Pastoral*. New York: New Directions, 1974.

English, James F. *The Economy of Prestige: Prizes, Awards and the Circulating of Cultural Value*. Cambridge: Harvard University Press, 2005.

Esau, Erika. *Images of the Pacific Rim: Australia and California 1850–1935*. Sydney: Power Publications, 2010.

Esposito, Roberto. *Bios: Biopolitics and Philosophy*. Minneapolis: University of Minnesota Press, 2008.

Evans, David. *An Introductory Dictionary of Lacanian Psychoanalysis*. London: Routledge, 1996.

Fabian, Johannes. *Time and the Other: How Anthropology Makes Its Object*. New York: Columbia University Press, 2002.

Falconer, Delia. "Elizabeth Harrower's *In Certain Circles* Is a Triumphant Final Fugue". *Weekend Australian*, 26–27 April 2014, 20.

——. "Grand Vision of Frank Moorhouse". *Australian*, 26 November 2011.

——. Interview: "Open Page with Delia Falconer". *Australian Book Review* 333 (July 2011). https://www.australianbookreview.com.au/abr-online/archive/2011/56-july-august-2011/445-open-page.

——. *The Lost Thoughts of Soldiers*. New York: Soft Skull, 2006.

——, ed. *The Penguin Book of the Road*. Melbourne: Penguin, 2012.

Fawkner, Harald. *Grasses That Have No Fields: From Gerald Murnane's* Inland *to a Philosophy of Isogonic Constitution*. Stockholm: Stockholm University, 2006.

Felsic, Rita. *The Uses of Literature*. Oxford: Wiley-Blackwell, 2008.

Field, Michael. "Eleanor Catton's Problem with New Zealand". Stuff.co.nz, 28 January 2015. http://www.stuff.co.nz/entertainment/books/65463098/Eleanor-Cattons-problem-with-New-Zealand.

Finch, Anne, Countess of Winchelsea. *Selected Poems*. Edited by Denys Thompson. Manchester: Carcanet, 1987.

Flanagan, Richard. Address to the 2015 PEN World Voices Festival. New York, 4 May 2015. https://youtu.be/C9nMfNQMiSE.

——. *The Narrow Road to the Deep North*. New York: Knopf, 2014.

Fletcher, Michael and Ben Guttmann. "Income Inequality in Australia". *Economic Roundup 2*. Canberra: Treasury of Australia, 2013.

Forrester, Viviane. *The Economic Horror*. London: Polity Press, 1999.

Forst, Rainer. *Toleration in Conflict: Past and Present*. Cambridge: Cambridge University Press, 2013.

Foucault, Michel. *Discipline and Punish*. Translated by Alan Sheridan. New York: Pantheon, 1975.

——. *The Order of Things: An Archaeology of the Human Sciences*. New York: Vintage Books, 1984.

Frank, Joseph. "Spatial Form in Modern Literature: An Essay in Two Parts". *The Sewanee Review* 53, no. 2 (1945): 221–40.

Franzen, Jonathan. "Rereading *The Man Who Loved Children*". *New York Times Book Review*, 6 June 2010, BR11.

Fraser, Nancy. "How Feminism Became Capitalism's Handmaiden – and How to Reclaim It". *Guardian*, 14 October 2013. http://www.theguardian.com/commentisfree/2013/oct/14/feminism-capitalist-handmaiden-neoliberal.

Freiman, Marcelle. "Seven Ways of Mourning". *Cordite Poetry Review* 46, May 2014. http://cordite.org.au/poetry/notheme3/seven-ways-of-mourning/.

Friedman, Susan Stanford. "Unthinking Manifest Destiny: Muslim Modernities on Three Continents". In *Shades of the Planet*, edited by Wai Chee Dimock and Lawrence Buell, 62–100. Princeton: Princeton University Press, 2005.

Frow, John. *The Practice of Value: Essays on Literature in Cultural Studies*. Nedlands: University of Western Australia Press, 2013.

Fukuyama, Francis. *The Great Disruption: Human Nature and the Reconstitution of Social Order*. New York: The Free Press, 1999.

Fuss, Diana. *Dying Modern*. Durham: Duke University Press, 2013.

Gabara, Esther. *Errant Modernism: The Ethos of Photography in Mexico and Brazil*. Durham: Duke University Press, 2008.

Gabra, Gawdat. *The A to Z of the Coptic Church*. Lanham: Scarecrow Press, 2009.

Gaile, Andreas. *Fabulating Beauty: Perspectives on the Fiction of Peter Carey*. Amsterdam: Rodopi, 2005.

Gammage, Bill. *The Biggest Estate on Earth: How Aborigines Made Australia*. Crows Nest: Allen & Unwin, 2013.

Gardiner, Judith Kegan. *Rhys, Stead, Lessing, and the Politics of Empathy*. Bloomington: Indiana University Press, 1989.

Geering, R. G. "The Achievement of Christina Stead". *Southerly* 22, no. 4 (1962): 193–212.

Gelder, Ken and Paul Salzman. *After the Celebration: Australian Fiction 1989–2007*. Melbourne: Melbourne University Press, 2009.

Gelder, Ken. "The Postcolonial Gothic". In *The Cambridge Companion to the Modern Gothic*, edited by Jerrold Hogle, 191–207. Cambridge: Cambridge University Press, 2014.

Genoni, Paul. "From the Nineties to the Noughties". *Westerly* 59, no. 2 (2014): 188–96.

Genter, Robert. *Late Modernism: Art, Culture, and Politics in Cold War America*. Philadelphia: University of Pennsylvania Press, 2011.

Ghosh, Amitav. "The Testimony of My Grandfather's Bookcase". *Kunapip: A Journal of Post-Colonial Writing* 19, no. 3 (1997): 2–13.

Gilbert, Helen and Chris Tiffin, eds. *Burden or Benefit: The Legacies of Benevolence*. Bloomington: Indiana University Press, 2008.

Gilbert, Sandra M. and Susan Gubar. *No Man's Land: The War of the Words*. New Haven: Yale University Press, 1989.

Giles, Paul. *Antipodean America: Australasia and the Constitution of US Literature*. New York: Oxford University Press, 2014.

Gilmore, R. J. and D. Warner. *Near North: Australia and a Thousand Million Neighbours*. Sydney: Angus & Robertson, 1948.

Glover, Douglas. "Australia On My Mind". *Chicago Tribune*, 19 February 1995, 5.

Grant, Bruce. *A Furious Hunger: America in the 21st Century*. Melbourne: Melbourne University Press, 1999.

Graves, Robert. *Selected Poems*. Edited by Paul O'Prey. New York: Penguin, 1986.

Gray, John. *False Dawn*. New York: Free Press, 2000.

Greenblatt, Stephen. *Marvelous Possessions*. Chicago: University of Chicago Press, 1991.

——. *Shakespearean Negotiations: The Circulations of Social Energy in Renaissance England*. Berkeley: University of California Press, 1988.

Greer, Germaine. "Old Flames: Rereading *The Thorn Birds*". *Guardian*, 10 August 2007. http://www.theguardian.com/books/2007/aug/11/featuresreviews.guardianreview21.

Grenville, Kate. *The Lieutenant*. New York: Atlantic Monthly, 2009.

——. *Sarah Thornhill*. New York: Grove, 2012.

——. *The Secret River*. New York: Canongate, 2007.

Griffin, Roger, ed. *Fascism, Totalitarianism and Political Religion*. London: Routledge, 2013.

Griffith, Michael. *God's Fool: The Life and Poetry of Francis Webb*. Sydney: Angus & Robertson, 1981.

Griffiths, Michael. Unsetling Artifacts: Biopolitics, Cultural Memory, and the Public Sphere in a (Post)Settler Colony. PhD dissertation. Rice University, 2012. http://hdl.handle.net/1911/71283.

Gunn, Kirsty. "*The Luminaries* by Eleanor Catton". *Guardian*, 11 September 2013. http://www.theguardian.com/books/2013/sep/11/luminaries-eleanor-catton-review.

Hage, Ghassan and Robyn Eckersley, eds. *Responsibility*. Melbourne: Melbourne University Press, 2012.

Hallum, Kirby-Jane. "'As Far Away from England as Any Man Could Be': *The Luminaries* as Sensation Sequel". *Journal of Victorian Culture Online* 19, no. 1 (2014). http://blogs.tandf.co.uk/jvc/2014/04/28/as-far-away-from-england-as-any-man-could-be-the-luminaries-as-sensation-sequel/.

Hamaker-Zondag, Karen. *Psychological Astrology*. New York: Weiser, 1990.

Harrex, Syd. *Inside Out*. Kent Town: Wakefield Press, 1991.

Harris, Margaret, ed. *The Magic Phrase: Critical Essays on Christina Stead*. St Lucia: University of Queensland Press, 2000.

Harrison, Martin. "Breakfast". Poetry International Rotterdam. http://www.poetryinternationalweb.net/pi/site/poem/item/786.

Harrower, Elizabeth. "Alice." *New Yorker*, 2 February 2015. http://www.newyorker.com/magazine/2015/02/02/alice.

——. *The Catherine Wheel*. Melbourne: Text Publishing, 2014.

——. *Down in the City*. Melbourne: Text Publishing, 2013.

——. *In Certain Circles*. Melbourne: Text Publishing, 2014.

——. *The Watch Tower*. Melbourne: Text Publishing, 2012.

Hart, Kevin. *A. D. Hope*. Melbourne: Oxford University Press, 1993.

——. *The Trespass of the Sign*. New York: Fordham University Press, 2008.

Harvey, David. *A Brief History of Neoliberalism*. New York: Oxford University Press, 2005.

Hassall, Anthony. *Dancing on Hot Macadam: Peter Carey's Fiction*. St Lucia: University of Queensland Press, 1998.

——. "Whatever Happened to Australian Literature in the Universities?" *Quadrant* 55, no. 10 (2011): 30–34.

Hazzard, Shirley. *Defeat of an Ideal*. New York: Little, Brown and Company, 1973.

——. *People in Glass Houses*. New York: Knopf, 1967.

Heighton, Steven. "Fire and Ice". *New York Times*, 27 September 2013, BR17.

Heiss, Anita. *Am I Black Enough for You?* Sydney: Random House, 2013.

Henderson, Ian and Anouk Lang, eds. *Patrick White Beyond the Grave*. London: Anthem, 2015.

Hendin, Josephine. "Perfecting Woman". *New York Times*, 19 July 1987. http://www.nytimes.com/1987/07/19/books/perfecting-woman.html.

Heyward, Michael. *The Ern Malley Affair*. St Lucia: University of Queensland Press, 1993.

——. "*Grand Days*, by Frank Moorhouse". *The New Republic*, 1 August 1994, 43–45.

Hile, Fiona. "A Portable Crush". *Overland* 216 (2014): 100.

Hirst, John. *Sense and Nonsense in Australian History*. Melbourne: Black Inc., 2009.

Hobsbawm, Eric. *The Age of Extremes: The Short Twentieth Century, 1914–1991*. New York: Vintage, 1994.

Hockey, Joe. "The End of the Age of Entitlement". Speech to the Institute of Economic Affairs, London, 17 April 2012. Published in the *Sydney Morning Herald*, 19 April 2012. http://www.smh.com.au/national/the-end-of-the-age-of-entitlement-20120419-1x8vj.html.

Hollander, Paul. *Political Pilgrims: Western Intellectuals in Search of the Good Society*. New Brunswick: Transaction Publishers, 1997.

Holquist, Peter. "The Origin of the Concept of Crimes against Humanity". Lecture, Janey Program of the New School, 12 December 2014.

Honneth, Axel. *The Struggle for Recognition: The Moral Grammar of Social Conflicts*. Translated by Joel Anderson. London: Polity, 1995.

Hope, A. D. *The Cave and the Spring: Essays on Poetry*. Sydney: Sydney University Press, 1974.

——. *Chance Encounters*. Melbourne: Melbourne University Press, 1992.

——. *Dunciad Minor*. Melbourne: Melbourne University Press, 1971.

——. "Standards in Australian Literature". *Current Affairs Bulletin*, November 1956.

Htun, Mala. "Political Inclusion: Women, Blacks, and Indigenous Peoples". In *Constructing Democratic Governance*, edited by Jorge Domínguez and Michael Shifter. Third edition. Baltimore: Johns Hopkins University Press, 2008.

Huggan, Graham. *Australian Literature: Postcolonialism, Racism, Transnationalism*. Oxford: Oxford University Press, 2007.

——. "Cultural Memory in Postcolonial Fiction: the Uses and Abuses of Ned Kelly". *Australian Literary Studies* 20, no. 3 (2000).

Hughes-D'Aeth, Tony. "*Salt Scars*: John Kinsella's *Wheatbelt*". *Australian Literary Studies* 27, no. 2 (2012): 18–31.

Hutcheon, Linda. *A Poetics of Postmodernism: History, Theory, Fiction*. London: Routledge, 1988.

Indyk, Ivor. "Gerald Murnane and the Provincial Imagination." Paper presented to the Writing and Society Research Centre, Western Sydney University, 2014. http://tiny.cc/indyk_2014.

——. "The Journals of Antigone Kefala". In *Antigone Kefala: A Writer's Journey*, edited by Vrasidas Karalis and Helen Nickas, 221–33. Melbourne: Owl, 2014.

Jach, Antoni. *The Layers of the City*. Melbourne: Hodder Headline, 1999.

Jacklin, Michael. "The Transnational Turn in Australian Literary Studies". *Journal of the Association for the Study of Australian Literature*, Special Issue 2009. http://openjournals.library.usyd.edu.au/index.php/JASAL/article/view/10040.

Jayasuriya, Laksiri, David Walker and Jan Gothard, eds. *Legacies of White Australia*. Crawley: University of Western Australia Press, 2003.

Johnson, Colin. "Dalwurra". *Antipodes* 2, no. 1 (1988): 3.

Johnson, Pauline. "Sociology and the Critique of Neoliberalism: Reflections on Peter Wagner and Axel Honneth". *European Journal of Social Theory* 17, no. 4 (2014): 516–533.

Jones, Ernest. *Hamlet and Oedipus*. New York: W. W. Norton & Co., 1949.

Jones, Gail. *Five Bells*. New York: Picador, 2012.

——. *Sorry*. New York: Europa Editions, 2008.

Jones, Philip. *The Italian City State: From Commune to Signoria*. New York: Oxford University Press, 1997.

Jose, Nicholas. *The Custodians*. New York: St Martin's Press, 1998.

——, ed. *Macquarie PEN Anthology of Australian Literature*. Crows Nest: Allen & Unwin, 2009.

Kane, Paul. *Australian Poetry: Romanticism and Negativity*. Cambridge: Cambridge University Press, 1996.

Kateb, George. *The Inner Ocean: Individualism and Democratic Culture*. Ithaca: Cornell University Press, 1992.

Kefala, Antigone. *Sydney Journals: Reflections 1970–2000*. Artarmon: Giramondo Publishing, 2008.

Kelly, Ned. *The Jerilderie Letter*, edited by Alex McDermott. London: Faber & Faber, 2001.

Kendall, Henry Clarence. *The Poems of Henry Clarence Kendall*. Melbourne: George Robertson & Co., 1903.

Keneally, Thomas. Interviewed by Mark Corcoran, *Foreign Correspondent*, ABC TV, 25 May 2004. http://www.abc.net.au/foreign/content/2004/s1115693.htm.

——. "A New Chant for Jimmie Blacksmith?" *Sydney Morning Herald*, 25–26 August 2001, *Spectrum* 4–5.

——. *To Asmara*. New York: Warner Books, 1989.

Kennedy, Rosanne. "Humanity's Footprint: Reading *Rings of Saturn* and Palestinian Walks in an Anthropocene Era". *Biography* 35, no. 1 (2012): 170–89.

Kent, Hannah. *Burial Rites*. Boston: Little, Brown, 2013.

——. Foreword to *Sight Lines: 2014 UTS Writers' Anthology*, edited by Kate Adams et al. Sydney: Xoum, 2014.

Kenworthy, Lane. *Social Democratic America*. New York: Oxford University Press, 2014.

Kinsella, John. *Divine Comedy*. New York: W. W. Norton & Co., 2008.

——. "For Beauty's Sake: Poetry and Activism". Keynote address to the Perth Poetry Festival, 14 August 2014. http://poetsveganananarchistpacifist.blogspot.com.au/2014/08/for-beautys-sake-poetry-and-activism.html.

——. *Full Fathom Five*. South Fremantle: Fremantle Arts Centre Press, 1993.

——. *The Hunt*. Fremantle: Fremantle Arts Centre Press, 1998.

——. *New Arcadia*. New York: Norton. 2007.

——. *Poems 1980–1994*. South Fremantle: Fremantle Press, 1997.

——. *Spatial Relations*, Volume 1. Amsterdam: Rodopi, 2013.

——. *Spatial Relations*, Volume 2. Amsterdam: Rodopi, 2013.

Kite, Lorien. "Interview with Booker Prize-winning Eleanor Catton". *Financial Times,* 18 October 2013. http://tiny.cc/catton_2013.

Knausgaard, Karl Ove. *My Struggle: Book 3*. Translated by Don Bartlett. New York: Macmillan, 2014.

Köllmann, Sabine. *A Companion to Mario Vargas Llosa*. London: Tamesis Books, 2014.

Kolodny, Annette. *In Search of First Contact: The Vikings of Vinland, the Peoples of the Dawnland, and the Anglo-American Anxiety of Discovery*. Durham: Duke University Press, 2012.

Kossew, Sue. *Lighting Dark Places: Essays on Kate Grenville*. Amsterdam: Rodopi, 2010.

Kowal, Emma. "The Subject of Responsibilities: Noel Pearson and Indigenous Disadvantage in Australia". In *Responsibilty*, edited by Ghassan Hage and Robyn Eckersley, 43–56. Melbourne: Melbourne University Press, 2012.

Kushner, Rachel. *The Flamethrowers*. New York: Scribner, 2013.

Lamb, Karen. *Peter Carey and the Genesis of Fame*. Sydney: Angus & Robertson, 1992.

Lambert, Constant. *Music Ho! A Study of Music in Decline*. London: Faber & Faber, 1934.

Lamond, Julieanna. "The Australian Face". *Sydney Review of Books*, November 2013. http://www.sydneyreviewofbooks.com/the-australian-face/.

Lanchester, John. "Money Talks: Learning the Language of Finance". *New Yorker*, 4 August 2014, 31.

Landon, Philip. "Great Exhibitions: Nature and Disciplinary Spectacle in the Victorian Novel". Doctoral dissertation, University of Rochester, New York, 1995

Langton, Marcia. *The Quiet Revolution: Indigenous People and the Resources Boom*. 2012 Boyer lectures, presented November–December 2012. http://www.abc.net.au/radional/programs/boyerlectures/2012-boyer-lectures/4305696.

Laski, Harold. *The Rise of European Liberalism*. London: Allen & Unwin, 1936.

Latour, Bruno. *We Have Never Been Modern*. Translated by Catherine Porter. Cambridge: Harvard University Press, 1993.

Lavalle, Ashley. *The Death of Social Democracy: Political Consequences in the 21st Century*. Aldershot: Ashgate, 2008.

Leane, Jeanine. "Rites/Rights/Writes of Passage: Identity Construction in Australian Aboriginal Young Adult Fiction". In *A Companion to Australian Aboriginal Literature*, edited by Belinda Wheeler, 107–23. Rochester: Camden House, 2013.

——. "Tracking Our Country in Settler Literature", *Journal of the Association for the Study of Australian Literature* 14, no. 3 (2014). http://openjournals.library.usyd.edu.au/index.php/JASAL/article/view/10039.

LeClair, Tom. *In The Loop: Don DeLillo and the Systems Novel*. Urbana: University of Illinois Press, 1988.

Lee, Theresa Man Ming. *Politics and Truth: Political Theory and the Postmodernist Challenge*. Albany: State University of New York Press, 1997.

Leigh, Andrew. "An Australian Take on Thomas Piketty's *Capital in the Twenty-First Century*".*Monthly*, June 2014. https://www.themonthly.com.au/issue/2014/june/1401544800/andrew-leigh/australian-take-thomas-pikettys-capital-twenty-first-century.

Lepore, Jill. "The Disruption Machine: What the Gospel of Innovation Gets Wrong". *New Yorker*, 23 June 2014. http://www.newyorker.com/magazine/2014/06/23/the-disruption-machine.

Lethem, Jonathan. *The Ecstasy of Influence*. New York: Vintage Books, 2012.

Lever, Susan. *David Foster: The Satirist of Australia*. Amherst: Cambria Press, 2008.

Levinas, Emmanuel. *Alterity and Transcendence*. Translated by Michael B. Smith. New York: Columbia University Press, 2006.

Levinson, Sanford. "Law: On Dworkin, Kennedy, and Ely". *The Partisan Review* 52, no. 1 (1984): 248–264.

Lewis, Brian J. *Deerpark*. Mount Pleasant: Arcadia, 2002.

Lewis, Jeremy. *Grub Street Irregular: Scenes from the Literary Life*. London: HarperCollins, 2008.

Ley, James. "I Refuse to Rock and Roll". *Sydney Review of Books*, 19 September 2013. http://www.sydneyreviewofbooks.com/i-refuse-to-rock-and-roll/.

Lindsay, Elaine. *Rewriting God: Spirituality in Contemporary Australian Women's Fiction*. Amsterdam: Rodopi, 2009.

London, Joan. *Gilgamesh*. Sydney: Vintage, 2001.

Low, Lenny Anne. "Harry Seidler's Life and Legacy Explored in New Exhibition at the Museum of Sydney". *Sydney Morning Herald*, 28 October 2014. http://www.smh.com.au/entertainment/art-and-design/harry-seidlers-life-and-legacy-explored-in-new-exhibition-at-the-museum-of-sydney-20141030-11d19d.html.

Lucashenko, Melissa. *Mullumbimby*. St Lucia: University of Queensland Press, 2013.

Macintyre, Stuart. *Winners and Losers: The Pursuit of Social Justice in Australian History*. Sydney: Angus & Robertson, 1986.

Macintyre, Stuart and Anna Clark. *The History Wars*. Melbourne: Melbourne University Press, 2004.

MacLulich, T. D. "The Alien Role: Farley Mowat's Northern Pastorals". *Studies in Canadian Literature* 2, no. 2 (1977): 226–33.

Maiden, Jennifer. *Friendly Fire*. Artarmon: Giramondo Publishing, 2005.

Malouf, David. *Remembering Babylon*. New York: Vintage Books, 1994.

Malraux, André. *Le musée imaginaire*. Paris: Albert Skira, 1947.

Mansfield, Nicholas. "The Only Russian in Sydney". *Australian Literary Studies* 15, no. 3 (May 1992): 131–140.

Manzer, Ronald A. *Educational Regimes and Anglo-American Democracy*. Toronto: University of Toronto Press, 2003.

Marginson, Simon and Mark Clonidine, *The Enterprise University: Power, Governance and Reinvention in Australia*. Cambridge: Cambridge University Press, 2001.

Marlowe, Christopher. *Four Plays*. New York: Bloomsbury, 2014.

Marx, John. *Geopolitics and the Anglophone Novel*. Cambridge: Cambridge University Press, 2012.

Maslin, Mark. *Global Warming: A Very Short Introduction*. Oxford: Oxford University Press, 2008.

Mateer, John . "Pinjarra". *Manoa* 18, no. 2 (2006): 21.

Matthews, Jill Julius. *Dance Hall and Picture Palace: Sydney's Romance with Modernity* Sydney: Currency Press, 2005.

Mbembe, Achille. "Necropolitics". *Public Culture* 15, no. 1 (2003): 11–40.

McCann, A. L. *Subtopia*. Melbourne: Vulgar Press, 2005.

McCann, Andrew. "Discrepant Cosmopolitanism and the Contemporary Novel: Reading the Inhuman in Christos Tsiolkas' *Dead Europe* and Roberto Bolaño's *2666*". *Antipodes* 24, no. 2 (2010): 135–41.

——. "How to Fuck a Tuscan Garden". *Overland* 177 (2004): 22–24.

McCauley, Stephen. "Pedant in Love". *New York Times*, 10 July 1988. http://www.nytimes.com/1988/07/10/books/pedant-in-love.html.

McCooey, David. "Contemporary Poetry: Across Party Lines". In *The Cambridge Companion to Australian Literature*, edited by Elizabeth Webby, 158–82. Cambridge: Cambridge University Press, 2000.

McCrea, Michele. "Collisions of Authority: Nonunitary Narration and Textual Authority in Gail Jones' *Sorry*". In *The Encounters: Place, Situation, Context Papers – Refereed Proceedings of the 17th Conference of the Australasian Association of Writing Programs*, edited by Cassandra Atherton, and Rhonda Dredge et al. Canberra: The Australasian Association of Writing Programs, 2012. http://www.aawp.dreamhosters.com/wp-content/uploads/2015/03/McCrea.pdf.

McCredden, Lyn. *The Contemporary Sacred*. Adelaide: ATF Press, 2012.

——. "The Quality of Mercy". *Sydney Review of Books*, December 2013, http://www.sydneyreviewofbooks.com/the-quality-of-mercy/.

——. "'untranscended / life itself': The Poetry of Pam Brown". *Australian Literary Studies* 22, no. 2 (2005): 217–28.

McCulloch, Ann. *Dance of the Nomad: A Study of the Selected Notebooks of A. D. Hope*. Acton: Australian National University Press, 2010.

McCullough, Colleen. *The Thorn Birds*. New York: Harper & Row, 1977.

McDermott, Alex. Introduction to *The Jerilderie Letter*. London: Faber & Faber, 2001.

McDonald, Roger. *Mr Darwin's Shooter*. New York: Atlantic Monthly Press, 1998.

McFarlane, Fiona. "Art Appreciation". *New Yorker*, 13 May 2013. http://www.newyorker.com/magazine/2013/05/13/art-appreciation.

McGahan, Andrew. *The White Earth*. New York: Soho Press, 2006.

McGregor, Craig. "Australian Writing Today: Riding off in All Directions". *New York Times Book Review*, 19 May 1985, 3, 40.

McLean, Ian. *White Aborigines: Identity Politics in Australian Art*. Cambridge: Cambridge University Press, 1998.

Mead, Philip. "Alexis Wright's Fiction and Sovereignty of the Mind". Paper presented at the 2015 Modern Language Association of America Convention, Vancouver, 10 January 2015.

——. "Connectivity, Community, and the Question of Literary Universality: Reading Kim Scott's *Chronotope* and John Kinsella's *Commedia*". In *Republics of Letters: Literary Communities in Australia*, edited by Peter Kirkpatrick and Robert Dixon, 137–155. Sydney: Sydney University Press, 2012.

Mehta, Suketu. *Maximum City: Bombay Lost and Found*. New York: Vintage Books, 2005.

Meisel, Perry. *The Literary Freud*. London: Routledge, 2007.

Mendelsohn, Daniel. "Uneasy Pieces". *New York Magazine*, 7 August 2000. http://nymag.com/nymetro/arts/books/reviews/3594/.

Mendelson, Edward. "The Sacred, the Profane, and *The Crying of Lot 49*". In *Individual and Community: Variations on a Theme in American Fiction*. Edited by Kenneth Baldwin and David Kirby, 182–222. Durham: Duke University Press, 1975.

Mercer, Gina. "Little Women: Helen Garner Sold by Weight". *Australian Book Review* 81 (June 1986): 26–28.

Michaels, Walter Benn. *The Shape of the Signifier: 1967 to the End of History*. Princeton: Princeton University Press, 2006.

Miller, Alex. *Coal Creek*. Crows Nest: Allen & Unwin, 2013.

——. *Journey to the Stone Country*. Crows Nest: Allen & Unwin, 2002. Kindle edition.

——. *Lovesong*. Sydney: Allen & Unwin, 2009.

Works Cited

Miller, John. *Australia's Great Writers and Poets: The Story of Our Rich Literary Heritage*. Wollombi: Exisle Publishing, 2007.

Miller, Tyrus. *Late Modernism: Politics, Fiction, and the Arts between the World Wars*. Berkeley: University of California Press, 1999.

Mills, Jennifer. "The Rarest of Birds". *Overland*, 19 September 2013. https://overland.org.au/2013/09/the-rarest-of-birds/.

Milman, Oliver. "Novelist Alex Miller Attacks Australia's 'Cruel and Inhumane' Refugee Treatment". *Guardian Australia*, 27 December 2013. http://www.theguardian.com/world/2013/dec/27/novelist-attacks-cruel-refugee-treatment.

Minter, Peter. "From *Incognita*, Book One". *Jacket2*, 24 January 2012. http://jacket2.org/poems/poems-peter-minter.

Moore, Nicole and Christina Spittel, eds. *South by East: Australian Literature in the German Democratic Republic*. London: Anthem Press, 2015.

Moore, Nicole. *The Censor's Library: Uncovering the Lost History of Australia's Banned Books*. St Lucia: University of Queensland Press, 2012.

Moorhouse, Frank. *Cold Light*. Milsons Point: Random House, 2011.

Moretti, Franco. *Atlas of the European Novel*. London: Verso Books, 1999.

——. *Distant Reading*. London: Verso Books, 2012.

Morgan, Patrick. "Getting Away from It All". *Kunapipi* 5, no. 1 (1983): 73–87.

Morrison, Fiona. "The Rhetoric of Luck in Christina Stead's *Letty Fox: Her Luck*". *Antipodes* 28, no. 1 (2014): 111–22.

——. "Unread Books and Christina Stead's *The Man Who Loved Children*". In *Republics of Letters: Literary Communities in Australia*, edited by Peter Kirkpatrick and Robert Dixon. Sydney: Sydney University Press, 2013, 127–36.

Motion, Andrew. "*Amnesia*: Turbo-Charged Hypernenergetic". *Guardian*, 30 October 2014.

Moyn, Samuel. *The Last Utopia*. Cambridge: Harvard University Press, 2012.

Muecke, Stephen. "Wide Open Spaces: Horizontal Readings of Australian Literature". *New Literatures Review* 16 (1988).

Mühlbauer, Peter Josef. "Frontiers and Dystopias: Libertarianism and Ideology in Science Fiction". In *Neoliberal Hegemony: A Global Critique*, edited by Dieter Plehwe et al. London: Routledge, 2009.

Murnane, Gerald. "The Breathing Author". In *Delphic Intimations: Dialogues with Australian Writers and Critics*, edited by Pradeep Trikha, 100–121. New Delhi: Sarup & Sons, 2007.

——. Comments at the Melbourne Writers' Festival. Transcribed by Breth Driscoll. "Gerard Murnane at the Melbourne Writers' Festival", Storify, 22 August 2015. https://storify.com/Beth_driscoll/gerald-murnane-at-the-melbourne-writers-festival-2.

——. *A History of Books*. Artarmon: Giramondo Publishing, 2012.

——. "Land Deal". In *Velvet Waters*. Ringwood: McPhee Gribble, 1990, 55–60.

——. *A Million Windows*. Artarmon: Giramondo Publishing, 2014.

——. *The Plains*. New York: George Braziller, 1985.

——. "The Three Archives of Gerald Murnane". *Music & Literature* 3, 2013. http://www.musicandliterature.org/features/2013/11/11/the-three-archives-of-gerald-murnane.

Murray, Les. *The Biplane Houses*. London: Macmillan, 2006.

——. *Collected Poems*. Melbourne: Black Inc., 2006.

——. *The Daylight Moon*. Sydney: Angus & Robertson, 1987.

——. *Fredy Neptune*. New York: Farrar, Straus & Giroux, 1999.

——. "Poemes and the Mystery of Embodiment". *Meanjin* 47, no. 3 (1988): 519–33.

——. *Poems Against Economics*. Sydney: Angus & Robertson, 1974.

——. *Selected Poems*. New York: Farrar, Straus, & Giroux, 2007.

Neill, Rosemary. "Lost for Words". *The Weekend Australian Review*, 2–3 December 2006, 4–6.

Ng, Lynda. "Inheriting the World: German Exiles, Napoleon's Campaign in Egypt, and Australian National Identity". In *Scenes of Reading: Is Australian Literature a World Literature?*, edited by Robert Dixon and Brigid Rooney. North Melbourne: Australian Scholarly Publishing, 2013.

Ngai, Sianne. "Merely Interesting". *Critical Inquiry* 34, no. 44 (2008): 777–817.

——. *Our Aesthetic Categories: Zany, Cute, Interesting*. Cambridge: Harvard University Press, 2013.

——. *Ugly Feelings*. Cambridge: Harvard University Press, 2005.

Nicholl, Jal. Review of *Liquid Nitrogen* by Jennifer Maiden. *Southerly* 73, no. 1 (2013): 234.

Nicolacopoulos, Toula and George Vassilacopoulos. "The Making of Greek-Australian Citizenship: From Heteronomous to Autonomous Political Communities". *Modern Greek Studies* 11 (2003): 165–76.

Nietzsche, Friedrich. *On the Genealogy of Morals: A Polemic*. Translated by Douglas Smith. New York: Oxford University Press, 1996.

Nixon, Rob. "Neoliberalism, Slow Violence, and the Environmental Picaresque". *Modern Fiction Studies* 55, no. 3 (2009): 443–67.

Nussbaum, Martha. "Compassion: The Basic Social Emotion". *Social Philosophy and Policy* 13 (1996): 27–38.

O'Reilly, Nathanael. *Exploring Suburbia: The Suburbs in the Contemporary Australian Novel*, Amherst: Teneo, 2012.

Ogien, Ruwen. "Neutrality Towards Non-Controversial Conceptions of the Good Life". In *Political Neutrality: A Re-evaluation*, edited by Alberto Merrill and Daniel Weinstock, 97–108. New York: Palgrave Macmillan, 2014.

Olmos, Liliana, Rich Van Heertum and Carlos Alberto Torres. *Educating the Global Citizen in the Shadow of Neoliberalism: Thirty Years of Educational Reform in North America*. Oak Park: Bentham Science Publishers, 2011.

Olubas, Brigitta and Elizabeth McMahon, eds. *Remembering Patrick White*. Amsterdam: Rodopi, 2010.

Ong, Aihwa. *Neoliberalism as Exception: Mutations in Citizenship and Sovereignty*. Durham: Duke University Press, 2006.

Ouyang Yu. "Bad English". *Cha* 4 (August 2008). http://www.asiancha.com/content/view/216/124/.

——. *The Eastern Slope Chronicle*. Sydney: Brandl & Schlsinger 2003.

——. *The English Class*. Melbourne: Transit Lounge, 2010.

——. *The Kingsbury Tales*. Kingsbury: Otherland, 2012.

——. *Loose: A Wild History*. Kent Town: Wakefield, 2011.

Packer, George. *The Unwinding: An Inner History of the New America*. New York: Farrar, Straus, & Giroux, 2013.

Pan, Lynn. "Of Shanghai and Chinese Cosmopolitanism". *Asian Ethnicity* 10, no. 3 (2009): 217–24.

Parks, Tim. *Translating Style: The English Modernists and Their Italian Translators*. London: Cassell & Co., 1997.

Pearce, Nick. "Thomas Piketty: A Modern French Revolutionary". *New Statesman*, Cultural Capital blog, 3 April 2014. http://www.newstatesman.com/2014/03/french-revolutionary.

Pender, Anne. *Christina Stead, Satirist*. Altona: Common Ground Publishing, 2002.

Perera, Suvendrini. *Australia and the Insular Imagination: Beaches, Borders, Boats and Bodies*. New York: Palgrave Macmillan, 2009.

Pettman, Dominic. *Love and Other Technologies: Retrofitting Eros for the Information Age* Stanford: Stanford University Press, 2006.

Pfau, Thomas. *Wordsworth's Profession: Form, Class, and the Logic of Early Romantic Cultural Production*. Stanford: Stanford University Press, 1997.

Phillips, A. A. "The Cultural Cringe". *Meanjin* 9, no. 4 (1950): 299–302.

Phillips, Adam. *Becoming Freud: The Making of a Psychoanalyst*. New Haven: Yale University Press, 2014.

Piaget, Jean. *The Theory of Stages in Cognitive Development*. New York: McGraw Hill, 1969.

Pierce, Peter. *The Country of Lost Children: An Australian Anxiety*. Melbourne: Cambridge University Press, 1999.

Piketty, Thomas. *Capital in the Twenty-First Century*. Translated by Arthur Goldhammer. Cambridge: Harvard University Press, 2014.

Pilger, John. *A Secret Country: The First Australians Fight Back*. Sydney: Random House, 1982.

Pilkington Garimara, Doris. *Follow the Rabbit-Proof Fence*. St Lucia: University of Queensland Press, 2013.

Poore, Charles. "Books of the Times". *New York Times*, 18 October 1940, 19.

Post, Chad. "Context #23 [Back!]". Three Percent blog, 3 November 2011. http://www.rochester.edu/College/translation/threepercent/index.php?id=3704.

Pulvers, Roger. Review of *The Narrow Road to the Deep North*. *Japan Times*, 9 November 2013.

Pusey, Michael. *Economic Rationalism in Canberra: A Nation-Building State Changes Its Mind*. Cambridge: Cambridge University Press, 1991.

Quiggin, John. "Globalisation, Neoliberalism, and Inequality". *Economic and Labour Relations Review* 10, no. 2 (1999): 240–59.

Rama, Ángel. "La guerra del fin del mundo: una obra maestra del fanatismo artístico". *Eco* 246 (1982): 600–64.

Rashbrooke, Max. *Inequality: A New Zealand Crisis*. Wellington: Bridget Williams Books, 2011.

Ravenscroft, Alison. *The Postcolonial Eye: White Australian Desire and the Visual Field of Race*. Farnham: Ashgate, 2012.

Reeves, William Pember. *State Experiments in Australia and New Zealand*. Cambridge: Cambridge University Press, 2011.

Reid, Ian. *The Shifting Shore*. Vancouver: Grange Press, 1997.

Rescher, Nicholas. *Studies in Idealism*. Berlin: De Gruyter, 2005.

Richardson, Henry Handel. *The Getting of Wisdom*. Melbourne: Text Publishing, 2012.

Ricoeur, Paul. *Freud and Philosophy*. New Haven: Yale University Press, 1977.

Riddle, Naomi. "Turning Inward on Himself: Male Hysteria in Elizabeth Harrower's *The Watch Tower*". *Southerly* 72, no. 1 (2012): 204–13.

Robin, Corey. "Nietzsche's Marginal Children: On Friedrich Hayek". *Nation*, 27 May 2013, 27–36.

Rocha, Carolina. *Masculinities in Argentine Popular Cinema*. London: Palgrave Macmillan, 2012.

Rodham, Hillary. "Children's Rights: A Legal Perspective". In *Children's Rights: Contemporary Perspectives*, edited by Patricia A. Vardin and Ilene N. Brody, 21–36. New York: Teachers College Press, 1979.

Roe, Jill. *Her Brilliant Career: The Life of Miles Franklin*. Cambridge: Harvard University Press, 2009.

Rofel, Lisa. *Desiring China: Experiments in Neoliberalism, Sexuality, and Public Culture*. Durham: Duke University Press, 2007

Romei, Stephen. "Books of the Year". *Weekend Australian*, 21–22 December 2012, 14–18.

Rooney, Bridgid. "Christina Stead". In *A Companion to Australian Literature Since 1900*, edited by Nicholas Birns and Rebecca McNeer, 235–46. Rochester: Camden House, 2007.

——. "Kate Grenville as Public Intellectual". In *Lighting Dark Places: Essays on Kate Grenville*, edited by Sue Kossew, 17–38. Amsterdam: Rodopi, 2010.

——. "Loving the Revolutionary: Re-reading Christina Stead's Encounter with Men, Marxism and the Popular Front in 1930s Paris". *Southerly* 58, no. 4 (1998): 24–102.

——. "'No One Had Thought of Looking Close to Home': Reading the Province in *The Bay of Noon*". In *Shirley Hazzard: New Critical Essays*, edited by Brigitta Olubas, 41–53. Sydney: Sydney University Press, 2014.

Rorty, Richard. "Deconstruction and Circumvention". *Critical Inquiry* 11, no. 1 (1984): 1–21.

Rowley, Hazel. *Christina Stead: A Biography*. New York: Henry Holt, 1994.

——. Interviewed by Leonard Lopate, WNYC radio, 22 August 2005.

——. "The Mocking Country". *Weekend Australian*, 25–26 August 2007, 8–9.

Royo Grasa, Maria del Pilar. "In Conversation with Gail Jones". *Journal of the Association for the Study of Australian Literature* 12, no. 3 (2012). http://openjournals.library.usyd.edu.au/index.php/JASAL/article/view/9828.

Rutherford, Jennifer. *The Gauche Intruder: Freud, Lacan and the White Australia Fantasy*. Melbourne: Melbourne University Press, 2000.

Ryan, Tracy. "Cold Greed and Rankling Guilt: a Re-reading of A. D. Hope's 'The Cetaceans'". *Southerly* 69, no.1 (2009): 146–69.

Ryan-Fazilleau, Sue. "Bob's Dreaming: Playing with Reader Expectations in Peter Carey's *Oscar and Lucinda*". *Rocky Mountain Review of Language and Literature* 59, no. 1 (2005): 11–30.

Salaita, Steven. *The Holy Land in Transit: Colonialism and the Quest for Canaan*. Syracuse: Syracuse University Press, 2006.

Salusinzky, Imre. "An Interview with Harold Bloom". *Scripsi* 4, no. 1 (1986): 69–88.

Sante, Luc. "O Canada!" *New York Times Book Review*, 25 July 1999, 6.

Sassen, Saskia. *The Global City: London, New York, Tokyo*. Princeton: Princeton University Press, 1992.

Saunders, Brian. *Discovery of Australia's Fishes: A History of Australian Ichthyology to 1930*. Collingwood: CSIRO Publishing, 2012.

Sayers, Stuart. "Books You Just Listen To". *The Age*, 23 August 1969, 10.

Scheckter, John. "The Pleasures of Structural Uncertainty". *Antipodes*, 28, no. 1 (2014): 237–38.

Schiller, Friedrich. *On the Aesthetic Education of Man*. Translated by Reginald Snell. New York: Dover Books, 2009.

Schmidt am Busch, Hans-Christoph Schmidt am. "Can the Goals of the Frankfurt School be Achieved by a Theory of Recognition?" In *The Philosophy of Recognition: Historical and Contemporary Perspectives*, edited by Hans-Christoph Schmidt am Busch and Christopher F. Zum, 257–83. Lanham: Lexington Books, 2010.

Scott, David. "Colonial Governmentality". *Social Text* 43 (1995): 191–220.

———. "The Tragic Vision in Postcolonial Time". *PMLA* 129, no. 4 (2014): 799–808.

Sedgwick, Eve Kosofsky. *Touching Feeling: Affect, Pedagogy, Performativity*. Durham: Duke University Press, 2003.

Seidel, Michael. *Satiric Inheritance: From Rabelais to Sterne*. Princeton: Princeton University Press, 1979.

Seiler, Claire. "The Mid-Century Method of *The Great Fire*". In *Shirley Hazzard: New Critical Essays*, edited by Brigitta Olubas, 97–110. Sydney: Sydney University Press, 2014.

Seymour-Smith, Martin. *Guide to Modern World Literature*. London: Macmillan, 1985.

Shahani, Nishant. *Queer Retrosexualities: The Politics of Reparative Return*. Bethlehem: Lehigh University Press, 2012.

Sharrad, Paul. "The Post-Colonial Gesture". In *A Talent(ed) Digger*, edited by Hena Maes-Jelinek, Gordon Collier and Geoffrey V. Davis, 134–40. Amsterdam: Rodopi, 1996.

Sheridan, Susan. *Christina Stead*. London: Harvester Wheatsheaf, 1988.

———. *Nine Lives: Postwar Women Writers Making Their Mark*. St Lucia: University of Queensland Press, 2011.

Sinnett, Frederick. "Fiction Fields of Australia". *Journal of Australasia* 1 (July–December 1856), 97–105, 199–208. http://tiny.cc/sinnett.

Slaughter, Joseph R. "Enabling Fictions and Novel Subjects: The 'Bildungsroman' and International Human Rights Law". *PMLA* 121, no. 5 (2006): 1405–23.

Slemon, Stephen. "Unsettling the Empire: Resistance Theory for the Second World". *World Literatures Written in English* (1990): 30–42.

Smith, Terry. *Making the Modern: Industry, Art, and Design in America*. Chicago: University of Chicago Press, 1994.

———. *Thinking Contemporary Curating*. New York: Independent Curators, 2012.

Smith, Vivan. *Remembrance of Things: Here, There and Elsewhere*. Artarmon: Giramondo, Publishing, 2012.

Smith, Wendy. "Tim Winton's Beautiful, Baffling *Eyrie*". *The Daily Beast*, 18 August 2014. http://www.thedailybeast.com/articles/2014/08/18/tim-winton-s-beautiful-baffling-eyrie.html.

Smith, Zadie. Commencement speech to the New School, 23 May 2014. https://youtu.be/pjdmo6EKn8I.

Snyder, Timothy. *Bloodlands: Europe between Hitler and Stalin*. New York: Basic Books, 2010.

Spektorowski, Alberto and Elisabet Mizrachi. "Eugenics and the Welfare State in Sweden: The Politics of Social Margins and the Idea of a Productive Society". *Journal of Contemporary History* 39, no. 3 (2004): 333–52.

Spivak, Gayatri Chakravorty. "Three Women's Texts and a Critique of Imperialism". *Critical Inquiry* 12, no. 1 (Autumn 1985): 235–61.

Stafford, Jane and Mark Williams, eds. *The Auckland University Press Anthology of New Zealand Literature*. Auckland: Auckland University Press, 2012.

Stafford, Jane and Mark Williams. *Māoriland: New Zealand Literature 1872 to 1914*. Wellington: Victoria University Press, 2007.

Standing, Guy. *The Precariat: The New Dangerous Class*. London: Bloomsbury Academic, 2011.

Stead, C. K. *Book Self: The Reader as Writer and the Writer as Critic*. Auckland: Auckland University Press, 2008.

——. "From Wystan to Carlos: Modern and Modernism in Recent New Zealand Poetry". *Islands* 5, no. 7 (1979): 467–86.

——. *Kin of Place: Essays on Twenty New Zealand Writers*. Auckland: Auckland University Press, 2002.

——. "*The Luminaries* by Eleanor Catton". *Financial Times*, 6 September 2013. http://tiny.cc/stead_2013.

Stead, Christina. *For Love Alone*. Melbourne: Melbourne University Press, 2012.

——. *Letty Fox: Her Luck*. Melbourne: Melbourne University Press, 2011.

——. *The Man Who Loved Children*. Melbourne: Melbourne University Press, 2010.

——. "Uses of the Many-Charactered Novel". In *Selected Fiction and Nonfiction*, edited by R. G. Geering and A. Segerberg. St Lucia: University of Queensland Press, 196–99.

Steiner, George. "Our Homeland, the Text". *Salmagundi* 66 (1985): 4–25

Stephen, Anne. *Modern Times: The Untold Story of Modernism in Australia*. Melbourne: Melbourne University Press, 2008.

Stephens, M. G. "The Dogs of Literature – Seymour Krim: Bottom Dog Part I". *The Hollins Critic* 51, no. 5 (2014): 1–16.

Stinson, Emmett. "Remote Viewing". *Sydney Review of Books*, 2 September 2015. http://www.sydneyreviewofbooks.com/million-windows-gerald-murnane/.

Stoljar, Jeremy. *My First Mistake*. Roseville: Simon & Schuster Australia, 1992.

Stratton, Jon. "Deconstructing the Territory". *Cultural Studies* 3, no. 1 (1989): 38–57.

Strongman, Luke. *The Booker Prize and the Legacy of Empire*. Amsterdam: Rodopi, 2002.

Szalay, Michael. *New Deal Modernism: American Literature and the Invention of the Welfare State*. Durham: Duke University Press, 2000.

Tartt, Donna. *The Goldfinch*. New York: Little, Brown, 2014.

Thatcher, Margaret. "Europe's Political Architecture". Speech delivered at the Hague, 15 May 1992. www.margaretthatcher.org/document/108296.

Thwaites, Frederick J. *The Broken Melody*. Sydney: Publicity Press, 1930.

Toltz, Steve. *A Fraction of the Whole*. London: Hamish Hamilton, 2008.

Trigg, Stephanie, ed. *Medievalism and the Gothic in Australian Culture*. Melbourne: Melbourne University Press, 2005.

Trilling, Lionel. *The Liberal Imagination*. New York: New York Review Books, 2008.

Tsiolkas, Christos. *Barracuda*. Crows Nest: Allen & Unwin, 2013.

——. *Dead Europe*. Sydney: Vintage, 2005.

——. *The Slap*. Crows Nest: Allen & Unwin, 2009.

Tulk, Niki. "My Self, My Country: Robert Dixon's Critical Collection on the Works of Alex Miller". Reading Across the Pacific (blog of *Antipodes*), 9 April 2014. http://antipodesjournal.blogspot.com/2014/04/my-self-my-country-robert-dixons.html.

Turner, Graeme. "American Dreaming: The Fictions of Peter Carey". *Australian Literary Studies*, 12, no. 4 (1986): 431–41.

——. "Nationalising the Author: The Celebrity of Peter Carey". *Australian Literary Studies* 16, no. 2 (1993): 131–39.

Works Cited

Turner, Jack. "Tim Winton's *Riders* Sends Father on a European Quest". *Antipodes* 9, no. 2 (1995): 148–49.

Upfield, Arthur. *Death of a Swagman*. Sydney: Angus & Robertson, 1980.

van Neerven, Ellen. *Heat and Light*. St Lucia: University of Queensland Press, 2014.

Waldren, Murray. "Distaff Side of Plato". *Weekend Australian*, 4–5 September 1999, 14.

Waley Daniel Philip. *The Italian City-Republics*. New York: McGraw-Hill, 1969.

Walker, Brenda. "Alex Miller and Leo Tolstoy: Australian Storytelling in a European Tradition". In *The Novels of Alex Miller*, edited by Robert Dixon, 42–54. Crows Nest: Allen & Unwin, 2012.

Walkowitz, Rebecca. *Cosmopolitan Style: Writing Beyond the Nation*. New York: Columbia University Press, 2007.

Walton, James. "Star Fiction". *New York Review of Books*, 4 December 2014. http://www.nybooks.com/articles/archives/2014/dec/04/luminaries-star-fiction/.

Wark, McKenzie. *The Virtual Republic*. Crows Nest: Allen & Unwin, 1997.

Watt, Ian. *The Rise of the Novel*. Stanford: Stanford University Press, 1957.

Welchman, John. *Invisible Colors: A Visual History of Titles*. New Haven: Yale University Press, 1997.

Welsh, Alexander. *From Copyright to Copperfield: The Identity of Dickens*. Cambridge: Harvard University Press, 1987.

White, Patrick. *The Burnt Ones*. London: Penguin, 1974.

——. *The Hanging Garden*. New York: Picador, 2013.

Whitehead, Anne. *Paradise Mislaid: In Search of the Australian Tribe of Paraguay*. St Lucia: University of Queensland Press, 1998.

Whyman, Tom. "Beware of Cupcake Fascism". *Guardian* online, 8 April centur2014. http://www.theguardian.com/commentisfree/2014/apr/08/beware-of-cupcake-fascism.

Wiener, Martin J. *English Culture and the Decline of the Industrial Spirit, 1850–1980*. Second edition. Cambridge: Cambridge University Press, 2005.

Wilding, Michael. "On Australian Publishing in a Global Environment". *Antipodes* 14, no. 2 (2000): 152–54.

Williams, Bernard. *Moral Luck*. Cambridge: Cambridge University Press, 1982.

Williamson, Geordie. *The Burning Library: Our Great Novelists Lost and Found*. Melbourne: Text Publishing, 2012.

Windschuttle, Keith. *The Fabrication of Aboriginal History Volume One: Van Diemens Land, 1803–1847*. Sydney: Macleay Press, 2002.

Winton, Tim. *Eyrie*. New York: Farrar, Straus & Giroux, 2014.

——. "Some Thoughts about Class in Australia". *Monthly*, December 2013, 24–31.

Wolfe, Peter. *Laden Choirs: The Fiction of Patrick White*. Lexington: University Press of Kentucky, 1983.

Wolpert, Stanley. *An Introduction to India*. London: Penguin, 2000.

Wood, James. "No Time for Lies: Rediscovering Elizabeth Harrower". *New Yorker*, 20 October 2014, 66–70.

Woodcock, Bruce. *Peter Carey*. Manchester: Manchester University Press, 1996.

Wright, Alexis. *Carpentaria*. Artarmon: Giramondo Publishing, 2006.

——. *The Swan Book*. Artarmon: Giramondo Publishing, 2013. Kindle edition.

Yelin, Louise. *From the Margins of Empire: Christina Stead, Doris Lessing, Nadine Gordimer*. Ithaca: Cornell University Press, 1988.

Yu, Pauline and Theodore Huters. "The Imaginative Universe of Chinese Literature". In *Chinese Aesthetics and Literature*, edited by Corinne H. Dale, 1–14. Albany: State University of New York Press, 2004.

Yu, Timothy. "On Asian Australian Poetry". *Southerly* 73, no. 1 (2013): 75–88.

Zahler, Diane. *Than Shwe's Burma*. Minneapolis: Twenty-First Century Books, 2010.

Index